MW01629896

"THANKS FOR LISTENING"

High Adventures in Journalism and Diplomacy

By

Patricia Gates Lynch

Foreword by

Justice Sandra Day O'Connor

"THANKS FOR LISTENING"

High Adventures in Journalism and Diplomacy

By

Patricia Gates Lynch

Foreword by

Justice Sandra Day O'Connor

Countinghouse Press, Inc.
Bloomfield Hills, Michigan

To Winifred and Gerald Clausing
With my very best wishes
and my thanks for all your help!
Warmly,
Pat Gates Lynch Ewell

THANKS FOR LISTENING
By Patricia Gates Lynch

Address inquiries to: Countinghouse Press, Inc., 6632 Telegraph Rd. # 311, Bloomfield Hills, MI 48301.

Telephone: 248.642.7191. Email: nuhuguenot@aol.com

First edition

First printing

ISBN: 978-0-9786191-2-1 hard cover
         978-0-9786191-3-8 trade paper

Printed in the United States of America by
Cover design by Sans Serif, Inc., Saline, MI.

This is a memoir. It does not claim to be, and is not, political, medical, or legal advice. The opinions expressed are those of the author. Trademarks and other proprietary marks used herein are the property of their respective owners.

Dedication

This book is dedicated to:

Ink Gates who shared with me "Duty, Honor, Country;"

to our children

Larry and Pam,

Jamye and Jeri;

and to our grandchildren

Emily and Sally;

to Bill Lynch, pioneer diplomatic spouse;

and to Ruth Boorstin,

who encouraged me to write this book.

Contents

Foreword   xi-xii
By Justice Sandra Day O'Connor

Epigraph   Xiii

Prologue   xv-xv11

Photo Gallery   xix-xxvi
Following p. 174

Part I   **The Early Years**   1

1 Growing Up   3-22
Little Girl in Connecticut — War Clouds Overhead — Crossed
Swords and Camp McCoy — The Long Wait: India and Burma

2 The Manhattan Project   23-36

3 Washington, Here We Come!   37-44
University of Illinois — The Washington Years

4 On to Europe   45-64
Munich — Paris

5 A Nascent Career   65-76
Kansas, USA — The Magic of the Microphone — Through the
Window Glass

6 Foreign Correspondent   77-92
Munich Revisited — The Czech Border — Dr. Von Braun —
Reunion and Discovery in Iran — Christmas Catastrophe in
Munich — The Passion Play and Royalty in Lech

7 Both Sides of the Iron Curtain   93-112
Berlin — I Cross the Barrier into the Soviet Union — Warsaw —
Budapest — Dachau

8 Paris to Fort Benning, Georgia   113-122
Dressed for Dior — North to Norway — Reunion in Italy- U.S.
Army Post

Part II   **Good Morning, World**   123

9 International Broadcaster   125-134
The Voice of America and I — Gateway to Science — My Soldier
Goes to Vietnam

10 Radio Waves   135-142
My Journey into Space — The Breakfast Show — Microphone
Memories

11 On the White House Staff   143-166
In Pat Nixon's East Wing — Duke Ellington at the White
House — Around the World with the President and First Lady —
Into Vietnam on Air Force One — From Thailand to India,
Pakistan, Romania, and England — Back in the East Wing — The
Astronauts Come to Dinner

12 Travels Far and Wide   167-184
Back to the Microphone — White House Wedding — To Africa
with Mrs. Nixon — End of a Love Affair — Breakfast Show World
Tour

13 Highs and Lows   185-200
Returned POWs at the White House — End of an Era — Freedom
Still Rings — The Spirit of '76 — A Full Mailbox — More
Microphone Memories

14 New Horizons   201-224
 Dartmouth Days — Bells Are Ringing — Presidents, Senators,
and Hostages — The Road to China — You Will Never Be the
Same — Nanjing University and Beyond — Home and Family

15 The Last Hurrahs   225-234
Is Anybody Listening? — My Solo Lecture Tour

Part III   **Diplomacy and Beyond**   235

16 One Ambassador, One New Voice   237-256
Microphone to Madame Ambassador — What Is an
Ambassador? — Advice and Consent — Goodbye Washington —
Ahoy Madagascar

17 Madagascar Discovered   257-278
Trooping the Line at the Palace — Cigars and Brandy — The
Residence — Exploring the Country — Safari into Lemur
Territory — Visiting my Comoros Embassy

18 On the Diplomatic Front Line   279-302
A Woman in the Lion's Den — Diplomatic Diversity — The
Exorcism — A Star for Christmas — Lemurs and Riots —
Celebrating the Fourth of July, the United States Constitution,
and More Visitors — The Seabees Land in Madagascar

19 Real Life Continues   303-316
Children, Grandchildren, Elephants, and Giraffes — Glasnost in
Madagascar — More Travels, and Champagne for a New
Bridge — Sandra Day O'Connor Visits Madagascar

20 Out of Africa   317-340
Home Leave and Pearl Harbor — The French Warship — From
the Ngong Hills to the Andringitra Mountains — U.S. Election —
Welcome Peace Corps in the Comoros — The Pope Comes to
Madagascar — Time Grows Short — Au Revoir, Veloma, Farewell

Part IV   **The Radios**   341

21 Once Again a New Career   343-354
Into the Corporate World: RFE/RL — Death Takes No
Holiday — Life Goes On

Coda   355-356

Bibliography   357-358

Acknowledgments

Ruth Boorstin, my highly respected editor, was not only a marvel at filling my script margins with invaluable criticisms, she was a source of constant encouragement. Her personal friendship and professional support have been joys of my life.

I thank the distinguished editor and publishing director of the Association for Diplomatic Studies and Training, Margery Boichel Thompson. Her skilled further editing and consultation have been indispensable.

My special thanks go to Faith Moore, whose devotion to the writing of this book made it all possible. Her computer skills as my assistant were remarkable, and her ability to laugh and to cry in all the right places is greatly appreciated!

An excellent agent is vital to an author and I have the good fortune to have a superb one, Diane Nine.

Above all, thanks to my wonderful husband, Julian Ewell, a man of great wisdom and great courage on the battlefield. I thank him for his encouragement and patience as I wrote day after day in my attic studio.

Generous friends have helped me with background information and observations and in numerous other ways. I am most grateful to them for their understanding and support:

H. E. Zina Andrianarivelo-Razafy, Permanent Representative of Madagascar to the United Nations; Bob Arnold, science editor and SETI analyst; Jeanne Viner Bell, president of Jeanne Viner Associates; George S. Blanchard, General, U.S. Army (ret.);   Rosanne McQuarrie Broughton, WFAX Radio partner; Jeri Charles, President, Worldwide Speakers Bureau; Winifred and Gerald Clausing; Frederick J. Clarke, Lt. General, U.S. Army (ret.); Peter Cochran; William J. Crowe, U.S. Ambassador to Great Britain and Admiral, U.S. Navy (ret.); John Russell Deane Jr., General, U.S. Army (ret.); Baudouin DeMarcken, Director, USAID, Madagascar; Lawrence Dunham, Assistant

Chief of Protocol, U.S. Department of State; Carroll Dunn, Lt. General, U.S. Army (ret.); Harvey R. Fraser, Brig. General, U.S. Army (ret.); Lawrence Alan Gates; Pamela Townley Gates; Jacob Glick, Brigadier General, U.S. Marine Corps, (ret.); Barbara Hemphill, Organizational Consultant, Author; Michael Hildebrand; Kiran Jagga, Information Officer, Embassy of India; Alan Jones, Colonel, U. S. Army (ret.); Daniel Raymond, Major General, U.S. Army (ret.); Samuel S. Rea, Director, USAID, Madagascar; Robin Rupli; Rex Scouten, former curator of the White House; Raymond L. Shoemaker Jr., Lt. General, U.S. Army (ret.); Helen McCain Smith, Press Secretary to Mrs. Nixon; Adrian St. John, Major General, U.S. Army (ret.); Gilbert Tannis, former Executive Officer and Director of Continuing Education, Dartmouth College; Anne Power Werner; George M. White, Architect of the United States Capitol; Howard Wickert, Colonel, U.S. Army (ret.).

Foreword

by

Justice Sandra Day O'Connor

I enjoy true stories about real people -- and, particularly, stories that end well. Pat Gates Lynch has produced a fine book about her own life as it unfolded in a remarkable way.

Pat Gates Lynch grew up in Connecticut and married a West Point cadet whom she met when she was learning to be an actress. With World War II breaking out, Pat's husband was sent to India and then to fight in Burma. Before the war ended he was assigned to the Manhattan Project, sparking her interest in people engaged in important work. Pat met many of the scientists and officials involved in the Project. In time, Pat's husband was assigned to the Armed Forces Special Weapons Project in Washington, D.C. They become parents of two children. The Army next sent Pat's husband and family to Munich, then Paris, and finally back to the United States.

With another Army wife, Pat found a small radio station in the Washington, D.C. area, which allowed the two women to have a daily radio broadcast doing interviews of people in the military service, as well as in the community. That program succeeded and led to opportunities to do interview programs from NBC, the Armed Forces Network, and her Washington, D.C. area station. Pat traveled in many areas of Europe, the Soviet Union, and the Middle East to do those interviews. She honed her skills with some fascinating interviews with a wide array of remarkable people.

The Voice of America producer of the Breakfast Show invited Pat to become part of that program on a regular basis. Her beautiful voice became America's voice heard around the world. In many parts of the world her voice and her program are still the things people remember most fondly about our country. Reading about the people Pat interviewed for Voice of America is a who's who around the world.

When Richard Nixon became President, Pat became Pat Nixon's press aide for radio and television. Her book takes the reader into the White House with some wonderful glimpses.

Pat's final post was a diplomatic one as Ambassador to Madagascar, where I had a chance to visit and to see Pat Gates Lynch in action. Her skills as an interviewer were very useful to her in her diplomatic post in what was then a Marxist State. She helped make the country's subsequent transition to democracy an easier one.

This is a story full of life, of people, of a woman who created a splendid career for herself at a time when women were seldom heard as broadcasters. The story is a reaffirmation of the progress of women in this country over the past fifty years. It is a story I enjoyed.

Seek therefore to find of what and how the world is made,

that you may learn a better way of life.

Attributed to Pythagoras

Prologue

Each of us paints a picture as we go about keeping our balance on the tightrope of life. I would like to tell you something about how I balanced on my own tightrope and enjoyed the crossing.

My first career was army wife, mother, and homemaker. My first big adventure was landing in the midst of the Manhattan Project.

The world of radio and television opened new doors. I hosted programs on public television and, while living in Europe, became a foreign correspondent. On NBC Radio, AFN, and WFAX, I talked about other countries and their cultures. Next, on international radio, the Voice of America, for 25 years, I shared with listeners around the world information about our country, its culture, its setbacks, and achievements.

On the White House staff, I learned something about the highest levels of government. As the United States ambassador to Madagascar and the Comoros, I was able to put all I had learned to use.

From Africa, I entered the corporate world in Washington as the U.S. representative of Radio Free Europe and Radio Liberty, which broadcast for many years from Munich, and now from Prague, into Central Europe and the countries of the former Soviet Union.

Still evolving as history unfolds from the twentieth century into the twenty-first, I mull over the past and realize that I have always kept one foot in the future. I have wondered why life and I seem to have such a good time together. It is only in retrospect that I hear recurring notes in my song of experience. How did a little girl from a small town in Connecticut become a workingwoman—unusual for the time—and in so doing find herself in places where history was being made?

* * * * *

When I was about ten years old my mother told me the secret of standing up straight and tall. "Imagine you are attached to the sky by a string," she told me, "and you will find it easier to walk and to stand; your feet will be on the ground, but you will feel almost weightless."

Well, I tried suspending myself from a cloud on a string and, to my amazement; it worked! I walked effortlessly. I liked the feeling of not hitting the earth too hard and of lifting my spirits, as well as my rather small body, up toward heaven.

All these years later I realize that the connection "on a string" has helped me get through the rough times, walking over and past the obstacles we all run into during a lifetime. It also has helped me appreciate the wondrous sights and sounds around me and enjoy the strength that seems to run down the line from on high on that little piece of string.

I never thought much about my navigation through the heavy and smooth waters of life until now, and I wonder if the sailors of old, with their tall ships and high sails, held tight to the ropes on deck, feeling connected to the heavens above.

I wonder if, when I die, God may reel me up to heaven on that string of mine, rather like the watermen I watch as they haul up the crab pots out of the Chesapeake Bay.

P.G.L

Part I
The Early Years

1

Growing Up

Life changed for this little girl in New Canaan, Connecticut, when Hitler marched into Poland in September of 1939. All the talk in our house on the radio was of war. I wasn't sure what "war" meant but knew my father could tell me. My father, Charles Lawrence, knew about everything and even as a schoolgirl I recognized that fact.

You have to understand that I adored my father and not only loved him but respected him greatly. He didn't think he knew everything, but I believed him to be more intelligent than most people, kind and filled with wisdom. If he didn't have an answer to one of my questions, he would find out for me or tell me how I could think it through myself. He was, after all, the man who had cautioned me not to jump off the diving board into the Long Island Sound off the Connecticut coast, saying the water was too low and I could break my neck. I gave it a try anyway when he wasn't watching, and even though I did a shallow dive it hurt my neck like the very devil. Thus had my father built up enormous credibility with me! Later in life, I admitted to myself that he wasn't perfect, but I never changed my mind about his being the most dear and dependable man I have ever known, quiet, strong, and steady. Imagine being so fortunate as to have a man like that as a father. My mother, Molly Lawrence, knew about his character long before I came along. Theirs was a serious love story through good times and rocky ones.

But back to war. My father told me about World War I (to me an eternity ago) and of how many people had been killed, about little planes dropping big bombs, and about earlier wars all through the centuries. Wars came and went, settling things for only awhile, but it was necessary to fight — for your country, your beliefs, your survival.

The war had a big effect on my life as it did for so many. It surely influenced my early marriage, my thoughts about public service, my way of fighting for my ideals, and my concern for people in other countries behind barbed wire, facing manmade hardship and dangers. I have almost never been discouraged about life on earth and guess I was born with "life-glad," a word used by the widow of Russian poet Osip Mandelstam. In her book *Hope Against Hope,* Nadezhda Mandelstam writes that the poet was *zhizneradostny* — "life-glad" — no matter what difficulties he faced. I like that word.

My parents never thought of women as inferior human beings. I am sure that helped make me more confident of my own abilities. At school, I was an avid reader. At one school, the principal, Henry Welles, had spent many years in China as headmaster of the American School in Shanghai. He gave marvelous talks about China to the students and planted the seeds of my interest in foreign affairs. Then, too, the radio at home brought us the news, and my mother and father expected their three children to know what was happening in the world.

Early on, I discovered that women had to be creative. They were not expected to be doctors or lawyers. They had to carve out a niche for themselves, just as enterprising entrepreneurs do. If they are creative, they find a need and come up with an idea and a business to meet it.

My mother was pretty special. She believed that children should have an "educated heart," which to her meant being sensitive to other people's feelings and walking in their shoes. She had one of those hearts herself.

My mother would take me shopping with her and show me how to buy something in an inexpensive store that would still look fine. She told me about the days when they had plenty of money and then about when the depression had come. My father was a stockbroker at that time, which was not good! Trained as an engineer, he then started has own business as a representative for General Electric Equipment. Then this war had hurt my father's business again. But it's always possible to manage, she said. I dreamed of making money to make life easier for her and my father. They wanted me to have a good education, so I went to a fine girls' school but ended up mostly on scholarship when money ran out. Among the few working women around, I knew at least two who were good family friends, one of them a managing editor of *Vogue* magazine.

My first creative impulse was to become an actress on the stage, and I stayed with that idea all through my school years. Marriage and motherhood could wait.

Having heard that actors make a good salary, I decided to explore a theater career so there would be no more financial worries for my parents! Well, I discovered that money doesn't just pour in that easily. Although I aimed for a life on stage, hoping I could go to England and work in a Shakespearean company for real experience, my dreams of "All the world's a stage" didn't quite work out that way. No great fortune came along but what a life!

I was in all the school plays, which parents so bravely attend. Because my school was just for girls, one time I was cast as the American patriot, Nathan Hale, who lost his life during the American Revolution. I remember saying his historic words, "I only regret that I have but one life to lose for my country." I knew that my sentiments would always be the same as his.

One day in New York City, I visited with the famous British actress Gertrude Lawrence, then starring in a musical called *Lady in the Dark*. My last name was Lawrence, too, which I thought was a good sign. Gertrude Lawrence gave me sound advice: to get work in summer stock, paint scenery, try for a part, and get experience at the grassroots level.

In a stroke of luck, I became a summer intern at the noted Westport Country Playhouse in Westport, Connecticut. One of the best in the country, it was owned and directed by Armina Marshall and her husband, Lawrence Langner, director of the Theater Guild in New York. That summer one of the plays was to be Hungarian playwright Ferenc Molnar's *Liliom*, later to become the highly successful Rodgers and Hammerstein musical, *Carousel*. Coming from California to star in *Liliom* would be the number one movie star in the country, Tyrone Power, and his beautiful French wife, the actress Annabella. I gave my mother all this information to convince her to drive me thirty minutes every morning to the playhouse and another thirty minutes every night to pick me up after the performance. I wasn't old enough to drive and without my mother and father's approval and assistance there would be no summer job.

I was the youngest child in the family—my brother Bill was seven years older than I, my sister Dorothy twelve years older. By the time I went to be an apprentice at the Westport Playhouse both had married and long since left home, so in a way I was like an only child. However, I had had the fun of growing up in a close family where I'd had a good look at teenagers and young adults before becoming one myself. I think I was a bit of a nuisance to my brother and sister because they were supposed to keep an eye on me even when they had plenty of their own activities.

Now that I am a parent myself I know that my parents must have worried about leaving me at a summer theater so far from New Canaan, but Mother agreed and drove me back and forth every day. She never stayed around but was always there at the appointed hour. I loved being on my own from early morning to late at night and getting to know so many people working in theater. And I met other young people like me working hard to learn all we could about the trade even as we painted scenery and did errands for everyone.

I was given a part as an extra in *Liliom,* the most important of the summer plays! That was a great day, and I thought I was on my way. Although I had no speaking part I was on stage in all the crowd scenes. Even better, an outstanding director, Lee Strasberg, took a great deal of time with the young people in the crowd scenes, wanting us to get it right. I was learning, and I was painting sets every day, too. When the play opened to rave reviews in the New York press, it was decided to keep it in Westport for a full month. I was especially pleased because I had become an informal assistant to Annabella, helping her with her changes of costume and running errands for her. She and Tyrone Power were down-to-earth people, intelligent, friendly, and considerate. Little did I imagine that one day Annabella would become a lifelong friend and that I would receive a postcard from Tyrone, signed by Annabella too, just before hearing the radio news of his death. But there was much to happen in our lives after Westport, for World War II was waiting in the wings.

The assistant stage manager for *Liliom* was a woman I liked very much, Elaine Anderson, who later married the famous author John Steinbeck. Eddie Knill, the playhouse's business manager, became a friend of many years, often finding me a seat for a Broadway play even when none were available. Once he put up a chair for me in the front row to see one of the big musicals, *Oklahoma!,* I think.

6

Life changed for me one August day that summer of 1941, though I didn't realize it until much later. The Powers were invited to bring the entire production of *Liliom* to the United States Military Academy at West Point for a Sunday performance and dinner. We were all excited, even the Powers. West Point is an impressive, beautiful spot on the Hudson River, filled with history, tradition, and cadets. When we arrived, the cast was divided into small groups, each escorted around the academy by a cadet first classman who was a member of the dialectic society and had volunteered for the assignment. To my surprise, the cadet with my group, Mahlon ("Ink," as he was always called) Gates, talked with me quite a bit and invited me to sit with him at dinner that night. He also asked me for my address.

Just before dinner Annabella said to me, "Ah ha, I see you have yourself a cadet!"

"Well, maybe for a football game sometime," I suggested.

Just at that moment, a strange cadet rushed up to tell me that my cadet dinner partner had been taken ill and could not join me. That, I thought, was the end of that, but I was wrong. I was not going to be an actress after all. My "constant" goal would fade from sight, for a year and a half later I was to marry that "no show" cadet. From that time on, my stage was all the world.

War Clouds Overhead

From our house in Connecticut we watched each step of Hitler's march toward war. There was no such thing as television then, but we had the *New York Herald Tribune* newspaper, and we had our Philco radio! We had spoken images from CBS Radio, with Edward R. Murrow reporting from London and William L. Shirer broadcasting from Berlin and Prague, where so much was happening. My father, mother, and I would have discussions every night before I did my homework. My father would tell me about the First World War. He hadn't gone because he was married with two small children (my brother and sister). He had worked, instead, as manager and assistant to the president of a huge shipyard that built Liberty ships to carry war supplies to Europe. Now, he was very much concerned that we wouldn't be ready for what he envisioned as an even greater war fast approaching. Only President Roosevelt seemed aware of the danger we faced; consequently, my father, although he had always been a Republican, became a supporter of the Democratic president.

The reason we were such loyal followers of CBS radio was that Murrow, Shirer, and the rest of their team took us right to the scene of events via shortwave to New York, then out to us. The news of Hitler's march into the Sudetenland, the important industrial area of Czechoslovakia, distressed us, and we thought the French and British capitulation at Munich a huge mistake that could only lead to full-scale war. Such was the influence of Murrow, Shirer, Larry LeSueur, and others like Marvin Breckenridge, a woman broadcaster, that I longed to be in Europe to see what they were seeing up close. I don't think it occurred to me, however, that I might someday be broadcasting over shortwave myself and that I would know Murrow, LeSueur, and Marvin Breckenridge Patterson. Little do we know the paths we may follow!

By no means was war in Europe the only thing on my mind. I was still young, working hard at school, active in sports, excited about learning French, and longing to go to school in Switzerland. I knew that money was tight in our house, but my mother always managed to save a little on the side and had been encouraging. That dream evaporated quickly when Ed Murrow via our Philco brought the news on September 1, 1939, that the Nazis had marched into Poland. But I had other dreams—my career in the theater, travel, marriage, and children. I would study, and nothing was impossible! I didn't know then that women couldn't always do what they wanted. In my girls' school everyone looked pretty capable to me. I was getting a good classical education, and we were all preparing for college, even though many women did not go on to college in those days.

The summer I interned at the Westport Playhouse and met a cadet at West Point turned into fall and back-to-school time. There were no more glamorous actresses and actors, just ourselves in our school Shakespeare plays. One day when I'd walked to the village post office to get the mail out of our box, there was a letter for me from Ink Gates, the "no show" cadet at the military academy! How about a football game date? Well, I wrote back, my mother and father were going to the Yale-Army game in New Haven and I could meet him there.

As planned, we lunched with friends of my parents, a tailgate picnic out of the car trunk in the parking lot. After the game, we met up again with my brother and his wife and went with them for a quick supper before Ink had to leave for the academy on the bus carrying the corps of cadets. It was all a roaring success. When the subject of my age came up, my sister-in-law gave me a new, two-year older age and that was the end of that.

Before long, this nice young cadet came to spend a weekend with us, and we all liked him even in his civilian clothes. I had no serious thoughts about our relationship for I had no intentions of being serious with anybody. However, I now had a friend who would be directly affected by a war if it should come. I was sorry about that.

One Sunday in early December 1941, the 7th to be exact, I went out with my father to do some errands. We were listening to a baseball game on the car radio when suddenly, an announcer interrupted to say, "The Japanese have just bombed Pearl Harbor!"

Most Americans can remember exactly where they were when they heard that incredible report. I remember how we both jumped out of the old Packard and rushed into the house to tell my mother the news and to switch on the radio as fast as possible.

A torrent of news on the radio and in the newspaper followed that first bulletin about the bombing of Pearl Harbor. President Franklin D. Roosevelt declared that we were in the war with Japan, and Germany soon declared war on us. We all feared there would be more bombings, perhaps even on the East coast, and volunteers were posted in every village and town to watch for unidentified aircraft. My mother signed up to be a volunteer.

My school was located on Long Island Sound in Stamford, Connecticut. Though it was a boarding school, I was a day student. We worried about German submarines getting into that large body of water and had blackout practice at school, leaving the black window shades down when darkness fell. We were beginning to feel an even closer kinship to the British. We had suffered for them vicariously during the Battle of Britain in the summer and fall of 1940 when Hitler's bombers and fighters fought the planes of the Royal Air Force in the skies over Britain. When Ed Murrow would come on our radio and say, "This—is—London," we could hear the air raid sirens and the bombs falling.

Would this war terror come to our shores? We were lucky here at home. It was our troops, crossing the Atlantic and Pacific Oceans that would be in the midst of the war.

Ink Gates phoned from West Point to tell me what was happening up there. The military academy professors were receiving orders to report for active duty, and a few of the higher-ranking cadets were being named as cadet instructors to help with the teaching. Ink had been made one of those instructors and was much pleased. The academy would let his class of '42 graduate on schedule, but the next classes would be speeded up and graduate ahead of time, as officers were needed quickly. The class of 1942 would suffer severe casualties during the war years. Many of the new young officers would die in the U.S. Army Air Corps during training; the planes were being turned out quickly and were not as safe as later models.

Life went on for the moment, and I was invited to West Point several times. Also, because of his teaching responsibilities, Ink had more free weekends than the other cadets and was able to visit us in Connecticut. There was, I thought, plenty of time before the war would reach us. Besides I was busy at school, and there was that career I was planning.

Soon, we all had ration books for buying gasoline and certain other things in short supply. My father was worried about his General Electric business, for he saw it gradually folding as some of his contacts were signing war contracts and turning away from all domestic production. What was he going to do to make a living? He wanted to serve and was excited when he heard that the navy was recruiting men with managerial experience to serve as lieutenant commanders. He applied quickly but missed the age cutoff by one year. I had a full scholarship at school now so he didn't have that particular worry. When he heard that the army engineers were looking for civilian engineers he signed up quickly. The drawback was that the job was in Bermuda, where our army was building a base. Details were secret.

My mother and father had never been separated and were devastated by the idea of being apart. They were a true love match, forever and always. But that's what happens in wartime, and my dad made plans to go to that British island where he and my mother had vacationed in better days.

Meanwhile, I was invited to June Week at West Point! And my parents were invited for the graduation ceremony. Ink's parents, the Gateses, were coming from Pennsylvania and his brother, a professor at the academy, would be there, too, with his family. We had a wonderful time at the graduation ball, where your date's friends would all sign up for a dance with you. The cadets were invited to bring their girls to the superintendent's reception, a memorable occasion. General George C. Marshall delivered the commencement address. The cadets talked of assignments and where everyone would be a year later. Would we help the allies finish the war quickly, or would it last a long time? West Point is a beautiful place and its tradition of Duty, Honor, Country is as sacred to me as it is to most cadets. After that June Week, I knew it would always be special to me.

It was some time after his graduation that Ink wrote and asked me to marry him. I remember sitting at my desk and reading the letter several times wondering how I should reply. I was in love but was I ready to marry? He was older than I but that was all right. He had integrity and intelligence and a good sense of humor. I liked the idea of army life but knew it wasn't easy, with many moves and not much income. I wanted to see the world; I wanted children. It would mean giving up my career, counted on for so long.

The next day I talked with my Latin teacher, who was to be another lifelong friend. I asked her if she thought I was old enough to marry in a year.

"Yes", she said, "you are. Every case is different."

I asked the headmistress, an English-born woman I admired, if it would matter very much if I did not go to college. She thought one of the main purposes of a university is to open your mind to constant learning and told me it would be all right, because she knew that I would never stop studying.

After more thinking on my part, for it was a big step, I said yes and was never sorry.

Crossed Swords and Camp McCoy

That first summer after graduating from West Point, Ink went to Fort Belvoir in Virginia for basic training at the Engineer Officers' School. He was pleased to have been assigned to the Army Corps of Engineers, which had been his first choice. You had to have a high class standing to make it. Located just outside Washington, D.C., Fort Belvoir was within driving distance of New Canaan, Connecticut, so Ink was able to drive up to see me almost every weekend. The trip took about seven hours, as there was a ferryboat then instead of the Delaware Memorial Bridge. It was a long haul for him and another lieutenant who shared the driving as far as New York City, where his girl lived.

After Fort Belvoir came our first real separation, for the new orders read, "Camp McCoy, Wisconsin," and the letters and phone calls multiplied. We had decided on a wedding the following June and announced our engagement in the *New York Herald Tribune* at Thanksgiving time. My mother and I were missing my father very much, for by this time he was working in Bermuda. I knew he would be home for the wedding and that was a comfort. But in wartime no dates are ever certain.

Sure enough, in early December Ink wrote that it looked as though his 44th Engineer Combat Regiment would soon be reorganizing into battalions and heading overseas. He might be leaving, he wrote, and didn't want to go to war without having married me first! Let's make it at Christmas time when he could get a few days' leave, he suggested. Suddenly all systems were go for a December wedding. My father, who was very fond of Ink, wrote from his wartime post in Bermuda that he understood and we should go ahead. I found it painful to visualize a wedding without my beloved father.

Something else was happening about that time—Mother and I were moving! Because of the acute shortage and high price of home heating oil, Mother decided it would be more practical to give up our house and move to nearby Stamford, Connecticut, where some new apartments had been built just before the war began. We were barely settled when the holidays were upon us.

Mother and I set off for West Point on a cold December day through snow and icy roads, taking with us a simple long white wedding dress. We had reservations at the Thayer Hotel and would meet Ink there. We had invited a few friends and family to drive over the next day and would drive back to the apartment in Stamford after the ceremony for a reception. I walked down the aisle of the stately West Point Chapel to thunderous organ music, the guests sat in the choir stall, and Chaplain Walthour pronounced us husband and wife. We walked back up that long aisle and out into the sunlight under four gleaming crossed swords held aloft by Ink's cadet friends from the class of '43.

Along with my family, Ink's mother and father had come up from Tyrone, Pennsylvania. I had met them during June week, and Ink and I had visited them in Tyrone during the summer. I fell in love with them both, and it was the beginning of a long friendship. My mother and dad gathered them into my family, and that made it comfortable for Ink and me. Mother Gates, as I called her, was a sweet, loving woman with kind thoughts for everyone and great fortitude in sorrow. She was to lose two of her three sons in the coming months, and both she and her husband twice experienced that dreaded shock of Western Union bringing an army telegram right to the front door, a telegram informing them of the death of a son. My parents and I were more fortunate than they, for my brother and my husband both came home safely.

On this happy December day, however, there was only joy. There were no forebodings then, nor any thoughts of another war in Vietnam, where Ink would be serving for almost two years and where he would become a general. No thoughts then either that his mother would be living with me during those Vietnam War years and longer. I was lucky with my new family and know it is not always thus!

After the ceremony, our little group, which included my brother, sister and cousin, drove back through the snow, through Bear Mountain Park and on into Connecticut for the party at our apartment. When Ink and I left for New York that evening, everyone came to the railroad station and threw tapioca at us instead of rice (it seemed there was a shortage of rice). Tapioca kept rolling around up and down the aisles of the train, and everyone smiled. We tried to be more dignified when we checked into the Biltmore Hotel in New

York, but even there a piece of tapioca fell out of Ink's pocket and bounced across the floor!

Wartime leave was almost always short. After a final fling at the Hotel Pennsylvania's Cafe Rouge, where we danced to Jimmy Dorsey's Orchestra, we were on the Pennsylvania Railroad's "Broadway Limited," en route to Chicago and the Palmer House Hotel. Soon after, we boarded another train that took us to La Crosse, Wisconsin, and Camp McCoy. We had rented a room in the little town of Sparta and that's where we arrived on Christmas Eve. Many people near army camps rented out rooms in their houses, both to help the war effort and to make extra money. We were lucky to have a room in a private home. We shared the bath with a total of eight people, including another army couple then away on Christmas leave. When they returned, I was delighted to have a new friend, Alice Hunter, wife of a lieutenant in Ink's regiment. Ink and I were quite alone on Christmas day, however, and as meals were not included with our room we went off to find a restaurant for our Christmas dinner. Not a place was to be found; everything was closed for the holiday, even the restaurant in the Sparta Hotel. We finally found a dairy open and bought some milk, cheese, and biscuits, which we took back to our room. We laughed at our first Christmas dinner together!

Ink was allowed off the base only three nights a week. In good weather, Alice Hunter would drive me to Camp McCoy whenever the men could meet us for dinner at the officer's club, which wasn't often. We ate most of our meals at the Sparta Hotel and were all quite taken with our jolly, pretty waitress there with the unique name of "Marvelous"! Because the thermometer greeted us many days with a 35-below-zero reading, walking to the hotel was an adventure. The roads were a solid sheet of ice, and Alice and I trod carefully, holding on to each other. It was impossible to drive on such roads unless you were in a big truck. We saw some people on ice skates.

At Camp McCoy, I met all of the regimental officers, in particular the ones in Ink's 236th Engineer Combat Battalion, from all over the United States. These men would go off to fight together and many of them would die. One of my favorites, Kahl Perlman, was a bachelor from Stamford, Connecticut, and I promised I would visit his mother and father in their jewelry store when I went home. Everyone liked

Kahl, for he was patient and kind. His best friend was another battalion officer, Joe Fallon from Boston. Fate would take a strange turn for them in the jungles of Burma.

One of the most liked couples in the battalion was Dr. Max Goldberg and his wife, Sid, from New Orleans. Max had given up a lucrative practice at home to join the army and serve his country, knowing that doctors were needed. And what a help Max was to everyone in combat! Dr. Don Green, a dentist from Hannibal, Missouri, saved lives in combat, too, once by performing a tracheotomy using a fountain pen to open the wind passage. Keith Esme, married to the pretty dark-haired Mary Ellen, looked more like an artist than a soldier. Ink told me later that, under fire, Keith was the bravest man of all and volunteered to go on missions into the jungle many times. It was in a jungle where Japanese soldiers hid in the treetops with their guns that a sharpshooter killed Keith one night.

Just as the weather started to warm up, the battalion was sent to Tennessee on maneuvers. I went home by train to Stamford, took my final exams, and graduated from school in June! Then I flew to Nashville, Tennessee, my first experience of air travel. Thunder and lightning filled the sky as our propeller plane lurched from side to side. I determined that if I reached the ground safely, I would never board another plane. It seems an absurd thought now when I reflect that I have flown many thousands of miles since that stormy afternoon.

Ink met me at the Nashville airport and took me to Convent Place and my new rented room. It was in a pretty house owned by Mr. and Mrs. M. O. Armstrong, who had never had strangers living in their home before and treated me like a guest. Ink could only come home one night a week, and after a few nights of watching me go out to a little restaurant a few blocks away, the Armstrongs decided I must eat at home with them. On Thursday nights when their cook was off they took me out with them. What happy memories I have of those fine people.

It saddened me when Ink one day told me I must move because the battalion would be changing its location and I would be too far away in Nashville. I was to live in a place called Mount Eagle-in-the-Mountains, between Nashville and Chattanooga. There I had a room in Mrs. Taylor's boarding house, with a bath down the hall. It was another adventure, complete with an older man (or so he seemed to me at the time) at dinner, who told us all about his having been in the Spanish-American War. Two older women boarders had a handsome convertible Buick but couldn't drive. They asked if I would drive them around the countryside from time to time. I was eager to chauffeur my new friends around the South, though I hadn't been driving very long and was very careful. Mount Eagle was close to Sewanee and the university there, so we attended some good concerts and lectures.

Ink came home only once a week; he had a rugged schedule with little free time allowed. Before maneuvers were over I had to change domiciles again, this time to Lebanon, Tennessee. I never made it to Memphis then but would many years later, to visit our son and his family. After Lebanon, it was back to Wisconsin and Camp McCoy. Good friends from the original Regiment had phoned to say that a room was available in Tomah near the camp. We would share a bath only with them, as it was a two-bath house, a funeral home! Such luxury and such an unusual experience!

I had been to very few funerals and knew nothing about funeral homes but soon learned that life can go on at full tilt even with death in the front parlor. The White family had been in the funeral business for some time and their children played on the staircase, made noise as all children do, except when there were services going on. Everything was quiet then and I could hear the words of the service coming up into my room through the heat ventilator.

Ink and I knew that he would be receiving his orders for overseas very soon. Would it be Europe? We had read in the newspaper about reports coming out of Europe of what Hitler was doing to the Jews in Germany and in the countries he was taking over. We read and talked about Hitler's drive for world domination and were convinced that this was a war that must be fought hard and won for sure. With the strength and optimism of youth, we were sure that Ink would come back alive and well, and I hoped we were right. With the way the regiment had been split up, there were now one group and two battalions. The group was going to Europe to be joined to a larger outfit. Where Ink would go we did not know. When orders came he was to report to a staging area in California, and that didn't sound as though he would be on his way to Europe. He couldn't tell me then but it was Riverside, California, and his destination turned out to be India and Burma, the CBI, or China-Burma-India theater.

Summer days were behind us, it was 1943, and this separation was the big one. I waved goodbye, packed up, and prepared to drive our Ford from Wisconsin back to Connecticut. Another army wife was supposed to drive with me for most of the trip, but at the last minute she had to leave me in Chicago. I didn't tell my family I was driving alone all the way from Chicago to New York where I would meet my father. I knew it was a little crazy to drive so far alone as a fairly new driver, but it was the only way to get the car home. You do what you have to do. I was learning the responsibilities of an army wife.

The Long Wait — India and Burma

What is it like waiting at home when your husband goes to war? Worrisome, lonely, frustrating, and, for me, constantly busy. Ink and I wrote each other every day (and continued to do so in years to come when apart). Filling my waking hours with activity helped, because I wished I could be overseas and have a hand in the war myself — impossible of course. The army was adamant that no army wives would be allowed to leave the country — not with the Red Cross, the USO, which was sending plays abroad to entertain the troops in combat areas, or any form of war effort — so that was that. To begin my own war effort, I took a course with the Red Cross and was soon working part-time as a volunteer Red Cross nurses' aide. Because of the shortage of nurses, so many having left the civilian hospitals for military duty, being an aide was much like being a nurse, except for not giving patients medication. It was hard but interesting work as we moved around from ward to ward, with the sick and dying, the not so sick, and the new babies in the maternity ward, everyone's favorite assignment.

So many families were watching, listening, and waiting. At home, we worried not only about Ink, but about my brother Bill, who had enlisted in the army because he thought that's where he should be and was stationed in Europe. He and his wife had a new baby girl, and he was sad to leave them behind. He wrote us letters from Europe, always writing of how much he missed us, his wife, and his daughter Kay. When he came back from the war, his marriage did not survive, a wartime casualty I have always thought, and we were sorry that we were not able to see much of his daughter as she grew up, although Bill worked hard to see her often.

When I heard that the Cushing Bookshop in New Canaan was looking for a part-time assistant manager, I signed on immediately, as I had long had a love affair with books. Growing up I had been a familiar sight at the local library, trudging up and down the steps with my arms full of books, and had been on the school library committee. I felt at home in the Cushing Bookshop, which was quite remarkable and different from other bookshops. Mr. Cushing's large collection of books on mountain-climbing was kept in the back room, where good customers were welcomed for a cup of coffee. Mr. Cushing himself was somewhere in Europe with the OSS, that glamorous-sounding but often dangerous forerunner of the CIA. We heard later that he had helped the actress Marlene Dietrich counter accusations that she had Nazi ties. Like so many others, he had apparently become enchanted with the famed Miss Dietrich, though I never knew the facts.

Our little village overflowed with authors, publishers, and editors, like the legendary Maxwell Perkins of Scribner's. When he visited the shop, he and I would have long talks about the publishing business and the war. He was the editor who discovered such great writers as Ernest Hemingway, F. Scott Fitzgerald, and Thomas Wolfe. Another of his finds, James Jones, wrote *From Here to Eternity*, a great success as a book and later as an Academy Award–winning movie. Mr. Perkins didn't live to see the James Jones book come out in 1951. That book was only one of many the highly respected Perkins selected for publication. He always worked with his authors, encouraging them and often bringing them fame and fortune. Another of his Pulitzer Prize–winning authors was Marjorie Kinnan Rawlings, who wrote *The Yearling*.

Maxwell Perkins and his wife, Louise, had moved to New Canaan from New Jersey with their young daughters because, as he later wrote, "It is the charm of New Canaan, a New England village at the end of a single-track railroad with almost wild country in three directions, i.e., wild to an Easterner. An ideal place for bringing up children in the way they should go, girls anyhow."

I liked that he felt that way about my hometown, because I thought it was a wonderful place to grow up. I have always been glad that I spent my early years in New England. The weather can be harsh or beautiful, and something about New England sinks into your bones and helps you through adversity or unexpected achievements.

Another Cushing regular was Alexander Kerensky, who had been prime minister of Russia briefly in 1917. He and his wife came in to buy books or to borrow one from our small lending library. They kindly took me to dinner with them one night at the nearby Silvermine Tavern, and I only wish I had known then what I know now so I could have asked some questions about those final days of the Russian Revolution. The pro-Western Prime Minister Kerensky had refused to make a separate peace with Germany, undoubtedly causing his downfall. We did talk a little about his early life in Tsarist Russia.

From my talks with Liam O'Flaherty, whose book *The Informer* had won a Pulitzer Prize, I learned that the mind of an Irishman can be stubborn and volatile as well as intriguing.

When novelist Faith Baldwin came in, I was always glad to see her. We had been friends since I interviewed her when I was twelve to earn my Girl Scout writer's badge. As part of her support for the troops Faith wrote frequent letters to my husband. Until the time she died, many years later, she would urge me to write a book myself.

While Mr. Cushing was off with the OSS, Mrs. Cushing came to the bookshop frequently. An author herself, Mary Watkins Cushing knew a great deal about her subject, which was opera. She had worked for one of the great dramatic sopranos of the Metropolitan Opera, Olive Fremstad, and after the war wrote a book about her called *The Rainbow Bridge*.

I found I was spending much of my salary on books. My first purchase was the huge *Columbia Encyclopedia,* which has moved with me almost everywhere. Tattered and old though it be, I still find it useful.

My first contact with the backstage wonders of radio came thanks to Cameron Mitchell, a young neighbor in our apartment house in Stamford. He was a struggling young actor about to burst on the Broadway scene, where he became a much admired star, playing one of the sons in the original production of Arthur Miller's *Death of a*

Salesman. Another successful play for him was Irving Berlin's *This is the Army.* He went on to make many films in Hollywood. When we met, he was putting on plays for the Stamford radio station. He needed a young woman to act in some of his radio dramas, one of the great arts of early radio. At his invitation, I auditioned at the station, was hired, and thoroughly enjoyed myself. Later, I would make a living broadcasting to people in countries far from Connecticut, but I have not forgotten my first introduction to the microphone.

From news reports coming in from Europe and from India and Burma, it looked as though the war would be a long one. I made frequent trips into New York, only an hour away, for Broadway tryouts. For plays like *Life with Father* and *Dear Ruth,* I would get callbacks, which meant I had a second chance; but I was never good enough to get the job. I realized that I was competing with young people who had had a great deal of training, so I took a few lessons from a coach in Westport, Connecticut, who introduced me to a good agent. Luckily, the agent took me on, but I discovered that I never did as well in a tryout as I did when actually on stage. An offer from the American Theater Wing to perform in some factories to raise money for Liberty Bonds turned out to be great fun. The man who played Lamont Cranston on *The Shadow,* one of our most popular radio programs, played a father and I his daughter in a one-act play. We raised quite a bit of money, which brought me a nice certificate from the Theater Wing.

When I tried out for a play called, *Harriet,* starring the great actress, Helen Hayes, I went backstage and talked with Miss Hayes, my favorite of all actresses. I told her I would like to play the part of her daughter in *Harriet.* She thought I looked very much as she had at my age. Looking at our two faces in the mirror, she said, "You see, we both have eyes that are far apart and a face that can be adapted to various characters," adding, "We're not ready to go into production yet, but I hope you'll come back and read for us again."

I never did go back because my life took another turn about that time.

On my frequent trips to New York, I would visit Annabella, who was living at the Hotel Pierre while starring in a Broadway play called *Jacobowski and the Colonel.* Tyrone Power had volunteered for the United States Marine Corps and was flying combat missions as a pilot. The separation was a difficult one, for I knew they were very much in love. Annabella also worried about her family in France. Unhappily, the Powers's marriage became another casualty of wartime separation, and eventually they divorced. For me it was difficult to understand how two people so much in love could not work things out somehow.

The bookshop gave my life some structure during my wait for Ink's return, and I found great satisfaction in my nursing work at the hospital. At a beach club I joined as a junior member, I found I was one of only a few army wives. I saw many young men arriving from their jobs in New York to join their wives and realized that not all young men were overseas. One woman sitting near me on the sand thought that facing death couldn't be as bad for regular army officers as it was for draftees, because the regular army prepared you to die and therefore death wasn't such a tragedy. I told her I strongly disagreed with her but knew that arguing the point would be useless. Ink had told me that West Point taught them not to expect great thanks for fighting for their country but to do it because it was necessary and because it was right.

The real combat for Ink's battalion began in Burma. He was now the battalion commander. He and his troops were sent in to replace Merrill's Marauders, which had suffered huge casualties on the Burma Road. All of his letters were censored, but I could discern that the risks were high and the foxholes deep.

My father had finished his tour of duty with the Corps of Engineers in Bermuda and was now working for the navy on Wall Street in New York City. I well remember coming home to our Stamford apartment one night from my job at the bookshop in New Canaan to find my father standing beside the garage where I parked my car. That was so unusual that I knew at once something was wrong.

He sat down beside me in the car and said, "It's not Ink, but Kahl Perlman has been killed in Burma. It's in tonight's newspaper. We must go right away to visit his mother and father. I found their home address by phoning the jewelry store."

Not only was I upset to hear about Kahl, but I knew that because he was operations officer for Ink's battalion, the battalion headquarters may have been attacked. We went right to the Perlmans' house, and it was a sad time. I told his parents how highly regarded Kahl had been by everyone in the battalion. I learned later from Ink that Kahl had volunteered to go out on patrol that night to take the place of his good friend, Joe Fallon, who was very ill. Ink was only five yards away from Kahl when the fatal shot was fired from a tree in the jungle. Some years later, when Joe Fallon had returned to his home in Boston, he named his baby son Kahlman for his dear friend.

We received two terrible telephone calls during the long wait. Both came from Tyrone, Pennsylvania, and both times it was Ink's father calling with tragic news. The first call concerned Ink's brother, Clayton, an army colonel, a brilliant man, and a former West Point professor. Dad Gates told us Clate was killed in a training accident just before his battalion was due to go overseas. The second call some months later was to tell us that the dreaded telegram from the War Department had arrived saying that the middle brother, Bernard, an army captain fighting in France, was also dead. Ink and I took Mother Gates to visit Bun's grave there many years later when we lived in Europe. Because Ink was the sole surviving son, the army ordered him home from his combat duties in Burma, a little earlier than he might have returned had his two brothers still been alive.

On a cold afternoon in February 1945, my father drove me into New York and left me at the old Biltmore Hotel, where I was to meet Ink on his return home. After a day in New York, we were to visit his mother and father in Pennsylvania, then come back to Connecticut before heading south to visit our widowed sister-in-law.

We were greatly saddened by the circumstances that had brought Ink home early but overjoyed to be back together. Ink was to report to West Point for duty, but first we were both to go to Asheville, North Carolina, to the Grove Park Inn, which the army had taken over for returning servicemen to have a brief holiday. We could hardly believe we would have a week together in such a beautiful place.

We saw all the families, holidayed in North Carolina, and then, before reporting to West Point, headed south in our Ford automobile to Tennessee. The long wait was over.

2

The Manhattan Project

*"It is an atomic bomb. It is a harnessing of the basic power of the
Universe. The force from which the sun draws its powers has
been loosed against those who brought war to the Far East."*
—President Truman, August 6, 1945

It was hard to believe that Ink was home and that we were driving together to a place called Oak Ridge, Tennessee, and from there to his next assignment, the military academy at West Point. We were together, but the war was not over. It was February 1945.

Our first destination was a mysterious place, not on any map. Oak Ridge, Tennessee, part of the Manhattan Project we were told. We wondered if it would rise up in a great mist like the mythical city of Brigadoon. We knew that the place was not far from Knoxville, Tennessee, and that our widowed sister-in-law lived there. We knew that she was the editor of a newspaper with a circulation of 75,000, strange numbers for a non-city.

Ink had talked to a general in Burma, who had been ordered to leave his assignment there and report to the Manhattan Project in Washington. The general told Ink he had no idea what it was except that it was something important. We were curious to discover more about Oak Ridge and why, if it were part of the Manhattan Project, it would be located down south in the state of Tennessee. As we drove through farmland, suddenly there it was, a gate, a guard, and a large wooden pole barring our way. We were expected so the pole was raised and on we drove into a city of dust and dirt and heavy building equipment. It could have been a western outpost years ago. Underneath it all we could see the plan of a neatly laid out small city. It had a bank, a filling station, and little houses and churches on the surrounding hills. The houses were designated As, Bs, Cs, and Ds, with As the smallest and the Ds the largest. Even the D was not very large.

The commanding officer, whom we knew quite well, was Colonel Kenneth D. Nichols, soon to be Brigadier General then Major General Nichols. His title of deputy district engineer and district engineer of the Manhattan Engineer District meant that he had responsibility for the design, construction, and operation of the gigantic plants for producing U-235 and plutonium, the fissionable material required by Los Alamos as the source of explosive energy ultimately used in the atomic bombs at the Alamogordo, New Mexico, test site, Hiroshima, and Nagasaki. Nick, as we called him, was the number two man in the Manhattan Project, directly under General Leslie Groves, who was headquartered in Washington. General Groves had already achieved renown for having built the Pentagon in record time, but it was the Manhattan project that would put him in the history books.

As Ink and I drove through the city, I looked around at the muddy streets and thought how glad I was that we didn't live there! We were heading to beautiful West Point in the Hudson Valley, close to Connecticut, New York, Pennsylvania, and our family and friends. Little did I know that this dusty corner of Tennessee would be the place where we would live among and befriend scientists, military, and civilians from all over the United States. We would see the end of World War II from here and know that we had played a part in making it happen.

Up the hill we drove, to Fran Gates's house on Olney Circle. Fran, Ink's brother Clate's widow, was raising their two young sons and running the *Oak Ridge Journal.* She rented a room to an army private and his wife. The private was a PhD, as were so many of the privates on duty there, and his wife took care of the boys when Fran was at work. We were glad to see them all and to discover that the Nicholses lived right next door.

"Nick wants to see you in his office," Fran told Ink and added that we would all be going to the Nichols house for drinks that night.

Colonel Nichols asked Ink if he would like to work at Oak Ridge as his assistant. The job would entail frequent travel to Los Alamos, New Mexico, the Hanford reservation in Richland, Washington, and other parts of the project around the United States. It would be a great career opportunity, he explained. He was looking for outstanding young officers, he said, and thought Ink had all the right qualifications. Changing the West Point assignment would be no problem, as Oak Ridge had priority over all assignments, authority direct from the White House (meaning President Roosevelt). Think it over, he told Ink. Talk it over with Pat and let me know tomorrow, in my office.

The next day Ink told Nick that although he had given the idea of staying in Oak Ridge serious thought and knew it would be good for his career; having just returned from combat in Burma he thought it best to go north for his teaching assignment at the military academy.

"You'll like it here," said Colonel Nichols. "Washington is preparing all the necessary papers and as soon as possible you'll be assigned a house. One's coming up in a couple of months next to ours, just behind Olney Circle on Outer Drive."

So, the deed was done. Being young, in love, and ready for adventure, we accepted the inevitable and found a room to rent in Knoxville, Tennessee, about a half hour away. After awhile we moved to a small apartment in Fountain City, and Ink commuted daily to Oak Ridge. I frequently went out to Oak Ridge with him, spending time at the hospital as a Red Cross nurses' aide, thanks to my early training.

One special couple we met, Arthur and Betty Compton, lived on Olney Lane, opposite the Nicholses. Arthur's code name in the Project was A. H. COMAS, but in reality he was Dr. Arthur Holly Compton of the University of Chicago, a Nobel Laureate for Physics in 1927 and one of the most important members of the project's scientific community.

Arthur and Betty were deeply rooted in their religion and, unlike some scientists, believed that God and science are completely compatible. The Comptons kindly lent us their house while they went on a trip for several weeks, by the end of which our little "B" house would be ready for us. I well recall one Sunday morning during our stay when Dr. Compton came by the house for breakfast. Among his mail was an invitation to give a speech in the Soviet Union!

His deep-set blue eyes twinkled as he said, "That is one invitation I better not accept."

I always enjoyed talking to the physicists, Dr. Compton in particular. We spoke of many things but never what was going on at Oak Ridge. I admired a photograph of Arthur Compton that hung on the wall of his house. He was extremely good-looking and had a remarkable brain. After the war, he became chancellor of Washington University in St. Louis, Missouri. His older brother, Karl Compton, was president of the Massachusetts Institute of Technology. Imagine my delight when I walked down the hallway of my club, the Cosmos, in Washington, some forty-eight years after Oak Ridge and saw that same picture of Arthur Holly Compton on the wall. It hung beside a doorway, along with all the Nobel Prize winners who have been members of the Cosmos Club. Just above Arthur's picture is that of another Nobel Laureate, President Woodrow Wilson. Arthur died some years ago, but he made his mark here on earth.

Ink and I would walk over to the Comptons' house once a week to look at the stars through the telescope in his front yard, and he and some of the other neighborhood scientists would explain the heavens to us. One man said he had built his own telescope, something I said I wished I could do, and lo, the next day, he sent me a little book on how to build your own telescope. Given the times, I was convinced without even trying that I could never do anything so complicated. Women were just programmed that way then! Gradually, I learned to have more confidence in myself. Now, though I rarely give up trying, I do know my limits and I'm afraid building a telescope is one of them.

My former high school math teacher, Mary Horne, later dean of the school, told me once that the FBI had come to interview her about me when I was going to work at the White House.

"I told them all kinds of good things about you, Patty dear," she said, and finally the FBI man asked, "Can you tell us something negative about her?" "I thought for a bit and finally replied, Well, she wasn't very good at math!'"

Among the Oak Ridge luminaries was Dr. Ernest O. Lawrence, professor of physics at the University of California and a Nobel Laureate for his work developing the cyclotron for experimental use in the treatment of cancer. The cyclotron produced new artificial isotopes of the chemical elements and proved of great importance in nuclear physics. E. O. Lawrence was one of the project's most distinguished scientists and spent a great deal of time at Oak Ridge working on the development of U-235. One night, Dr. Lawrence and his wife Molly came to our house for an outdoor picnic. I told Molly that she had the same name as my mother, Molly Lawrence. A coffee connoisseur, she liked my coffee and wondered what kind I used. She was surprised when I told her it was inexpensive, freshly ground "Eight O'clock" coffee from the A & P.

I never met the famous Dr. J. Robert Oppenheimer, but Ink would sit in on conferences with him in Los Alamos. "Oppie" would sometimes bounce a rubber ball while he was talking, Ink said. Not a typical habit of most scientists!

We made many fast friends in Oak Ridge, most of them our neighbors, and our first year went by quickly. Ink was gone a great deal of the time, traveling with General Nichols to every part of the United States. Normally, he could not tell me where he was going, but once he contacted me to ask me to come to Buffalo, New York, where he was hospitalized with a severe recurrence of the malaria he had contracted in India. I immediately boarded a train and headed for Buffalo, where I had once lived as a child, and made plans to stay with good friends of my parents while visiting Ink in the hospital.

My recollection of the day I arrived in Buffalo is a vivid one, because it was April 12, 1945, the day that President Franklin D. Roosevelt died. President Roosevelt had been our great war leader along with Winston Churchill in Great Britain, and it was a sad day. Ink recovered after about ten days and returned to duty in Oak Ridge.

When Ink could get away, which was seldom, we would visit the nearby Great Smoky Mountains, which had not yet become a big tourist area. We stayed in Gatlinburg in a charming old rustic inn and swam in a nearby natural lake. The Great Smokies are a beautiful sight to behold.

When the phone rang in our apartment in Fountain City on the morning of August 6, 1945, it was Ink calling from his office in the Oak Ridge headquarters building. "Turn your radio on right away," he said. "President Truman is about to make a very important announcement. You will hear all about what we have been doing in the Manhattan Project and understand why we are so excited out here and think the war will be over right away because of our efforts.

I have to go now but get ready to come out here to the Nicholses' house tonight."

I rushed for the radio and heard President Truman announce that the United States had dropped a powerful new weapon, an atom bomb, on the city of Hiroshima, Japan. Even without television in those days, the word traveled fast around the world and was met with shock and relief. It looked as though the devastation from that one bomb would cause the Japanese to surrender and save many lives. It took another atom bomb, however, dropped on Nagasaki a few days later, to convince the Japanese to give up. World War II was over. That day, another phone call from Ink told me that he was on his way to Washington, D.C. with Nick Nichols, and I would have to be content to listen on my radio to the cheering in the streets. While Ink was in Washington, I spent most of my time in Oak Ridge with the wives of the other officers who were gone.

Dr. Stafford Warren, medical section chief at Oak Ridge, whose wife Vi was one of my special friends on the base, left immediately for Japan to assess the radiation damage. Dr. Warren had previously headed the radiology department at the University of Rochester Medical School. When he was brought into the army for the Manhattan Project, one story goes, he was made an instant full colonel. While walking down the street in uniform near the bank in Oak Ridge, a soldier passed him and saluted. "Staff" had a handful of change in his right hand and didn't know what to do, so he dropped the change on the sidewalk and saluted the soldier.

When the war ended, Dr. Warren became the founding dean of the University of California at Los Angeles medical school. When I visited him there, he explained that much of his work concerned cancer. He showed me a huge oil painting of a striking blond woman on the wall of his office and asked me if I knew who she was. "That's Marion Davies, the mistress of William Randolph Hearst," he said. I had seen the film *Citizen Kane*, the fictionalized story of the life of Hearst, so I knew about them both. "That lovely woman," he said, "has made this hospital possible for she gave us all the money to build it." When John F. Kennedy was president, he brought Staff Warren to Washington to head his newly formed Mental Retardation Program.

After the bomb, many of the original scientists and reserve officers left Oak Ridge, and we were sorry to see them go. New people moved onto Olney Lane and into other parts of the city. Ink had been one of the first officers from the regular army at Oak Ridge, but more soon arrived, among them Colonels Harvey Fraser and Donald Williams, who had seen combat in Europe. They were reunited with their wives, Jean and Madge, after years of separation, so it was a happy time. On Saturday nights, we took turns hosting potluck dinners at each of our homes, with lots of bridge and good conversation. The hostess would cook the dinner and the men would clean up afterwards.

When our beautiful baby girl arrived one rainy afternoon, we felt additionally lucky because until then all Gates family children and grandchildren had been boys. Our Pamela Townley Gates was born in the state-of-the-art Oak Ridge Hospital, designed for those involved in the vital Manhattan project. During the first three years after the hospital was built almost three thousand babies were born there. My army doctor at Oak Ridge, William "Bucky" O'Connor, had retired a few months before Pam's arrival to set up a private practice in Oak Ridge, but we decided to stretch our meager budget and keep him for Pam's delivery as did our good friends, the Frasers. Jean had her baby first, and I learned all about new babies from watching her. She was already an experienced mother, having raised three and a half year old Harvey Jr. alone while Harvey Sr. was off in Europe fighting War World II with the combat engineers. (Harvey Fraser became a West Point professor and later president of the South Dakota School of Mines in Rapid City. Many years later, in 1999, he received the George S. Patton Award for his heroic actions in combat during World War II.)

Don Williams, the other newly arrived colonel, was a splendid pianist and played as a soloist in the newly formed Oak Ridge Symphony Orchestra. He later headed the Hanford Operation, site of the plutonium production plants. We all grieved when he died of Alzheimer's many years later.

Other special friends included A. V. "Pete" Peterson and his wife, Marie Louise. Pete Peterson held a pivotal responsibility as the central liaison between the Metallurgical Project and the army. Later, he became a highly esteemed consultant on atomic energy matters.

When the Comptons left Oak Ridge after the war, Colonel Staunton Brown, his wife Fannie, and their two (later three) girls moved into the Comptons' house on Olney Circle. Staunton Brown was another one of the highly regarded engineer officers brought into the Manhattan Project. As Colonel Nichols was winding up his responsibilities at Oak Ridge, Ink became Staunton Brown's assistant operations officer, working on the big plants at Oak Ridge, K-25, Y-12, and others. Preparing our nuclear defenses for the years ahead left much work to do.

A man at Oak Ridge whom I admired and liked tremendously, although many in the outside world considered him a prickly character, was Admiral Hyman (Rick) Rickover, father of America's nuclear navy and undoubtedly a great American. Ink met him first when he was assigned to show then Captain Rickover through a secret room at Oak Ridge, so secret that it was totally wired up in case of a break-in. (One time, in the middle of the night, Ink was phoned to come at once because the alarm had gone off in the never-mentioned room. The intruder turned out to be a mouse!) But back to the VIP visitor's tour. Ink told me when he came home that day that he had just met a most exasperating and difficult man. Every time Ink started to explain something, Rickover would say he knew all about it and more. Truth be told, he really did know it all, and Ink came to admire Rick, as we called him, as much as I did.

We came to know Rickover well through navy commander Louis Roddis, who worked for him, and through our sister-in-law, Fran Gates, the *Oak Ridge Journal* editor. Rickover was good about explaining atomic energy to lay people like me. He also took an interest in our young school-age nephews, Sam and Dick Gates, explaining atomic energy to them in great detail—after the bomb had been dropped, of course. Rick didn't arrive in Oak Ridge until June 1946, by which time it was quite safe to talk about the Manhattan Project.

During the many good evenings together at our house, Rick told us how lucky he was to have been brought to the United States from Poland when he was six years old. His father was a Jewish tailor who moved his business to Chicago, Illinois, after four years in New York City. I have always loved Rick's story about coming here and the fact that he contributed so much to our nation of immigrants. Many years after Oak Ridge, in a speech he gave in Washington, he told the story he had once told me. His account of his early life and why he loved this country so much, touched me most:

> [America] has allowed an immigrant boy to realize every opportunity available to individuals who work hard. I was born in Poland, then a part of Russia. I was not allowed to attend public schools because of my Jewish faith. However, starting at the age of four, I attended a religious school where the only learning was from the Old Testament, in Hebrew. School hours were from sunrise to sunset, six days a week. On the seventh day, we attended Synagogue a good part of the day . . . . My father immigrated to the United States shortly before 1900 and saved enough money from his work to send tickets for my mother, my sister, and me. . . .
>
> I started grammar school at the age of six and a half in Brooklyn, knowing only a few words of English. Shortly thereafter, my mother, who worked at a Catholic hospital washing clothes, brought home for me a number of old *St. Nicholas* magazines, given her by the nuns. It was my first gift. I read them avidly. They greatly helped me learn English. Twelve years later at the naval academy, I finished near the top of my class in English.

Though Rick lacked good looks and had a somewhat abrasive and egotistical personality, to me he was a thoughtful friend and a splendid man who accomplished miracles, building for us a strong, indomitable nuclear navy. Undoubtedly, his Jewish roots may have caused some of his troubles, as prejudice was said to have played a part where promotions were concerned. Fortunately, some naval officers who recognized Rick's genius and wanted him promoted to admiral were helped by members of Congress who admired him enormously. I've met many men who took great pride in having worked for Rickover, having passed his difficult tests. These men had to work ten or twelve hours a day, seven days a week, as did Rickover. How lucky we are to have men like Hyman Rickover who give so much to our country! Happily, I believe there is less prejudice in the armed forces today than in the past.

One of the last times I spoke with Admiral Rickover was following his heart attack in 1972. I phoned him at Bethesda Naval Hospital, and we talked for a good half hour. As we spoke of Oak Ridge, he said some kind things, which I appreciated, about my role as an army wife. He was glad Ink had become a general and liked what I was doing at Voice of America. I praised his outspoken concern on the state of education in the public schools of America. He believed strongly that changes were needed, that we were on the wrong track for reading and writing and for producing mathematicians and scientists. Today, there is loud complaining about schools, but Rick's was an early voice raised.

From his hospital room, Rick was working long hours every day walking outside the hospital doors, with his aide taking notes as they walked. I suggested that he might live a great deal longer if he would cut down on his working hours. He laughed and said, "Pat, I would die immediately if I didn't stick with my regular routine."

Several months after leaving Bethesda Naval Hospital, Rick, who was a widower, married his nurse, Navy Commander Eleonore Bednowicz. He continued to work at a fast pace just as he had promised and lived until 1986. Rick and the extraordinary colleagues he trained had produced the world's first nuclear-powered ship, the *Nautilus,* followed by many more nuclear-propelled submarines and ships. Vice Admiral Charles Griffiths, then deputy chief of naval operations for submarines, delivered one of many tributes:

> "One name will always be associated with the history of nuclear power. Over the entire life of the nuclear-propulsion program, Admiral Hyman G. Rickover has been its single continuous thread of genius. He has made the navy the world's foremost source of knowledge in the design, construction, and operation of nuclear power plants. His demanding leadership has molded the Navy Nuclear Power Propulsion program. His technical leadership, open and frank exchanges with Congress and dogged pursuit of excellence have had a profound effect on the entire navy. His influence has reached into many areas of American life."

When Rick retired from the navy in 1982, the United States Congress authorized the presentation, on behalf of the Congress, of a specially struck gold medal honoring Admiral Hyman George Rickover and calling him "a man of vision, steadfastness, high principles, thorough devotion to his duty, during his illustrious career of more than sixty-three years in the United States Navy. Admiral Rickover is a national treasure."

After the war, visitors to Oak Ridge, always asked us why the name "Manhattan Project?" The answer went back to 1942. The government, fearing that Germany would produce an atomic bomb before we did, charged the U.S. Corps of Engineers to produce U-235 and plutonium and build an American atom bomb. Our best scientists worked together tirelessly with the army, meeting in New York in the Engineers' Manhattan District headquarters. For security reasons, the original name was kept, as the geographical locations spread out.

The extraordinary teamwork by the people in the Manhattan Project succeeded in producing the atom bomb that helped end the war. Japan surrendered after we dropped the second bomb, saving an estimated hundreds of thousands of American lives. Although the debate continues to rage, a Japanese woman at the Red Cross headquarters in Tokyo told me years later that the Japanese people are aware that the swift end to the war also saved many Japanese lives.

At Dartmouth College, where I was attending a seminar at the Dartmouth Institute some thirty years after the war, the professor said to our class of business CEOs and executives, "Now we are marking an anniversary of that dreadful day when the United States dropped the atomic bomb on Hiroshima." The classroom fell silent. Finally, I could stand it no longer and raised my hand.

"I was in Oak Ridge, Tennessee, that day," I told the professor. "It was a great day, not a dreadful one. We were ending the war. I knew people like my brother waiting to invade Japan whose lives were saved."

One by one, the men in the room raised their hands.

"I was in the Pacific," said one. "I was jubilant."

"I would live," said another. "I was awaiting orders for the invasion."

Another said, "I knew the Japanese would fight to the last person. The bomb was a godsend."

The decision to drop the bomb, all there agreed, was a courageous and right decision for President Truman to have made. The work of the Manhattan Project, of hundreds of organizations and thousands of individuals, deserves praise. A dangerous war had ended, a new era had begun.

"Why," I later asked Tom Vargish, the Dartmouth professor, "did you ask the question in such a negative way?"

"To get a discussion going," he replied, "and it turned out to be even better than I had hoped."

Many people connected with the Manhattan Project went on to have brilliant careers in the postwar years. To me, the hero of the Manhattan Project was General K. D. Nichols, who became one of America's foremost authorities on nuclear power. Scientists and army officers don't always see things in the same light, but the scientists in the project had great respect for K. D. Nichols. He made things work and helped everyone get along together. After Oak Ridge, he became consultant to the U. S. delegation to the United Nations Atomic Energy Commission and the U. S. Congress's Joint Committee on Atomic Energy, chief of the Armed Forces Special Weapons Project, and chief of research and development for the U. S. Army. After retiring from the military, he served as general manager for the U. S. Atomic Energy Commission and later as chairman of the Westinghouse International Atomic Power Company, Ltd., in Geneva, Switzerland, and lived on into his nineties.

Concerned about the peaceful uses of nuclear energy, he had high hopes for its use in the future. In one of our many conversations over the years, this time for my radio program, I asked Nick about his qualifications in nuclear physics. In the beginning, he said, he had absolutely none because he had been educated as an engineer. In his assignment to the Manhattan District, his job was in engineering, in charge of construction and operation of the production plants.

He went on to say, "Early in the game, I discussed with Arthur Compton, one of our scientific leaders, the need to educate me if I was to do my job. So he took the time, and whenever I was in Chicago, others like Enrico Fermi would take me to a room and give me a nice easy blackboard lesson on the fundamentals of nuclear physics."

I commented that Fermi was quite a teacher to have and Nick said, "Oh, he was a wonderful teacher, and he simplified things so an engineer could understand them. Others did the same, Ernest Lawrence and Oppenheimer. The main job, in fact one of the main jobs in the District, was to establish an understanding, a relationship between scientists, engineers, and industrial people. Many of the nuclear physicists had not done many practical things in their life and had no experience whatsoever working with industry. So our job was to get the two together and from a complicated theory arrive at practical solutions on how to build plants to produce U-35 and plutonium."

I suggested to Nick that he could have been called Dr. Nichols, as he did have his doctorate, but he preferred using his military rank. He emphasized that reactor design is really power plant design and that bomb design is a distinctly different field. He believed that it was unfortunate that nuclear energy was born in war, leading people to insist on connecting nuclear energy with nuclear weapons.

General Nichols worked well as the number two man to General Groves, who was not always easy to work with. The two men had much respect for each other.

Of Robert Oppenheimer, General Nichols said, "Although Oppie had a problem record as far as security was concerned, everyone agreed that Oppenheimer was the only one who could do the job in the time required, that he was by far the best man, and that we should approve him." Some years later, Oppenheimer was denied top clearance. In spite of his involvement in the denial of that clearance, General Nichols always believed, he said, that Oppenheimer had never been disloyal to the United States. However, he explained, security risk is different from disloyalty. When I commented that it never comes out in the plays and books written about Oppenheimer that General Nichols felt that way, he said, "No, because most people don't understand the difference between loyalty and security."

Nick and I agreed that our world cannot put the nuclear genie back in the bottle. We can only try to make sure that another nuclear device will never be used.

It was time for us to move on. The army wanted Ink to get his master's degree in civil engineering, with three additional months for a course in atomic physics, and sent him to the University of Illinois in Champaign-Urbana. We said good-bye to Oak Ridge and to 88 Outer Drive. Many of our friends were also going on to universities for graduate studies. Our house had been simply furnished, but the crib, the Magnavox stereo, and the books were ours and we packed them all up. It was our first big move together and the first of many more to come. Best of all, we had our Tennessee baby girl with us, not to mention our cocker spaniel. We had loved Oak Ridge, but the road ahead surely would lead us to other remarkable adventures. We were on our way!

3

Washington, Here We Come!

The day we arrived in Champaign, Illinois, the rain came down in angry sheets. In the middle of a June afternoon, I looked from the window of the Hotel Tilden-Hall onto total darkness. Illinois looked pretty grim—flat, so different from Connecticut and the hills of Tennessee. With no alternative, I quickly became accustomed to it.

Ink was off signing in at the armory, which meant he was back on duty, this time academic duty. I was alone because we had left our baby Pam in Connecticut with my mother and dad. They were to drive out with her as soon as we were settled. Ink arrived back at the hotel with the news that Champaign had just been hit by a tornado a few blocks from the hotel! No sooner had he made his announcement, than the sun came out, we hopped in the car, and were off to see our new house—actually half a house.

On a quick trip to Champaign before we left Oak Ridge Ink had found us a place to live. His judgment was good and I always liked the houses he chose, though sometimes there was little choice. Both Champaign and Urbana, the twin cities of the university, had a housing shortage and he was lucky to find even half a house to rent. An army officer lived downstairs who was just moving out when we arrived. The landlord lived next door and rented the downstairs of the house to us and the upstairs to another army couple, the Reynoldses. We had a common front door and stairway, one telephone between us in the hallway, and a small shared backyard. I was delighted when I saw it, for although just a matchbox, it had a tiny room with a window for Pam and a small master bedroom just big enough for a bed and a wardrobe trunk with drawers. The trunk served as Ink's bureau, and we bought a small dresser for me. Beside the bed we used orange crates, the widely known army substitute for end tables. We bought a table and chairs for the small dining room, a day-bed sofa for the living room that made into a double bed for guests, a round mahogany leather top coffee table, and a chair. Ink had a small chair and desk in the dining room for his homework, and that's where we put Pam's playpen.

We were overjoyed when my mother and father arrived with Pam just a few days after we moved in. I bathed Pam in the kitchen sink because we had only a shower, but sometimes the Reynoldses would let me take her upstairs to their bathtub. It certainly wasn't fancy, but we loved it and were happy being together. We had a good time there with many friends coming and going.

Here we were, at one of the best universities in the country and I wanted very much to be a student myself. We had found a good babysitter, but to hire her full time for my classes would have cost more than our budget would allow. Pam needed me at home with her, I knew, and I thought there might be a chance some time in the future for me to attend a university, so I was not too unhappy staying home. As it turned out, I never did find a time to get my degree, and I've always wished that I might have had that luxury. College, I've always thought, must be a great experience of concentrated learning. But I was self-taught and perhaps benefited from having to do it on my own all along the way. I had gone to a school with high academic standards, devoted to college preparation. I was a good student, but certainly far from the best.

I have thought often of Miss Tilley, the headmistress at my school, who told me I would be all right without college because I would never stop educating myself. "The purpose of education," she said, "is to teach you to do just that—read, think, watch, listen." The professors at Dartmouth had told me the same thing when I attended the Dartmouth Institute. "Some people can learn on their own," they told me, "and you are one of them."

Often through the years, I have been asked to speak to college students. I know the women graduates struggle with the problem of how to use their education and still be wives and mothers. I tell them they have time to raise their children while young and then pick up their careers again or start anew. Children are with you only seventeen or eighteen years, and women live longer now, allowing time for both children and a career. In my case, I point out, my most productive working years came when I was older. Once the children were in school, I worked part-time but was always available to attend their school activities and take them to the doctor or to piano lessons. It is certainly more difficult for single mothers. I suggest they work from home if possible, or get a job where the hours would fit the children's needs. I still marvel at how single parents cope with full-time jobs and full-time children's demands.

We went to all the university sporting events with our student tickets, and they were something to see. The Midwest is famous for its football, baseball, basketball, high jumps, low jumps, almost anything you can think of.

Ink worked hard on his civil engineering courses and especially enjoyed his classes in atomic physics. An "A" student, he excelled at every school. He always had time for me, and I appreciated him. I saw other marriages that were not as solid as ours, and I was sure ours would last forever.

Life was never dull for me in Champaign. I went to Sunday lectures at the university and sometimes invited home for tea a foreign student I would meet there. Ink brought home a classmate, Y. C. (Eugene) Chang, from China. We liked him and continued to see him occasionally for several years, for he stayed in this country working for a large engineering firm. He told us he could never go back to China because his mother's house and all her land had been taken over by the communists. He would raise his children here in the United States, which is exactly what he did.

I signed up for a course in child psychology at the university and found a good babysitter for that one course. My professor lived across the street from us, and I used to watch her children playing in her front yard, screaming, yelling, and allowed to do whatever they wished. I marveled at this lax discipline from a woman who made a life's work of the study of children. In class, the professor was interesting, but as I made notes, I wondered if total freedom without much structure is what children really need and want. I wanted to be a good mother so I kept my notes as we moved around. In about five years, I looked at them one day, laughed, and threw them out! We wanted to enjoy our children while they were growing up, not let them run wild and turn out fine years later. There is no perfect answer to raising children. It is an enormous responsibility, but those notes weren't much help!

After fifteen months in Champaign, Ink received orders to go to Washington, D.C., to our delight. Ink would be working for AFSWP, the Armed Forces Special Weapons Project, which was established early in 1947 by the secretary of war and the secretary of the navy. General Groves had been the first chief of AFSWP, responsible for the armed forces' participation in the military uses of atomic weapons. General Nichols was now chief and had requested that Ink come work for him. We would see old friends and make new ones. I had always wanted to live in Washington and Ink was eager to work in the Pentagon. Housing was a big problem because Washington, which in those days was still more like a small town than a big city, had been expanding rapidly since the end of the war. We had the good luck to rent an apartment in Arlington, Virginia, just across the Potomac from Washington, thanks to some friends of my family who were just leaving Barcroft apartments on Route 50. I have always remembered those friends, not just for the apartment but because they called me an idealistic realist. I had never heard that expression and have wondered from time to time if it were an accurate description. It probably was, although I had to toughen up a bit as the years went by to survive the hard knocks along with the many good happenings.

When orders come, it's always an exciting time for everyone. Moving is part of the difficulty and the joy of army life. It's not always easy for children to leave their schools and their friends, but mine said in later life that the moves were all worthwhile, because they had new adventures and made new friends. The moving van came and we three were on our way to Connecticut, where we would visit my parents before heading for Washington and our new life.

The Washington Years

When I was twelve years old, my parents brought me to Washington and I was dazzled by it. Our hotel was near Union Station, and from my room I could look out at the Capitol building with its lighted dome. It was an inspiring sight with the Statue of Freedom standing proudly on top. Freedom, my father had told me, was what our country is all about. I still love to see our Capitol. Nowadays when I come over the bridge from Maryland, the road curves for a moment and there it is, that dome straight ahead. Or I will be in the car crossing Pennsylvania Avenue and look down the avenue to see the Capitol on the hill in all its glory.

Orders for Washington meant we were going to live there for several years, and I would be able to explore everything. The first year I would get lost every time I drove to a new place, but that was a good method of learning my way around. One day a week was my day off, when my cleaning woman would look after Pam. I volunteered at Walter Reed Hospital and once gave a course to teenage girls in a city high school about self-improvement and dating. I had been given a book to use called *The Stork Didn't Bring You.* We were a little ahead of the times! I also volunteered at an early television studio, where we produced a children's program based on fairy tales.

In 1950, when Pam was a little over three years old, Lawrence Alan Gates (Larry), was born in the army hospital at Fort Belvoir, Virginia. What good luck! We had two children, one girl, one boy, they were fun, and we adored them. Suddenly, our apartment was too cramped and we found a small house to rent, also in Arlington, near an elementary school close enough for Pam to walk. She joined up with Kate Blanchard, and they both felt grown up being first-graders. Kate's father was also in the military (most of our neighbors were not) and eventually became commander of all U.S. troops in the European Theater.

First-grade mothers are most always enthusiastic about school activities and in no time, I found myself serving on the board of our Parent-Teacher Association. Harold Johnson, a pleasant, intelligent, army colonel, was on the board with me. He and I were upset by the statements of the school principal that the new idea for running a school was to have no competition between children. But competition, we disputed, was part of the American way of life. Eventually, the school leadership changed. I admired Harold Johnson and his wife, Dorothy. He had been a prisoner of war in the Philippines and Ink told me that former POWs were often overlooked for promotion. I need not have worried because Harold K. Johnson became a four-star general and chief of staff of the army!

Ink and I liked living in neighborhoods where people came from different walks of life—such as doctors, lawyers, and businessmen— rather than always being on army posts. Ink would take the bus to the Pentagon to leave me the car, and life was busy. Washington can be hot and humid in the summer, but there was almost no home air-conditioning in those days. I would drive with the children to pick up Ink at the Pentagon almost every night, and he would come out of his air-conditioned building looking cool and handsome in his uniform to a wilted wife! The Nicholses were the first of our friends to have a bedroom air-conditioner. It sounds funny now but when they had friends for dinner we would all troop into the one cool room for the early part of the evening.

When my mother and father came to visit us from Connecticut in 1949, we took the children to the Inaugural Parade of President Harry Truman. When Dwight Eisenhower became president four years later, I took Pam and Larry to the Lincoln Memorial to see him lay a wreath for some special occasion, and one Easter Monday we went to the White House for the Easter egg roll on the White House lawn. President Eisenhower was right there on the lawn with us with his daughter-in-law Barbara, whom I knew because she was an army wife. Very briefly, for there was a big crowd, she introduced me to the president.

I mention these special events, because it was a unique city for a young mother to share with her children. Military bands gave free concerts positioned on a barge beside the Lincoln Memorial. We would take the children to the evening concerts and sit on the big stone steps leading down to the water. Or sometimes, we would rent a canoe from the Potomac boathouse and join all the other boaters pulled up near the steps to listen. We didn't need much money for entertainment, and that was good because we didn't have much.

We would visit Ink's parents in Tyrone, Pennsylvania, or mine in Connecticut for our vacations or go to my older sister's house on the New Jersey shore. We loved the ocean, and all the children needed there was a bathing suit and a sand bucket.

The Washington years flew by. Ink was sent to Fort Belvoir, Virginia, for ten months at the engineer school and commuted from Arlington instead of moving out there. It seemed easier to stay in our house because of Pam's school, but we went to Fort Belvoir often and gave parties in our house for Ink's Belvoir classmates. We met Kay and Frank Little from Nebraska, thanks to that Belvoir year. He was another engineer lieutenant colonel, and they would become very important to us in future years.

That time was rolling around again for orders. We had been in Washington for five years, longer than I had dared hope. Would we come back again? I hoped we would.

The year was 1953 and many of the engineer officers were being sent to Korea. Finally, Ink's orders came, and they were for Germany. Frank Little had orders for Germany, too. Frank was to go to Stuttgart, Ink to Munich. The bad news was that no families were allowed to come to Germany for a year because of a housing shortage. I was crushed. I told Kay Little that there must be a way, and we decided to buy inexpensive passage on a small, slow ship and go to Germany on our own. Ink would find a little apartment to rent, and we would sail for Europe as soon as possible.

The first step on the grand adventure was seeing Ink and Frank off on a military ship sailing from Hoboken, New Jersey. Kay and I waved good-bye as the ship, loaded with army troops, slowly pulled out of its berth and the band played "Anchors Away." It was a highly emotional moment. There is something sad about a ship separating so majestically from the shore, with the waving and the shouted good-byes, as little by little, it edges out into the harbor and disappears from sight. I thought of all the separations of men and women through the centuries when the trumpet sounded. The men departed on foot, on horseback, by ship, but almost always, it was the women who stayed behind. I felt connected to all those waiting women. Although many women are part of the military these days, many others still wait, hoping for a reunion.

Kay went home to Lincoln, Nebraska, to pack for our trip, and I filled a footlocker and some suitcases with what I thought we would need for three years in Europe. Our passage was booked on the Holland-America Line, one cabin for the four of us, and the ship was the S.S. *Ryndam*, a dandy little ship. In nine days we would arrive in Rotterdam, The Netherlands. All was ready, and my father and mother took us to the ship. This time, we were the ones leaving the dock and heading out to sea.

4

On to Europe

The children took to an ocean crossing like seasoned travelers and made friends with all of the ship's complement. Pam was six, Larry three, and Kay and I were careful never to let them out of our sight. We didn't want to lose them overboard! We awoke one morning to the green, misty shores of Ireland, our first glimpse of land after a week at sea. Despite a hard rain, the sight was just as I had pictured it. We imagined a wee elf peering at us from a thatched roof. Our disembarking passengers were taken to shore on a tender. The next few hours were rough sailing as we neared the English Channel. About 10 p.m., the sea calmed down, the moon came out, and I brought Kay out on deck to catch our first view of England. The next morning, we sailed into Southampton, where many passengers went ashore.

Sailing out of the harbor in sunlight, we had a good look at the English villages along the shore, a pretty sight, with seagulls providing a picturesque escort. Next morning our excitement reached fever pitch as we reached Holland, gliding for what seemed an eternity through the long canal into the port of Rotterdam, viewing the Dutch countryside at close range on each side of the ship. Holland recalls the picture books at school. The windmills still stand but are no longer used to hold back the sea; that is the job of the dike system. Beautiful flowers and neat little farms abounded. How different that first arrival in Europe was from my many future trips by air, so quick and convenient but missing the atmosphere of the shoreline.

From the deck of the *Ryndam* Kay and I felt disappointed that in the waving crowd on shore there was no one to meet us. We had hoped to see Kay's husband, Frank Little, but there was no sign of him. Even after we docked, it was an hour or more before we could get off the ship. Suddenly, we noticed some men had been allowed to come on board, and in the crowd Kay ran right into Frank. He had corsages for us all, even Pam, and a wooden ship for Larry. Best of all, he brought the news that Ink would meet us in Munich and had a two-day leave. Immediately, it became imperative that I change our reservations on the Rhinegold Express to a night train to arrive in Munich early the next morning.

Time was short and Kay and Frank devoted their entire day to helping me. We went in Frank's car to the Hotel Atlanta and put our luggage in the Littles' room, canceled our train reservations for the next day, managed a 6:20 p.m. sleeper reservation with a change of train in Utrecht. Meanwhile, we lunched at the hotel and briefly walked Rotterdam's main street. The traffic was harrowing, whether on foot or by car, bicycles all over the place and no signal lights, everyone just going. My children blended right in with the blond Dutch girls and boys. We saw heartbreaking war destruction everywhere, but on every corner, construction was bringing order out of chaos. The friendly Dutch people made us feel welcome from our first step ashore.

Kay stayed at the hotel with the children, while Frank and I tracked down our six pieces of transit baggage, had it taken from one railroad station, where the ship had sent it, to another station, where it was weighed, checked on my ticket, and loaded onto our night train's baggage car. Later, Kay and Frank put us on the train with our five pieces of hand luggage, and I told the children to hang on to my skirt. We were on our way!

Riding through the countryside, we saw canals, fat black and white cows, and flowers on every farm. We reached Utrecht at 7:02 p.m., right on schedule, but the American Express agent had misinformed us — instead of twenty minutes between trains, we had only seven. No porter in sight. People everywhere, no one speaking English. The conductor finally found me a porter, told him where to take me, and we dashed downstairs into a busy terminal where our train was about to pull out. I looked as helpless as possible, what with two children, five bags, coats, camera, pocketbook, and corsage. I still thought I was taking a 7:20, not a 7:10 train, and might yet be standing there but for a thoughtful Dutch woman who spoke no English but practically shoved me onto the outgoing train. I kept saying München, the German name for Munich, to make sure it was going to the right place, but didn't find out until ten minutes after we had pulled out whether or not our compartment was on it. We just sat on our suitcases until a sympathetic conductor led us through six cars and brought our bags back for me. Our room was all made up and made our stateroom on the ship look like a palace. I put the children in the lower bunk, one at each end, and myself in the side less upper. Before long morning came, our ten-day journey was over, and Ink greeted us at the Munich railroad station with open arms!

We had a little apartment there in a small hotel, Torbrau Am Isartorplatz. Our building had survived the bombing raids, but all around it lay rubble from crumbled, less fortunate structures. In the midst of the debris stood kiosks selling all kinds of things. We arrived on a streetcar, or *Strassenbahn*, that pulled up right in front of the one building still standing in a rock-covered field. The day after our arrival, I bought Pam and Larry jump ropes from one of the kiosks and watched them frolic amid the rocks.

It was our good luck that Ink had met the mayor of Munich, who helped him find us a place to live. We had two rooms and a bathroom. Ink and I slept in the living room, with the children on cots in the other room. Every morning a maid came to make the beds and clean the rooms, and that was the luckiest stroke of all. Ink had been told just after our arrival that a house would be coming up in Grünwald, one of the residential sections of Munich. Now that I was on the scene it would be assigned to us. Evidently, his name was high enough on the list, with more houses expected to be available soon, so he was given the house right away. He had also learned that it was very difficult to find a housekeeper. Luckily, our hotel maid, Hedy, knew of someone who would like to live with an American family.

That's how wonderful Anni Haindel came into our lives. She came to our apartment for an interview, talked with me and with the children in German, which we did not speak, although Larry at three and one-half was learning fast. I hired Anni on the spot and began planning for her to move in with us as soon as we went into our house the following month.

The house was on Grünwalderstrasse in a pretty residential section of Munich. Although it had been confiscated by the American occupation, the army paid rent for it to its German owner, which greatly improved his financial situation. It was not lavish but had plenty of space, with separate bedrooms for Pam and Larry and us and one for Anni. Best of all were our neighbors, a German doctor, Dr. Georgi Maurer, and his wife, Erika. They had three children, Peter, Monica, and Eva. The youngest, Eva, was Pam's age, and they became good friends. I did not meet Erika and Georgi, however, until one night when Pam was late coming home for dinner. I went over and rang the bell at the big gate in the surrounding fence, similar to ours, and I asked the maid Dora for Pam.

"Yes, she's here," said Dora, "but Frau Dr. Maurer says please come in for she would so like to meet you."

It was that night that I discovered that the German custom regarding new neighbors is quite the opposite of ours. It is the newcomers in a neighborhood who must call on their neighbors if they wish to be friendly (later we found the same custom in France). If Pam hadn't been late coming home for supper, I might never have met and made friends with a most remarkable woman. It was from Erika that I learned much about Germany and the war years for her, when she lived with her husband south of Munich in an old farmhouse while Georgi was stationed there with the German army. We always reached a point when talking about the war when I hesitated to ask questions. How could the Germans, who loved children and music, animals and art, have been so brutal as to exterminate human beings in concentration camps? I had not yet visited Dachau, the notorious camp close to Munich. (That would come eight years later, when I lived in Munich once again; only then did I realize the full horror of the story.) Erika seemed to sense my concerns about the war and would tell me how mistaken the German people had been about Hitler. In the midst of great poverty in Germany, he had promised to improve the lives of everyone but then turned out to be evil, wreaking havoc on the country and its people.

By the time we came to Munich, Georgi had become one of Germany's most distinguished surgeons and headed the large city hospital, Rechts Am Isar, in Munich. He lectured at conferences all over the world, including Moscow and Washington. On one of my trips back to Munich some years later, I learned that Georgi had been working night and day in the hospital, saving the lives of some of the British Manchester soccer team players injured in a terrible plane crash in Munich. For his superb efforts and for his wartime help to

British soldiers at Dunkirk, Queen Elizabeth II invited the Maurers to England; Georgi was honored in Manchester and received the Order of the British Empire from the queen. I think that Georgi was the only German to be honored with both Germany's Iron Cross and Britain's OBE.

Erika took me with her all around Munich, to operas, operettas, and concerts, and to their little farmhouse in the mountains. Ink and I included the Maurers frequently when we entertained. Their young son, Peter, would come over and practice his English with me to augment what he was learning from textbooks. Later, he would attend medical school and become a highly regarded surgeon like his father, even becoming head of surgery in the Rechts Am Isar Hospital. To this day, he is a dear friend and visits me in America with his wife when he comes to lecture at medical conferences, like his father before him.

At a Christmas party for the children at the Maurers' house, a doctor from the hospital said to me, "I want to tell you something about Frau Dr. Maurer. During the war, at great personal risk, she helped me and other Jewish doctors escape over the mountains to Switzerland. She was living near Bad Tolz where the S.S. troops were located, but she was able to save our lives. She is a great and courageous lady!"

Erika had traveled to many parts of the world with her father and spoke five languages. She was beloved by those who knew her, and I have always been grateful for our friendship. Unhappily, though Erika and Georgi were devoted in many ways, he fell in love with another woman and they divorced after we had left Germany. Erika died at an early age and Georgi was devastated but it was too late. Their story certainly is not unique to Germany, for I have observed it in many parts of the world.

Ink was away with his battalion most of the time on maneuvers with the 43rd Division, but once in a while he would have a day off. On our first trip to the mountains, the magnificent German Alps, we took the scenic winding mountain road via Mittenwald. Our destination was Garmisch, the famous resort and site of the 1936 Olympics two hours' drive from Munich. Our first view of the Alps was only a few minutes' drive from the city, and what a view it is. In the lovely town of Mittenwald, with its pink, brown, and green buildings with pictures painted on them, and a tall pink, painted church, Bavarians walked the narrow streets dressed in their Sunday best.

In Garmisch, we dined at the Hotel Von Steuben and optimistically made reservations for a weekend in January at the Rissersee Hotel on the side of a mountain (Americans ran both hotels at the time). We planned to take the children with us so we could take skiing lessons and skate on the lake. Ink and I skated that first day and were pleased that we could stay upright after many years on land.

It was a pleasure to observe the good relations between the U.S. Army and the Germans, both the officials and the general population. We have all read enough history to know that most occupying forces of vanquished countries were anything but interested in getting along. Certainly in the ancient Greek wars, prisoners were taken and either kept or shipped off as slaves. In modern times, people feared being occupied by Russian troops, whose reputation in Germany was very bad indeed. The Americans stayed in Germany in part to keep the Soviets from rolling their conventional forces over West Germany and other territories. I was pleased to see that Americans of all nationalities were a new breed of victor.

Former German officers we met tried not to offend. Few would admit to fighting Americans, saying they had "fought on the Soviet front." One retired German army general however, spoke to me frankly about Adolf Hitler. After dinner in a German home, the general told me he had fought against the Americans in Africa. He was, he said, of high enough rank to know Hitler and to request an audience with him upon his return from Africa. He felt it imperative that he tell Hitler that things were not going well for the Germans, that the war would be lost, and that he was sure Hitler was not being given the truth of what was happening in the field.

"I came into the Führer's office," he said, "ready to tell him the truth, what I and many officers out there truly believed. We wanted to save Germany, while there was still time. Hitler was gracious, Hitler was listening, and then, in two minutes, he was telling me I was wrong, here was the plan, here's what is really happening. Hitler was charming, he was extraordinarily convincing. Even though I believed him to be wrong, I was convinced he was right. The man was not like any other man. He filled the room with optimism, with confidence, with power. Hitler was a marvel and even while doing evil and leading his followers to disaster, he was absolutely mesmerizing."

I took German lessons twice a week, but never reached the proficiency of my young son as he progressed from nursery school to kindergarten, nor of Pam, who was in the American school but speaking German with her playmates. Anni and I spoke together only in German and do to this day on the telephone on birthdays or Christmas or in my visits to Germany or hers to us in the United States.

I bought my first huge German Christmas tree in the middle of the city on our first Christmas there. I was alone that day because Ink as usual was out in the field. While I was in the city, I noticed the beginning of a tremendous reconstruction effort with bomb rubble being hauled away. It was during that next year of 1954 that the vestiges of war began to disappear. The celebration of Christmas itself was very much like our Christmas at home, as were the music and the family gatherings.

In the fifties, the horses still pulled delivery wagons in downtown Munich. We could stand before the Rathaus, or town hall, and watch the Glockenspiel, an intricate old clock with its figures going round as the chimes rang out eleven o'clock. Shoppers had little money, and could not imagine the sights I would see on these same streets years later, when the extraordinary opulence of the shops would outdo Paris. Cars would become ubiquitous, the horses would be gone, the sound of deutsche marks would jangle in almost every pocket. But now, I was a young woman still in my twenties, learning, watching, being part of another culture, and always disturbed about the war years.

When we could, we traveled on a shoestring, but that was the wonder of it. American tourists had to come across the ocean and stay in expensive hotels. We lived here and could learn about places to go from our friends or books. I would read how to find inexpensive hotels or inns with atmosphere. We drove to Rome, Florence, and Sorrento in Italy with my mother and father, leaving the children in Munich with Anni. Ink and Dad would go into a little place we would find and ask for rooms with balconies, and as we were "off season," they would come up with wonderful rooms for little money. One of our best experiences was in Rome. Mother had been given the name of her Italian shoemaker's nephew, who worked somewhere in the Vatican. When we looked him up, to our surprise and delight he was commander of the Pope's guard, the Caribenieri! He treated us royally, taking us through the Pope's private quarters and throughout the Vatican. We saw the Pope speak from his balcony. Although we are not Catholic, seeing the faces of the people in the square made me understand what the Pope means to them, how he stirs their soul, and how he gives them spiritual strength. One day, I was to meet the Pope, a different one, hold his hand, and speak with him in the home of his ambassador to Madagascar.

I drove to Holland to meet my mother and father when they arrived in Europe. It was their first trip across the Atlantic and much longer than when they had gone by ship to Bermuda. (Once they had taken me with them to Bermuda when I was eleven, and looking back, I can see that my journalistic mind was working even then. The manager of the Coral Island Club where we stayed had taken me to meet the famous American naturalist, William Beebe, in his laboratories. I was curious about everything in that remarkable place with hundreds of fish in big tanks. Dr. Beebe decided to put a deep-sea diving helmet on me to explore the sea around us. I loved walking on the ocean floor and seeing the wondrous sights so far from the sandy shores. I am sure I would have been happy exploring the seas or outer space. At least, I learned a little about each area in the years ahead, thanks to my work. But all that adventuring was to be much later. Right now, I was discovering Europe.)

When it was time for my parents to go home, we drove them to Paris, where we spent two nights and saw our French army friend, Major Théodore Brodin, and his wife Yvonne, who had spent a year at Fort Belvoir at the Army Engineer School. Ted was soon to go to Vietnam, where the French were at war. The Brodins had made reservations for us at a little hotel run by two widows on the left bank. We took bus tours to see as much as possible in a short time, and dined with the Brodins at a restaurant beside the bookstalls on the River Seine just across from Notre Dame.

We were all enchanted by Paris and I said, "The dream of my life is to live in this beautiful city." The few times I have expressed such enormous wishes, it seems they have come true, so I am always careful not to be greedy and wish for too much! But, as Carl Sandburg wrote, "Nothing happens unless first a dream."

To me, each day is a gift, and that's what it was like living in Europe. For Ink, it was hard work and long hours the whole three years but he enjoyed being there too.

Our time in Munich was all too short. In less than a year Ink received orders to report to European headquarters in Heidelberg. He was sorry to leave his troops but looking forward to the experience of a good staff job in an important headquarters. We were sad to leave our house but had been promised a large apartment in Heidelberg. Anni agreed to come with us, and that was good news. We were to be in Heidelberg only a few months but it gave us a chance to see another part of Germany. Certainly Heidelberg is one of the most historic of all the old German cities. Its famous university was still welcoming students from all over the world.

Ink's mother and my dear niece Jeri visited us there. We drove Mother Gates to the Army cemetery near Metz, in France, to visit the grave of her middle son, Bernard. She traveled to Berlin with a group of Americans and liked everything she did during her visit. Jeri's plan to go to school in Switzerland changed because of difficulties her mother was having, so instead she went to school in Germany and lived with us. We were thus raising a teenager long before Pam and Larry had reached that stage! She was like our own child.

While Ink had been at the Pentagon, he had worked for Colonel Harold (Sam) Donnelly, who was now stationed at SHAPE (Supreme Headquarters Allied Powers Europe) in Paris as air force chief of policy, plans and operations for General Alfred Gruenther, the SHAPE commander. One day, Ink announced that he'd had a call from Sam Donnelly: "He wants me to come work for him in Paris. Would you like to go?"

He knew the answer before I gave it. He also knew that I spoke a little French, having studied the language for six years in school. Ink said it would be difficult to leave Heidelberg, where his general would not be pleased to have him transferred, but Sam Donnelly had said SHAPE had priority over all other headquarters. It was delicate, and the general couldn't understand why we would want to go to Paris, where living was far more difficult than in Germany. But we said good-bye at his house and remained friends over the years.

Once again it was moving time. We said Auf Wiedersehen to Germany and were on our way to Paris!

Paris

We arrived in Paris on New Year's Eve with the children and Jeri but without our beloved Anni. She was to marry a young German engineer and could not move so far away. Ink had traveled to France before our move and found us an old house in Le Vesinet, a delightful French village just outside Paris. The kitchen had no heat, the furniture was sparse but adequate, and I fell in love with the house in a split second. The doors of the living room opened into a beautiful garden, where Larry could ride his bicycle along the garden paths. A large iron-gated fence surrounded the house, running from one block to the next. A gardener and his wife, George and Georgette, came with the house and lived in a small gardener's cottage in the front garden. We were the first tenants of our landlady, Madame Bel. She and her family had had a difficult time during the war years and now she was using her old family home to supplement her income.

The house was three stories high and had a room for Jeri on the top floor, a room for Pam on the second floor, and a tiny room for Larry also on the second floor. Our bedroom looked out over the chestnut trees in the garden and was cold like the rest of the house. Coal was expensive and we had to watch our budget, so we kept the house quite cool, but to my surprise, we stayed healthy. By healthy I mean we had few colds. But . . . we had only been there about two weeks when Larry came down with the mumps. Not too long after that, Pam had the French measles. Then Ink had the mumps. We rushed him to the hospital but it was not serious, and he soon came home.

All three children went to French schools, and that was one of the best things about living in Le Vesinet. We rented a piano for Pam and found her an excellent teacher, Mademoiselle Rondel, a graduate of the French conservatory. She wanted Pam to study to be a professional pianist but Pam had other ideas.

How is it that one can fall in love with a city? I'm not sure. I only know that I fell in love with Paris, as historians, poets, artists, students, scientists, and so many others have been enchanted by this beautiful city. The river Seine, the great cathedrals, the Opera House, the museums, and the parks, the people, I loved them all. It took me no time to know that Paris was my city and that its tiny suburb, the village of Le Vesinet, out beyond the Bois de Boulogne, beyond St. Cloud and Chatou, would stay in my heart always.

Le Vesinet was home to us for almost two years, and our old French house was filled with love and laughter. Years later there was another house, a log house on the Chesapeake Bay in Maryland, and it is called "Le Vesinet." Friends ask about the unusual name and sometimes I let them read my *cahier*, a big book of once blank pages where I try to explain its meaning on the first page. Once in a while, I look back and read the pages myself.

> Le Vesinet is a village near Paris, in France.
> In this village there are brooks and lakes,
> and memories of children skating in winter,
> near an old man selling warm chestnuts.
> Memories of friends and an old French professor
> coming on his bicycle to a house behind an iron gate,
> a house filled with love.
> Le Vesinet is also a little American house on a cliff.
> There is a beautiful bay just beyond the garden.
> And there is a ravine, like a rain forest on a tropical
> island.
> There are memories of those last days
> before the children grew to be adults
> and went out into the world.
> Le Vesinet is a dream,
> an old dream that shattered and broke many hearts.
> But in such a special place there is strength enough
> to make new dreams, and build a new life.
> Remembering the memories, the chestnuts, the children,
> the love to be found in every Le Vesinet.
>
> --P. G. L.

Before I wrote those words about the two Le Vesinets, many earth-shaking events had occurred. There were wars and separations, and there was heartbreak. Yet, there was much joy, and I would like to tell you about living in Paris in the 1950s.

Parisians still recovering from World War II and concerned about the future of Europe worried about the omnipresent Soviet threat. Supreme Headquarters, Allied Powers in Europe, known as SHAPE, at Rocquencourt near Paris, sought to guard against that threat. At these headquarters Ink worked with other American and NATO officers.

The original countries of NATO (North Atlantic Treaty Organization)—Belgium, Canada, Denmark, France, Iceland, Italy, Luxembourg, The Netherlands, Norway, Portugal, the United Kingdom, and the United States—were joined in 1952 by Greece and Turkey. A semicircle of flags of each country flew in front of SHAPE headquarters. People whose countries don't always get along, nonetheless, worked and talked together in this headquarters. The people at SHAPE lived in nearby villages, as did we, or in SHAPE Village, which included families of all nationalities.

On our first Fourth of July in Le Vesinet, we held a garden party and invited many of our friends at SHAPE. We included the first SHAPE representative from West Germany, Colonel Von Plato, who had just arrived. The year was 1955 and West Germany had just joined NATO, an historic occasion. I had watched the German flag being raised into that semicircle of flags in front of headquarters and found it remarkable indeed to see the French and German flags flying together. When Ink started to give the colonel directions to Le Vesinet, Colonel Von Plato said he did not need directions, because he had been stationed at a German headquarters in Le Vesinet during the war.

The party was a success and we enjoyed bringing so many nationalities together in our garden. In one awkward moment, one of our French friends, Germaine, began a conversation with our German guest, telling him about her service in the French Underground during the German occupation. She told him some uncomplimentary things about the Germans, at which point the colonel drew himself up, clicked his heels together, bowed, and said, "Madame, I apologize for my countrymen."

Germaine spoke to me later of her embarrassment. She had risked her life many times as a freedom fighter in the underground and so was strong enough to recover from the incident! Colonel Von Plato later became a general and was once stationed in Washington.

General Alfred M. Gruenther, the Supreme Allied Commander in Europe, had succeeded its first commander, General Dwight D. Eisenhower. All the officers at SHAPE admired General Gruenther greatly, and all who went to his briefings were impressed by the general's extraordinary grasp of the world situation and of each man's responsibilities at SHAPE. He asked penetrating questions at briefings, and everyone took care to be well prepared.

General Gruenther and his wife, Grace, gave many receptions at their home. We were always delighted when we were included, as the Gruenthers were warm and gracious hosts. I had a delightful conversation one evening there with the famous British General Bernard Montgomery, one of the most important people at SHAPE. Standing beside a little pond, we discussed not World War II but the fish in the pond!

General Gruenther left SHAPE in the fall of 1956 and returned to Washington, where he succeeded Ellsworth Bunker as president of the American Red Cross. In 1959, on the tenth anniversary of NATO, I interviewed him in his Red Cross office for a special documentary radio program. NATO, the general explained to my radio audience, was a collective security defensive operation. One of its outstanding accomplishments was that not one single inch of a member country's territory had been given up to Soviet imperialism.

"The strategy of NATO," Gruenther said, "is presented in terms of the sword and the shield. The sword represents air power and guided missiles; the shield represents troops in forward areas, including ground troops, air forces, and some naval forces."

The general further explained that NATO "provided a force of such strength that any foray or raid or probing effort would be stopped. It caused the Soviet Union to stop, think, and listen. It raised the price of entering Western Europe to a point that the Soviet Union would be inviting deliberate retaliation. . . . The Soviets did not want everything they had been working on to be destroyed."

Gruenther considered collective security pacts absolutely essential to the security of the United States, saying we need the assistance of our allies "as much as they need us. The days of an isolation state are gone forever." Today, although a Soviet Union no longer exists, and our relations with the Russians have improved, I am sure General

Gruenther, now no longer living, would still be proud of NATO's accomplishments.

We had been in our French house only a few months when our beloved Anni Haindel came back to us. Her fiancé had died after a bad automobile accident. His last words, she said, were, "Go to Frau Gates."

Ink, Jeri, Pam, Larry and I, all went to the railroad station to meet Anni, and everyone cried when she stepped off the train. We rented a sewing machine for her and gave her the little room next to Jeri's on the third floor. She and I continued speaking German to each other and were both learning French. She helped me glue our dining-room table around the edges before dinner parties to keep the food from falling into a guest's lap, as it had one night. Anni was a good cook, and we entertained frequently. The kitchen was warm now, heated by a portable "Aladdin stove." She was also a good housekeeper, and the children adored her.

When young Jane Crookenden, aged four, pushed Larry, aged four and a half into a creek near our house, her parents came from across the street to apologize. The children's water episode began a lifelong friendship between our families. Napier Crookenden, then a colonel in the British Army, worked at SHAPE. He was a great success in the British Army, becoming Lieutenant General Sir Napier Crookenden and, in retirement, a well-known author, writing about the war years. For six years, he served as Lieutenant of Her Majesty's Tower of London, a high honor indeed that came with an apartment in the Tower, where we visited him.

Pat Crookenden and I explored Paris together, with and without the children, going to all the museums, driving to the Palace at Versailles, and even taking a sewing course in French at Singers in Paris. I learned in both French and English that I had no talent for sewing!

The Gateses, including our Jeri, and the Crookenden children, including Jane and a son James (Jamie), went to L'Ecole Jeanne d'Arc in the village. They learned to speak good French and became immersed in the culture. At a lively dinner we hosted for Jeri's classmates, everyone brought a present. The nuns came on their bicycles bringing bottles of wine.

Ink took French lessons at SHAPE every week, and I studied with Monsieur Mesnil who came to the house twice a week on his bicycle. In cold weather, he wore a long black cape. He had fought in World Wars I and II, had been wounded at Verdun, and I adored him. We read Balzac together, and he made me write compositions to improve my grammar. Best of all, he invited us to come to his small house for dinner to meet his family. Such an invitation was not usual for his students, and we were honored. To this day when I journey to Le Vesinet, I visit the surviving son and two daughters of the Mesnils. It was a privilege to know these splendid families and learn from them about French ways.

The Mesnils had lived in England between the two World Wars and in London, Maurice Mesnil, my professor, had been manager of Yardleys. They returned to Le Vesinet after the World War II with no fortune and no complaints to live near their relatives in a small house on a big estate.

Daughter Marie Rose Mesnil worked many years with Schlumberger, and her sister, Colette, worked for the president of France in the Elysées Palace. That was exciting for us, because Colette would get permission to give us the president's box at the Paris Opera House when it was not occupied. We invited our friends and, seated in splendor in the gilded box of the old opera house, saw beautifully staged grand operas.

Sometimes we would go to nightclubs with the Crookendens. As we didn't have much money between us, we would buy one bottle of champagne per couple, the required cover charge, and make it last all evening. Going out on the town meant less money for coal, making the house colder and us healthier! At a party in Le Vesinet one night, we met the famous French singer and film star, Maurice Chevalier. We would meet again.

Sam Donnelly, who had arranged Ink's being ordered to Paris, was by now a brigadier general in the Air Force. Sam and Dotty enjoyed coming to our house in Le Vesinet, which was a small, quiet village compared to busy Paris. We loved visiting them in their Paris apartment near l'Arc de Triomphe. At one of their exciting parties, the Duke and Duchess of Windsor were among the guests. I found it rather sad to see the former King Edward VIII of Great Britain with the woman he loved and for whom he had given up his throne. They looked subdued and rather like wax figures.

It was while we were in Paris that we met Annabella once again. She came to our house often, and I visited her mother in her house in St. Cloud. Annabella was much respected in France as one of their all-time great stars of the cinema. She had divorced Tyrone Power, but they remained the closest of friends. One day she told me that Tyrone had invited her to England for the weekend, and she had every reason to believe that he was going to ask her to marry him again. She was not certain what she would do. They were still in love, but she was reluctant to live again under the Hollywood influence. She came to see me right upon her return and said she had been right. He did want them to marry again, but she had said no. For many years afterward she wondered if she had made the right decision. Perhaps she thought if they had remarried, he would have led a less turbulent life and not died at such a young age.

Just before his death, Tyrone and his new wife visited Annabella at Contremundo, her farm in the South of France. He and Annabella wrote me a postcard that I received in Washington just after he had died. He had been making a film in Spain and died of a heart attack on the set after many retakes of a sword fight. Not long after his death, his wife gave birth to their son—the son he had always wanted, to carry on the acting tradition of his father and grandfather. One reason Annabella had left him was that she was no longer able to give him children. She had one wonderful daughter, Anne, whom Tyrone had adopted, but she knew he desperately wanted a son. He married a second time, had two daughters, divorced again, and in his third marriage finally produced a son—too late.

Ink and I took Jeri on an automobile trip through the magnificent Loire Valley, after which we put her on the train back to Paris, as her school holiday was over. We drove on to Spain together, following advice from the Crookendens, and stayed in what was then an undiscovered town called Torremolinos.

Before arriving in Torremolinos, we visited Gibraltar, where in the car beside us at a red light I recognized Lawrence Langner, president of the Theater Guild and owner of the Westport Playhouse in Connecticut, where I had apprenticed and where I had met Annabella and Tyrone Power and Ink, when Langner took our play to West

Point. I leaned out the car window and said, "Aren't you Lawrence Langner?" At that moment, the light changed and our cars sped off in opposite directions.

Hours later, we arrived at our hotel in Torremolinos and there, much to our surprise, we found the Langners, Armina and Lawrence, with their New York friends Tony and Fran Minor. In the early days of television Tony had produced *Studio One,* the first important drama show on television. Lawrence said he had worried all day about the woman who had called him by name in the middle of Gibraltar. For the next few days, we had a happy time together. We all rode to Grenada in our convertible, singing popular songs all the way, dined together, and later, in America, had many reunions.

On our trip to Spain, we stopped to visit a remarkable *finca,* Pascualete, an ancient estate and farm dating to the fifteenth century that belonged to the Count and Countess de Quintanilla. The countess was an American, Aline Griffith from Pearl River, New York, and a friend of Annabella's. Aline had been sent to Spain as a member of our OSS, our World War II intelligence agency. At the end of the war, she met and married the Count de Quintanilla. We had stopped first in Madrid to have lunch with Aline and her husband, and she asked us to take along to the finca the young son of one of the farm staff. She had brought him to Madrid to see the doctor, and it was time for him to go home. With Annabella as her guest Aline and her husband had made the first trip to the finca by any member of the family for more than one hundred years. When they arrived, the house on the finca was ready and waiting, with the household staff whose families had served there for generations hoping that some day someone would come. Aline fell in love with the huge farm and proceeded to make it livable.

Ink and I drove to Pascualete in about three and half hours with our young guide, taking the highway toward Portugal, and arrived in the Province of Estremadura around dinnertime. It was like entering another world many centuries ago. We saw ancient farm equipment in the fields, with flocks of sheep and olive trees everywhere. We were in the Middle Ages. The staff expected us and had dinner waiting, serving us in front of a huge fireplace. The stone walls of the finca were impressive and the room was cool, but we did not mind because under the tablecloth a brazier filled with hot coals kept our feet warm. The next morning we toured a part of the farm on horseback, again having the sense of being in a time warp.

We took our first trip to England with Pat Crookenden and daughter Jane. Ink and I were going over to visit some American friends, so we took Pat and Jane in our car and put it on the ferry across the channel to Dover. We saw the white cliffs so famous from the wartime song. From Dover, we drove to Leigh near Tonbridge, site of Ramhurst Manor, the home of Pat's parents, Nan and Hugh Kindersley. We had met Lord and Lady Kindersley in Paris when they visited the Crookendens, and they had invited us to come visit. Hugh Kindersley was a great figure in that era of British history. As an army brigadier, he was one of the first officers to land on French soil the night before D-Day. After the war, he was head of Lazard Frères and chairman of Rolls Royce, among many other responsibilities, and was one of the finest men I have ever met. He and Nan were splendid hosts. Strolling the beautiful gardens of historic Ramhurst Manor was to see the aristocratic side of England at its best. Ramhurst also had a ghost that roamed about ever since one wing burned down, but I didn't see her. I have returned to England many times through the years and treasure each visit.

On a small table in the front hall of our house in Le Vesinet sat an old-fashioned black telephone, the kind where your left hand curled around a tall base with a little speaker cup on top and a cradle on the side to hold the earphone, which you held up to your ear with your right hand. When you picked up the earphone to make a call, an operator came on the line and asked in French, of course, what number you would like to call. There was no dial, just you and the operator.

I remember holding the phone with both hands when Kay Little, my shipmate, called from Stuttgart, Germany. "Frank was killed this afternoon during an exercise," she said, "in an air crash. Two military planes collided, killing a whole company of men in Frank's Engineer Battalion and Frank. I am devastated."

"Kay," I said, "we'll be there as fast as we can get a train to Germany. Ink will help with all the arrangements and I'll help you and the baby. We'll be there by tomorrow morning."

We were heartbroken. I thought of the day Frank had met us when our ship docked in Holland. I thought of Kay during our long voyage across the Atlantic and how much she had helped me with Pam and Larry. She and Frank had wanted children of their own but that was not to be. However, a year ago, after a tremendous effort, they adopted a German newborn baby and named him Stephen. I had driven to Stuttgart with Larry from Munich to see the baby right after they brought him home. I was his godmother. What would happen, I wondered, with the adoption papers not yet final because their home state, Nebraska, had been slow getting the paperwork done to send to Stuttgart.

Ink and I packed quickly, and Ink borrowed money from Sam Donnelly to buy our railroad tickets, as it was too late in the day to cash a check. We left the children with Anni and knew they would be safe with her. We caught the last train out of Paris that night and were in Stuttgart the next morning, where we were met by an army car.

Fifty-six men had been killed in this enormous catastrophe. It was, we were told, the largest ever peacetime military crash in Germany. German officials were everywhere, as relations between the German and U.S. military were very good. An impressive outdoor memorial service was held for all the men lost. It was a tragedy for all. Plans were under way to send home all the widows, but there was a major hitch in plans for Kay's departure. She wouldn't leave without the baby, needless to say, and the German government refused to let him go without formal adoption papers being signed. Ink went to the highest office of government in Bonn to ask that the president of Germany intercede, and he did. Then someone in the U.S. Congress cleared up the Nebraska problem and the baby was granted a visa. Kay and Steve were on their way.

We visited the Normandy beachheads with Anni and the children, a never-to-be-forgotten experience. We could almost see and truly could feel the presence of the soldiers and the ships coming to shore under fire on D-Day, June 6, 1944, when the allied troops landed in France.

My parents came to visit us for Christmas one year in Paris, and they too were enchanted by Le Vesinet. Our French friends welcomed them and our children were overjoyed. Christmas was never quite the same after my parents died, for they would always visit us wherever we lived, or we would visit them in Connecticut for holidays. How could they now be just pictures on the wall when they were once so alive and so loving? The love goes on I know, but I miss their smiles and their mellifluous voices.

Jeri went back to the States a little before we did to be with her mother, and we missed her. She had become a real member of our family.

The months in Paris went far too fast. Though Ink was asked to stay for another year, the army personnel people, certain that Ink had a great career ahead, thought it was time for him to go to the Command and General Staff College at Fort Leavenworth, Kansas. So, in the summer of 1957, it was au revoir Paris, hello, Kansas!

5

A Nascent Career

After three years in Europe with no trips home, arriving back in the United States was a truly special event, especially passing the Statue of Liberty. Ink and I stood on deck with the children, greeting her with pride and appreciation.

We sailed into New York Harbor on the *S.S.United States*, the fastest passenger ship afloat at the time, crossing in four and a half days. Given the army's space available arrangement, we were lucky to be on board at all. We had headed for the port of Le Havre in France by train with our French shepherd dog, Lady, and were given the good news at the last minute. Lady had first class accommodations, but we had only second and needed special permission to visit her!

During our voyage we had seen a film about a ship sinking at sea and had to reassure the children not to worry because ships were safer now. Well, no sooner had we arrived in Connecticut with my parents, who had met us in New York, than my father turned on the news on that "new invention" television, only to see the lead story: "Tragedy in the Atlantic". The Italian ship, the *Andrea Doria*, the ship that was sinking at that very moment, had been sailing along at full tilt while we, too, were at sea. Pam and Larry reminded us we had assured them these accidents no longer happened. So much for parental credibility!

Though I was sorry to leave Paris, I knew I had enjoyed living in Illinois and correctly guessed that I would like returning to the Midwest. From a landscape dotted with tall round crop-storage silos, Kansas farmers ship their wheat all over the world. The friendly Kansans in the town of Leavenworth were content to have an army post in their midst. They admired the army, so that made for a pleasant atmosphere.

Our house was small, three bedrooms, a living room, a bathroom, and a kitchen squeezed into one thousand square feet. But we were glad of a house instead of the crowded apartment complex where most students lived. Ink studied in a small laundry room off the kitchen, keeping his books on the washing machine. Several houses exactly like ours had big square green lawns in front where children played. Our dog Lady would trot along beside Larry, enjoying the excitement.

Leavenworth included students from other countries and two faculty liaison officers from France and England. One night as dark clouds gathered, we invited these visiting officers for dinner with several of our neighbors. The radio had been broadcasting tornado warnings for Kansas City, about fifty miles away. By the time our guests arrived, we could see tornado funnels forming in the sky, and the English colonel asked if we would like to transfer our supper to his quarters because he had a basement where we could go if the tornado came our way. The French officer was not worried and said it would be much nicer to die together in a storm than alone. We stayed in our house and, luckily, the urgent warning signals did not sound for us. But Kansas City suffered many casualties that night when the tornado touched down there.

Pam and Larry were happy in their Leavenworth school but I was sorry to see them losing their French and German language skills. Because Ink was home studying by the time the children came home from school each day, I knew it would be all right for me to be away for a few days. Taking advantage of a $99 round-trip train fare to San Francisco I made a weeklong visit to friends in California, my first time out West. I stopped overnight in Tucson, Arizona, with an older couple from New Canaan days. They drove me into Mexico for lunch, so I was not only discovering more of my own country but also adding a new one to my list of foreign travel. I was glad I stopped over in Tucson for it was the last time I ever saw them. In San Francisco, I stayed with my old wartime friend, Alice Hunter, and we reminisced about our days in Sparta, Wisconsin, when our husbands were stationed at Camp McCoy before going off to India and Burma.

Back in Leavenworth, the director of the Little Theater asked me to try out for the leading role in *Janus,* a play he was producing. Another woman reading for the part, Rosanne McQuarrie, was a better actress than I, but I was given the part. I always figured it was type-casting because I was a small blue-eyed blond and she was a tall brunette. Rosanne was cast in the other female role, however.

Rosanne and I became great friends. When Ink and Jock McQuarrie were both assigned to the Pentagon, Rosanne and I decided to go into the radio business together. We spent hours planning a thirty-minute interview program that we would sell to a radio station to bring us enough outside income to take our children to operas, ballets, and plays. We mapped out a formidable guest list centered around military interviews, knowing such a program did not exist in Washington at that time. What we did not know was that it was almost impossible to get on the air in Washington, especially for women. In our blissful ignorance, we continued our planning, adding other categories of interest to a cosmopolitan audience. We would interview prominent members of the military, we would tell about women doing volunteer work, we would talk about developments in the medical world, we would interview people from other countries and the stars of plays at the National Theater in Washington.

Without realizing it, we were shaping a morning program format that would later become a staple for network television. We each had had a dash of professional theater experience in New York, and I had had a little radio experience in Stamford, Connecticut. We had plenty of enthusiasm and high hopes without realizing how many doors would be closed to us.

At the end of nine months, we packed up our small collections of furniture, books, and children and headed for Washington. Housing was still difficult in the nation's capital, but good army friends had found us a little brick house in Arlington Forest in Virginia. While Ink and Jock toiled at the Pentagon, the children would go to schools in Arlington, and Rosanne and I would seek our fortune in Washington radio. The hunt began but our program proposal consistently met with "No."

The Magic of the Microphone

To our great good fortune Rosanne and I discovered a small radio station in Falls Church, Virginia, with power enough to cover the entire Washington area. Genevieve and Lamar Newcomb were the owners of WFAX, and Genevieve also served as program manager. Rosanne and I told her about the program we proposed and showed her our guest list. She decided to take a chance on us. I have read that when women with little experience try to break into the work place, it helps to have a woman at the top believe in them. I will always be grateful to Genevieve Newcomb, who made possible my long career in radio and all that followed. I have tried ever since to lend a hand to young people starting off in their careers, remembering my own experience.

It is quite true that you need experience at a small station before going on to a big one. In my life I have worked for a small station and for the largest station in the world and found that the joys and problems are the same, just magnified at the big one! Engineers are vital no matter where you are and I have been blessed with good ones. Later in television, I discovered the importance of the director, the camera crew, the sound people, everyone on the team. The performer is only as good as his or her support. When I worked at the White House, one of my most treasured letters of congratulations came from a cameraman with whom I had worked at American University. In volunteering when requested, I had picked up many hours of on-camera time as what was called "the talent" part of the team. But I'm leaping ahead of myself, for the hard work was just beginning at WFAX.

Rosanne and I wrote, produced, and took turns interviewing our guests. We called our program, *U.S. Lady on the Air*, having sought permission from *U.S. Lady* magazine to use its title. At the end of the first year, we had interviewed almost every guest on our proposal list, and the Newcombs were pleased. We had established good relations with the public affairs people in the military. We had to be careful not to involve our husbands in any of our contacts, for in those days it was frowned on for army wives to work. The public affairs people did not frown; they were absolutely delighted to get airtime for the military of all ranks. They knew that we were more knowledgeable about military activities than most other broadcasters, and they knew we cared.

We became expert jugglers, a necessary skill for working women everywhere. We juggled our time between being good mothers, good wives — and in our case, that meant going to meetings of army wives' groups — entertaining, doing volunteer work, and having a professional career.

Our career centered around an extraordinary electronic invention—the microphone—that sat on a table in the studio. In reduced form, held in a hand, it reached out to pick up the voices of two people conversing. A microphone has the magical quality of carrying spoken words, music, sounds of everyday activities. What an instrument it is! The microphone makes possible communication over great distances; it demands precision, compassion, clarity. More than electronic genius, a microphone is magic. Using this modern miracle well is a great responsibility, and to me living with the microphone for so many years has been one of the great joys of my life.

An interview must be compelling to capture the attention of an audience. I soon learned that a good interview demands a momentary, intimate connection between the interviewer and the guest. As the person controlling the questions, you want to make the guest dominant. You are not at the microphone to show how much you know about a subject but how much your guest knows. You must be well informed to ask the right questions, but it is the guest you want to have shine. My questions flow from the direction of the conversation rather than from a prepared list. I'm curious about everything and genuinely interested in people. Most of all, an interviewer must listen carefully to what others are saying. Once I was not listening carefully when my guest said she had broken her arm. I said, "Good," and went on with my question. "What do you mean good?" she said, "I told you I broke my arm!" From that time on, I never forgot to listen.

I learned as I went along and had no studied technique.

Sometimes Rosanne or I went out alone, sometimes together. Most of our guests on WFAX came to the studio for interviews, but sometimes we two lugged our cumbersome portable studio tape recorder to them. The size of portable recorders has changed so much, it's hard to remember how large, heavy, and awkward the old ones were. One day, we interviewed Julie Harris, one of our finest actresses, at the National Theater. After the interview we played back a bit of tape to make sure it had recorded our words. To our great distress, it had not! But Julie Harris offered to do it all again. The day was saved, our deadline was met, and we took greater care with our recorder from then on. As the years went by and tape recorders became smaller and smaller, I learned that by buying my own machine, I could keep it in dependable shape.

On one occasion we rushed off to the White House to do a commentary on Princess Elizabeth's visit to Washington. I can still see the future queen of Great Britain, tiny and beautiful, coming onto the front steps of the White House wearing a long gold gown covered with pearls. Regulars in the White House press corps were as impressed as we were by this enchanting young woman, soon to have so much responsibility thrust upon her. The White House portico and those steps became familiar in later years, when I could walk anywhere I wished within those historic walls, but this first time was special.

The day we received the United States Army's Outstanding Public Service Award in a special ceremony in the Pentagon office of General C. K. Gailey had to be one of the great moments in our joint radio venture. We were honored that the military appreciated our efforts to inform the Washington community about the military men and women in its midst.

There came a time, to our mutual regret, when Rosanne felt she must give up broadcasting. Her husband pointed out that while my children were in school, she still had a small daughter at home. Even working part-time was a strain on her family life. So it is, even today, for a woman with a career. Rosanne continued to help me with interview ideas both in the United States and in Europe. Our theme song for *U.S. Lady on the Air* was the same as that used on *The News Hour with Jim Lehrer*, so the melody lingers on!

Through the Window Glass

Lamar Newcomb, the owner of WFAX, had the idea of putting a little studio behind the plate glass window of a big music store in the new Seven Corners Shopping Center. Nowadays, we see people on such television programs as *The Today Show* talking on their microphones behind windows so people can gather round outdoors and watch them interviewing famous guests. In the late 1950s, however, it was a pretty wild idea.

In the beginning, the window revealed only a big studio table with a microphone and two turntables for playing records. The manager of the store, called Music Time, was delighted to have a man sitting in the shop window for two hours every afternoon, operating this miniature studio, which was actually broadcasting from the WFAX tower several miles away.

When Rosanne retired from our microphone, Mr. Newcomb decided to bring the man in the window back to the main studio and send me over to Seven Corners. Would I go? I could interview my guests right there at Music Time in full public view, and the engineers would teach me to operate the remote control table. I could play any records I chose from the store's enormous collection and fix the window up any way I wanted. I liked the idea of a new adventure and, although not sure I could conquer the electronic gear on my own, I would give it a try!

The manager of a nearby furniture store agreed to lend me some attractive furniture for my window set in exchange for free advertising on WFAX. The photographer in another store took a picture of me to put in the window and made a sign inviting people to come by from 1:00 to 3:00 p.m. every weekday afternoon to watch and listen to a live broadcast. A loudspeaker just outside the window enabled the crowd to hear the music and the interviews. Would it work? To our surprise and pleasure, it took off like a rocket. No one could see the knots in my stomach while I was learning to operate those turntables, but soon it became second nature. My guests, it turned out, enjoyed the unique experience of being viewed through a glass brightly!

Who were some of the guests?

One of the most memorable, that great entertainer Maurice Chevalier, enthralled not only me but also the crowds that welcomed him to Seven Corners. Maurice Chevalier was a charming, delightful, talented man of the twentieth century who loved America. He was in Washington to perform a one-man show at the Shubert Theater, and his new movie, *Gigi*, had just opened. His manager, Monsieur Vals, had told me on the telephone that Maurice Chevalier did very few radio interviews because he could fill a theater without them; but he had liked my letter reminding him of our meeting in Le Vesinet, France, and would cross the Potomac River to see me. A small notice in the newspaper and a sign in my window had announced his upcoming appearance. When his car arrived just outside my studio, the crowd parted, applauding vigorously as he walked through the path they had cleared for him.

In the interview Chevalier said the show at the Shubert would run for a short time only, after which he would take it to New York for another short run and then back to Paris for the opening of *Gigi*. I had seen the film, a charming story by Colette, with Leslie Caron in the role of Gigi and Louis Jourdan as her suitor and music and lyrics by Alan J. Lerner and Frederick Lowe. The song Chevalier liked singing best in the film, he said, was "Thank Heaven for Little Girls." He also enjoyed singing "I'm Glad I'm Not Young Anymore" but was not too sincere about that! He denied being sad about getting old. A walk around the White House the afternoon before his opening at the Shubert had given him the idea of imitating chiefs of state, and he had tried it out on opening night, doing a friendly parody of great men. I told him the audience had loved his interpretations. I particularly liked a charming song — "How Is the Weather in Paris? — about a provincial boy and a Parisian girl who meet and fall in love at the seashore. Chevalier said of it, "Sometimes you look for a knockout in a song but also there must be some moments when people can be relaxed and think about the things of life." For some reason I've always remembered that song.

A year or two later I reminded Chevalier of the song we had both liked when I visited him in Marnes la Coquette, just outside of Paris. His house, La Louque was next to the house where President Eisenhower had lived while serving as commanding general at SHAPE. The very hospitable Maurice Chevalier showed me all around his house. While we were having tea, I noticed on one of his tables an autographed photograph of Elvis Presley. "There," Chevalier said, "is a very talented young man who has changed the course of all contemporary music." It was a lovely afternoon.

Now, back to my Falls Church, Virginia, days. Some years ago, two of the most admired singers in American films were soprano Jeanette MacDonald and baritone Nelson Eddy. Their music, much of it by Victor Herbert and Sigmund Romberg, may seem old-fashioned now, but then everybody knew "Ah, Sweet Mystery of Life" and "I'm Falling In Love with Someone" from *Naughty Marietta* or the title song from the film *Rose Marie*. MacDonald and Eddy were sensational together at a time when romance was in fashion. Incidentally, Jeanette MacDonald had previously starred with Maurice Chevalier in the film *Love Me Tonight*.

When Nelson Eddy was in Washington to sing at the Shoreham Hotel, he came to my Music Time studio for an interview, generating another crowd around the window (though not one as reverential as Chevalier's). Eddy talked about his films with MacDonald and how much he had enjoyed his many USO tours during the war to entertain the troops. At another time in another place I interviewed Jeanette MacDonald.

Another memorable guest was British playwright Robert Bolt, who was destined to go down in theater history as one of the great playwrights of the twentieth century. Bolt was in Washington with his gentle play *The Flowering Cherry*, following its successful run in London. He had high hopes it would go over well in New York after a Washington opening. Ink and I had attended and enjoyed that first U.S. performance, but the Washington critics were not kind, the New York ones even less so. Bolt was deeply disappointed, as he wrote to me in a November 1959 letter from his home in Surrey, England. He despaired of any future American success, saying, "My plays seem progressively to pursue finer and finer distinctions, not bigger and bigger bangs. If they thought this one 'small' they'll think the next one invisible."

He was wrong about that. In November 1961, when he brought his next play, *A Man for All Seasons*, about Sir Thomas More, to New York, the critics were overwhelmed. They shouted from the rooftops that here was a play that comes along only once or twice in a lifetime. It was also made into a successful film. Bolt took the title from a passage by Robert Whittington designed for Tudor schoolboys to put in Latin: "More is a man of angel's wit and singular learning; I know not his fellow. For where is the man of that gentleness, lowliness and affability? And as time requireth, a man of marvelous mirth and pastimes; and sometimes of a sad gravity; a man for all seasons."

I also interviewed a great British actor, Sir John Gielgud. I think I went to him. Our listeners loved him and his always magnificent voice.

I had the good fortune to interview many of the big stars of the day who performed at the Shoreham Hotel in Washington, indoors in the Blue Room in winter and on the Shoreham Terrace in the summer. Patti Mauldin, the Shoreham's public relations person, called her press table "The Golden Circle," the lucky group she granted interviews with "her" celebrities. My husband joined me for the Blue Room and Terrace evenings. Another couple, Liz Carpenter and her husband Les, were the Washington editors of *Variety*, the premier magazine read by theater pros as well as by the public. When Liz, a remarkable woman, left the magazine, she went to work for Senator, then President, Lyndon B. Johnson, and later became press secretary for Lady Bird Johnson. It was Liz who wrote the powerful words Lyndon Johnson spoke on Air Force One when he was sworn in as President of the United States, en route back to Washington from Dallas, Texas, following the assassination of President John F. Kennedy.

Meanwhile, back at the Shoreham, I often arrived in the late afternoon to interview that evening's guests. When I went to interview the famous French singer, Edith Piaf, her manager asked if I would speak to her a little in French before the interview to relax her. Our casual conversation in French went fairly well, but when I switched to English for our conversation on the air, I had trouble finding the right English words! Piaf sang superbly that night. Listening to the timbre of her voice and her heartbreaking interpretations of the melodies, tears started rolling down my cheeks, especially when she sang "La Vie en Rose." Piaf was exceptional. She looked tiny and vulnerable, dressed simply in black, giving her heart to her craft and to her audience. She had risen out of poverty from the streets of Paris to be recognized everywhere for her talent. I doubt that her fame and fortune brought her much happiness, a circumstance I have seen with other famous people.

One of my most memorable interviews was with Fred Astaire, one of the great dancers of our time, Astaire danced across Broadway stages and movie screens and his performances continue even today on television. He never watched his old movies, he said, but was glad that other people enjoyed them. Fred Astaire in person, sitting at my microphone at the Shoreham in June 1959, was much like the characters he played on screen, natural, debonair, warm, and

74

enthusiastic, moving effortlessly with grace and dignity. For the big reception at the Shoreham for his just published book *Steps in Time*, publicist Patti Mauldin had invited Fred's sister, Adele. I shared with Fred that my parents had told me what remarkable dancers he and Adele were together long before his acclaimed partnership with Ginger Rogers.

Mine was one of only two interviews Patti had arranged for Fred Astaire, the other being with NBC host Patty Cavin. I went up to Fred's suite and we sat at a table with my portable microphone between us. We talked about the book, his interest in singing as well as in choreographing his own dances, and his thoughts on music of the fifties.

When we had finished the interview, he said, "Come on downstairs and meet my sister, Adele, I want her to meet you." (He was a gentleman to the very toes.) He led me by the hand to the elevator, not walking I was sure, but floating along. We all grew up dreaming that we too, would dance like Fred Astaire—impossible of course. But he always lifted your spirits, if not your feet, off the ground!

I enjoyed interviewing many other legendary film stars in those years at WFAX. People always gathered round outside my unique window studio because they never knew who might be there. Among those who came were actor Pat O'Brien, singers Steve Lawrence and Eydie Gorme (his wife), and my old and good friend, Tyrone Power who came through town while on a theater tour.

Charles Laughton gave me a memorable interview when he was in Washington filming *Advise and Consent*, in which he played a senator. I still recall the way he said, "We live on a quiet street in Hollywood." I instantly felt the atmosphere of his street from the way he spoke the words. Even now when I say the word, "quiet," I try to remember how soft it should sound to convey its true meaning.

One day my husband Ink informed me that he was being sent on a "hardship tour," meaning a year in a faraway country without family. All officers were expected to take a turn at this not very desirable situation. His tour was to be in Iran with the U.S. Army Corps of Engineers to supervise a large construction project for the Shah of Iran funded by the United States. An American construction company would be building housing for Iranian troops.

Although I loved my work and my microphone, I decided to move with the children to Munich for the year that Ink would be away, hoping I could visit him in Iran. I wanted the children to regain some of their German and planned to send Pam to France for a time to brush up her French. I also planned to send some interviews back to WFAX from Germany.

When word got around that I was leaving, I received a call from NBC in New York from the young man who as an army private had arranged all the military interviews we requested when Rosanne and I were broadcasting *U.S. Lady on the Air*. Having served his time in the army, he now worked for the vice president of the NBC network. He invited me to New York to meet with his vice president, Buck Prince, who wanted me to do interviews for NBC while I was living in Europe. After that meeting in New York, I was assigned as an NBC free-lance reporter. Amazing!

Once again I was on my way to Europe with the children, no husband, but this time with my portable tape recorder and microphone.

6

Foreign Correspondent

The year of "hardship tour," from the middle of 1960 to the middle of 1961, turned out to be one of the most productive years of my life. While living in Munich, I represented three radio stations: NBC (the National Broadcasting Company), WFAX in the Washington area, and AFN (the Armed Forces Network — Worldwide). My broadcasting travels took me to Berlin during intense times, Austria, Iran, Turkey, and behind the Iron Curtain to Moscow, Kiev, and Leningrad in the Soviet Union, Budapest in Hungry, and Warsaw in Poland. I also took my microphone to Norway, and the children joined me on journeys to Switzerland, Italy, and France. At first I was lonely, not an uncommon feeling for an army wife whose husband is serving far away. The great demands of motherhood and work, however, made the lonely months pass faster than I had dared to hope, and then the year of separation was over.

In July 1960, as the hardship tour began, the children and I were excited to be living in beautiful Munich again. This time we were on our own, with no house awaiting us. Fortunately, our former German neighbors, Professor Dr. and Frau Dr. Maurer, lent us a pretty fifth-floor walk-up apartment they had bought as an investment. They let us live in it rent free, paying only the utilities. The flat was situated on the main street in a section called Harloching. A gas heater in the kitchen heated the whole apartment. The main room had a slice of window, from which I could see out by standing on a small stool. Pam's bed sat in a small alcove in that room, where I hung curtains to give her privacy. I slept on the sofa in the same room but kept its big feather comforter in the closet during the day. I bought a five-foot sleeper couch for Larry and put it in an alcove in the square front hall. To this day Larry says that he grew up in the smallest room of every house we ever lived in! The flat also had a small bathroom.

When Pam saw the kitchen, she asked, "Where is the dishwasher?" I said, "You are the dishwasher!" In fact, I handled the kitchen chores while the children studied.

We lived on the top floor and had no elevator. If you have ever walked up five flights of steps several times a day, you will know it is not easy at first. In the beginning I huffed and puffed, but after a few weeks I would run up the steps to recover forgotten car keys and not mind at all!

I had bought a little Volkswagen when we first arrived. Thank goodness Ink was with us for a day or two before flying off to Teheran so he could help with the voluminous paperwork involved in registering a car in Germany. There were tearful farewells at the airport. A year was a long time to be separated, but we hoped I would be able to visit Iran, and that did happen.

The Maurers treated us well and always made us welcome at their house. Dr. Maurer, along with his daughter, Eva, would pick up Pam every morning to drive both girls to the *Gymnasium,* their German high school. Eva and Pam, now about fourteen years old, were friends from our earlier days in Munich. The following spring Pam went to Paris for a semester in a French school and lived with the Vincents, the French family we had known there.

Larry walked to school over the nearby hills, and I could watch him go if I stood on my window stool. On his back he carried a German book bag, which seemed very practical to us but was not yet widely used in the United States. Larry's school was the local *Volksschule,* which had been run by Americans just a few years before when Pam had been a student there! Now, it was all German, and Larry had to work hard to regain his kindergarten German plus an eleven- year-old's vocabulary. It wasn't easy being an American boy in an all-German school, but he finally earned acceptance by becoming a good *füssball* (soccer) player on his class team. He stayed after school for what was called the *Hort,* a study period with a teacher on duty to answer questions. I hired young Francine Vincent to tutor the children in German twice a week. Francine, the daughter of our French friends in Paris, was in Munich studying at the university.

A short time after Francine graduated from the University of Munich, Princess Grace of Monaco (the former film star Grace Kelly) hired her to tutor the royal children in French. I dare say the palace at Monaco was quite a change from our apartment in Munich! Francine married the court doctor, Bernard Robin, and was godmother to her pupil Princess Caroline's first child.

Before the school year had begun, when we were all adjusting to our new life, I accepted an invitation from my good friends Molly and John McChesney, who were staying in St. Moritiz in Switzerland. John had been a legendary English master at the Hotchkiss School in Lakeville, Connecticut. Going across the Alps would be a test for my little Volkswagen. We were short on funds and I was hoping that our friends had meant our hotel room was their treat (of course it was!). I knew we could swing the cost of the gasoline and expenses. Later, my NBC and other checks would start coming in, but right now, Ink and I were living frugally on his army pay.

What an adventure it was seeing Switzerland through the windows of our little car! From southern Germany, we had entered Austria, taking the Fernpasse through Landeck, and before we knew it were in Switzerland, going higher and higher. A big, beautiful Swiss cow walking down the center of the road was followed, on the next curve, by little goats herded along by a Swiss boy surely no more than four years old. It looked like a scene from *Heidi*, a book all three of us loved.

Sometimes, we had to hold our breath, as two cars would meet along the narrow road, where the houses seemed to reach out and touch over our heads. On one turn, we looked down into the valley and saw an emerald lake so brilliant I hoped I could come back someday for another look. Higher and higher we climbed until frequent signs announced "St. Moritz," and at last we arrived in the village we had heard so much about. Though traffic had increased, the village still displayed its characteristic charm. Despite our hunger pangs, it was difficult to drive away from that breathtaking view. A mountain stream tumbled toward us and the fir trees looked very friendly.

When we finally reached our hotel, the Suvretta House, perched on the mountainside, our hosts were resting. We were given two rooms, one for the children and one for me, and there were flowers in my room. Though unaccustomed to such luxury, it didn't take us long to adapt! At dinner with our friends, we found that in St. Moritz everyone speaks so many languages that dining is an education. German was spoken by all, English by many, Italian by several (the Italian border is close by), and some French. But the real language of this small corner of Switzerland was Romanche, which is close to Latin! The food was delicious in all languages.

After a good night's sleep in a feather bed, it was time for a pleasant walk in the mountains with our hosts and a picnic at ten thousand feet above sea level. We took a little train and then a cable car for part of the way. As the train chugged happily up the narrow passes, we saw a magnificent glacier out the window. A cable car, we discovered, wasn't half as frightening as it looks. Swinging through the air with no tracks beneath but nice sturdy cable lines above, it was too exciting to worry about. Those Swiss cows grazing on the mountains looked smaller from above but the view was breathtaking on every side. Back to earth, we found a walking stick a great help.

The McChesneys took us for the customary afternoon tea in the village before returning to the hotel. It was hard to say goodbye to St. Moritz. Now it was the time for the children to go to school and for me to go to work.

The Czech Border

One of my first contacts in Munich was with retired Major General C. Rodney Smith, whom I had known in Paris. A highly respected engineer in his army years, he now headed Radio Free Europe (RFE), whose work I was eager to report on for my American radio stations. At the time, Radio Liberty, also located in Munich, had not yet joined with Radio Free Europe. When I went to see General Smith at RFE headquarters in the Englischer Garten, Munich's beautiful central park, he immediately invited me to attend the morning staff meeting, where his public affairs people began to educate me about RFE's mission.

David Grozier, RFE's public affairs chief, told me about an important upcoming helicopter journey that the Fourth Armored Division would be taking to the German-Czechoslovak border and invited me along with my microphone. Fortunately, I had a splendid microphone and a small, battery-operated tape recorder, an English-made Fi-Cord I had bought in London, which was quite revolutionary at the time. It was smaller than a shoebox on a strap, and I carried it over my shoulder. The trip to the border was being specially staged for what were called "Crusade Leaders," people from the United States who supported Radio Free Europe in its mission of broadcasting behind the Iron Curtain. Among the U.S. guests were Eleanor Dulles, sister of Secretary of State John Foster Dulles, and Esther Van Wagoner Tufty, a friend from the Washington Press Corps.

With the Bavarian Alps in plain sight we took off from Munich in twelve military helicopters, engines roaring as we rose above the ground and mist rising up toward us. Sometimes we saw no sign of life, as though the fields were tilled by night and left in perfect order for all flying over to see. Two thousand feet above the land, we could see below clearly while sensing the vastness of the earth and the sky, the closeness of the two, and the beauty of it all defying the dangers and threats of the moment.

Our remarkable journey to a location still dangerous during the Cold War was made possible by the cooperation of the 4th Armored Division under the command of Gen. John K. Waters, son-in-law of General George Patton. General Waters accompanied us to the border, where heavily armed Soviet and Czech guards stood atop tall towers just beyond an electrified fence. The fence served to keep people from leaving Soviet-occupied territory and entering the free West. The Germans and the Americans also had troops at this and other points along the German side of the border in case Soviet tanks started to roll.

Gazing down as we flew, I saw neat little houses that resembled toy villages in electric train sets, rich black earth, and forests that looked blue. I saw neat rows of hay stacked in fields, tiny lakes sparkling in sunlight, and here was I flying in a watchful army sky bird over all this beauty of the earth below. Through the mist, I saw country roads, superhighways, magnificent cathedral spires, and fat little steeples with onion-shaped tops. Our H-34 helicopter floated up and down gently, flying in close formation with the other sky birds. With snow below us, we dropped suddenly as we flew over valleys and rivers with World War II bridges. I could see the Danube from every window.

General Waters told me about the troops of the 11th Armored Cavalry, a specialized organization in an isolated area. It was these troops, guarding the border, which we were visiting. A fighting machine used for transporting men or supplies to the border, the 11th could be in the field in less than two hours. At the border, its mission was security, surveillance, and training. German border police were also active in the area. In this milieu, Radio Free Europe, with its message of hope, served as an intangible but powerful force.

Back on earth, buses took us close to the barbed wire marking the Czech border. Guards on the towers trained machine guns directly on us. I learned that you can be inside Iron Curtain territory before you reach the barbed wire, so it was important to watch where we stepped. Being under the gun was definitely not fun and games. I had time to interview just one of our border guards before we headed back to Munich. As darkness fell and fog closed in, patterns of a town and one church spire came into view as we approached Straubing, then all light vanished. We were in the lead ship, a mother-bird with its flock following, an armada of twelve. We landed in what seemed a different world. I would not soon forget the air of bleakness and tension that permeated the border we had just left.

Dr. Von Braun

My career as an NBC correspondent began when I interviewed Dr. Werner Von Braun in Munich the day after the opening of *Aim for the Stars*, the film of his life story. As associate director of the National Aeronautics and Space Administration (NASA) in Washington, D.C. and director of the Marshall Space Flight Center in Huntsville, Alabama, Dr. Von Braun was best known for directing the team that designed and built the Saturn 5 Rocket that carried men to the moon. During World War II he had been responsible for designing the V-2 rockets that descended on Great Britain, killing and injuring thousands. At the end of the war Von Braun had surrendered to the Allies with his engineering team. In the eyes of many scientists he was redeemed by his contribution to our space program. After meeting this interesting scientist, so absorbed in helping man ascend into space, I found it difficult to imagine him working freely for the Nazis. I cannot resolve in my own mind this difficult paradox.

Von Braun, who had a quaint sense of humor, was once quoted as saying, "Gravity we can overcome, but paperwork is often overwhelming." Sometimes I recall that remark when I feel overcome by paperwork and smile to think that even scientists can be bothered by it. Werner Von Braun died in his early sixties, well remembered for his contribution to space exploration.

Reunion and Discovery in Iran

One reason I had moved to Munich for the year of the "hardship tour" was the hope that I could visit Ink in Iran. After several months, he sent the great news that he had permission for me to pay him a two-week visit and stay with him in Ajabshar. I made arrangements for Anni, my housekeeper, to care for the children while I was away.

As the jet took off from the Munich Airport, I saw ripples in a mirror caused by the vibration, then the glass was clear again. I watched baby clouds scooting along like cotton geese, massive clouds looking like a delicious French mousse. Such beauty, this world of ours! We climbed higher and higher until the earth was lost from sight. I saw the first star come out, and it looked as though we were only an escalator ride from the moon. We remained above the sunset, creating a radiant scene when the wings dipped. If man can fly like this, what limits are there to what he can do?

Ink met me at the airport in Teheran on October 25, 1960. It was a joyous reunion! Luckily, friends had lent us their small apartment right in Teheran. Next day, when we lunched at the Semaramis Hotel, crowds filled the streets for the Shah's birthday. To glimpse the Shah pass by on his way to a celebration in the stadium, I was eager to get up close along the curb to have a good view of the motorcade. But Ink said, "No, we will stay back here against the buildings. You will see why in a few minutes."

Hundreds of people were gathering along the street, excitedly waiting for their leader. Soon we saw a Rolls-Royce surrounded by truckloads of soldiers. Police were everywhere, some in tanks with guns and whips, which they used to keep the crowds from surging into the street. The unlucky people on the curb being pushed from behind were the victims of many a slash. How glad I was not to be in the front row!

We drove around the city that afternoon, and it was time for me to do some work. The government had given me a guide, an intelligent young woman. She was Muslim but did not wear the chador, the traditional long cloth that envelops the body and covers all or part of the face. She told me that only recently had women been allowed to have important jobs. "The Shah," she said, "was changing life for women, giving them new opportunities."

My guide had arranged for me to interview a professor of English at the University of Teheran, a modern university in an ancient country. The professor told me he had earned his Ph.D. in American Literature at Indiana University in the United States. He invited me to lecture to his class of one hundred students after we had completed an interview for NBC. I talked to the students about the current presidential election in the United States. John F. Kennedy was to be our next president, but we didn't yet know it that day. The students had many questions about the United States, including the American electoral system, and I did my best to answer them.

In a bazaar, Ink and I lunched on a Kebab made of raw egg, butter, powder, rice, and lamb flank barbecued after soaking three days in yogurt. Later we visited a mosque, where I covered my head, and the Golestan Palace for more interviews and to see the Peacock Throne.

Also in Teheran I interviewed Maj. Gen. John C. Hayden, chief of the Army's Mission and Military Assistance Advisory Group in Iran. The mission, which included U.S. Air Force and U.S. Navy representatives advising the Iranian forces, was stationed in Iran at the invitation of the Iranian government.

After four days in Teheran, we boarded a Trans-Iranian-National Railroad train for Ajabshar in northwestern Iran, where Ink had his headquarters. We shared a small compartment on the train with others, making for a long, interesting overnight trip. On the train, I interviewed a Mr. Johnson, the man in charge of the American construction company at Ajabshar that was building army quarters for the Shah with American money. Ink was there representing the Army Corps of Engineers to make sure the job would be done as economically as possible. As the officer in charge, he was able to save the United States considerable money. He also won friends among the Iranians, I was told, because whenever possible he would dig a ditch to channel excess water, a much needed commodity, to the farmers.

At Ajabshar nothing was elaborate. The buildings were quite simple, as was Ink's office. We toured the building site. About noon that first day, word arrived of the birth of the Shah's baby boy, Crown Prince Cyrus Reza. The date was October 31st, and it was a big occasion in Iran. The baby's mother was the Empress Farah, the Shah's new wife. (Later, in Munich I would meet Saroya, the woman he had divorced because she could not have children. She lived next door to the U.S. consul general, whom I knew.)

Iran, old Persia, is an intriguing country with rugged mountains, deserts, and plains, where many languages are spoken. When I was there, I spoke both English and French, which many Iranians speak, and I do not speak Farsi, their most often used language.

Traveling through the mountains and to little villages to see the countryside, we climbed high enough to see the lake and to look down at the construction site. The women in the countryside wore chadors, which covered the head and part of the face, sometimes with only one eye showing. We saw a man making bricks for his house out of mud and water. He framed them and dried them in the sun. At the construction site, I talked with Paul Kleimans, the operator of a concrete mixer who was building a large foundation for a water tower; with Clark Kemp at an open-hearth blast furnace; and with Rex Lane, who operated a well-drilling rig.

One morning in perfect weather, Ink and I left early for Tabriz, the second largest city in Iran, accompanied by a driver and my Armenian translator. The roads were dusty and bumpy, but the scenery was striking. In Tabriz we visited an old Turkish fort, a donkey caravansari. We saw flat bread being made, and I did an interview about the unusual clay furnaces placed down into the ground, with goat hair on top and small holes on the side for even heating as the bread baked, clinging to the oven's sides.

Another destination was the city of Rezaieh, a small city on the Great Rezaieh Salt Lake, marked on many maps by its old name, Urmia. To reach Rezaieh, we crossed a lonely road over a desert where smugglers were known to bring in goods and drugs from other countries. We had been warned of possible attacks by bandits. I was wrapped in a sheet from head to toe to protect myself from the blowing sand and was careful to hold my microphone and tape recorder in my arms beneath my large white cover.

We reached Rezaieh in late afternoon. Our first stop was the ancient Zoroastrian St. Mary's Church, the alleged burial place of one of the biblical Three Wise Men, or Magi. Zorastrianism, the religion of Persia before the conversion of the Persians to Mohammedanism, was founded by its great prophet, Zoroaster, a sixth century b.c. teacher sometimes called Zarathushtra. This ancient Persian religion was characterized by the worship of a supreme deity who requires men's good deeds for help in the cosmic struggle against evil. The Three Magi were known to be of the class of Zoroastrian priests among the Medes in ancient Persia and were reported to possess supernatural as well as astrological powers.

The story of my interview at that church in Rezaieh is one of my favorites. The church sat in the middle of a large dusty square covered with brown dirt well packed into the earth. I saw that in the little tower of the church was a large, old bell. Because NBC, for whom I was doing the interview, liked to have a "you are there" sound at the start of each interview, I asked the church's pastor if he would kindly ring the bell so I could tape the sound.

That would be impossible, he told me with great regret. He could only ring the bell when somebody died or it was time to call people to morning services. Could I come back in the morning? I said we would be on the road in the morning and he explained, "I cannot confuse the people."

I told him that we would go ahead with the interview and he invited me down the steps into the church, which was underground. At that very moment, a young boy came racing across the square heading right to the priest. After a rapid exchange of words in Farsi, the priest turned to me and said, "There is news! Someone died, we can ring the bell!" He quickly added, "I do not mean to be happy about anyone's death, but this man who died was very old, very sick, and had lived a good life. His death was not unexpected."

And so the bell rang, and we did the interview. On Christmas Eve that year, NBC broadcast my conversation with the priest inside the church about the Wise Man buried there. I have thought many times about the tolling of that bell for a man I did not know. His bell tolled all across the United States that Christmas Eve, and later, when I replayed the interview on my Voice of America program, it tolled all over the world, reaching many more millions of listeners of all nationalities.

I knew about my interview being heard on Christmas Eve in the United States because my father had bought a small tape recorder after NBC notified him it would be airing one of my interviews that night. My family gathered around the radio in Connecticut and my father made a recording in the midst of what they told me was considerable excitement at hearing my voice coming in from so far away.

As a foreign correspondent, I was able to see much of the world up close, but the far northwestern corner of Iran was one of my most memorable stops.

Leaving the Great Salt Lake in Rezaieh, we drove to the Russian border. We did not cross it, of course, for that was forbidden. A man at the border was selling samovars, which he had set up on a little table near his house.

"I am looking for a fat one, not a tall one," I told him.

He ran into his house and came out with a graceful samovar of the Czarist era stamped with a coin of 1903, which I gladly bought. Later an American professor of Russian literature, who came to our house for dinner, said the samovar was a very good one.

On our trip to the northwestern corner of Iran, we stopped in Marand, the smallest site of the construction project. There we met with the American construction chief, Mr. Johnson, his wife and his son, Jeff, who later visited me in Munich. After tea at our interpreter's house back in Rezaieh, we supped and stayed the night at a Point Four program guesthouse.

We next stopped at the American missionary grounds, which had been used between 1832 and 1932. It was now an agricultural experiment station, with hens from America and bulls from Yugoslavia and Belgium.

When we visited Hasanlu, one of the oldest known excavations was taking place. The chief archeologist, whom I interviewed, let me walk through the digs, which dated back four or five thousand years to the time of the Median Empire. The Syrians had tried and failed to capture it, but managed to set fire to the fort. Now the University of Pennsylvania had sent people and financial support to Iran to work in this quiet yet exciting place of discovery. I brought a rock back in my pocket, as I always did when I traveled. Because I didn't mark each one, I no longer know which is which, but I love them all.

In a small Turkish village along the way, I did an interview in a building where Persian rugs were being made. In the workshop a foreman was giving instructions by song in Turkish. I watched the workers tying the knots in the hand-dyed string, following the number of knots and the colors in the pattern in accordance with the chant instructing them. Most of the rugs are exported, although some are kept in Iran.

At Maregeh an Iranian general hosted a dinner party in our honor. Among the guests were the governor general of Rezaieh, and women were also included. Farsi, French, and English were the languages spoken at dinner.

A place where there were no women and perhaps never had been until I entered its door was a teahouse in a village. My interpreter took me into it and we did an interview there. It is in just such a teahouse that the news of the day is heard, with people singing their tales, both of ancient and current history. No newspapers here, but a custom passed down from father to son through the ages remained in good working order.

Another interview I especially enjoyed was with an overseer of water buffalo that were plowing fields. The buffalo worked best, he told me, when love songs were sung to them asking them please to work well and happily. At the beginning of the tape for my NBC sound, the men around us sang some love songs to guide the buffalo in their work. When we finished talking, I noticed the buffalo approaching us from the fields and asked the men if they would like to hear the tape.

"Oh, yes," they said, "please play it for us."

We had done all the talking through the interpreter, but the love songs I played back were in the Persian language. All of a sudden, the water buffalo perked up their ears at the sound of the tape and, being unattended for the moment, took off across the fields following their musical instructions. All the men chased after them, and it was a sight to see.

Iran held many sights to see. I was always impressed by the contrast between the old and the new. Yes, there were camels, sheep, goats, donkeys, and water buffalo, but there was also a modern airport, much modernizing construction in Teheran, and everywhere signs of a country on the move. We saw no outward signs then of the chaos to come years later when the Shah would be overthrown, along with freedom of the press and freedom for women, and a break with the United States would become part of the new Iran. American hostages would be held in our embassy, and even after the hostages returned home, relations between our two countries remained tense. I hope that someday we will once again become friends.

At the end of my maximum two-week visit, I boarded a plane at the Mehrabad airport (a newer airport there is named Khomeini) and headed home to Munich via Ankara, Turkey. Ink and I would have to wait until the summer of 1961 to see each other again, so I planned to continue reporting for NBC New York, WFAX, and the AFN in Europe. Lucky for me, the children awaited me in Munich, eager to hear about my adventures in Iran and my plans for trips we would take together in the months to come.

Christmas Catastrophe in Munich

"The smoking skeleton of a U.S. Air Force twin-engine Convair lies in the downtown area of Munich tonight, and the holiday atmosphere of the city has changed to one of great sadness.

"Black-helmeted German firemen in long black slickers are working side by side with U.S. Army soldiers of the 508th M.P. Battalion. As I watch, the workers have succeeded in raising a shrouded streetcar onto its tracks, a Strassenbahn they call it here in Germany, and this one is Number Ten. It is still filled with Christmas shoppers who were electrocuted instantly when the plane crashed into it.

"Inside the plane are the bodies of the U.S. Air Force crew of seven and approximately sixteen American students of the Munich branch of the University of Maryland bound for England to spend Christmas with their military families. Searchlights are everywhere, aiding the German and American rescue workers. My eyes pick up the sight of a dozen or more Christmas turkeys, which the students had been carrying home. They were roasted from the heat of the smoldering plane."

I wrote the above report at the time of my visit to the crash site. I was late arriving at the scene, for I had just returned home with the children and knew nothing of the chaos in the city until an engineer from VOA laboriously climbed the five flights of steps and knocked on my door. He offered to take me to the accident and suggested I do a story about it for NBC. He had come to see me earlier as I could not be reached by phone (which I did not have, as the waiting time for a phone was nine months), but no one had been home. It might be too late to get the report to New York but I would try.

As I walked through the crash area, an army escort told me that all the bodies were being removed and that he would lead me to where the mayor of Munich, Hans Johann Vogel, was surveying the damage. I expressed my sympathy to the mayor for the death of the thirty or more Munich citizens who had been engulfed in flames on the Strassenbahn, and he expressed sympathy to me for the collision of two planes in New York City shortly before this tragic accident. At one point, I tripped on a wire cable and it cut into my leg, not doing much damage, but the mark of that wire lasted a year. It was a reminder of a tragedy I would not forget and a realization that "hard news" reporting was not for me. I preferred to stick with human interest stories and interviews.

The Passion Play and Royalty in Lech

The children missed their father almost as much as I did, so I tried to think of working trips that could include them and be fun for us all. Down we would come from our fifth-floor apartment lugging our bags and my recorder. We would load up our little Volkswagen and head for the Alps.

One early destination was the Bavarian village of Oberammergau, to see the world famous Passion Play that is performed only once every ten years. The tickets are usually sold out years ahead of time. I called the village mayor, told him I would like to do a story about the play for my radio programs, and said my children would like to come with me to see the play. He came up with three tickets, and we had a grand experience.

The Passion Play stars local residents of Oberammergau. The tradition of performing it for around one hundred performances once every ten years at the beginning of each decade goes back about four centuries. Performed outdoors on a huge stage, the whole play is based on medieval passion plays. It tells of the crucifixion of Christ as related in the four Gospels. The production includes a large orchestra and chorus and a cast of around two thousand people, about half the population of Oberammergau. People of all faiths go to see it, as it is a most unusual production.

En route to our hotel in the village, we drove through a big traffic jam. We came up to an intersection where a policeman was directing traffic. I pushed my left-hand turn signal, which in those days was a wooden stick mounted outside the left car window to be raised and lowered on command. Another such stick was mounted on the right. In my excitement at seeing the policeman and not knowing exactly which way I wanted to turn, I accidentally gave both sticks the command to go up and down. The policeman stood looking at me and laughing. He raised both his arms and waved them like a windmill, imitating my wooden sticks and called out to me in German, "What is this up and down signal? Which way do you want to go?"

"Left," I told him, and he waved me on. I found the hotel and still recall not only the play in Oberammergau but also my wild wooden sticks trying to communicate with a patient police officer.

As Christmas drew near, we were invited to our housekeeper's apartment for Christmas Eve. Anni lived in the middle of Munich, and we loved going to visit her. The children were always happy when she took care of them in our apartment during my travels. She had a daytime job sewing in a dress factory but would arrive to take care of the children just before they came home from school and stay all night and on weekends.

Not long before Christmas, my German friend Erika Maurer, who owned our apartment, said, "Come with us to Lech in Austria where we will ski over the holidays."

I told her that we would love to join them, but first I would have to find an inexpensive place for us to stay. We would also have to rent ski equipment there. She assured me that no matter where we stayed we could join them in their hotel for after-ski dancing and informal dinner. I was sure there would be good interviews to do in Lech, so I called the tourist bureau and procured one room big enough to hold the three of us in a little inn at the edge of the village.

As soon as I told the children about our reservations, Larry told a neighbor in our building that we would be skiing for Christmas. This friendly neighbor took out her ski poles and taught Larry how to balance on wedged-shaped pillows. "Pretend you are on skis," she said, "coming down a steep hill and figure out how to keep your balance." By the time we arrived in Lech, Larry was starting to get the hang of how to ski, and I agreed to pay for a few lessons on the slopes for both children.

Larry took to the snow as though he had been born in the Alps. Two instructors even approached me to ask if I would leave him with them for a few weeks so they could teach him more because he had the makings of a champion skier. Flattering but, of course, out of the question. Pam did pretty well too, remembering a bit from being on skis one weekend in Garmisch, the first time we had lived in Munich.

We were joined one night at dinner by a Dutchman and his son, friends of the Maurers. The boy was about Larry's age, and he and Larry struck up a conversation in German as the boy didn't speak English and Larry didn't speak Dutch. Suddenly, Larry understood why he was working hard to learn languages other than his own.

The Dutch father said to Larry, "I saw you on the mountain today with a Dutch woman giving you some lessons. Do you know who that woman is? She is Princess Beatrix of the Netherlands, who will one day be queen. She and her sister are here at Lech with the royal family for the holidays." Larry still likes hearing that story.

We all loved Lech and our holiday there with Erika and her children. When we returned home to Munich with empty pockets, we ate lots of breakfast cereal to economize on grocery bills. We were always tight on funds but never on fun!

7

Both Sides of the Iron Curtain

Berlin

In February 1961, I took Pam and Larry to Berlin for a brief holiday from school. We would visit my old radio partner, Rosanne McQuarrie, and her husband Jock at U.S. Army headquarters of the Berlin Brigade. Pam and I traveled by train, but Larry preceded us by plane to give him more time with his good friend, the McQuarrie's son, another sixth grader. My mother and father, reading the newspapers at home about continuous tensions in Berlin, were aghast that I was going there and taking the children. I wrote back that things were seldom as bad on the spot as in the papers. Because they were used to my plunging ahead, they soon relaxed and asked to hear all about the trip as soon as I returned to Munich. My tape recorder went with us.

I conducted many interviews in this historic city run by the Four Powers—France, Britain, the United States, and the Soviet Union. In addition to interviewing General Ralph Osborne about his responsibilities as commander in Berlin, I also looked at the lighter side of Berlin—how the Americans were living, the little league baseball groups, and the everyday life of the troops.

In East Berlin I saw the extraordinary contrast between the east and west portions of the city. East Berlin still bore the ravages of war, in the midst of which stood the German State Opera House of Berlin. Rosanne and Jock took us there to the best performance I have ever seen of *Gajaneh*, an exciting ballet by Aram Khatchaturian. After the rude shock of the Berlin Wall on August 13, the opera house was closed to the western sector of the city. I felt fortunate to have had that one evening there.

I followed closely the first news reports of the Wall but it wasn't until I talked with Army General John Russell Deane many years later that I heard firsthand how our Army handled the dramatic events of that time. General Deane remembered well that August day when the Berlin Wall went up before dawn. It started out as a barbed wire fence all along the twenty-nine- mile border between East and West Berlin. The barbed wire soon became a ten-foot-high, solid concrete wall, manned by guards in observation towers with floodlights and electrified fences. Anyone trying to escape was killed. The Wall cut off Soviet-occupied East Berlin from the American, British, and French sectors of West Berlin.

Jack Deane was then colonel in command of the 2d Battle Group of the 6th Infantry Regiment, having assumed command just before the Wall's construction. An exercise in progress at the time was named "Alerts." These alerts were called on an unannounced basis by the Supreme Headquarters Allied Powers, Europe (SHAPE), by the U.S. Army, Europe (USAREUR) and by the Berlin Brigade. When an "Alert" was held, the units had to be assembled in full battle gear with trucks loaded with ammunition, rations, gasoline, and all the rest and ready to move to predesignated battle stations within a specified period of time, about an hour. Deane conducted frequent "Alerts" until his men were ready to go in less than half the allotted time. This preparation stood him in good stead in the days after the East German forces erected the Berlin Wall.

Back in February 1961, some of the army families in Berlin seemed apprehensive, but conditions then were actually not too bad, according to Deane. However, attitudes changed when the Wall went up and the East German government announced on their public radio that anyone who came within one hundred meters of the Wall would be shot. The most sensitive place along the Wall for our troops was "Checkpoint Charlie," the crossing point from the American Sector of West Berlin to the Russian Sector in East Berlin. After the Wall, the crossing points were drastically reduced to further impede the escape of East Germans to the West. Only Checkpoint Charlie remained in the American Sector.

The Americans, Jack Deane said, could not let stand the Soviet threat to shoot anyone who came within one hundred meters. Deane took his troops right up to the Wall to patrol it. He told them they were not to fire unless fired upon. He explained to them the possibility that the East Germans would carry out their threat, although he did not think they would. Just to show how strongly he felt, Deane himself led the patrol. He radioed the Berlin Brigade that the patrol was moving out to accomplish the assigned mission, namely, to show that we would not stay one hundred meters from the Wall but would patrol it. He and his troops were close enough to reach out and touch the Wall. The East Germans watching, apparently stunned, did not know what to do. They appeared confused and afraid to fire. The Americans patrolled for about two miles, at the end of which Jack radioed the brigade that he believed we had made our point.

Patrols continued on a regular basis, with occasional incidents, once during the changing of the guard at Spandau Prison, where Rudolph Hess was held. A tank confrontation occurred in October, pictures of which appeared in newspapers throughout the world. Russian tanks filled the street leading to their side of Checkpoint Charlie. Their guns pointed at the U.S. tanks that filled the street on our side of the checkpoint. This tense situation went on for several hours, with Colonel Deane reporting by phone to the Berlin commander, who in turn was on the phone with Heidelberg, SHAPE, the Pentagon, and the White House. Finally, both sides moved their tanks back from Checkpoint Charlie.

On a later visit to Berlin, during a business trip to Germany after I had returned to the United States, I saw the Wall for myself and visited a pre-Wall mosaic factory built right up along its side. One night, the factory's owner told me, his employees went to their homes, some in East Berlin, some in West Berlin, but when they started off to work next morning, the East German workers were unable to get to the factory. The Wall had been erected during the night! There would be no more escape to freedom through West Berlin without fear of being shot by the guards posted atop the Wall.

Today in my library, I have some small pieces of that Wall, torn down in 1989. These remnants of an unhappy artifice in world history were sent to me by Ambassador Hans Gunther-Hasse, a European colleague and advisor for Radio Free Europe and Radio Liberty. So much to remember looking at those tiny jagged pieces of the Berlin Wall.

I Cross the Barrier into the Soviet Union

The Soviets said I could come! For a matter of only a few weeks, they were letting some correspondents into the Soviet Union on condition that we tell the outside world what it was like to tour in Soviet territory. The Armed Forces Network director who had assigned me made all the arrangements for me to go in with my tape recorder, explaining that the Soviets were eager to attract visitors and needed exposure. Because of the uncertainty of Soviet promises I would not know for sure whether I could bring my tapes out after doing the interviews. My trip would be paid for by AFN, which would use all of my material, and I would also send it on to NBC in New York. I would fly into the Soviet Union with a group of American teachers from American schools abroad.

I asked Radio Free Europe for a briefing before my departure, which helped me greatly in carrying out my assignment. Radio Free Europe was sending news of the Free World to the Soviet satellite countries twenty-four hours a day. At RFE operational headquarters in Munich, Germany, I had watched Hungarian, Romanian, Bulgarian, Czechoslovakian, and Polish men and women from their strangled countries work with fervor and dedication aiding the American staff in achieving its goal. I had also met with former Soviet citizens now broadcasting back into the cities from which they had fled. I had done interviews at Radio Free Europe, which I had sent back to NBC in the United States and to AFN in Europe.

I was about to do something forbidden to those emigrés at RFE, who spoke to me before my departure with sadness, a bit of envy, and eagerness. Could they through me vicariously visit the lands they had left, such as Poland and Hungary, two of my destinations? These Eastern European countries under Soviet control were spoken of everyday on the RFE airwaves. They lay such a short distance from Munich in miles, such an eternity away in reality.

What could I bring in the way of up-to-date news to the Hungarian who told me of his beautiful Budapest? With tears in his eyes and fear in his heart, he dared not give me the address of any relatives there, because of danger not to me but to anyone I would contact. For them it might mean endless hours of questioning by the police, loss of privileges, and all kinds of possible trouble. Everyone warned me not to do any interviews behind potted palms, because that would make it appear as though I were hiding from the Soviet authorities. I would of course be followed at all times on my visits to Kiev, Moscow, Leningrad (now once again St. Petersburg), Warsaw, and Budapest.

As our adventure began, the teachers and I met at the airport in Munich. From there we took off to the forbidden Soviet Union, flying directly to our first stop, Kiev, capital of Ukraine, on the banks of the Dnieper River. People in Kiev maintain a constant effort to keep folk traditions and customs alive. In Kiev, World War II was still fresh in people's minds. In the center of the city, 140,000 citizens killed by Germans between 1941 and 1945 were buried.

My hotel roommate was a teacher from Illinois, Ann Covington. We agreed that rather than both of us keeping notes, she would do the writing and give me the notes at the end of the trip. Ann was excellent company, and we had a good time sharing the impressions of our journey. Another extremely helpful American schoolteacher was Nancy Phillips, who was teaching in Norway. I gave her some rolls of 35-millimeter film I had brought along and asked her to take pictures of me doing interviews whenever possible. There was no way I could carry a camera along with my recording equipment.

People told us of their pride in Kiev University, built in 1834, where more than 700 teachers served over 6,000 students. Though under the wing of Intourist and its official Soviet guides for foreign visitors, we were free to walk around on our own. We were not, however, completely on our own. On our first night in Kiev, we walked into the wrong hotel then turned around and came outside. There under a tree stood a man, watching us and smiling; he knew we would come back out and followed us into the correct hotel.

On our first day, I visited a Russian school, where a ticking clock chimed every fifteen minutes. The school's director, a short, stocky woman wearing a purple suit with a white lace collar, had a sweet, deeply lined face. Tasseled white draperies hung at the windows, and those large potted palms made the room seem smaller than it was. High-backed wooden chairs stood on the red varnished floor.

The director answered my questions through an interpreter, telling me that this grammar school taught students from seven to eighteen years of age. She suggested we walk through the building. The school was crowded, with narrow classrooms

 but wide hallways. The children, dressed in dark uniforms, lined up in one central hall as I passed. At the end of the hall, I saw busts of Stalin, Lenin, and Khrushchev, then leader of the Soviet Union. Boys and girls were separated at the fifth-grade level, the director explained, but here in the corridors we saw both girls and boys hurrying to class. In the school library, girls worked on factory-sized sewing machines. In the next room, boys were learning to work with factory lathes. Lessons of labor, these classes were called.

On our first night in Kiev, we went to a ballet, "Heart of the Forest." There we met a charming couple, an engineer and his young wife. They had probably been seated next to me on purpose, for they spoke good English and were very friendly. After the ballet, they invited my roommate and me to join them at a restaurant. Irina, the woman, said she was studying mathematics, although she had also studied music. They took us to Pektopah at the top of a hill, where we were served vodka and mineral water, bread and butter, cucumber salad, and later champagne with chocolate wafers. We stayed quite late and then went for a walk. Irina showed me the hall where Van Cliburn had played. She thought him a marvelous pianist.

As we walked along the streets, Irina said, "You are the first Americans I have ever seen. Please, let us ask you, why do you not want peace?" Obviously, the Soviets were being told that we wanted to fight with them. I could only hope they would believe me when I said that was untrue.

After more interviews in Kiev, we flew to Leningrad on a Russian TY-114 jet. It was a foggy Easter Sunday morning, and we couldn't land in Leningrad on our first try, so we turned around, went back to Kiev. When the fog cleared, back we went to Leningrad. On both flights we noticed a great deal of vibration, not quite enough cabin pressure, and a lot of noise, but we did arrive safely. En route I interviewed the woman pilot.

Leningrad is a beautiful city, often called the Venice of the North because of the many canals and islands. Situated on the Neva River, it was built by Peter the Great in the 18th century. In the twentieth century, it was the city the Germans besieged for nine hundred days.

After the Soviet Union collapsed, the city reverted to its former name of St. Petersburg. Only a few miles from the Gulf of Finland, it is the gateway to the Arctic. Of its many museums, the greatest of all is the Hermitage, the palace of Catherine the Great, which ranks with the Louvre in Paris and the Vatican in Rome. I spent a long while inside the Hermitage interviewing the curator. Nowadays many paintings continue to be added to the collections, but even at the time of my visit, there were an extraordinary number of famous artists represented. Most, like the sixteen Picassos, were paintings from their early days. The Soviets did not approve of modern paintings. Among other great works were those by Cezanne, Gaugain, Matisse, Van Gogh, Renoir, Bonnard, forty-nine paintings by Rubens, twenty-six Van Dykes, and twenty-four Rembrandts. I prepared a special program on the Hermitage.

Leningrad had many colleges, many libraries, and glorious architecture dating to the days of the czars. I went to the circus, the People's Circus it was called, and sat in the bleachers, all bundled up against the chilly weather. This was a one-ring circus, with trapeze artists, horses, jugglers, clowns, and seals. It was fun to watch and discouraging to discover later that what the clowns were saying was all Soviet propaganda aimed at the children.

Then off we flew to Moscow. I have never forgotten the grimness of Moscow at that time. The Intourist guides politely informed us that the Soviet Union would be taking over the United States, winning the Cold War by proving itself superior economically. They were peace-loving people, we were told, while we were the war-oriented nation. It was distressing listening to their viewpoint, but with the newspapers saying dreadful and untrue things about the United States, such twisted ideas about the West were not surprising.

In Moscow we stayed at the Hotel Ukrainian. Everything in the city is built on a massive scale, including the hotel, which looked like a skyscraper apartment house. We did get a beautiful panorama of the entire city from our front window. There were snow flurries everyday, and the atmosphere was heavy. I was busy doing my interviews, though not behind large plants. We saw displays of the Soviet Space Program in the great Exhibition Hall, which contained a replica of *Sputnik*. Only after my return to Munich did the rest of the world and I learn that the Soviets had launched a man, Yuri Gargarin, into space. This Soviet cosmonaut flew on April 12, 1961, but there was a news blackout at the time.

I conducted an interview on the Kremlin Museum, which houses elaborate, jeweled-encrusted gifts to the Czars from other crowned heads around the world. The spectacular collection included jeweled robes, thrones, carriages, and harnesses belonging to Peter the Great, Catherine the Great, Ivan the Terrible, and the Romanovs. They used twenty-six horses to pull a large coach and changed the horses every three hours going from Moscow to Leningrad.

We visited the Great Mausoleum, where bodies of both Lenin and Stalin then lay in state. Our Intourist guide led us past the long queues waiting to go in and through an inside passage. Seeing those two bodies was a strange experience. They certainly looked real, and they certainly looked dead. At several churches we visited in Red Square, it seemed that only old people were worshiping. To worship in a church was frowned upon and had severe consequences for young people. St. Basil's was the most beautiful.

I visited the American Embassy in Moscow, where two American correspondents, John Chancellor of NBC and Marvin Kalb of CBS, took me to lunch in the cafeteria. They were eager for news of the outside world, even if only from as far away as Munich. I would meet them both again in future years.

In the great Moscow Metro, our guide took us down a tremendously long escalator at terrific speed. I saw Moscovites reading books on the way down the escalator and sometimes eating ice cream. The Russian people were friendly when I spoke with them. Only the officials were often cold. Some Metro stations looked like museums, with rich carvings and mosaics. Many people stopped to look at the pictures, a happy break in the drab socialist day. Most stations looked rather dingy. People I noticed had stoic gray faces. The trains came every three minutes. There was a modern train with vents on the outside top turned toward the wind to receive fresh air and reversed on the other side to emit stale air, a built-in air-conditioning. During the rush hour 100,000 people go through the Metro, we were told.

Recently, I saw a spectacular performance of *Don Quixote* by the Bolshoi Ballet at the Kennedy Center in Washington. It brought back to me the extraordinary evening I spent at the Bolshoi in Moscow, at a performance of the opera *Aida*.

The Bolshoi Theater is breathtaking in its glittering gold and crimson decor. Five regal red velvet tiers rise from the huge auditorium, which holds two thousand people. The stage is as large as the theater itself. I was seated in the third tier and just below me, on the right, I had a clear view of the state box, where the President of the Soviet Union, Leonid Brezhnev, sat. In his party, I recognized the minister of culture, Madame Katherina Furtseva, an imposing figure of a woman who had recently allowed such innovations at the Bolshoi as a rock and roll number.

The Bolshoi has always been closely associated with classical Russian opera and ballet. It has also featured the works of some Western composers, including classical operas by Mozart and that night's *Aida* by Verdi. The opera orchestra boasted 250 musicians, and the scenery, the lighting, and mechanical effects were most impressive. At that time the Bolshoi employed more than five hundred people of different trades, such as expert shoemakers and costumers, and printed the programs in its own plant.

It's not difficult to visualize the high fashion days at the Bolshoi. On this night, however, people were simply dressed, many of them wearing high, black boots. Looking around me, I saw people from many lands, as well as Russian students and older Russians. One very old Russian woman came over to speak with me, saying she was eager to speak with an American if only for a moment.

On our last evening in Moscow, we went to the famous Puppet Theater, a fascinating place, and saw something called "Take-off on Hollywood." It was not at all complimentary to movie producers, playwrights, and actors. The audience included many young people, and everyone laughed heartily. Backstage a stagehand told us a little about the productions. As many as three people work on making one puppet; the voice recording is synchronized with the acting, and the puppets are worked on long sticks.

Earlier that day, we made a quick visit to the GUM Department Store, an old building with stone steps inside worn in deep ruts where thousands have walked. Long arcades, two stories high with arched bridges, led from one side of a balcony to another. In the center of the building stood a large fountain, and a skylight over the top of the entire store was designed to save electricity. What little merchandise the store had to offer was all quite expensive. I bought some books in Russian with good black-and-white pictures of the city and a set of the famous nested wooden dolls. In later years, my granddaughters played by the hour with those little dolls.

One episode in Moscow had made me uneasy. I carried in my handbag a letter of introduction to two doctors from my good friend in Munich, the highly respected Dr. Georgi Maurer. Georgi wanted me to call on these doctors, Professor Boris A. Petrov and Professor Dr. Vladimir Kovanov, at the Medical Institute in Moscow. He had met them at medical conferences and was sure I would find them most interesting to interview. When I entered the Soviet Union, I had been asked in no uncertain terms if I carried any letters for anyone. Realizing that the inspector at the airport was deadly serious, I handed him my letter of introduction. After a few questions, he returned it to me but not before he had called over his supervisor and made a written report of it.

When I went to the Medical Institute and asked to see the doctor, there was quite a stir of activity. A nurse, whose kind eyes I could see above her medical mask, explained that I could come to the professor's office with her and perhaps telephone him from there. However, he was not at home and not in his office that day. Before we reached the professor's office, a young doctor barred my way and started asking me questions.

"What do you have for the doctor? Who has sent you?" As he spoke, I looked above his medical mask to see dark, cold, suspicious eyes glaring at me. This man was not giving me a warm welcome.

In the hallways, I had noted dirty, bloody rags and a lack of what we would consider sterile conditions. I liked the professor's office, redolent of the old world, with an oriental rug and interesting pictures. There was no answer on his home telephone. I suspected he had been ordered to stay home that day and was hoping I had not caused him any trouble. Back in my hotel room, several times I noticed what seemed crossed wires on my telephone when I tried to call the front desk. Each time I overheard discussions in Russian mentioning the names of the two doctors I had tried to find. Obviously, someone was listening to see if I would try to contact the doctors for some subversive reason.

Back in Munich, I told Dr. Maurer that I had had no luck seeing his friends to give them his regards. In recent years, I have seen newspaper clippings announcing the death of one or possibly both of them. I was sorry the system would not allow me to see them. After that day in the hospital, I was especially careful to be in plain sight when holding my microphone.

Snow fell gently over Moscow and cold winds whipped around us at the airport as we took off for Warsaw.

Warsaw

Warsaw, warm and beautiful in the sunlight, was only a short flight from Moscow, but how far apart its atmosphere. We had gone from winter to summer, from cold to warm. Here the sun shone, people smiled, and we were welcomed in a flower-bedecked air terminal. Churches were open and people worshiped in them. We visited the church where Chopin had played the organ and fallen in love with a beautiful girl in the congregation. Later on in the park, we saw a fine statue of Chopin with his garments flowing and the tree behind him blowing in the same direction.

Warsaw was badly destroyed during World War II, with signs of warfare abounding. The city was unquestionably dominated by the Soviets at the time, but I noticed immediately the proud Polish spirit that somehow managed to raise its head. Still, the many restrictions kept us aware that we were still well behind the Iron Curtain.

Something forceful showed in the pulse of the capital city of Poland, the least subjugated of the satellite countries. A hat store caught my womanly eye on the way into town from the airport. The hats were chic, and people were actually wearing them. It surprised me that some people could afford to buy these hats, for in many Soviet satellites the store windows often displayed goods that were way beyond the possibility of purchase. Polish shoes were sturdy and good, the coats of decent quality, people looked busy, and churches held services, not museum tours. I knew that behind this façade of freedom lay many restrictions that cut into the life of the Poles; but the city of Warsaw appeared to be undergoing reconstruction bit by bit. Ordinary people's lives improved day by day. Yet I worried lest a people apparently making do under communism might forget the way life once was without restrictions.

I stood where the Warsaw Ghetto had been, where thousands of Jewish Poles had been forced to live and to die. Nothing remained but the blood-stained stones and a huge statue, originally ordered by Hitler as a Victory Statue for Berlin but later set in place as a monument to the many Jews who had died in the 1942 Warsaw Ghetto uprising. Remembering what had happened in the Warsaw Ghetto was a deeply moving experience.

"Do Polish people listen to radio from other countries?" I inquired. In spite of Soviet jamming, people told me yes, they listened to VOA, BBC, sometimes AFN, but mostly to Radio Free Europe. It was RFE, I was told, that gave them news of their own internal affairs and made clear to them that Poland was receiving economic aid from the United States, a fact not well advertised by the Soviets! The Polish spirit seemed alive and well, jokes were told that made fun of the Soviet system, and there seemed to be little acceptance of communism.

A haunting thought as I traveled was of the constant and steady flow of refugees from such countries as Poland and Hungary to the West. How homesick those people must have been for the old precommunist days in the beautiful cities I was able to visit, cities to which they might never return. No wonder my slightest descriptions of a reconstructed building in an old part of their city brought them joy. What fortitude these refugees possessed to live and work outside their countries, giving of their knowledge and ability to such organizations as Radio Free Europe in Munich, which employed so many refugees.

I interviewed many people in Warsaw before heading for our last stop, Budapest. So far no problem had arisen with my carrying tapes through airport customs. The final test would come when leaving Hungary for Germany.

Budapest

We flew to Budapest in a turboprop Hungarian airliner and landed at the impressive Budapest Airport, where every facility was available and only air traffic notably absent. Our plane was the first planeload of Americans to land in Budapest since the Hungarian revolution in 1956. Several months earlier a bus had brought in Americans, but our pilot was pleased to bring in the first plane with Americans aboard.

As we approached Budapest at night, I stood in the cockpit where the navigator excitedly pointed to his radar screen to show me his city. "We are 231 kilometers from Budapest," he said. "She is beautiful and I hope you will like her." And I did, from the moment I turned to see the lights of this proud, broken, beautiful capital city, once the queen of all Europe.

As an American, I met Budapest with tangled emotions. Here were the people who had called out to America in their bid for freedom and received no answer. That moment had been a black one for RFE. Accusations had been heaped upon this radio station that the Hungarians had been promised help in case of an uprising and that no help had come. RFE had come forth with proof, miles of tape recordings of exactly what had been said over the air and was finally proven not guilty of promising help. As so often happens, an accusation overpowers the proven denial, and even today I hear people blame RFE for planting an idea that was after all the American tradition of standing strong when human dignity is threatened. Hungary's idea of taking a stand for freedom was its own. I wish we could have helped.

On my first day in Budapest, I stood near the square where Hungarian Freedom Fighters had pulled down a statue of Stalin. Somewhere near this spot, a young Hungarian Freedom Fighter standing beside his tank had been monitored on the air reciting Abraham Lincoln's Gettysburg Address, a crackled, halting version garbled by gunfire.

Everywhere I saw other reminders of the communists' ubiquitous presence. Building after building carried the Red Star on its back, a large glassy star glowing in the night, throwing deep red shadows on the waters of the rivers. On one side of the river is Pest, and on the other Buda. The contrast between Warsaw and Budapest, then the more suppressed city of the two, was apparent everywhere I looked.

"Life must go on," one attractive Hungarian girl said to me, "and what is life for us?"

And so life went on and people gathered to visit together in the little cafes on the main square. At one cafe where I stopped for a delicious Hungarian torte, I sat at a little table on the sidewalk beside the busy square, watching people hurrying along the street. The women dressed simply but with an obvious flair for style. Their true beauty lay in their charm and the quality of their voices, which seemed to vibrate with emotion and sincerity.

Sipping my Hungarian tea, I suddenly became aware of two handsome Hungarian children standing near my table, eyeing me as somewhat of a curiosity. I spoke to them in German, our only common language. The little girl was eleven years old, she told me, her brother eight. Their father was a doctor. They were dressed in grey flannel suits, he in smart short pants, she in a neat flared skirt, both wearing long white socks. The little girl's braids were long, her eyes eager and intent when I spoke of America. We said goodbye and I watched them return to their mother at a nearby table. In a short while, my little friends were back. They had gone to a lady beneath a big umbrella in front of the cafe and bought from her a beautiful bouquet of daffodils. This bouquet the boy solemnly presented to me in hopes that I would remember Budapest. How could I ever forget it when welcomed in such a way!

"I hope you can visit my country someday," I told the children.

The little girl shook her head and said, "I am afraid that is not possible."

Ordinarily to an eleven-year-old, anything is possible. I hope that somehow she and her brother did come to the United States and find yellow daffodils everywhere. I took a picture of my daffodils, and when I look at the photograph, I wonder about the children, now grown. I wonder if they remember, too.

I could tell my Hungarian friend at RFE about the children and about the early morning streetcar ride I took far out into the suburbs. On board the streetcar, I saw young mothers taking their children to day care centers before going to their factory jobs. A very young woman sat next to me and smiled. We spoke briefly. She did not work, she told me, which was lucky as the schools for the very little ones were quite bad and she was glad she could keep her two children with her. She was the exception, however she said, for most mothers must work to help the families exist.

"The beautiful blue Danube" (which to tell the truth is more brown than blue) flows up to Vienna from Budapest, but no one was allowed to sail so far. Standing on the deck of a small boat on the Danube, I looked at the scarred buildings of Budapest as the boat passed beneath the Chained Bridge that first united Buda and Pest. I felt the oppressive presence of the huge, hated "Liberation" statue towering over the city—the figure of a woman holding an olive branch above her head, a Russian soldier at her feet. It was whispered in Budapest that the woman must hold the olive branch out of reach or the Russian soldier would take it from her! This once proud city seen from the Danube looked to me like the ghost of a city seen on the screen of the past.

I left Budapest with the sounds of gypsy music lingering in my mind. Some of the music I heard in Budapest sounded American. I discovered that the musicians had learned about American music on shortwave radio, especially from the Voice of America. The friendliness of the Hungarian people had touched me. I felt there was no resentment in their attitude toward the United States, no servitude in their feelings toward the Soviet Union. At the time of my visit to Hungary, Soviets were in every shop and on every street corner.

As a postscript, some years later, while the Soviets were still in control, I had a call from my friend, Assistant Secretary of Labor Esther Peterson, who had just returned from a trip to Hungary. At that time, I was broadcasting around the world for the Voice of America. Esther was excited about something that happened to her in Hungary. She had gone into a music shop in Budapest where the Hungarian salesman had said to her, "I have a friend in the United States, Pat Gates. I really don't know her but I listen to her on the Voice of America."

When he asked Esther if she knew me, she had replied, "Yes, I do!" I was understandably delighted by this news.

Going through customs at the Budapest Airport, I had a tense moment as customs looked at all my tapes but left them untouched. True to their word the Soviets had given advance orders that I was to be allowed to exit with all of my material.

As we boarded our plane for Munich and our return to the West after the great adventure, we rejoiced that we were free to leave Soviet Territory and happy that we had been able to see the stark difference between oppression and freedom. Now it was time to prepare for an interview with actor James Cagney, who was in Munich making a film and who would send me on a sad journey.

Dachau

Never will I forget my visit to Dachau, the infamous Nazi concentration camp. Even now years later, I find it difficult to express the horror I felt seeing the ovens into which human beings were turned into ashes. My eleven-year-old son walked beside me on a sunny day, and the buildings before us glowed in the sunlight. It was surreal to hear the German version of the song "Charlie Brown" blasting over a loudspeaker and see families sitting on the porches of old houses still standing within the gates. They were refugees from Soviet satellite nations such as Romania and Bulgaria that had been swallowed up by the Soviets. It gave the place an eerie feeling of continuity. Here and there were German tourists, some quite young, perhaps in their twenties. The year of our visit was 1961, and this was a new generation growing up after the war.

Larry and I followed the signs, and our steps grew heavy along the way. Here on the walls were pictures of the prisoners of Dachau. And then we saw the gas chambers and the showers. The sense of human life and death was strong. Holding hands, my son and I remained silent.

We were the lucky ones, we came to see and remember. Though not part of the Holocaust, we could reach out and feel it. A small sign told of the ashes floating through the air and into a small pond. We stood beside that pond in sorrow.

Why were we in Dachau, Larry and I? We had been living in Munich for the second time and had never visited the camp, which is right outside Munich. I kept postponing driving to Dachau because I dreaded seeing it, although I knew I must go someday. On this day we were there because of the well-known movie actor, James Cagney, whom I had interviewed at his hotel in Munich. When we had finished our interview, I noticed the book sitting on the table beside Mr. Cagney's chair, William L. Shirer's *The Rise and Fall of the Third Reich.*

"It's a fine book," Cagney said and added, "My wife and I are very much interested in the history of the war. This week we visited Dachau. As you live here, I am sure you have been there."

"No," I told him. "I have not gone to Dachau yet because I know it will be overwhelming, and I keep putting it off."

He replied, "You are wrong not to go now. You owe it to the people who died there to pay them a visit. You must go." He was deadly serious, and I knew he was right.

"I will go tomorrow," I told him. "It is a Sunday and I will take my son with me." Pam was away at school in Paris or I would have taken her too. She would go later.

Neither mother nor son has ever forgotten the experience, and Pam still speaks of her own everlasting memory of the visit she made to Dachau. Over forty years later, Pam said to me, "I have just heard Mayor Giuliani speak of Dachau on television from New York City. He compared the tragic events of September 11, 2001 (when terrorists flew into the World Trade Center), to Dachau, as 'two horrifying experiences, which should never be forgotten.' " People do tend to shove terrible events out of their minds.

Looking back on that day inside the gates of Dachau, I find it impossible to put into words the emotion I felt standing on the actual ground where such monstrous deeds had taken place. I have been told that a visitor today sees a slightly more sanitized version than what Larry and I saw, and I wonder if those visitors also have a sense of the smoke in the air and of mothers and children being torn apart at the last moment, all to go to their death.

We had entered a new century when I attended a lecture just outside of Washington about the liberation of Dachau. As I listened to retired American Army Lt. General Ray Shoemaker, I recalled my visit to the concentration camp many years before. General Shoemaker, in 2002, spoke about April 1945, when American troops came upon Dachau in the closing days of World War II. He was then a 25-year-old lieutenant colonel in the Field Artillery, commanding the 105th Field Artillery Battalion attached to the U.S. Third Army. The general's words were as important to hear in this century as they had been in the last. He stressed that we must not forget what happened to the sixteen million people killed so ruthlessly by the

Nazis in the twentieth century, men, women, and children, six million of them Jews.

To ensure that the largest number of people possible knew about Dachau, General Eisenhower had issued orders for all nearby commanders to tour the camp. Shoemaker was among the first to go in.

Although senior commanders had been told something about Dachau, Shoemaker told us, "No verbal briefing prepared us for what we would see. There was the smell of death," he said, "and in my mind, I can hear even now the strange sound—it was a high, quavering, barely human sound of the survivors trying to say thank you. Bodies were stacked in groups; some in the stacks were still living." Even as he spoke well over fifty years later, tears came to the general's eyes, and he had to stop speaking for a moment.

"The commanders were taken through the barracks," he continued, "and I asked, seeing some people still crowded on to beds, why everyone had not gone outside. I was told that many of those I saw in bed were dead. Then we came to the gas chambers. Twelve hundred bodies were left there. Two thousand bodies were in a deep ditch. There were bins of shoes and clothing and eyeglasses, all carefully put aside, but the human bodies had been cast aside like cord wood. The American soldiers were hardened battled troops, but no great battle had prepared us for what we saw at Dachau."

Yes, I can understand what shock the soldiers must have experienced. The prisoners were gone when I visited this monstrous camp, and I find I am still at a loss for words when I try to explain my feelings as I stood before the gas chambers.

"Dachau was founded in 1933 by Hitler himself," General Shoemaker had explained, "and it was the first and largest of all of the camps. Himmler supervised the construction, which was designed for two thousand prisoners. There were thirty thousand there at the time of liberation. The chancellor of Austria, Kurt von Schuschnigg was a prisoner there. Leon Blum, president of France was there. There were poets, scientists, teachers, the finest brains of Germany, and, let us not forget, thousands of little children who lost their lives at Dachau."

A man in the audience that day, Major General Daniel Raymond, had been in Nuremburg and then Dachau during the severe fighting of the war's final days. General Raymond later described to me not only Dachau but also the last-ditch battles fought in Nuremburg, which was already a pile of rubble from bombing. The American troops cleared the Adolf Hitler Platz and later entered the Zeppelin Stadium, which had on its topmost walls a huge swastika circled by a wreath. After fierce fighting in the stadium, the Americans finally took control.

The American forces used the stadium briefly for the presentation of important medals, some of them Medals of Honor. General Raymond, then an army captain, commanded Company "B" of the 10th Engineer Battalion, part of the Third Infantry Division, supporting the 15th Infantry Regiment. After the medals ceremony and just after the troops marched out of the stadium, Captain Raymond's company blew up the swastika. It was a symbolic act captured on camera and soon seen in print around the world.

After Nuremburg, on the way to Munich, Raymond and his company ran right into Dachau. He had not known of the existence of this camp before that day of discovery.

"I believe the higher-ranking officers had been given word under strict security, "he said, "but I had not heard of it. When we saw the barbed wire and the buildings, we thought at first that it might be a prisoner of war camp but then realized as we entered the gates that it was something different, something horrible."

The 42nd Division had come upon the concentration camp several hours earlier, and the men of that division were the first to see Dachau. Raymond remembered that some of the troops had offered food to the barely moving, starving survivors, but that goodwill gesture had been stopped quickly because sudden food could have proved fatal. The doctors explained that when people have gone without food and then are given too much all at once, their bodies can't handle the sudden change.

"After the war's end," General Shoemaker had explained, "a trial at Dachau was conducted by the American military, which meant appeals were possible. The Court at Nuremburg used a different system. Of 1670 Germans tried in Dachau, 428 were sentenced to be hanged, 299 were hanged after appeals."

Young people today have difficulty understanding what happened in places like Dachau, and some people still find it difficult to believe that the Holocaust really happened. But the facts testify to the painful reality.

8

Paris to Fort Benning, Georgia

Dressed for Dior

My assignments were certainly diversified. Leaving Berlin and the Soviet Union behind, I was next on my way to cover the world of 1960s fashion in Paris for my radio program in the States. Based on my notes at the time, the trip's success owed much to a versatile Italian knit dress I had rolled into my bag at the last moment! Traveling to Paris from my apartment in Munich, I arrived in France in an international frame of mind for my introduction to the fashion toast of Paris, Marc Bohan, designer for Dior.

What does one wear to a Paris haute couture collection? Judging from the mink coats surrounding me at the showing, I would say the more "haute" the better. A hat is not necessary unless one's coiffure is in a hectic state, then the coverall chapeau saves the day. And by all means, if one should arrive at the eleventh hour with an overstuffed bag of recording or other equipment under one arm, hide it immediately. I checked all I could spare at the Hotel George V across the street, in the heart of the fashion houses.

Back to that knit dress in the plaid suitcase: When I reached the vital second of decision on what to wear, there was no time to dawdle. My train was leaving the Paris suburbs for the Gare St. Lazare in five minutes and only the Italian knit was miraculously without a wrinkle. Besides, my first day in Paris was to be spent not at Dior's but Balmain's. I could always keep my coat on at Balmain's, and my new black shoes would be all that showed!

I was given the seat of honor at Balmain's, but alas, someone whisked off my coat before the first model slunk forth in all her *jolie madame* glory. After all, I realized, a grey knit dress would scarcely be noticed in all the excitement. The pleasant French lady beside me had been relieved of her pale blonde mink, and I admired her gorgeous pale blonde Balmain suit, which matched her pale blond hair. We chatted about the lovely fashions and her house at Monte Carlo. Although a Balmain customer, she confessed, she found her neighborhood dressmaker much more practical.

Before leaving Balmain, I met the dynamic Directrice, Madame Ginette Spanier, author of *It Isn't All Mink.* She introduced me to a pretty young American girl, who turned out to be the wife of the American humorist Art Buchwald. (I was relieved to see that she, too, wore a cloth coat.) I interviewed Madame Spanier, a dream of a subject as she whirled through an explanation of how the models perform on what they call the camembert, the round head of the runway, which does indeed look like the cheese!

Returning to the George V with my Italian knit dress now covered by my coat, I bailed out the bulk of my recording equipment and went to meet my friend, Annabella, that famous French actress, for tea at Fouchet's. She was as beautiful and charming as ever. A dinner with American friends living on the Avenue Suffrin turned out to be an elaborate dinner party. That black dress in my suitcase in Le Vesinet would have been just the thing. The dinner party proved to be such fun, I missed the train to Le Vesinet so I spent the night at Annabella's apartment in town. Came dawn on the Seine and what to wear to Dior's? The knit dress, of course.

Backstage at Dior's, I felt quite at home in my simple grey knit, microphone in hand, taping sounds of the seamstresses at work. Through winding passageways, I followed Mademoiselle Widmer, a sweet, dignified lady who had been private secretary to Christian Dior and who was wearing what was surely a simple little Dior suit. Ah well, I still hadn't wrinkled, and the cheerful, nimble girls whipping up gorgeous creations in the workrooms were too intrigued by my tape recorder to notice I was not wearing anything with a French accent. Back on the worldly side of the building, the Duchess of Windsor passed me on the staircase. Not a pleat out of place, she looked as though she couldn't possibly need a new suit but had obviously come for a fitting.

Now the portals opened and the grey knit carried me forth to meet the rage of Paris, Dior designer Marc Bohan. He looked surprisingly timid and kind, artistic and wise. I liked him, and he gave me one of the very few interviews he'd granted. I told him I was sorry to come to Dior in an Italian knit dress, but it would have to do until the Dior-Bohan models were copied en masse! He was most gallant and said he found the dress charming. By the time I sailed out of Dior's, the aura of fashion seemed to be seeping into my knit.

Later, boarding the train for my return to Germany with no time to change, I found the knit dress and I about to face a new adventure. I had reserved a "couchette" for the night—a suspended strip of what feels like solid marble, nestled into a second-class compartment along with five other suspended strips, sans curtains but graciously provided with a blanket and a pillow. The arrangement is strictly coed. I happened to share my voyage with four French women and one German gentleman, who kindly helped his harem hoist suitcases up and down from the ceiling. My couchette was the uppermost of three. The idea is to mount a folding-type ladder, leap into your couchette before the ladder slips out from under, cover up with the blanket, completely dressed, and close your eyes quickly before the customs men start flashing on the lights at the border. At that point, everyone grabs the passport, says "Merci" or "Danke" depending on how clearly you can see the uniforms in the confusion, and finally, after the third man at the border has run through this theme, everyone lurches back to sleep.

Arriving in Frankfurt for a new day in the knit dress with not a wrinkle in sight, I headed for a full day's work in the studios of the Armed Forces Network. Finally in my car, I headed for Heidelberg and an evening with friends, who kindly admired my knit dress while clamoring for news of the Paris fashions. A rest for the dress as I slept in Heidelberg, but it seemed only natural to let it bring me past the finish line in Munich the next day.

North to Norway

Back in Munich, I received an assignment from the people at AFN in Frankfurt for a week of interviews in Norway for them and for NBC. Fortunately, school was still in session for Larry, and Anni could stay with him.

On my quick trip to Paris, I spent time with my 14-year old daughter Pam, who was studying there in the Mortefontaine School. Thanks to my French friend, Colette Mesnil, who worked for

President DeGaulle, we spent an evening together at the opera. The tickets were delivered by uniformed guards of the Elysée Palace! The opera was *La Bohème,* which to this day, is Pam's most cherished opera. We loved sitting in the president's seats.

In Norway, land of the midnight sun, I would take my microphone above the Arctic Circle for the first time. AFN arranged my transportation to Norway on the H.M.S. *Kron Prins Harald* of the Jahre Line, on its maiden voyage from Kiel, West Germany to Oslo.

As we sailed into Oslo harbor, I saw many tiny red houses, most with their own Norwegian flags snapping in the wind. From Oslo I would catch my plane to Bodo, capital town of the county of Nordand. Since the wartime bombardment that destroyed the town in 1940, Bodo had been completely rebuilt.

Landing at midnight wearing sunglasses can be most disconcerting. Is it the wrong year, the wrong day, the wrong planet? No, you are in Bodo, Norway, where the sun never sets during the summer months. Fatigue seemed to vanish as we drove up the mountain above the city and the rosy glow of midnight took over. I saw a woman beating a rug in her backyard as we passed, not seeming to mind that it was midnight. Far north of the Arctic Circle, there, like a giant stone set in the prongs of the mountains, gleamed the sun. We drove to a small chalet, where young and old Norwegians were enjoying an evening together. The young danced as the older people sat quietly by the windows drinking a bit of wine or beer. My fascination and admiration for Bodo kept me awake until 3:00 a.m. The next morning, I was ready to do my interviews. All too soon, it was time to board my flight back to Oslo via Trondheim. It was breathtaking crossing Norway over the mountains and fjords. I could hardly take my eyes from the window.

In Oslo, I took a tram to Lijorndet to visit my old friends, the Pettersens, Thor a distinguished Norwegian admiral, and Luli, his wife, both old friends from SHAPE in Paris. When I returned to the city at midnight, people were out walking through the park. Students wore red caps with tassels sporting ties or knots to indicate how many times the student had been up all night.

Norway had much to see and many people to interview. I traveled by bus, plane, and boat. Bergen and its fjords, indeed mountains and waterfalls everywhere, all produced memories of Norway's extraordinary beauty. On a trip to Voss, I discovered a thriving farm district. By bus from Sogndal to Lom over mountains, roads were narrow, sometimes snowy. At the Nidaros Cathedral in Trondheim, the third largest town in Norway, I talked with the master stone carvers at work. Just before my arrival in the town of Mo i Rana, which has a large steel mill, a tremendous electrical storm had demolished the power in the mill. All the molten lead in the vats had solidified, and men stood in the vats chipping away. When I interviewed the manager of the mill, we ignored the immediate crisis and focused on the general operation of the plant, the only steel mill in the country at that time.

I recall going out in a small boat on an Arctic lake. It was the first time out for the newly constructed boat, with five of us on board including the boat's owner-builder, his wife and dog, and two rather large Englishwomen. I was concerned when I saw that the boat was riding very low in the water and asked the owner how long it would take to swim to shore in case of trouble. It would be impossible to make it to shore, he said, because the water was so cold we would be frozen in a few seconds! One of the women patted me on the knee and said, "My dear, never trouble trouble 'til trouble troubles you." I have repeated that phrase to myself many times during the ensuing years.

While sailing out of the Oslo harbor en route back to Germany, holding my beige umbrella over my head up on deck in a rainstorm, I waved goodbye with the umbrella and it flew right out of my hand into the deep water below. I am always losing umbrellas, but this was a new experience. Several weeks later, I received a package in Munich. Lo, there was my umbrella! How it had been retrieved I do not know but I thought it a most thoughtful gesture, for someone must have put to sea to save it.

While in Norway and then working in Copenhagen, Denmark, on the way home, I stayed several times with families who opened their homes to me. Some were farmhouses, some town houses, some more elaborate than others. I found my hosts gracious, well informed, and most hospitable. Some of them I interviewed about politics and business. I am glad I had time for that last assignment.

Back in Munich I packed for Italy, where the children and I were to meet my husband. After that happy family time, there would be more memorable events for this newly minted foreign correspondent.

Reunion in Italy

The "hardship tour" was over! Ink was flying into Rome from Iran, and the children and I boarded the train in Munich to meet him there. We traveled second-class, stretching out our funds as far as possible. Larry brought a portable chess set with him, and the Germans on the train were fascinated that an eleven-year-old boy could beat them in chess. They shared their fruit and wurst with us.

When Ink stepped off the plane, he looked painfully thin. I was afraid he might be unwell, but after a few days in Terracina, Italy, he looked relaxed and happy to be back with his family. The Maurers had loaned us their villa on the Mediterranean for our reunion and it was a dream place to be.

Soon it was back to Munich to pick up our footlockers and our Volkswagen and head for Bremerhaven, from which we sailed home on an Army ship. It was an adventure, with the children and I way down in the bottom of the ship with other wives, and Ink on the top deck with three other officers. Our destinations were New York and then Carlisle, Pennsylvania, and the Army War College, where we would spend a busy year before returning to Washington.

It was 1962, the year Astronaut John Glenn became the first American to orbit the earth in a spaceship. We drove to Washington with the children to see the parade given in his honor upon his return to earth. Pam and Larry were back in American schools, and I could see that they had an especially good foundation in reading, writing, and arithmetic as well as in history, thanks to their European school experiences.

Our house at Carlisle was one of the smallest we had ever lived in, but it had an attic of sorts. I set up my radio equipment there and was soon doing interviews in Pennsylvania, editing them with a little knife (no digital cutting back then). On my weekly drives into Washington, I frequently stopped in Gettysburg for breakfast with my friend, Barbara Eisenhower. She and husband John lived in a house on President Eisenhower's farm. John was out of the army then and working on a book with his father. In Washington, I would spend the night with my niece Jeri, do more interviews, then come home the next day. I managed to carry on with my army wife duties at the same time. Because we had rarely been stationed on an army post, it surprised me that we wives in those days were included in our husbands' evaluation reports. Luckily, I passed, even though in those days army wives who worked were sometimes frowned upon. The approval or disapproval of working wives seemed to depend upon the commanding officer.

The year itself was a hard one. My father died, and I flew to Florida to spend the last ten days of his life with him and my mother. When I returned to the War College from Florida, my heart was heavy. The next day I met an unusual person, who saw my grief and helped me by something she said. Life can be strange, I thought, for she was the daughter of the famous German general, Heinz Guderian, the tank commander known as the father of the panzer corps. After the war, she had married an American army officer and happened to be visiting friends at Carlisle. When her father had died it was the most difficult time in her life, she said, and she could not see how the sorrow would ever diminish. But she had discovered that as time passed, her father seemed to be with her more and more and lived on strongly in her memory. I found her words comforting.

In the middle of the year our house was being renovated and I lost my attic in the move. My sister-in-law, Marge, who had remarried and lived in Tyrone, Pennsylvania, informed us that Ink's mother was having more heart trouble and had been advised by her doctor to go into a nursing home. I said that wouldn't do, that instead she could live with us. But first came another move, this time to Fort Benning, Georgia, where we would have real army quarters for the first time and Ink would have an important job as commander of the 151st Engineer Combat Group. His mother would join us in our house on Lumpkin Road. What lay ahead would be parachutes and the Cuban Missile Crisis.

U.S. Army Post

It didn't take us long to spread out in our gracious Fort Benning house, where Ink's mother joined us right after we moved in. We had a large living room with a fireplace and a separate dining room, which enabled us to entertain the people working for Ink and many of our neighbors. Pam and Larry liked their new schools and their new friends, and Lady, our French shepherd dog, seemed delighted to be spending what turned out to be the last year of her life in that house. My mother came to visit from Connecticut, and it saddened me that my father would never see our first real army quarters on this pretty post.

Ink went to paratrooper school, the oldest man in his class but still running and keeping up with the young men being transformed from huffing, puffing recruits into able young soldiers. I would sometimes watch the training and was there for the first jumps. It was a proud day for everyone in the class, including Ink and me, as the men became airborne and earned those treasured paratrooper wings.

Fort Benning experienced considerable tension at the time of the Cuban Missile Crisis. President John F. Kennedy warned the country of possible dangers ahead. Within a few hours, Ink's combat-ready outfit quickly began to dispatch men to the Florida shores to be positioned if needed. Some of the wives came to my house that day to tell me they had come home at lunchtime to find notes from their husbands saying goodbye. Other wives telephoned me for solace and information. One woman was expecting a baby any minute. If the Soviet weapons in Cuba had been used, I would have had to comfort those wives in tragedy while worrying deeply about my own husband. He would, I knew, lead his men in battle. I would have left my basement, with the cots and bottles of water we had been told to prepare, to do what I could. At the airfield I had seen the pilots sleeping beneath the planes flown in to be ready. We were on the brink.

On that day when Ink's 151st Engineer Combat Group prepared for action, his troops were all in combat uniform, including William H. T. "Bucky" Bush, a young captain we admired. He was an outstanding officer whom we wished would stay in the army, but he and his wife Pat decided to leave the military at the end of his Fort Benning tour. Captain Bush's brother, George H.W. Bush, would one day be president of the United States, as would a nephew, George W. Bush. We thought this Bush could match anyone in his family.

120

Fortunately, the crisis ended with no need for combat. It had been a close call, but both countries were spared. Life returned to normal, which for us included another move, this time back to Washington. We had buried our dog Lady in the Fort Benning pet cemetery. She had been with us since Paris, and it was hard to say goodbye.

Part II

Good Morning, World

9

International Broadcaster

The Voice of America

At Fort Benning, under contract with the Voice of America, I had sent interviews from Georgia, just as I had done from Carlisle, Pennsylvania. Already my life with VOA had begun. Once back in Washington from Fort Benning, my long, happy relationship with the Voice of America, its people, and its listeners around the world began in earnest. How did this critical turn in my life come about?

In Munich, VOA had asked me to do a Christmas program in its studios there. The money this earned me bought two snow tires for my Volkswagen. I enjoyed reading the script about Christmas customs around the world. The broadcast aired worldwide, and someone in Washington was listening.

As it happened, one of my WFAX projects had been a documentary about the Voice of America. People in the Washington area had heard of VOA, but they did not understand what it did. Ann Hagen Randall, public affairs director for the United States Information Agency, had asked me to do a program about the mission of VOA, which was under the USIA umbrella. She would line up guests for me, she said. When everything was ready, I drove to Independence Avenue in Washington and taped a special program on how VOA sends its story about the United States all round the world. Walking down the handsome halls of this enormous government building, seeing the master control panel, then the largest in the world, I thought I would like to broadcast from there some day. And now, several years later, my life had become intertwined with VOA and its listeners.

My radio life always fit in well with my life at home. By balancing my schedule, I could be home when my children returned from school or my husband came home from work and be available for medical checkups, piano lessons, school plays, and sports days. Ink often came home very late from the Pentagon, for the demands on him were great. He liked to relax in the evening and enjoyed going to the theater or out to dinner with friends. Television was tempting. While under contract to VOA and still working part-time, I did quite a bit of television for Washington public television station WETA, including hosting some programs. But my heart always belonged to radio.

Upon returning from Munich and before heading to the Army War College, when Ink and I were spending a few days in Washington, I received a call from Cliff Groce, the Voice of America program director. Would I come in to talk with Al Johnson about his new VOA program, "The Breakfast Show"? Johnson had heard my Christmas broadcast from Munich and wanted to discuss my working for him. Walking once again into that big government building, with its impressive WPA paintings in the entrance hall, I recalled the special documentary I had done on VOA and how I had wished I could be part of our government's worldwide network. I was excited by the idea of telling people in other countries about us, just as I had broadcast for NBC from abroad to the USA about other nationalities.

I admired Al Johnson right away and also VOA director Henry Loomis. The other host on "The Breakfast Show" was Phil Irwin. He and Al would host and produce the show on alternate days. Al hired me at that first meeting on a contract basis to interview for the program. I explained that I would be living in Carlisle, Pennsylvania, for a year while my husband studied at the Army War College, but that after a possible brief duty assignment we hoped to be stationed back in Washington. I would drive into Washington from Carlisle one day a week, spend the night with Jeri (the niece who had lived with us in Europe), and return home the next day.

I conducted many of my interviews in Pennsylvania and some in Washington, where I interviewed cabinet officers, stars of the plays at the National Theater, artists, and policemen. Eventually, I became host of the two-hour Sunday program. The indispensable engineers were most helpful and seemed to be caught up in the spirit of "The Breakfast Show." Different from other VOA programs, the show was informal, with many interviews and some music, which we each chose for our own programs. Then, too, there was informative, relaxed conversation. Al had started something new, talking about his Swedish family's migrating to America and about his own adopted children. He encouraged me to do the same, saying, "Let yourself go, Pat, and be yourself. Let your sense of humor show."

Along with the more serious interviews he wanted us to talk about everyday life in the United States. Phil would talk about his farm in Virginia, I about Pam and Larry at school and little happenings in our lives. Soon the letters began to pour in to each of us. The news people were amazed. How could letters and surveys put this program out in front of all the others? And it was to remain out in front for the ensuing years. New VOA directors would come and go with each change in administration, but they didn't tamper with "The Breakfast Show," their number one program, ahead of even the highly successful and famous "Willis Conover Jazz Program."

As program director Cliff Groce used to say, "The myth may be Conover but the reality is 'The Breakfast Show.'"

Coming in ahead on all the surveys kept us on our toes. We were always adding new features, experimenting with new ideas. We talked with people in American industry—nothing new about that now, but it was then. We went all out for the space program, too. NASA gave us a knowledgeable man, John Hammersmith, each week to answer questions we invited from listeners about U.S. space activities. We each also aired extensive interviews with experts from NASA. People all over the world sent in their questions as they followed the U.S. space program with rapt attention.

On "The Breakfast Show," we brought in people from all walks of life, not the ones you see in the movies sent all over the world but everyday Americans—farmers, artists, students, business people, scientists, diplomats, teachers, politicians, secretaries, sailors, soldiers, and marines, firemen, people of all colors and ethnic backgrounds, people who share the hopes and dreams of men and women the world over.

Gateway to Science

One of the most respected and talented producers at the Voice of America was Mary Shen, an Asian American. Mary had come to this country on a scholarship and had married Raymond Graham Swing, known as the dean of American broadcasters during World War II. Despite the great difference in their ages, they were happy together. I was privileged to know them both before his death. Mary hired me to do some programs for the VOA Asian service, which she headed. I was not yet a regular staff member so was free to accept separate contracts. Mary wanted me to write and voice a science program that would include interviews with scientists and news of scientific developments.

"But Mary," I said, "I am not a scientist. How can I do a science program for you?"

Mary replied, "If I had two scientists speaking together in their own special language of science, no one anywhere would understand what they were talking about. You will be the one who will make it all understandable and interesting as well as educational!"

Mary Shen gave me the confidence I needed to enter a new world, one that had always fascinated me ever since my years with nuclear scientists at Oak Ridge, Tennessee. I called my program "Gateway to Science" and started it off saying: "Science has changed man's life in many ways. It has made life easier; it has brought him communication, transportation, medicine, education, industry, and an understanding of the universe."

In one program I visited the ARMCO Steel Corporation in Middletown, Ohio, where men and machinery worked side by side manufacturing one of the world's most vital commodities. I wore a hard hat and safety glasses while touring the plant and rode in a panel truck for a rough ride to the Works #2 open-hearth hot strip mill. Taking my microphone, I looked into the open-hearth furnace and watched the steel ingots roll along their fiery track like an express train before being flattened and coiled into a workable portable state.

In my two days at ARMCO I interviewed people at all levels of the company and talked about the products produced at ARMCO's many overseas plants. I talked with a machine shop apprentice's wife in their home about family social life and economics, so listeners would know how the family of an American working for a steel company actually lives. I talked with the head of ARMCO international about their extensive overseas training program and interviewed ARMCO president William Verity, who some years later would become the United States Secretary of Commerce.

I was amused to read ARMCO's story about my visit. The manager of the works had said, "This gal carried her tape recorder and microphone like it was part of her arm. When she wanted to know something she would stick that mike in front of the nearest panel operator or foreman and fire away with questions, and the men enjoyed every minute of it."

ARMCO's management had a history of being concerned for the welfare of its employees, and I found them the epitome of a people-minded U.S. company. "It's important," I told them, "that our overseas listeners, especially those behind the Iron Curtain, have the opportunity to know this kind of history."

In a picture taken with Mr. Beech Moore of Works #2, we are both wearing hard hats. He was explaining the use of oxygen in steel-making, and because I was holding my microphone his voice was heard throughout the world over the roar of the furnaces.

Mary Shen also assigned me to cover certain state visits at the White House. On one such occasion, dressed in a long evening gown and carrying a notebook in my evening bag, I arrived at the White House and went directly to the library, where the White House women's press corps gathered. Here in the library we listened on a remote speaker to President Lyndon Johnson toasting the state dinner's guest of honor, President Tubman of Liberia, who responded with his own toast to President Johnson. I made notes during the toasts for my broadcast script. As soon as the dinner ended, we women reporters (about ten of us) were escorted into the main foyer to mingle with the guests and go down the receiving line to meet President and Mrs. Johnson, then into the East Room for the after-dinner entertainment.

That night's performance was by the noted composer, conductor, and pianist Duke Ellington and his Orchestra. Mr. Ellington, who had performed in Africa, told me that one of his selections at the White House that night would be an excerpt from his *Liberian Suite*, first performed at New York's Metropolitan Opera House. Years later I was to attend a spectacular dinner party for Duke Ellington at the White House given by President and Mrs. Nixon, which I will tell you about later.

In my script, I told about some of the guests at the dinner, among whom were William Tubman, the Liberian president's son, the U.S. vice president Hubert Humphrey and Mrs. Humphrey, Secretary of State and Mrs. Dean Rusk, and Ambassador at Large Henry Cabot Lodge talking with General Maxwell D. Taylor about their experiences in South Vietnam, where both had been U.S. ambassador.

My Soldier Goes to Vietnam

Ink was working in the Pentagon as assistant to the director in the office of the Joint Chiefs of Staff when orders came for him to go to Vietnam at the end of his Pentagon assignment. The year was 1966. I had dreaded this day. It would be like War World II again, living with the constant worry of each day and the difficulty of separation.

One big decision we had to make before Ink left was where "the girl he left behind" would live. Our rental house in Falls Church, Virginia, had been good for us. We had given Ink's mother the master bedroom, each child had a bedroom, and Ink and I had space of our own, a bedroom and family room downstairs. I had set up a small studio in the cinder-block basement with exposed beams and hung draperies around for better sound.   I taped my WFAX programs in the basement studio from a table with a microphone, lent to me by the station, and edited many of my Voice of America tapes there.

Pam was away at Briarcliff College in New York State, and Larry at the Hotchkiss School in Lakeville, Connecticut. He had been in nine different schools in nine years and, with his father about to leave the country, it seemed best to have him in a good boarding school where he would have several years in one place. Now, with our landlord returning to Washington, we had to move. We found a newly built townhouse in Falls Church and bought it. It was the first house we had ever owned. The house would work well during our separation, although it would be too small when Ink returned. Mother Gates would have the master bedroom and bath, the children would have their own rooms when home from school, and I would fix up the basement room, which had a fireplace, for my bedroom and office. The house was small but it worked.

Often I have thought of those six years when my mother-in-law shared her life with us. It must have been hard for her, except perhaps for the year at Fort Benning, where other mothers lived with their children. In Virginia, she must have been lonely when I was at work and she was home with the television and the dog. She never complained. Although she had lost two sons in World War II and had no other child but Ink, she was a remarkable person with a deep faith and an acceptance of life and death. Though unsophisticated, she had the capacity to help others who had suffered loss. Long before I met her, she had had a severe nervous breakdown from which she had completely recovered. Our friends commented often on her serenity and understanding of life, which for her had been hard, most of it spent in Tyrone, Pennsylvania, a very small town. As my father said, she was a born lady, even without a great deal of travel and experience.

So I said goodbye to Ink at Dulles Airport, he flew off to Vietnam, and we were back to writing letters. Fortunately, my work kept me busy, and I was very much involved with a group called American Women in Radio and Television. I enjoyed the stimulating, active women I met, all dedicated to introducing Washington to radio and television women and learning from one another about our own profession. When I became president of the organization's Washington chapter, I loved every minute of the responsibility involved.

The one bright spot about duty in Vietnam was "R&R" in Hawaii. A serviceman was allowed five days in Hawaii about halfway through his twelve-month tour for rest and recreation, and his wife could meet him there. One day in Houston, Texas, where I was doing a series of interviews for VOA, I received a telephone call from Ink with good news and bad news. It was most unusual to receive a telephone call from Ink from Vietnam but somehow the call had been relayed by the Pentagon to where I was staying in Houston. The good news—Ink was being promoted to brigadier general, big news indeed in the army. In Vietnam, however, the promotion meant no R&R yet and required an additional year of war duty. That was the bad news. He had a good new assignment, though, as commander at Cam Rahn Bay, a large and vital port.

A few months after that phone call we did have an R&R in Hawaii. Ink had been away for nine months and the reunion was a happy time. I had earned my way to Hawaii by going out a week early and doing many interviews about that Pacific paradise. I remembered the time in my early radio days when I had interviewed author James Michener about his book *Hawaii,* which had given me a sense of the islands' history.

By the time Ink arrived I had learned my way around a bit, thanks to Dee Prather Smyser of the visitor's bureau, who became a good friend. Dee arranged many interviews for me on several of the islands and invited me to her home, something she said she rarely did with visitors. When I flew by helicopter into a rain forest with a man from the U.S. Geological Survey, it was like being thrown back in time. Few people had trod on the land where we had set down. I visited a volcano and a pineapple plantation and learned about the sugar industry, the East-West Center, and the Asians and pioneer Americans who had made the 50th state great. I returned several times in later years but that first trip was the best.

On my overnight flight back to Dulles Airport from Hawaii, the plane was filled with servicemen just finished with their tours in Vietnam. I told no one that I was an officer's wife as I talked with several of them on the flight. I had been put into first class as a courtesy, and a young soldier was seated next to me. The heating equipment was not working on the plane and the plane had no blankets. We talked about how cold it was after the warmth of Hawaii and about Vietnam. He had heard that people at home were angry with the American army for fighting there. As the plane became colder and colder, the soldier said he would like to offer me his jacket if I wouldn't be embarrassed to wear it because he had been in Vietnam. I told him I would be proud to wear it. It broke my heart. Where was the band to meet him and the others on their return home? Where was the hometown parade?

I went to the big parade in Washington at the end of the first Gulf War, where units with men who had fought in Vietnam at long last received applause. I stood and cheered when they passed my stand. I was not embarrassed to shout "Bravo!"

It was hard coming home after R&R in Hawaii and realizing that Ink would be gone for a while longer. I felt very much like a single mother with all of the responsibilities of the children and my mother-in-law. I had to help Larry choose a university and attend Pam's graduation from Briarcliff without Ink. My mother came from Connecticut, and that was good. Friends were always helpful, but the months passed slowly.

Just before Ink returned from Vietnam, I rented out our townhouse and moved us into Prospect House, in Arlington, Virginia, just above the Iwo Jima Memorial. The view of Washington from our eighth floor balcony was spectacular—I could see the Lincoln Memorial, the Washington Monument, and the Capitol as well as many other Washington landmarks. I rented a separate apartment on a lower floor for Ink's mother and Pam, as there wasn't room in one apartment for all of us. Everyone in the family loved the apartments from the first day, and when Ink came home he fully approved of my decision. He was glad to be home but not sorry for one minute that he had been able to play his part in Vietnam. It had been a sad time for this country, and Ink felt that was where he should have been. Later, he was truly sorry at the war's unhappy ending, both for our country and for South Vietnam.

While Ink had been gone we had written to each other almost every day. What a worrisome time! Each service wife goes on with her life, but underneath the daily routine lie the ever-present questions: Will he come back? Will he be wounded? When my soldier did come home, his temper was shorter with the children and with me. Things were not quite the same, although I had no doubts that our marriage was as strong as ever. There was still so much love. Each war takes its share of a man's heart. There are often changes, sometimes slight, sometimes intense.

Later, I myself would go to Vietnam and fly in a small helicopter with the pilot on my left and a Secret Service agent on my right, with his machine gun at my feet and two wives of presidents sitting within arm's reach behind me. I would look down at the green earth below and think of the men who didn't make it. I would meet some of the wounded in the hospital who would soon be taking a helicopter ride out. They were all heroes of my country. Some would become bitter, but most, I believe, would come to understand that with or without glory and thanks they could say to themselves that they proved their courage when tested.

Not long after Ink came home, he was assigned to the Huntsville, Alabama, logistics command as commanding general. We commuted back and forth every weekend for about ten months, with Ink coming home or me going there. We were entering the modern world of commuter marriage. It was the first time for us and worked out fairly well. Ink would be coming back to Washington in less than a year, to serve three years in the headquarters of the Army Materiel Command.

Soon after Ink's return from Vietnam, his mother became quite ill. I had taken her to the hospital for frequent checkups for her heart problems over the six years she lived with us. At one point she had a blood disease that was successfully treated by her drinking what was called a radioactive cocktail, a substance put together at the laboratories at Oak Ridge, Tennessee, where we had lived during the building of the atom bomb. Amazing that Oak Ridge would come back into our lives in such a medical miracle way! We were grateful. But now time had taken its toll, and in March 1968 she died, to our sorrow. It was a hard time.

10

Radio Waves

My Journey into Space

The children were now grown, and I joined the regular staff of the Voice of America, working full time. Although I conducted interviews for all the programs, the two-hour Sunday Breakfast Show was still mine to produce and broadcast. Later, I would have more programs of my own. VOA gave me special permission to continue my weekly program on WFAX, which I taped at home, reviewing Washington plays and operas.

It was good to be a real staff member on the VOA team. I liked and respected my colleagues Al Johnson and Phil Irwin. We agreed we would make the Breakfast Show the best program, the most listened to, and the one with the strongest message about our country on the Voice of America. To our great joy, that's exactly what happened.

We were part of VOA's Worldwide English Division, in which many experienced people broadcast many fine programs. It boasted a first-rate newsroom and engineers who made it all possible. Staff members helped us, and technical people at our transmitters in many countries sent our programs worldwide.

Here on earth we have a project called SETI, the Search for Extraterrestrial Intelligence. The distinguished radio astronomer, Frank D. Drake, once wrote, "It may be possible for us to eavesdrop on local planetary radio communications of a distant civilization. Conversely, our civilization may be detectable over interstellar distances even though we make no effort to announce our presence. We may imagine our earliest radio transmissions, for example, traveling forever at the speed of light across interstellar space. A relatively nearby civilization in substantial advance of our own may be able to detect some of our domestic radio transmissions."

As people here on earth search for radio signals from other planets, I find it fascinating to imagine that earthly voices once transmitted into space by a microphone stay out there for years. Our international shortwave broadcasts carry much information about our civilization's cultural and scientific advancements. Some scientists say there is no limit on the number of years voices will stay out in space. Energy dissolves but signals do not decay entirely. They can be reconstructed with the proper receiving equipment. There is no recalling these voices. Radio signatures from earth may have been picked up already. I can't help but wonder if the voices of people I have brought to my VOA microphone are still floating around out there. Artists leave their paintings or films behind, and poets leave their poems; but what can voices leave behind? I had accepted the idea that my work was transitory, yet I hoped it would make a difference. Some day, somewhere, perhaps, our voices may be heard.

My friend Bob Arnold, once a VOA science editor and later associated with the SETI Institute, wrote to me that he had just received sad news of the death of Cyril Ponnamperuma, a professor doing research into the beginnings of life. Bob called him a great thinker. We both remembered that he used to appear with me on "The Breakfast Show," now, Bob said, "wafting its way through interstellar space."

Who are these people I chose to be travelers in space in these times of electronic marvels, poverty and plenty, wars and peace, and medical marvels? Do they all have something in common, a thread that weaves them all together? Some are famous, some not. When I traveled, listeners told me they remembered best the voices of everyday people, yet they also wanted to know about well-known persons. What voice went with the familiar name, what would it say to a man in India, a woman in Moscow, a student in Djarkarta, a couple in Bucharest? What was the human thread that made people in China understand a scientist in Chicago?

I would like you to know something about these voices, what they said to us and about us. And I would like you to know more about my own spaceship, the Breakfast Show.

The Breakfast Show

"Good morning, and welcome to the Breakfast Show on the Voice of America!" For many years that is how I began my broadcast to the world on the global radio network of the United States. Being part of the Voice of America is like being part of a large family of people of many cultures and many languages. The common hope of my colleagues and I was to promote understanding abroad for the United States. After broadcasting the Sunday Breakfast Show for several years, I became a permanent staff member, broadcasting three programs of my own. The two-hour Sunday Breakfast Show was always my responsibility, and my weekly shows, alternating days with my male colleagues, each lasted one-and-a-half hours. I brought Americans and sometimes visitors to America to my VOA microphone. We were heard in English in every country of the world, and I think it is a surprise to some people that English is now the second language everywhere it is not the mother tongue. On the Breakfast Show, we had a five-minute newscast on the hour. I would introduce the newsreader and return after the news report. We had features on science, economics, sports, business, theater, interviews on every imaginable subject, and conversation. The Breakfast Show was so much a part of my life that my conversations about my children (to illustrate everyday American life) followed them from elementary school to high school and college, and into the business world. When I traveled abroad, people asked me about Pam and Larry, recalling my accounts of their growing up, even their weddings, which illustrated American customs and traditions.

Everyday was a busy one at VOA. At election time I would talk with American politicians and voters, never promoting any one candidate. VOA does not belong to any president but to the American people, supported by their tax dollars. Although VOA editorials relay government policy, its reports and news programs remain independent. U.S. citizens abroad can listen to VOA by shortwave, but VOA does not direct its programs toward them.

My colleagues and I had the privilege of choosing our own guests and subjects. In my twenty-five years at VOA never a day went by that I didn't learn something. VOA began my transition from home to the public arena. You had to prove that you were good, and you almost had to be better than your male colleagues to progress professionally. Dependability was one key to success. It was a man's world then, and still is, but I think men now understand that women want to walk beside them, not in front of them.

Although I admire reporters who cover the daily happenings in big cities and small, I think the lasting story, the human story, is the one that has heart. I have found that even in the short space of an interview, my guest and I somehow touched a familiar human chord right away, better than if we had been speaking casually for years. I always strove to help the listener to see and hear the true person at my microphone. I also hoped I was asking the right questions. After years of asking many questions, one comment that pleased me immensely was when a Soviet scientist said to me, "When I listened to you talk with a scientist I would sometimes think, if only I were there I would like to ask that person a question, and just then you would ask the question I had in mind."

At the end of my program I would say, "This is Pat Gates on the Voice of America saying thank you for listening, and if you see someone without a smile, give him one of yours."

I was amazed at the universal acceptance of my sign-off. I had heard it somewhere and liked it, and people wrote to me about it. A woman doctor in Pakistan said, "I think your philosophy about the smile is very important." From Sussex, England, came a letter from a Professor Bruce Copen, enclosing a magazine he published called *The Seeker*, saying, "I have quoted your remark which I have heard on your program. I hope you do not mind my using this, because I think it quite apt." In *The Seeker* he had written, "I heard a VOA announcer the other day say 'If you meet someone without a smile, give him one of yours.' . . . Is there a better use of time than making a pleasant world to live in?"

From the letters we received and visitors from abroad we knew we were getting through. People were not only listening but cared about us as people.

During International Women's Year, 1975, I presented a special series featuring outstanding women. I talked about women from all over the world and asked people to nominate a woman they admired, perhaps a teacher or a homemaker, in a small village or in a big city. Men and women wrote volumes of letters. In one case a man voted for a woman mountain climber from Japan. A special panel of persons not related to VOA chose three letters every week, and each week I read the three winners' letters on the air and sent them each an International Women's Year pin and a letter from me. At the end of the year we announced the name of the woman who received the most nominations, and it was Mother Teresa of India. I wrote to her and have a picture of her receiving my letter and the pin from an officer of the U.S. Embassy.

Microphone Memories

It was always a pleasure to take my microphone to the White House, the president's home. I recall taking it there on the day that "Lady Bird" Johnson, the First Lady, announced the beginning of Project Head Start, which she had helped stimulate. Head Start is an educational effort to make available preschool and pre-kindergarten education for children beginning at age four. A federally funded eight-week summer program would be followed by year-long Head Start centers involving a hoped-for 150,000 children. Volunteers would be called upon to help the teachers in charge.

The kick-off for Head Start was in the White House Red Room. I sat on a red damask-covered settee beside the famous film star, Danny Kaye, whom I interviewed. Known for his talent and his great heart, Danny Kaye was to be the spokesman for Head Start throughout the country. He was also unofficial "ambassador" for the United Nations

Children's Fund and traveled the world with his film crew, recording UNICEF projects in clinics helping to rid small children of diseases like malaria and diphtheria.

We heard that morning at the White House of Head Start classes to be conducted throughout the United States, starting with 40,000 teachers. Pre-kindergarten children were to be taken to theaters, libraries, farms, and zoos. Schools, churches, and farm buildings would be used; townspeople had already offered space and given equipment and toys. When my church in Washington opened some of its rooms to Head Start classes, I volunteered once a week to spend an hour with the children with my microphone. I recorded them on tape and let them hear their voices and taught them some songs in French and German as the Christmas holidays approached. Head Start proved highly successful and continues to this day, with American children of all races and national origins.

Sometimes I went to the White House without my microphone, to report for example on state dinners. President Johnson was deeply concerned in those days about our involvement in Vietnam and knew that my husband was serving there. The women of the Press Corps were invited to mingle with the guests after dinner while the dancing went on in the main foyer.

To give you an idea of how thoughtful a president can be when he has the weight of the world on his shoulders, I will tell you that this night, President Johnson had Vice President Humphrey dance with me, then danced with me himself. The president loved to dance and did so expertly, but I know that he danced with me that night because he knew my husband was serving in the country he was so deeply concerned about. What a night!

One day I had a telephone call from Liz Carpenter, Mrs. Johnson's press secretary. Liz and I had been good friends since the days when she and her husband Les had been the editors of *Variety* Magazine. She was an invaluable aide to both the president and the first lady. It was Liz who had made me a member of the White House Women's Press Corps. Liz's call concerned a young U.S. Marine who had become engaged to marry the president's daughter, Lynda Bird. I had requested an interview with him, and Liz wanted him to have his first media interview with me in my Voice of America studio.

Captain Charles Robb of the United States Marine Corps had met Lynda Bird Johnson when he was a White House aide and officer-in-charge of the White House Color Guard. His fulltime occupation was as adjutant of the Marine barracks in Washington, D.C., the Marine Corps' ceremonial post. Chuck, as he is called, talked to me about his family in Milwaukee, Wisconsin and about the imminent wedding, after which he was going to Vietnam.

I had heard that Chuck was interested in politics. "Yes, I am thinking about entering the political scene someday," he said, "but it has little to do with my marrying the daughter of a president. It is a family tradition to be in politics, as members of my family were involved in Virginia politics many years ago." After his tour of duty in Vietnam and his departure from the Marine Corps, Chuck Robb became governor of Virginia and United States senator.

My last time at the Johnson White House came when Liz Carpenter invited me to come with my husband as guests for the "after-dinner entertainment" at the Johnsons' final party. It was a memorable affair, with the United States Marine Corps Band playing in the grand foyer for the dancing. Because the Johnsons were leaving the White House, an Auld Lang Syne atmosphere pervaded the evening as the family celebrated the good times they had had in this historic home. Luci Johnson told me they wanted to show everyone that the Johnsons really knew how to give a good party, and they did. The president was happy to see that Ink was home from Vietnam and treated us both graciously.

I was thinking I might not be coming back to the White House very often and would miss it. Little did I know that in only a few months I would not only be back but this time looking from the inside out. I did not yet know the Nixons but would soon know them, their children, and the White House staff. I would be one of them.

11

On the White House Staff

In Pat Nixon's East Wing

We never know what life has in store for us. For me life has always seemed a series of adventures. One spring day in 1969, I was astounded to find myself at the White House instead of at my microphone at Voice of America. Gerry Van der Heuvel, press secretary to President Richard Nixon's wife, Pat, had asked me to work in the East Wing to help Mrs. Nixon with radio and television! So here I was at my new desk on the White House staff, a press aide dealing with the White House Press Corps, on radio, television, and wherever else I could be helpful. My first meeting with the First Lady was right after I joined her staff at the White House.

I liked Mrs. Nixon from the very beginning, and the better I knew her and the more I traveled at her side, the better I liked her. In this first year of the Nixon administration, the American public, I sensed, did not know her well and had not seen enough of her warmth, her devotion to her family, and her dedication to running the White House as the people's house. Aside from her immediate family, Mrs. Nixon's great interest was in children. She loved them, and they knew it. Perhaps because she had been a teacher, she had a natural and genuine rapport with young people, especially little children. Later she would set up White House tours for blind children, with special explanations in each room.

After a short time in the East Wing, I received a call from Frank Shakespeare, director of the United States Information Agency. He had talked with Mrs. Nixon and convinced her that I could help with her demanding microphone confrontations. She would be calling me to come up to the White House family living quarters, and I should be ready to be her teacher!

To me the microphone is like an extension of my body. At VOA I worked with it every day to deliver what I wanted to say to millions of people. Far from being afraid of it, I was grateful to it. Sitting at my desk a bit shaken by the call from Mr. Shakespeare, I realized that what I had been thinking about my own relationship to this electronic genie was the answer to what I would tell my first pupil. Soon the call came from Mrs. Nixon, who liked to call members of her staff directly. "When can you come up? Tomorrow morning?"

The date was set. To arrange the scene I called the U.S. Signal Corps Presidential Unit, which keeps the president in contact with his staff and the rest of the world at all times, wherever he may be. It is an awesome task to be the president's primary communications contact, and the Signal Corps handles it with great skill. It was no trouble for them when I requested that a microphone be set up in the middle of the Yellow Oval Room, the formal drawing room for the president's family and the reception room for foreign chiefs of state and heads of government before state luncheons and dinners. The microphone was for Mrs. Nixon, I explained, so they should set it for her height. I asked that they also send up a tape recorder.

The next morning arrived and I felt not half so confident as I had the day before. As a newcomer I was a bit apprehensive, but I had planned what I would do and could only hope it would work. The White House family elevator whisked me up from the ground floor past the first floor, with the state dining room and other official rooms, to the third floor, my first time ever up there. The man who ushered me in was most reassuring. I think he knew that I was a little jiggly inside.

I entered the oval living room from the center hallway. Mrs. Nixon had decorated this formal room in the same yellow that Dolley Madison had used in 1809. The furnishings included a golden yellow carpet, gold curtains at the window, a formal Louis XVI style sofa in front of one window, two comfortable yellow sofas in the center of the room, one beside and one facing the fireplace, and two French chairs, a pretty russet color, facing one of the sofas. A handsome chandelier hung over this entire splendor, and just beneath stood the microphone I had requested!

I looked out a window at the breathtaking view of the city I love so much and said a little prayer that all would go well. I felt as though I had been shot from a cannon from my old house in Connecticut only to land in the president's home. Just then in came Mrs. Nixon. As soon as we had said good morning, I asked her to take off her shoes! With her shoes off, I suggested, she would be more comfortable and feel more at home with the microphone. The microphone, I told her, was her friend, no need to fear it. I assured her she had good things to say, she cared about people, she would not like it if her words were lost in a corner of a room somewhere.

Our lesson began, with a stocking-footed First Lady standing in front of the microphone. The top of the microphone obscured her head, which was set up much too high for the speaker (especially a shoeless one). She must be master of the instrument, I told her, not the other way around, and I showed her how to lower it until it was at a comfortable level and to speak about twelve inches away from it. Then we did some recording so she would hear her voice and inflection. Her voice, with its Midwestern, slightly flat twang, had a good quality, strong and true, just like the woman herself. She was pleased that she sounded good on the tape we made and picked up quickly on the idea of relaxing and not suffering through the experience but having fun communicating.

"No one has ever shown me how it all worked before," she told me, "and I didn't know that I could adjust the microphone up or down. I like the poem you brought for me to practice on 'I Am an American.' It says plenty of good things about this country of ours. I feel better already about making speeches." Hearing her words, I too relaxed. We had several of these sessions, and I think they gave her greater confidence.

In the White House, surrounded by people, Pat Nixon was nonetheless alone. She was a private person who had always had a great deal of responsibility behind the scenes. She loved to laugh and loved to be with her family. Here in the White House, however, her husband was totally preoccupied with affairs of state, and she was not included in policy meetings as some future First Ladies would be. However, she and her husband always found time to attend events involving parents at their daughters' schools. They were a close family.

Mrs. Nixon believed she should stand back and let her husband shine. She did everything she could to help him whenever he wanted something done that was within her domain. This concern for the president was a driving force behind all she did. People sometimes write, mistakenly, that she must have been disillusioned with her husband at the end when everything capsized. But she always believed in him and considered him an extremely intelligent man whom the country needed.

The president, as might be expected, left the running of the house to his wife, and she did it well. Clem Conger, then the White House curator, thought her taste impeccable. He told me she did almost as much for the redoing of the White House official rooms as had Jackie Kennedy, with whom he also had worked closely. Mrs. Nixon did the redecoration with so little fanfare that she never received the credit he thought she was due.

Mrs. Nixon arranged the first White House art exhibit. She brought the paintings of Andrew Wyeth to the East Room, invited people to come see them, and opened the exhibit to the many tourists from all over the United States. She saw to it that the presidential yacht was used for underprivileged children on a regular basis and that, for the first time, military veterans were entertained once a week aboard the yacht. Mrs. Nixon made it possible for cabinet wives to attend a cabinet meeting. She publicly supported the Equal Rights Amendment for women. She was the first to add military women to the once all-male group of White House military aides present at official social functions. Mrs. Nixon's influence is also evident in the American flag that now flies twenty-four hours a day atop the White House. It used to fly only in the daytime until Mrs. Nixon pushed to have lights installed so the flag could fly at night.

Rex Scouten, White House chief usher, managed everything and everyone. He was highly respected by the White House staff and by consecutive first families with whom he worked. He told me he found it a joy to take instructions from Mrs. Nixon. He later succeeded Clem Conger as White House curator. Conger had become curator of the State Department, where he brought to magnificent life the official rooms of the department's eighth floor.

I was constantly surprised at the rudeness of White House chief of staff Robert Haldeman, who did not believe in any special treatment for the First Lady. But after she did so well on her own on her African journey, he suddenly saw her as a vote-getter. I was chagrined that Haldeman should be considered an authority on the Nixons when he published a book not long before his death. I had watched him cause much grief to staff members, as when I observed someone blanch while talking to Haldeman on the phone. Haldeman would use foul language to tell people they were not performing well, when we all knew the people at whom he shouted were doing a great job. He left me alone, I think, because I had the ear of Mrs. Nixon. He was not much respected by most of the staff.

President Nixon enjoyed tremendous respect from his staff. When passing me in the hall he would always stop and talk for a moment, asking me how things were going in the East Wing. I would hear from members of the Secret Service who were with him at all times how much they admired him. I noticed that he frequently stopped to talk to the men and women cleaning the hallways.

"What is Mrs. Nixon really like?" was a question I was asked over and over again. I can tell you something about her. She was a woman of courage. When mobbed in Venezuela and threatened by a rock-throwing crowd along with then vice president Nixon, she never lost her cool. She was a devoted wife and a loving, imaginative mother, with a great deal of responsibility that she carried with remarkable grace.

I often saw her in the family quarters talking with her daughters, listening to their problems, showing interest in their activities. I enjoyed knowing both girls, though I knew Julie the best. Julie is a serious, well-informed woman with unusual writing ability. She and her husband, David Eisenhower, are an affectionate, well-matched couple who enjoy parenthood. In those later years, Mrs. Nixon told me how much she and the president enjoyed being grandparents to both Julie's and Tricia's children.

When I first came to work in the White House, I was assigned to rewrite Mrs. Nixon's autobiography for the press. She was born in a miner's shack in Ely, Nevada, a small mining town, on March 16, 1912, and christened Thelma Catherine Patricia Ryan. Her father, Will, coming home past midnight from his work in the copper mines and learning of her birth, called her "St. Patrick's Babe in the Morn." He called her Pat and decided they would celebrate her birthday on St. Patrick's Day. Her mother, Kate Halberstadt Bender Ryan, was born in Hessen County, near Frankfurt, Germany, and died in California in 1925, when young Pat was only thirteen.

After her mother died, the young teenager took care of her two brothers, did the housework, and, when the family moved to California, she worked after school and helped with the truck farm they had bought. After her father died when she was seventeen, she worked for two years as an X-ray technician in a New York hospital and saved enough money to attend the University of Southern California as a scholarship student. Aside from her classes she worked as many as forty hours a week doing various jobs. In one job, she was hired as an extra and a potential starlet at Universal Studios. Many years later, Universal director Alfred Hitchcock gave a big luncheon for then First Lady Pat Nixon, and I was there. I found it hard to associate Hitchcock, a round, jolly man, with his tremendously successful, scary, heavily dramatic films.

With all of her responsibilities, young Pat Ryan managed to graduate cum laude with a Bachelor of Science degree in 1937. After graduation, she taught commercial subjects at Whittier High School. While performing in an amateur play, she met Richard Nixon, a recent graduate of Duke University Law School.

Mrs. Nixon had been a beautiful young woman, and those of us who worked for her thought she was a beautiful older woman too. She was genuinely interested in people and displayed great dignity and real grit. To me she had the attributes of the early American pioneer woman. I remember once how comfortable she looked on a working trip out west as she rode in a covered wagon.

When Pat Nixon talked to people, she gave each person her complete attention. When she traveled, she was interested in what she would see and do. Children of all colors, shapes, and sizes seemed to love her, and you could see the love she had for them as she put her arms around them. She showed warmth and understanding of other people's pain and suffering; she knew about difficult times from her own hard childhood.

When I first came to the White House, I thought I should keep a diary. After a long day and often a long night, however, I had only enough energy left to keep notes. But I do have memories! At the Nixon "Western White House" in San Clemente, California, Mrs. Nixon showed me around the summer home she and the president loved so much, where she loved to do much of her own gardening. It was President Nixon who named it *La Casa Pacifica,* the peaceful house. It was in San Clemente that Richard Nixon had asked her to marry him. From the Spanish-style house, with its white stucco walls and red-tile roof, one could see the mighty Pacific Ocean.

President Franklin D. Roosevelt had come to the house once during a campaign train trip. He had the train stopped so that he could pay a call on the then owner of the house, Hamilton Cotton. President Roosevelt was brought up the cliff by pulley from the ground below to play a game of poker with Mr. Cotton. The room in which they played then had become President Nixon's bedroom. We both savored that historic tidbit.

Duke Ellington at the White House

The Nixons gave wonderful White House parties. One of the best, in 1969, honored Duke Ellington, composer, conductor, and pianist, on his seventieth birthday. As a native Washingtonian, Ellington knew all about the White House. His father, James Edward Ellington, had been a White House butler during the Harding administration. Now his son was being toasted by another president as the most famous of all jazz musicians.

Helping to arrange that evening was presidential counselor Leonard Garment, a jazz musician himself, who played his saxophone that night. Decades later he was planning to open a jazz museum in Harlem. What a good idea!

President Nixon presented Mr. Ellington with the Freedom Medal, our government's highest civilian decoration, for his contribution to American music It was the first Freedom Medal Nixon had presented to anyone.

Before dinner, President and Mrs. Nixon received Duke Ellington and his sister, Miss Ruth Ellington, in the Yellow Oval Room on the second floor of the White House, then descended the grand staircase to receive the guests in the East Room before going into the state dining room. In toasting Duke Ellington, the president had said, "In the royalty of music, no man swings more than the Duke." After dinner, it was back to the East Room for a concert of Ellington music performed by outstanding American musicians. This "White House Jazz Festival" was hosted by the president and by Willis Conover, whose popular jazz program was heard in many parts of the world on the Voice of America.

The president played "Happy Birthday" on the Steinway grand piano, and then the jazz began. Louis Bellson, former drummer with the Duke Ellington Orchestra and his assistant-composer arranger, was joined by Earl (Fatha) Hines, who had great influence on the development of jazz piano styles around the world, influential baritone saxophonist Jerry Mulligan, pianist Billy Taylor, former Count Basie singing star Joe Williams, and many more. How the guests applauded, and how they loved it! Someone said it was the best party they had ever been to in the White House. The Nixons stayed up until midnight, and the guests didn't leave until quarter past two in the morning. What a great evening!

Around the World with the President and First Lady

Though I could hardly believe it, I was on the list to go around the world with the president and Mrs. Nixon! The White House name for the trip was "Moonglow: A Journey in Quest of Peace." It was a goodwill trip to Asia and Europe, and we visited eight countries in eleven days. It was first of all a welcome home to the astronauts who had just made the first walk on the moon. The president left Washington on Air Force One to rendezvous with the U.S.S. *Hornet* in the Pacific, where the astronauts would splash down to be picked up and taken aboard the aircraft carrier. I was lucky enough to fly with Mrs. Nixon on what we called informally Air Force Two, along with a small group that included Adele Rogers, wife of the secretary of state. En route the pilot came back into the cabin and asked us to look out the window, where we saw Air Force One slightly ahead of us at a higher altitude, the sun glistening on its silver wings, a long jet stream marking its course toward Guam.

While stopping in Hawaii the nine of us gathered in Mrs. Nixon's hotel room to watch the president on television as he greeted the astronauts. We all stood up when the Star Spangled Banner was played on board the *Hornet*. Next day we flew on to meet President Nixon in Guam, where Governor and Mrs. Canacho invited me to dinner along with other staff members. At the state dinner in the Philippines, I remember sitting at a round table watching the Filipino dancers and suddenly becoming so tired that I tipped to one side and started to fall off my chair sound asleep. The admiral on my left very kindly pushed me back to the center. I opened my eyes wide and decided that must never happen to me again!

As we flew round the world in eleven days listening to speeches everywhere we went, I was always running to arrive ahead of Mrs. Nixon. Like Mrs. Nixon, I changed into a long dress and long white gloves for these state dinners. I once asked Mrs. Nixon how she could dash around in the heat all day and stay awake at a late affair. She concentrated hard on not falling asleep, she said, because she knew she simply could not. Another time, when I asked her how she managed to eat strange foods even when she was not feeling well, she said it helped to distribute the food a little around one's plate. She had a great sense of humor.

In the Philippines Mrs. Nixon kept busy every minute visiting welfare projects and villages, accompanied everywhere by Imelda

Marcos, wife of President Ferdinand Marcos. I was surprised that Mrs. Marcos seemed more intent on spending money on grandiose projects than she did on helping some of the poor people in the villages.

Soon after arrival at our next stop, Jakarta, Indonesia, President Nixon met with President Suharto at the Merdeka Palace. President and Mrs. Suharto took the Nixons to the Jakarta Fair, where we were told to expect about one million people. I have a vivid recollection of walking through that fair. Including the Secret Service agents, there were only about five of us accompanying the Nixons. In the middle of the fairgrounds friendly onlookers eager to get a look at the president of the United States began moving in on us. Suddenly, we realized we could quite easily be crushed to death as these thousands of people closed in. At this point, the Secret Service agents went into high gear. They formed a circle around the Nixons and asked the rest of us to join them. We locked hands to form a human barrier, each of us determined to defend the president from being trampled to death. Gradually, people eased back, and the Indonesian guards ensured us a safe exit.

After our adventure at the fair, we attended a reception given by President Suharto at the Negara Palace followed by the state dinner. This was my first of three trips to Indonesia. On this trip, Mrs. Nixon was constantly on the go and I was always with her. Somewhere around this time, I told a friend in the president's press office about my trouble getting from airports to Mrs. Nixon's destinations before she did. I explained that the chief of protocol had knocked on my door at 3:00 a.m. one morning saying he had to be sure that the official gift would be there when needed and knew he could depend on me. He had asked if I would take on the responsibility of getting each official gift to Mrs. Nixon on time so that she might present it to her host at whatever project she was visiting. Of course I said yes, but I needed help and transportation to arrive each time before she did. I also wanted to be available in case she needed my help or had any questions. It was a good thing I spoke up, because from then on a car and driver met me at each stop in each country so I would be first on the scene before Mrs. Nixon and the members of the press arrived.

In Bangkok, Thailand, Queen Sirikit took Mrs. Nixon to the Serpentarium, where we looked down, reluctantly, into a pit full of serious-looking snakes. When told that the venom of these snakes was extracted for antitoxins, I felt friendlier toward them and took another look. While we were busy with Mrs. Nixon's schedule, the president and the king went to the Pan Fah Bridge Pavilion, where, as was usual, Lord Mayor Chalit Kulkanthorn presented President Nixon with the key to the city. I'm only touching on some of the activities in each country. Now the big unannounced stop—wartime Vietnam—lay just ahead.

Into Vietnam On Air Force One

None of us was told until the very last minute that the Nixons would leave Bangkok early in the morning on Air Force One to spend one full day in Vietnam. The big plan for a wartime trip was kept secret because of the dangers involved. President Nixon had been to Vietnam approximately six times between 1953 and 1967, but this was his first time as president of the United States.

An NBC crew, coming in on a separate plane, was assigned to follow Mrs. Nixon around with her planned activities. President Nixon was to spend the day with the American troops. Because of limited space the plans did not include anyone assigned to Mrs. Nixon. Only at the last minute was her press secretary, Gerry Van der Heuvel, told she could go on the press plane. I was greatly disappointed. I thought perhaps someone on the press plane would be ill at the last moment (the heat was intense) and if I were there I could be put on board. The president's assistant press secretary, Jerry Warren, a friend, told me there would be no room for me on the press plane but that he really wished I could be there to help Mrs. Nixon. He had his car and driver take me to the runway where Air Force One would be awaiting the president's arrival and suggested that I ask the pilot, Colonel Albertazzie, if he could find me a place on the plane.

So off I went to the landing strip with my walkie-talkie radio in my hand. I stood for a long time in the burning sunshine in my little straw hat afraid to leave the foot of the runway to seek shelter inside a nearby building. The pilot told me that he might have a place but that I would have to have permission from General Hughes, whom I knew only slightly and who would be arriving shortly with President and Mrs. Nixon. I would have only ten seconds to ask him because the boarding must be swift.

As General Hughes approached, I stepped forward and said, "General, Colonel Albertazzie says he has room for me to go if you say it is all right."

"No," said General Hughes in his most emphatic tone.

He went up the ramp and the president, just behind him, said, "Good morning, Pat."

Mrs. Nixon right behind him said, "Good morning Pat, are you coming?"

I told her, "No, I wish I were coming because I think I could be of help."

"You always are," she replied.

With that she clambered up the steps behind her husband and tapped him on the shoulder. Then she turned around and called out to me, "Come on Pat, Dick says you can come."

When the three of us reached the top of the ramp, Mrs. Nixon said, "If there's no place for you there, you can sit with me up front."

The pilot found me a place for takeoff, and once we were airborne, Mrs. Nixon sent for me to come to her private compartment. We visited for a while and then she sent me to invite U.S. Ambassador to Nepal Carol Laise Bunker to come join us. Ambassador Laise was married to Ellsworth Bunker, the U.S. ambassador to South Vietnam, who at that moment was meeting with President Nixon, General Creighton Abrams, U.S. military chief in Vietnam, Marshall Green, the assistant secretary of state for East Asian and Pacific affairs, and National Security Advisor Henry Kissinger. The president had a section to himself, which made a good meeting place.

In no time we were landing at Saigon's Tan Son Nhut airport, where helicopters were waiting. I had been assigned to Mrs. Nixon's helicopter along with the pilot and Secret Service agent Verne Copeland. I knew Verne well because he was almost always along when Mrs. Nixon was out of the White House. Our helicopter took us directly to the palace in Saigon. Sandbags surrounded the entrance of the palace and fighter jets roared overhead. Here President Nixon joined us and the president of South Vietnam, Nguyen Van Thieu, and Mrs. Thieu hosted us all at tea. Strange to have tea with a war raging close by, but the palace was secure and it was a good place to start our exciting long day's journey. I could not help but think that at last I was seeing the country where my husband had served for two years.

After this reception, President Nixon flew off in his helicopter to spend the day with the American troops. Mrs. Nixon and I boarded our small helicopter once again and this time there were three of us in the front seat and three in the back, for Mrs. Thieu and Ambassador Laise had joined Mrs. Nixon for our trip. I was between the pilot and Verne Copeland. As we took off, I started to put Mrs. Nixon's raincoat on top of a small box at my feet. Verne told me not to put it there because he might need to get into that box quickly. It contained a machine gun, he said, explaining, "We do not know what kind of ground fire we might encounter even though there has been much careful preparation for our flight."

I asked him if he was carrying a gun also and if he would like me to use it in case he had to use the machine gun. "Yes," he said, "I will hand it to you immediately, and it will be ready to shoot if I do."

We flew first to an orphanage, with the NBC TV crew right behind us. The orphanage housed 745 children who had lost their parents in the war. The American GIs gave whatever time they could and whatever money they could to support this orphanage. As the doorway already was blocked, I, who could not ordinarily lift anything heavy, found the strength to help haul large men laden with camera equipment through the window. The children put on a little Vietnamese operetta for Mrs. Nixon. The children loved her, and she loved them.

Leaving the orphanage, we flew north to Long Binh and the 24th Evacuation Hospital, where Mrs. Nixon would visit the severely wounded American soldiers. She was the first wife of an American president since Eleanor Roosevelt to visit a combat zone. When we arrived at Long Binh, several general officers greeted us. I went ahead to some of the wards and explained to the wounded men that Mrs. Nixon was in Vietnam with the president and would be coming in to visit them. She followed soon after. At each bed she would slip down on her knees to speak more closely with the men. Big smiles lit their faces, for here was a voice from home and that of an important person besides. But Pat Nixon was not thinking of herself as someone important. This was a very emotional moment for her, as she cared deeply about these soldiers. The patients felt her compassion and were encouraged by her warm smile. It was a good experience for us all.

The day was almost over when we boarded our chopper again. We had instructions to go direct to Air Force One and run aboard as fast as we could. The president would arrive just after us, and the minute he did the door would shut and we would be airborne. On the way to the airport, I looked down at the green land below. No one had ever told me how beautiful this country could be without gunfire. I was glad to have had one long memorable day in Vietnam.

We landed near Air Force One, ran quickly aboard as we had been instructed, watched the president board shortly after us, and were on our way back to Bangkok.

On to India, Pakistan, Romania, and England

With the Vietnam trip behind us, it was time to leave the Mandarin Hotel for the Bangkok Airport. Our destination this time was New Delhi, India, and I was back on the press plane for the flight. I was always amazed at the efficiency of the White House travel people as we moved from one place to another. The logistics must have been complicated, but all that the rest of us—press and staff alike—had to do was put our bags in front of our doors at the hotel. When we arrived at the next stop, there they were in our hotel rooms.

On Thursday, July 31, 1969, we left the hotel at the crack of dawn. We were all aboard the TWA and Pan Am press planes ready to depart by midmorning, and before we knew it we had arrived in New Delhi. The President and Mrs. Nixon arrived fifteen minutes after we did, as planned, to enable the press to cover the president's arrival.

Airport arrival ceremonies were always impressive, with the playing of national anthems, a review of the troops by President Nixon, statements, in this case by India's acting president, Mr. M. Hidayatullah, and President Nixon. Prime Minister Indira Gandhi was also there to meet the plane. The motorcade soon had us on our way to Rashtrapati Bhavan, the official residence where President and Mrs. Nixon would stay. As usual, the motorcade was quite a show, with two photo trucks, two wire cars, the press pool bus carrying fifteen members of the U.S. press and fifteen from the Indian press. President Nixon called on the acting president after getting settled in his suite and then the press buses took us to the Ashoka Hotel, where we were staying.

In the middle of the afternoon, President Nixon and Prime Minister Indira Gandhi met for substantive talks. Afterwards, the president laid a wreath at the Gandhi Memorial and planted a tree next to one President Eisenhower had planted when he visited India. The big event of the day was the state dinner in the official banquet hall, with after-dinner speeches and entertainment. The day ended about 11:00 p.m., a long, action-filled day so typical on such trips.

After years of reading letters on The Breakfast Show from friends in India and Pakistan, visiting those countries was a special joy to me. Our stops were much too short yet I was pleased to even briefly glimpse these countries I had never seen. In India as I traveled about with Mrs. Nixon I met villagers and saw some of the countryside. Many people I met told me they listened to The Breakfast Show. At the banquet given for the president and Mrs. Nixon, some Indian army officers who saw my name on the guest list asked me if I were the one they listened to on the Voice of America. I was delighted to know that we had listeners not only in India's capital city but also all over the country.

One of my main responsibilities on this world trip was making sure that UPI correspondent Helen Thomas and AP correspondent Fran Lewine were seated up front and center wherever we stopped so they could get their stories back to Washington as quickly as possible. I told these two distinguished reporters, whose enormous influence mattered greatly to us, that I hoped to emulate my friend Liz Carpenter in making sure that the press received plenty of information and help along the way. Liz Carpenter, Lady Bird Johnson's press secretary, was respected by the press perhaps more than any press secretary before or since. "Tell me anytime how Liz would have done it and I'll try to do the same," I told them.

Helen and Fran were not shy about speaking up so I learned a great deal working with them. Having been on the broadcasting side of the fence, I knew how vital it was to get the story. This time what mattered most to me was ensuring that all the members of the traveling press got Mrs. Nixon's story.

Sleep or no sleep, we left New Delhi for Lahore, Pakistan, where President Nixon was greeted by Pakistan president Gen. Yahya Khan. Lahore was even hotter than New Delhi. Throughout this trip, Mrs. Nixon never seemed to tire. In Lahore I asked her how she was able to walk most of the day through 125-degree Fahrenheit heat and never complain. I could hardly move as I put on my long dress and long white gloves for the state dinner that evening, but Mrs. Nixon looked relaxed when we met at dinner. Her secret, she said, was that whenever she was as hot as she had been that day, she thought of the coldest things she could possibly conceive of—igloos, ice, snow, Antarctica, and such thoughts helped her feel a bit cooler.

In the reception hall of the president's residence, I was offered a cool drink with tinkling ice cubes. The White House doctor had warned us ahead of time that we would not be used to the water, including the ice, in all the countries we were to visit, and if we did not stay healthy the plane would take off without us. It wasn't easy, but I said "no thank you" to the tempting drink and shortly after, President Nixon's doctor, Walter Tkach, fortified my strength by giving me a most unappetizing salt tablet.

All day long, Mrs. Nixon and I visited schools and the West Pakistan Society for Rehabilitation of the Disabled. She was especially interested in examining the locally made prosthetic and orthopedic devices used in the treatment of disabled persons. We watched people studying arts and crafts and children at play on equipment especially designed for the handicapped. In one of the primary schools we visited, numerous art works in crayon showed men walking on the moon. Clearly, the landing on the moon had been of great interest to children and adults all over the world. I was proud of America's extraordinary voyage.

Late in the day, when we returned to the lawn of Government House, the photographers were in heaven, even dripping in the heat. Before us trooped splendidly costumed military bagpipers and with them the Khattaka Dancers. The bagpipes sounded better than any I have heard, and the players, though aging, marched with a steady step in the steaming sun. Without even a wisp of air, the afternoon held a solemn beauty. With our tiny figures on the great lawn, bagpipers marching before us, only the Pakistan president's air-conditioner fanning us and the Secret Service walkie-talkies reminded us that we were in the twentieth century.

Mrs. Nixon, after a long day's hard work, sat calmly. She looked pleased to be enjoying outdoor entertainment before the state dinner, which would mean an earlier bedtime for all of us. She even managed to look fairly rested.

En route to the dinner that night in my long dress, I rode the buses with the cameramen. Sometimes I went ahead of the press with a car and driver to make sure all was in readiness, but this night was so hot I rode with the crews, because it would be too galling to them if I were to ride in splendor in an air-conditioned car. These cameramen, who worked so hard carrying such heavy equipment, were always gallant, thoughtful, and a pleasure to work with. I had had a run-in with one CBS man when I tried to move him after he had positioned his camera—I didn't know the unwritten law that only one cameraman can ask another to move after he is positioned—but I made a friend, learned a valuable lesson, and didn't repeat that mistake.

When the -president moves, a fantastically well-organized unit moves with him—his communications team, his military, his State Department advisors, the Secret Service, and staff members, all of us realizing that everyone must help on every level. The miracle is that the president and the first lady perform admirably while on stage constantly and under a great deal of pressure. The president's life is eased in many ways by aides, but Mrs. Nixon had no one to pack her bags, help her with quick changes, or save her those extra steps. One time I offered to press a dress for her, but she declined, saying she would do it herself. She drew upon her tremendous stamina, willpower, and sense of humor to keep going. A woman of deep humility, she seemed determined to remain natural and genuine, at ease with people of all nationalities. She had a mind of her own and not much escaped her notice. I found her fun to be with under any and all circumstances.

That night at the pre-dinner reception, as I was on duty with little time to socialize, Mrs. Nixon introduced me to the president of Pakistan as a member of her staff and a military wife. She knew I would be especially interested in meeting him, as indeed I was. We talked just before I checked to see if dinner were about to be served, at which moment I would give the signal to the camera crews at the foot of the staircase and hurry them in for a two-minute session of picture-taking before escorting them back out.

The next morning, we set our clocks back three hours for a flight of almost six hours to Bucharest, Romania, landing at Otopeni Airport. President Nicolae Ceausescu greeted President Nixon as the first U.S. president to visit a communist country. Nixon had been in Romania in 1967 as a private citizen. The official party, including me, all stayed at the Romanian State Guest House. A disheartening ride from the airport revealed a grim, sad city, more barren than any of the communist-controlled countries of Eastern Europe I had seen.

Sunday morning, I awoke early and raised the window blinds in my room to look out into the garden. As I went into my bath, I suddenly heard someone in the bedroom. Returning quickly I found a guard in my room putting down all my blinds. He said no one was allowed to raise the blinds until later in the day! This rather startling

160

and unpleasant intrusion made me acutely aware that I was in a communist country.

Mrs. Nixon and the press visited the Pioneer Palace, the center of a boys-and-girls' communist organization. All neatly dressed in white shirts, the girls wore white hats and dark skirts, the boys dark hats and dark trousers, and entertained us with folk dancing, fine arts, science projects, and physical fitness exhibitions. The children were well trained and seemed pleased to have us there.

After President Nixon hosted a luncheon in the state dining room of the Guest House, we all headed for the airport, next stop Mildenhall Air Force Base in England, and it was still Sunday. Prime Minister Harold Wilson met President Nixon at the airport, where they held private talks in the base commander's quarters. Before we knew it, we were back on board headed to Andrews Air Force Base in Washington. We arrived around midnight, so tired that none of us knew exactly what time it was. But what a trip it had been!

In the view of many of us, the first lady had been a rousing success as an ambassador for the United States. She was a seasoned traveler, at home wherever she was. Many people didn't realize it but she had already traveled to fifty-three countries before making this world trip, dubbed "Moonglow." Now, she was beginning to shine on her own.

Back in the East Wing

A splendid woman, Helen McCain Smith, shared an office with me in the East Wing of the White House, both of us there to help Mrs. Nixon and her press secretary. Our responsibilities were almost interchangeable. Helen had not gone on the world trip but she would more than make up for mileage missed in the years to come, when she would become Mrs. Nixon's press secretary long after I returned to the Voice of America.

Mrs. Nixon's press office was small with just the press secretary, two secretaries, Helen and me. The secretaries had been in the White House through the Johnson years and were our "institutional memory." When Mrs. Nixon once asked me if I thought people held over from the last administration could be loyal to the current one, I told her absolutely yes. The White House at that time had many long-serving persons loyal to whatever administration they were serving. Just down the hall from us was the office of social secretary Lucy Winchester, who planned such social activities as state dinners. We worked closely with her and her staff.

One day, I said to Mrs. Nixon, "Last night I was watching the television series about Henry the VIII, which showed a great deal of maneuvering for power in the court. It reminded me of the White House, especially some of the pushing and shoving between the West Wing and the East Wing. Some things never change!" We both laughed.

What did I do all day? Everything imaginable. Arriving at the office at 8:45 a.m., I immediately started taking phone calls, clearing up requests by mail or phone, helping the press secretary in any way possible on crash projects. A typical day might also include asking the White House curator for the history of paintings hanging in family quarters for a member of the press doing a story for an art magazine about Mrs. Nixon's interest in White House paintings.

Some days I would spend time with Mrs. Nixon discussing radio and television programs and which requests for interviews she should accept. Often, there was no time for lunch, especially when an event had to be covered and I needed to be with the press. I might work in the afternoon preparing for a trip, digging up background information, perhaps attending a pertinent meeting. Sometimes I would talk with people from the Midwest or California concerned about volunteer projects, Mrs. Nixon's big interest.

I also worked on technical aspects of radio and television, occasionally visiting local television studios, and spent much time on the telephone with network people both locally and nationally. For example, TV correspondent Barbara Walters once called and asked my help in arranging an interview with Mrs. Nixon, which I gladly did.

Usually, I would leave the office around 6:00 or 6:30 p.m. except when evening activities were scheduled. Helen and I filled in for the press secretary and answered calls from members of the press, radio, and television at home as well as in the office on evenings and weekends. Weekends were rarely free because, like most White House staff, we were on call all the time. When Mrs. Nixon would call me at home, the amazing White House operators found me wherever I was. They recognized almost everyone on the staff by voice and could find people for the president anywhere in the world in a short time. One day, I went down to visit the operators at their switchboard in a basement corner of the White House. Like everyone else on the staff, I thought they were indispensable. There were operators on duty twenty-four hours a day then. In a later administration, they were replaced by modern technology and voice mail, though I think there are more human voices on the White House switchboard now than at the time of the first clumsy efforts toward modernization.

Before the world trip, I had accompanied Mrs. Nixon and Julie on a four-day trip out west. My role was to help the press. Mrs. Nixon visited ten grass-roots volunteer projects in California and Oregon that received no help from the government. The members of the press wrote glowingly of her concern for the volunteer workers and admired the way she hugged countless children in schools in nurseries for the deprived and schools for the blind.

Helen Thomas of UPI wrote in her syndicated column, read worldwide, "Radiating warmth and friendliness, Mrs. Nixon's First Lady image came into focus under the glare of the spotlight as she traveled to schools and social centers in the Los Angeles ghetto areas. Her human touch came through when a little boy clasped her hand and said 'Let's do a soul brother shake.' " You could see why I always made sure Helen could stand right where she wanted to be, in the front row as the press crowded around!

After the trip west, Mrs. Nixon was more convinced than ever of the value of concentrating on volunteerism, which became her main focus. Everywhere we had gone on the Moonglow world trip, she had inquired about people's interest in volunteerism and asked to see their volunteer projects.

The Astronauts Come to Dinner

Back from the western and world trips, we immediately began preparing for an official dinner to honor the Apollo II astronauts, to be held at the Century Plaza Hotel in Los Angeles on Wednesday, August 13, 1969. It would be as close to a White House state dinner as could be held outside the White House. Approximately fifteen hundred guests would be invited. Lucy Winchester and those of us in the press office were hard at work preparing for the event.

It was a coveted invitation. Members of the cabinet would attend along with Supreme Court justices, NASA officials, ambassadors from around the world, forty-four of the fifty state governors, the Senate and House leadership, members of the space committees of both houses, and, of course, the astronauts themselves. The Marine Band would perform as well as the Marine Drum and Bugle Corps, the Army Air Force Strolling Strings, and the Army Chorus. Plans also called for a six-foot high forty-pound replica of the Apollo II Seal made entirely of sugar ice and different varieties of chocolate. A future president would be among the guests. Finally, the stage was set and what an evening it was! How lucky I was to be there!

Before the astronauts had set off on their flight to the moon, the president had recognized their predecessors in space in an official statement: "There is no national boundary to courage. The names Gagarin and Komorov, of Grissom, White and Chaffee, share the honor we pray will come to Armstrong, Aldrin and Collins." Suspenseful days later, Armstrong and Aldrin walked on the moon, while Collins stayed aboard the Apollo II landing craft to assure the astronauts a safe return to their spacecraft after the moonwalk.

Now, less than a month later at the Century Plaza Hotel, the astronauts Neil A. Armstrong, Edwin E. Aldrin, Jr., and Michael Collins and their wives joined the President and Mrs. Nixon in the Presidential Suite and thence to the head table. Millions of viewers watched the live television coverage throughout the dinner, for the moon landing had been a closely followed event. Governor Ronald Reagan toasted the Nixons, and the President presented each astronaut with the Medal of Freedom.

During the evening, the television crews interviewed many of the guests. The NBC crew asked if I could bring the governor of California over to their cameras. I approached Ronald Reagan, and he agreeably followed me across the room. That was my first meeting with the man who would become president and later would play such an important role in my life. Little did I know what the future would hold when I introduced myself to him that evening.

12

Travels Far and Wide

Back to the Microphone

My White House days passed quickly, as I accompanied Mrs. Nixon on many short trips. At the urging of the West Wing, Mrs. Nixon chose a new press secretary. Mrs. Nixon wanted to keep me on her staff, but it seemed to me time to return to my microphone at the Voice of America. It did not mean goodbye to the White House. Mrs. Nixon and I kept in touch, and before too long there was another change. My good friend Helen McCain Smith became the first lady's press secretary. I had said to Mrs. Nixon before I left her staff that she could trust Helen to be a true friend and a great help to her. The members of the press liked Helen and had faith in her, knowing she would do her best to help both Mrs. Nixon and the press.

After I had left the White House staff, I gave a birthday party for Helen in our apartment. Mrs. Nixon and the president sent a delicious, decorated birthday cake for the occasion, and most of the members of the press covering Mrs. Nixon were there. My great friend, U.S. Representative Charlotte Reid, dressed as a French maid, helped serve the food, and no one recognized her at first. What a surprise!

Not long after I returned to VOA and The Breakfast Show, we all suffered a dreadful loss. Al Johnson, the originator of The Breakfast Show, died of a heart attack. He was the program's leading broadcaster and producer. Among other things, he would speak to the listeners about his family, including his young children, and his spirit permeated the program from its conception. It was Al who had hired me. For eight years, I had the good fortune to work for a man who had absolutely no prejudice against working women, an excellent leader of his team, consisting of Phil Irwin and me, and with much to teach when I had much to learn. Our listeners all over the world adored him. When he died, they wrote letters of sympathy telling us how much he would be missed. When I broke the horrific news of Al's fatal heart attack to his wife, she was at home with their three adopted children under five years old. I will never forget the anguish of that day.

After Al's death, Bill Reynolds came to run The Breakfast Show. He understood the spirit of the program and was himself a fine broadcaster. He helped us through difficult days and into more good years for the program. I was given the responsibility of hosting and producing more of our daily morning programs. Through all the years, we maintained our rating as the most listened to show on the VOA.

One of many more trips to come was to Africa with Mrs. Nixon, but first she asked me to come on a trip out west with her, along with a contingent of some twenty White House press corps. Whenever I left Washington, I would prerecord my programs. Mrs. Nixon and the president were interested in the environment even before it became a key issue in politics. This trip covered five states in three days, and her mission was to turn over federal lands to state and local governments for development as parks and recreation areas.

At one rather remote airport, the plane took off ahead of time without me! I was phoning my office and knew I still had ten more minutes on the ground, but the head count had been inaccurate and I was left behind. I rushed to the control tower and requested that someone contact the pilot and ask him to come back. At that moment, I thought I might never get home again. To everyone's surprise, the plane, which had flown almost out of sight, turned around and flew back to the airport to pick me up. When I came on board, quite out of breath, everyone applauded, and I thanked Mrs. Nixon for giving the pilot permission to come back for me.

We traveled across the United States from the Atlantic Coast to the Pacific, and Mrs. Nixon received an enthusiastic welcome at the new parklands wherever we stopped. The cross- country conservation tour ended with an unexpected visit to Mexico, where we were mobbed by a delighted crowd of Mexicans. That was the end of the trip for Mrs. Nixon, who proceeded to the western White House in San Clemente. For me, it was back to VOA to report on the trip at my microphone.

White House Wedding

White House weddings are few and far between, and undoubtedly all have been memorable. The one I remember was that of the Nixons' youngest daughter, Tricia, who married a young lawyer, Edward Finch Cox, on Saturday, the 12th of June 1971, in the White House Rose Garden.

To my delight, I was one of only four or five correspondents invited to the wedding. Luckily, I had a seat right in the Rose Garden. As it happened, I was on a dual assignment. Besides my Voice of America report, the Mutual Network had hired me to do a broadcast with their man on the scene, Forrest Boyd, who was waiting for me out on the lawn to give him a firsthand report immediately after the ceremony. During the wedding, I was busy writing in my head what I would say.

Being married in the Rose Garden may sound idyllic, but in this instance it was a cliff-hanger. At the appointed hour that afternoon, the rain poured down in a most determined fashion. However, meteorologists had reported to the White House that the black clouds overhead would vanish if we would all just be patient. Like a space shot held for a dark cloud to pass, there was a "hold" on the time of the wedding for thirty-two minutes. Tricia and her family remained calm and optimistic, while we guests waited indoors until the "go" signal, when dry chairs were set up in the garden and the ceremonies began.

Tricia Nixon was a beautiful bride as she walked down the white-carpeted aisle of the Rose Garden on the arm of her father, the president. I don't think I ever saw the president as relaxed and happy and having as good a time as on that wedding day. He talked with the press before the wedding when the weather was threatening and he was hoping for sunshine and a Hawaiian rainbow. Four hundred guests attended, all of them friends of the Nixons and the Coxes. This was a personal, not an official wedding, although the dean of the diplomatic corps attended, representing all countries on this special day.

The entire diplomatic corps had shared an evening with Tricia and Ed just a few days earlier at a party given by Adele Rogers, the wife of Secretary of State William Rogers. At that reception, I heard the president say that he sincerely hoped that his daughter and new son-in-law would meet many people from all countries of the world as he and Mrs. Nixon had had the good fortune to do.

Tricia was the eighth presidential daughter to be married in the White House and the sixteenth White House bride. The last wedding before this one had been that of Lynda Bird Johnson and Captain Charles Robb, now guests at Tricia's. Another White House bride was also a guest, President Theodore Roosevelt's daughter Alice Roosevelt Longworth, was married there in 1906.

There followed a reception in the East Room with dinner, music, and dancing, magnificent flowers everywhere, and a six-tiered, old-fashioned pound cake baked at the White House. All the bridal customs were followed, and when the bride and groom left the White House, we showered them with rose petals.

Many Americans shared the presidential family's happiness by means of radio and television. History recorded the moment because it was a White House wedding but the story was a familiar one to people everywhere.

To Africa with Mrs. Nixon

The sound of jet engines at Andrews Air Force Base warming up to take the wife of the president of the United States on a journey to Africa told me it was time to get on board. It was the first day of 1972.

I was going along to report on this trip for the Voice of America, and Mrs. Nixon had asked me to be on hand to give her guidance from time to time. Although she had confidence in herself, I think sometimes she found her responsibilities exhausting. When she looked pale and thin, I would worry she was asking too much of herself. I was assigned to fly with her on the presidential plane commonly called Air Force Two, although officially it was known only by the number 970.

Mrs. Nixon had been asked by the president to be his personal representative at the inauguration of the new president of the Republic of Liberia, William R. Tolbert, Jr. Invitations quickly followed for Mrs. Nixon from Ghana and the Ivory Coast, where she hoped to meet and talk not only with heads of state but also with local citizens.

Extensive preparations for the journey began once the decision had been reached that Mrs. Nixon would go to Africa. One of the first steps taken when the president or his wife travels abroad is to send an advance party to the countries to be visited to make plans with the host countries. Everything was arranged; from where Mrs. Nixon and the members of her party would stay and who from the press would be invited to come along, to arranging security matters. The president wanted the trip to be substantive, not just social, so Mrs. Nixon was briefed for serious conversations with chiefs of state and prepared to discuss the president's forthcoming trip to China.

At the hour of departure, my husband delivered me to Andrews Air Force Base to wave me off. For Mrs. Nixon and the press, however, the important man saying goodbye was President Nixon. His helicopter landed beside her plane at the foot of the runway for a brief ceremony at which they both greeted the ambassadors from the countries she was going to visit. Among the official delegation on board was Billy Graham, the American evangelist. He spoke with each of us from time to time during the trip.

Although Mrs. Nixon was the most traveled of any American president's wife, this was her first trip abroad where she would be called upon to make speeches and return toasts at formal occasions. Never at ease discussing politics, she seemed a bit nervous about what lay ahead. In each of the African countries she visited, Mrs. Nixon was accorded the honors of the highest-ranking dignitaries and entertained on the level of a head of state. Upon landing in Monrovia, capital of Liberia, after an all-night nonstop flight, she was met by the President of Liberia and Mrs. Tolbert, reviewed the troops, and addressed the large crowd gathered to welcome her. The motorcade departed for the executive mansion, always an exciting ride with people lining the streets and waving. I was riding near the back of the motorcade enjoying my first glimpse of Liberia.

The Grambling College Band from Reston, Louisiana, given air force transportation by President Nixon, performed on Sunday morning for a large crowd. They were terrific, and I could see why they had been invited.

Later that day, a press coffee with Mrs. Nixon included many newsmen and women in Liberia to cover the presidential inauguration and the celebration of Liberia's 150th anniversary. Mrs. Nixon answered questions about President Nixon's projected trips to Peking (Beijing) and Moscow and about economic development and aid. As at every press conference or special occasion, Mrs. Nixon spoke without notes. Once after her news conference, a newsman who had come to Liberia from London representing *Newsweek* asked me if Mrs. Nixon was always that good. "She gives an excellent press conference," he said, "and I had no idea she could do that." I informed him that Mrs. Nixon was quite capable of handling a press conference but usually stayed in the background, hence the press often failed to perceive what she could do.

Also on that busy first day when we were still jet lagged, a mid-afternoon church service was held with ministers of several faiths, including the Reverend Billy Graham. The next morning, a cannon announced the dawn of this important day. At mid-morning inaugural ceremonies President Tolbert was officially sworn into office in Monrovia's Centennial Memorial Pavilion. There was an afternoon inaugural parade followed that evening by an inaugural ball hosted by the president and his wife. I did not foresee then what difficult days lay ahead for Liberia but was disturbed nonetheless by the obvious disparity between rich and poor.

At our next stop, Accra, the capital of Ghana, Mrs. Nixon spoke with many people involved in volunteer work. She saw an old friend, Chief Nana Asse-djan, then eighty-three years old and blind, who remembered meeting her on Ghana's Independence Day in 1957. He and many other chiefs greeted Mrs. Nixon in the Botanical Gardens of Aburi, where they had gathered in her honor for a Durbar, a colorful ceremony reserved for special guests. It was quite a sight, with warrior dances and traditional drumming.

After President and Mrs. Edward Akufo Addo gave a luncheon for Mrs. Nixon in their home, she held official talks with the prime minister. Mrs. Nixon gave a dinner for the prime minister and Ghanaian officials at the residence of the American ambassador, Fred Hadsel. This was my first visit to Ghana, though I would later return.

The White House team arrived ahead of us everywhere. When we arrived at our final stop in Africa, the Ivory Coast (or Côte d'Ivoire), cars and buses were waiting as we stepped off the plane, microphones were in readiness, and our baggage was always in our hotel room when we arrived. As usual, everything appeared in the right place at the right time as if by magic. After ceremonies at the airport and the official motorcade, Mrs. Nixon arrived at the presidential palace in the capital, Abidjan.

At the Hotel Ivoire, where I stayed with the press, was my friend Fannie Granton, assistant editor of *Ebony* magazine. I had asked Fannie to come on this trip and bring her excellent photographer Maurice Sorrell with her, and *Ebony* obliged. Fannie Granton and I had known each other since my early days in American Women in Radio and Television. When I worked at the White House, I invited her to come as often as she could as a member of the press corps. I liked *Ebony* and thought it would be good to have Mrs. Nixon's events covered in the country's major African-American magazine.

Mrs. Nixon made a skillful transition from visits to special projects to meetings with presidents and prime ministers. That evening, the president, Félix Houphouet-Boigny, and his wife hosted an official dinner at the presidential palace. Next day Mrs. Nixon again met with the press. As at other press conferences on the trip, Mrs. Nixon said she was looking forward to going to China soon with the president and hoped to meet women leaders there. That coming trip was to be the historic visit to China.

As we flew back to Washington, I asked Mrs. Nixon if she had found her trip satisfying. She had enjoyed every minute, she said, and expressed her belief that nothing improves understanding better than people-to-people contact.

It was nighttime in Washington as the big 707 touched down at Andrews Air Force Base. The president had come to the landing strip with their daughters to welcome his wife home with smiles and hugs. My husband was there to meet me, and I too felt it had been a great trip.

End of a Love Affair

It had been almost thirty years since my marriage to Ink Gates, and our children were now in their twenties, with Pam working in Sun Valley, Idaho, and Larry a senior at the University of Virginia. For Ink and me, it had been a long love marriage. But there were problems I could not overcome that led me to divorce my husband. I had always dreamed of being married for at least fifty years as my mother and father had been, but it was not to be. I had lost twenty pounds grieving over how I could save my marriage. My mother told me later I was so thin she thought I was dying of cancer and would not tell her.

I have been told that anyone writing about the death of a marriage should lay out all the reasons, especially in this era when people lay bare their personal lives for all to see. In this I must disappoint.

My colleagues at The Breakfast Show showed great understanding of my grief over my divorce and of my absence for legal proceedings.

My American Red Cross International Committee in Washington was extremely helpful to me during this time. One member who had recently lost her husband shared many of her interests in the art world with me. The chairman was sensitive and kind and gave me a great deal of responsibility. Not long after she left Washington I became chairman of the committee. Women from many embassies

Patricia Gates Lynch, United States Ambassador to Madagascar and the Comoros.

Tyrone Power with Pat painting scenery at Westport Playhouse, Connecticut.

Pat broadcasts in the window for WFAX with Nelson Eddy.

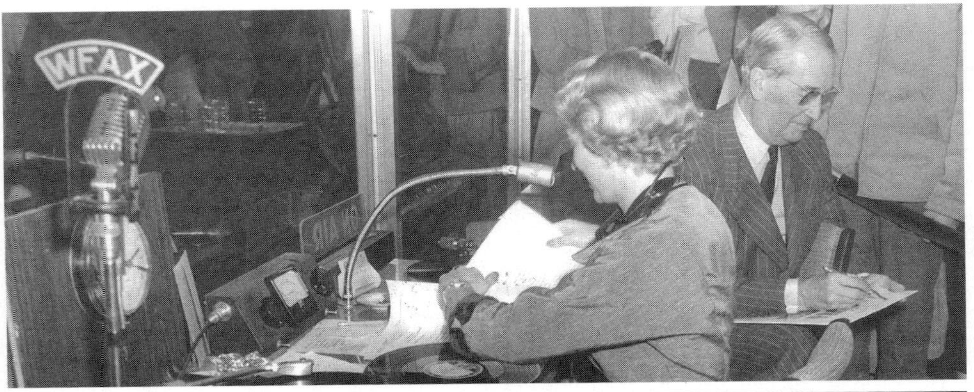

The famous French actor and singer, Maurice Chevalier, visits Pat at her WFAX window studio.

Ink, Pat, and Larry Gates with Ed Sullivan, on the stage of "The Ed Sullivan Theatre," in New York.

Pat with President Lyndon B. Johnson at the White House.

Barbara Bush, Chairman of the Red Cross Congressional Wives Committee, George Elsey, President of the American Red Cross, with Pat at the Capitol.

Pat, President of AWRT, with Senator Charles Percy and Loraine Percy.

Bob Hope comes to Pat's VOA studio for an interview.

Pat Nixon joins the musicians in Lahore, Pakistan. Background, left to right, Fran Lewine (AP), Pat Gates (staff) with sunglasses, Helen Thomas, (UPI) , Nancy Dickerson (NBC), 1969.

Supreme Court Justice Sandra Day O'Connor swears in Patricia Gates Lynch as United States Ambassador, with Bill Lynch in center, and on the left, the Honorable Timothy L. Towell.

Ronald Reagan welcomes his new ambassador to the Oval Office.

President Ratsiraka welcomes Pat to Madagascar.

Annabella visits Pat in Madagascar.

Pat greets Pope John Paul II in Madagascar.

Pat with Gene Pell, President for Radio Free Europe/Radio Liberty, the interpreter, and Lech Walesa, President of Poland at RFE/RL office in Washington.

Pat with Daniel Boorstin, Author and Librarian of Congress Emeritus, on the beach at Scientists' Cliffs, Maryland.

President George H. W. Bush talks with Pat Gates Lynch and Bill Lynch.

While at VOA, Pat goest to Nancy Reagan's Christmas party at the White House and meets J. R. (Larry Hagman) of TV's Dallas fame.

In 2004, the 101st AIRBORNE'S Lt. General Julian J. Ewell celebrates the anniversary of D-Day with Pat Gates Lynch.

Pat interviews Mr. Liu, the Vice President of All China Federation and Commerce, at his home in Beijing, October, 1982.

Pat at the Social Service Center of the Stalla Maris College, Madras, India, with student volunteers and their wards.

Pat visits a Malay woman in her house at Kampurg Surgai, near Kuala Lumpur. Malaysia.

Pat Gates and Voice of America's Phil Irwin visit the East Africa Flying Doctor Service, in Kenya.

General G. C. Gailey, then Commanding General of M.D.W., presents the Army's Outstanding Public Service Award to Pat Gates and Rosanne McQuarrie, who wrote, voiced and produced the radio show in 1960, "U. S. Lady on the Air," WFAX, Fairfax, Virginia. U. S. Army Photo.

The Ambassador (Pat Gates Lynch) feeds the Lemurs in Madagascar.

volunteered their time at Red Cross headquarters and my committee included wives of officials like the secretary of state, the chairman of the military joint chiefs of staff, several ambassadors' wives, and others. When you are alone, you meet new people and find new strengths.

A thoughtful navy wife, Kay Gayler, invited me and my children to visit her and her admiral husband Noel in Pearl Harbor for that first Christmas after my divorce. Larry was already there as a lieutenant in the army. And so our first Christmas was not dreary at all. Admiral Gayler as CINCPAC (Commander in Chief Pacific) commanded all United States forces in the Pacific. We stayed in their guesthouse and had all our meals with them in their navy quarters. Larry joined us whenever he could. The ships in the harbor were decorated with Christmas tree lights, which considerably brightened up a sad time for me.

The admiral piloted me in his helicopter over the USS *Arizona*, the battleship sunk when Pearl Harbor was attacked in 1941. Looking down, I could see the outline of the sunken ship most distinctly, sobered by the knowledge of the many bodies still on board left to rest in peace.

Among the Gaylers' many guests at a reception during the holidays was former congresswoman and ambassador Clare Boothe Luce. She suggested to Pam that she consider staying in Hawaii to work. Mrs. Luce had Pam and me for lunch at her house so Pam could talk to her assistant about how to find a job. Soon Pam did just that and spent two years working in Hawaii. I would be traveling myself in the next few years and was able to come through Hawaii while both children were there.

I was learning how a newly single woman copes in a variety of business and social situations after thirty years of being a "couple." Sometimes I felt like only half a person until good friends assured me that I was fully accepted on my own. Eventually, I learned that being single was not necessarily a permanent state. Meanwhile, plans were underway at The Breakfast Show for a remarkable trip to far-off places.

Breakfast Show World Tour

Bill Reynolds, our Breakfast Show chief, was eager for my colleague Phil Irwin and me to travel around the world to talk about our program, meet our listeners, and have them meet us. Our embassies were enthusiastic about our visiting their capitals, and soon cables were flying back and forth as plans took shape.

Phil and I took off on Pan American Airways for Accra, Ghana, first stop on our world trip. Pan Am had photographed us waving goodbye at the top of the plane's steps several weeks before the journey began. The whole scene was blown up to poster size with our names and the VOA logo on the bottom. Beneath the picture, it said, "Pat Gates and Philip Irwin, stars of Voice of America's Breakfast Show, will be here soon." The poster was sent to all the U.S. embassies and diplomatic posts we would visit, and everywhere we went we would see it prominently displayed, in hotels, embassies, and USIA libraries. It was a new experience for us to see Indian, African, and other newspapers writing about our visit and, sometimes, putting our pictures on the front page.

After our month-long trip many evaluations came in saying our visits had proved successful beyond all expectations. One wrote, "The informal evenings attracted capacity crowds. Many fans traveled two to three hundred miles to attend. Question-and-answer sessions revealed genuine interest in VOA programs and things American."

Another evaluation said, "As it turned out we filled the 650-seat hall and to our considerable surprise the audience included dozens of members of primary importance (judges of the Supreme Court, senior government officials, university professors, students, etc.)."

Back home, our chief, Bill Reynolds, wrote, "The tour took the two major "Breakfast Show" hosts to twelve cities in nine countries in thirty-two days of tightly scheduled travel. The trip was proposed as a personal appearance and goodwill mission with several aims:

> To honor the many requests from VOA listeners that Pat and Phil visit their countries, cities, villages, and even homes;

to afford the hosts an opportunity to renew that vital "sensitivity to audience";

To show interest in local activities and projects particularly those which "The Breakfast Show" has featured and fostered, such as volunteer work and environmental concern;

And to promote interest in not only "The Breakfast Show," but the Voice of America, the United States Information Service, and the nation itself.

In Accra, Ghana, Phil and I were met by a large group of listeners waving signs. That night, we gave a two-hour performance at the Open Air Accra Art Center. The evening was emceed by a popular Ghanaian radio personality, and included a live band. Phil and I danced the national dance, the Hi-Life, with many people, which was great fun. Phil told some of his jokes, and I gained an appreciation of his humor when I saw the audience response. I talked and read a poem, "Desiderata" (author unknown), and we gave away a shortwave radio and other gifts. Listeners had small gifts for us too. Everything was filmed for a later broadcast. It was quite a night.

During our stay in Ghana, we toured an industrialization center and other sites, but soon it was time to leave for Lagos, then capital of Nigeria. The audience in Lagos of about 250 was drawn mostly from a youth club composed of university students and young professionals, but also included a few older people, some from considerable distances. The program was televised, we were interviewed the next day, and there were more visits to projects. Then we flew to the city of Kaduna in northern Nigeria to give another performance.

After many meetings and talking with "Breakfast Show" listeners, we were off to Nairobi, Kenya. Because the VOA radio signal there was weak, fewer listeners showed up than in the other cities we visited. We thus concentrated on local radio interviews and a live TV show. We conducted an interview of our own with the Flying Doctor Service that flies medical aid to remote areas, a humanitarian effort supported by the United States. One night at a mountain lodge outside of Nairobi, we saw a family of elephants gathered at a water hole. What a great experience it was to see elephants in the wild for the first time.

On we flew to Karachi, Pakistan, for more on-stage appearances. We were pleased that all the tickets had been taken for our performance, so a second program was hastily arranged. We happily met with the second crowd, which included many university students. Phil and I took questions on all aspects of American life.

We did Radio Pakistan interviews, and while Phil visited several environmental research and city-planning organizations, I toured social welfare projects. For the first time in my life, I visited a leprosy hospital, where I spoke with the woman doctor in charge. She spoke of new highly effective drugs and regretted that outsiders lacked confidence. Many of the patients had been cured of leprosy and were eager to meet me. It would help, she said, if I would shake hands with them. When I held out my hand, I felt as though I were leapfrogging over centuries of anguish into a new and wondrous era.

I was much impressed by the women of South Asia, where the volunteer concept is very much alive. I heard one woman say, "When you start to volunteer one day a week, soon you are working every day."

I was graciously received by the governor of Sind, the Begum Liaquat Ali Khan. She had just moved into the governor's house the day before our meeting. Her husband, now dead, had been a prime minister of Pakistan. She hosted a tea in my honor, where I met a stimulating group of women. Most were members of the All Pakistan Women's Association (APWA). One woman who had studied for her doctorate in the United States told me to my great pleasure, "You do a great service for humanity with your program. I especially like your philosophy when you say 'If you see someone without a smile, give him one of yours.'"

Then off we flew to India. At our first stop, New Delhi, we gave a performance on the lawn of the U.S. Information Service. Phil spoke of American life and something about his life on his farm. Everywhere people asked him about the farm, and they asked me about my children and my house on the Chesapeake Bay, all subjects they had heard us talk about on The Breakfast Show. I also gave my views on the similarity of aspirations among people all over the world, and again I read that poem everyone seemed to like called "Desiderata," which can be found in many American kitchens, usually on the refrigerator. When I'd read it one day on the Breakfast Show, people wrote in from everywhere asking for a copy, so I thought it appropriate to read during our evening programs. Its familiar opening lines—" Go placidly amid the noise and haste, and remember what peace there may be in silence"—suggest its wise and uplifting spirit. Its ending, in particular, reflected my own philosophy: "With all its sham, drudgery, and broken dreams, it is still a beautiful world. Be cheerful, strive to be happy."

At the headquarters of the Indian Red Cross, I talked about my work with the Red Cross at home and learned about the many Red Cross activities in New Delhi and visited a childcare center. We met with listeners under a Shamiana, a beautiful canopy, and were touched by a student who had traveled 250 miles just to meet us.

On a trip to see the magnificent Taj Mahal, as we drove along crowded roads, I spied an elephant whose owner held a sign saying travelers could ride the elephant. I didn't care how much this looked like a tourist stop, I had always wanted to ride an elephant, and we stopped. With great effort I climbed up to the elephant's head over his rear quarters. Soon I was lumbering along high above the cars and the people. The ride was short, but I was delighted and felt safer on the back of the elephant than in the back seat of the car in which we'd been traveling.

In New Delhi, I discussed nuclear power plants in the cities of the future with a young city planner. Next we performed in Bombay. As in many of our "Evenings with Pat and Phil" in country after country, more than six hundred people attended. Phil and I were always pleased when our hosts found our visit proved successful beyond expectations.

When we arrived in Bombay, I was thrilled to see from my hotel window the great stone "Gateway to India." Pictures I had seen could not begin to capture it, with hundreds of people walking around it on the docks and with big ships and little boats in the harbor. Bombay is a great metropolis inhabited by extraordinary people. Shocking poverty also dwells there. Everywhere in the city, I talked with people dedicated to helping ease this terrible poverty and visited a family-planning training and research center.

At a workshop for the blind I had one of my greatest experiences as a broadcaster. I had read that these much-needed workshops were well organized and well run. As I was finishing my tour, a blind young man came out of the administrative office where he worked as an assistant. I remember the moment I met him as clearly as if it were occurring this very instant. He took my hand and said, "I have listened to you on the Voice of America for years, but I never dreamed I would ever meet you. I cannot see you, yet I know you."

I told him in turn that when I say, "Good Morning" on the Breakfast Show, "I cannot see you, yet I know we have shared many thoughts and experiences. I will think of you now when I am broadcasting."

I suddenly realized that our conversation was important but wasn't sure why. Thinking about that blind man while watching the clouds out the window flying home, illuminating ideas began to form. *That's it*, I thought, *I know why that man is so important. He has shown me that I too am blind when I sit in front of my microphone. I cannot see the people around the globe who write and tell me they are listening. Millions of people? That's what I'm told. But I always talk to only one person, or at most to one family. It is because I can't see them and they can't see me that we connect, more than if we were watching each other on television in the same room. When I'm broadcasting, I try to put myself into the mind of my listener, to think what he or she would like to know about my country, or would like me to ask a guest to discuss. We are visualizing each other directly, without the interference of thousands of miles between us. We connect instantaneously, although we are blind.*

Visitors to our studios in Washington would affirm the connection. One university student from India wanted to talk with me, he said, because he had listened to the program since he was a young boy. He had learned about America from the Breakfast Show, which now was a help to him as a student at Harvard. We had connected.

A man from Romania came to visit my studio when the Iron Curtain was still drawn tightly around his country. "I am here on a conference," he said, "the first time I have been allowed out of my country in years. Please don't tell anyone I left the conference briefly to come here to see you and tell you that when you travel with your microphone, you take me with you on your trips. That is when I am able to see and do things I cannot do at home." We had connected.

At the microphone, I often thought of the blind man in India, whose name I do not know. Today, my VOA microphone sits in my little studio at the Bay, reminding me of the day I learned from a man who could not see that I too was blind and that my not being able to see him helped create that strong bond—that connection—between us.

In Bombay, several guests had come from as far away as Poona and one young man had come from Kolhapur to see our performance. We posed for pictures with many of the people in the audience and received beautiful bouquets of flowers. We gave away some books and presented a transistor radio to one listener who had been awarded it almost two years before in a VOA listeners contest. But long customs delays had held up the actual arrival of the radio until that evening.

Mrs. J. R. D. Tata, wife of India's leading industrialist, told me she had been listening to The Breakfast Show for years. One woman in the audience told me she saw a strong blue aura around me, stronger than any she had ever seen before. Sometimes now when I am tired, I think that the aura might be fading! As our car pulled away after the performance, some people ran after us throwing flowers. People in the United States never knew us as we were known in cities around the world, so for us this was a most unusual experience.

We headed south for the city of Madras. According to the post report, we met our "most enthusiastic response in India in Madras. Many invitees overstayed the function (An Evening with . . .) to collect autographs and talk personally with Pat and Phil."

In Madras, we were interviewed by All India Radio and were invited to join the radio's orchestra. Though we weren't very good at playing their strange instruments, we tried and had a fine time.

At the Social Service Center of the Stella Maris College, we visited with student volunteers and the little children they cared for. We observed a growing volunteer spirit in the south, as we had everywhere we visited in Pakistan and India.

In a cover story in the *Radio Times of India,* S. M. Muzumdar wrote, "One reason why 'The Breakfast Show' remains popular is that it always focuses on people — their foibles, successes, problems, failures, hopes and dreams, and their achievements." Phil and I were always happy to read that people had sensed what "The Breakfast Show" was about.

We were scheduled to go to Dacca, the capital of Bangladesh next. But it was election time there, and because of unrest and anti-American attitudes in some quarters, we were advised not to go by the post in Dacca. We were disappointed. In an article about the cancellation of our trip, the *Los Angeles Times* wrote that the American embassy did not want us to take unnecessary risks.

Once again we were on our way, this time to Colombo, capital of the country once known as Ceylon and now called Sri Lanka. Here "Our Evening with . . ." was in the Lionel Wendt Theater, where every seat was taken. The audience included university professors, students, lawyers, people from every walk of life, and the questions as always were challenging. Among projects we visited, Phil went to Boys' Town, I to a handicraft and agricultural project, where my host was a member of Parliament.

In Kuala Lumpur, Malaysia, we were greeted warmly at our performance. I well recall visiting a Malaysian woman at her small house at Kampung Sungai. I took off my shoes to enter her house, where she stood in her bare feet, her slippers at the door. She made me feel very much at home. There we were, two women worlds apart in our cultures and yet friends.

And then there was the rubber tree! After many unsuccessful efforts and several demonstrations by my new Malaysian friends of how to draw latex from a tree, I cut a knife into the side of the tree and out came the latex. When shown how to draw water from a well at the home of a resident of Kampung Mindah, I discovered it was not an easy job at all. On the first two tries, I lost all the water just as I pulled the bucket to the top of the well. Finally, I made it without losing a drop. The women gathered found me quite funny and not very adept!

In Singapore there was no performance, and we had a bad initial experience. The embassy officer who met us told us several times that he was much too busy to spend time with us and made us feel extremely unwelcome. We did not appreciate his rudeness. We also felt exhausted because of our strenuous schedule. All other official welcomes on our trip had been warm and welcoming, I'm happy to say! Thanks to advance efforts by His Excellency Ernest Monteiro, at that time ambassador of Singapore to the United States, we were met by leading citizens, shown around the city, and taken to the Kidney Foundation hospital. We also visited Radio-TV Singapore, the university, and the industrial complex.

Our next stop was Jakarta, Indonesia, my second visit to the country and a busy one. Here we were warmly greeted at the airport by American embassy official Ivan Campbell and his wife Carroll. We had been greeted all along the way by American embassy officers, usually from the U.S. Information Service. We started off at Radio Republik Indonesia (RRI). Although all Indonesian government offices closed on Friday afternoons, RRI was kind enough to devote the entire morning hours to us that Friday. The director of radio, Abdul Hamid, escorted us into a meeting with fifty of his key radio personnel. For more than two hours we exchanged views on broadcasting, with the Indonesians actively participating.

Director Hamid presented Phil and me with Wayang Golek wooden puppets as souvenirs from Indonesia. To this day, my puppet sits on a table in my office. Later that day, we lunched with more radio people, and in the evening attended a reception given for us with forty Indonesian guests. At that time, we were told, radio was by far the most important of all media in Indonesia as a source of news and information, with the greatest impact on attitude and opinions.

I liked Jakarta, a city growing at a great rate. It had changed even from the time I had visited before. I did not know then that I would be coming back. But now, it was time to return to Washington, my family, and my microphone at the Voice of America.

Despite the unbelievable hours of work and travel, this world trip was an extraordinary experience. I discovered that the United States had many friends and could make many more if we continued to value the importance of good communication, both on the air and on the scene. In the twenty-first century, we would need good communication more than ever.

13

Highs and Lows

Returned POWs at the White House

What an extraordinary evening it was! I was back at the White House for the largest dinner ever held there until that time. It was May 24, 1973, the prisoners of war (POWs) were home from Vietnam, and they all knew that President Nixon had worked hard to free them. When the guests began arriving at 6:30 p.m., the former prisoners were escorted up to the Nixons' personal living room on the third floor, where President and Mrs. Nixon gave them an especially warm welcome. I went with them and watched President Nixon greet them. It had been several weeks since I had seen him, and worries about the Vietnam war and his Watergate problems weighed mightily upon him. He looked quite aged and tired, with a heaviness in his face that I had not seen before. Yet this night, he was greatly bolstered by the former prisoners, who were thanking him and praising him for his efforts on their behalf. They were happy to be home and wanted him to share their happiness.

The guests, from every station of life and all parts of the United States, included officers and enlisted men, many in uniform, some in civilian dress. The women wore long dresses, beaming with pride and happiness to have their men by their sides. The evening saw many reunions. Men who had been prisoners together introduced their wives to each other with great joy. Many came up to Secretary of State Henry Kissinger, patted him on the back, and thanked him for all he had done for them. He was obviously pleased by the attention.

One of the returned POWs, Lt. Commander John S. McCain III, in dress white navy uniform, had been a prisoner in Vietnam for several years, enduring severe hardship. He would later become a United States senator and make a try for the presidency.

Music filled the air, with the Air Force Band playing at the East Gate entrance, the Navy String Group in the East Wing corridor where the state flags hung, the Marine Orchestra in the Grand Hall, and the Navy Band playing on the balcony as the guests descended for dinner on the South Lawn. A gigantic striped tent bedecked with flowers and chandeliers sheltered the guests from the rain outside, as the president expressed the nation's pride in that evening's honored guests. For two hours before the dinner, every room in the White House, including the family quarters, had been opened to the more than three hundred guests. The men and their wives were delighted to see the Lincoln Room, the Treaty Room, the guest rooms, in addition to the private sitting room where the president had greeted them. Many of the guests appeared overwhelmed by meeting the president and just being in the White House.

After dinner, Bob Hope served as the master of ceremonies for the entertainment in the tent, which presented some of America's best known entertainers—Jimmy Stewart, John Wayne, Irving Berlin, Sammy Davis Jr., and many others. Each took a moment at the microphone to hail this night as a career high point. The guests gave standing ovations to the president, the entertainers, and the hard-working White House staff.

For me, one of the high points of the evening came when I slipped away for a moment to the library, where I frequently sought a few moments of reflection in my White House days. The library was an intimate room with soft grey and rose paneling and rose and green draperies. The Gilbert Stuart portrait of George Washington hung over the mantel, portraits of American Indians on the wall. Bookcases held a good selection of reading matter, and a round-top Duncan Phyfe table stood in the center of the room. On this night, I felt pretty sure the library would be empty and I could sit there a few minutes to reflect upon the evening. I was wrong.

There in front of the fireplace sat the great songwriter Irving Berlin, who beckoned me to sit opposite him by the fire. We spoke about the historic event we were witnessing that night. I told him of how my admiring parents had told me the story of his romance with Ellin Mackay, who became his wife. I recalled but didn't say that the story had been about how the socially prominent father of Miss Mackay had objected strenuously to his daughter's friendship with a Jewish immigrant songwriter and how everyone cheered when they married in spite of the hurdles. When I asked Mr. Berlin whether the song he wrote for his wife during their courtship had been the one that began "Remember the night, the night we met," he replied, "No, the important song I wrote for her began. 'I'll be loving you, always.' And I meant it."

 I still think of Irving Berlin when I hear his many beautiful songs, especially the one we sing perhaps more than any other, "God Bless America."

The homecoming of the prisoners of war had moved America. This emotional evening at the White House, with its undercurrent of thanksgiving, was truly one of the greatest celebrations.

End of an Era

President Nixon resigned as president on August 9, 1974. I remember the day well. I was at the White House in the office of Walter Tkach, the president's doctor. Even after I had left the staff he had continued seeing me as his patient, which wasn't often.

On this day of my last visit, Dr. Tkach told me they were all urging "the Boss" to hold on, "to fight the impeachment threat," because they were sure he could win. I replied that it was all over out there, and there was no hope of his not having to resign. The president would resign, he said, if necessary to keep the country from going through any more turmoil. The doctor still hoped it wouldn't be necessary for the president to give up.

Shortly after our conversation, the announcement came from the White House that the president had resigned and would be addressing the nation that evening. His speech was a thoughtful one, and I recall thinking of how it would sound as it went out across the world on the Voice of America. The next morning the now-resigned president gave another speech, as he and his family stood in the East Room ready to leave. This time his speech was rambling. He was sad and broke down.

My son Larry was with me as we watched the farewell on television in my apartment overlooking Washington, from which I could see the trees in front of the White House. As the White House helicopter began its lift-off from the White House lawn I went to the window and saw it rise above those trees and vanish on its flight to Andrews Air Force Base, where the Nixons would board Air Force One and fly to their home in California.

Larry felt sorry for me knowing that I was saying goodbye to friends as well as to a president. I telephoned the doctor's office and Genevieve, his nurse, answered the phone. She was crying hard and told me all the staff had gathered to wave goodbye, with many tears. The doctor had left with the president and would accompany him to California on Air Force One.

Over twenty years later, I had lunch with Rex Scouten, then about to retire from his post as White House curator. We talked about his time in the White House and especially about the Nixons. Rex had served ten presidents, beginning with President Truman, having been chief usher before becoming curator. Before that he had been a Secret Service agent and traveled to forty-two countries when he was assigned to Vice President Richard Nixon. They went to Hanoi and further south when the French were still fighting there. He said he thoroughly enjoyed his time with the Nixons, both in those early days and later at the White House.

In the years following his resignation, Richard Nixon regained his stature as a statesman and seemed to prove his mettle in adversity. He wrote books and advised his successors who sought his counsel, especially concerning foreign relations. Nixon and Henry Kissinger had worked well together and forged a coherent foreign policy. Nixon's capacity to look ahead could be seen, for example, in his opening the way to relations with China.

I was touched by President Nixon's handwritten note to me on the bottom of his more formal thank-you for the letter I had written him at the time of Mrs. Nixon's death. He wrote of my friendship meaning a great deal to her. He always remembered those who had worked at the White House.

Freedom Still Rings

The Breakfast Show listeners said they liked hearing about American history and about those things that make our country what it is. One guest on my program, General Harold K. Johnson, served this purpose well. (He had been the colonel with whom I served on a PTA board years earlier when our girls attended the same grammar school.) One night he had come to dinner with his wife Dorothy and had looked out the window of my apartment in Virginia, which had a spectacular view of the city of Washington. In front of us lay some of our country's most important monuments.

Pointing to the Lincoln Memorial he said, "In that building we have the compassion and the humanity of a great American, President Abraham Lincoln. In the Washington Monument, we can see the courage and stick-to-itiveness of George Washington, the man who really made us a nation. Then, in the great Capitol Dome, our senators and representatives have an open discussion and reconcile our inevitable differences. It is essential that these differences be reconciled." The general added another building—the great cathedral high on a hill over Washington, where, he said, "You can see the spiritual role integral to the creation of our nation! With these four monuments, you see the major part of the strength and substance of our country." I so liked what General Johnson had to say about them that I invited him to share his explanation of what these buildings stand for with my Breakfast Show audience.

The "Spirit of '76"

Phil Irwin and I were eager to do something special for the bicentennial celebration, the two hundredth birthday of the United States. We hoped to tell our listeners about all the exciting things that would be happening on the Fourth of July 1976! We couldn't be everywhere at once, we knew, but as it turned out we almost were. We went to Philadelphia, the birthplace of our Declaration of Independence, about a week before the big day and from Independence Hall taped the story of the Declaration to be played on the Fourth

We talked about one of the great American icons, the Liberty Bell, visible to us from Independence Hall. Across the top of the bell are the words "Proclaim liberty throughout all the land unto all the inhabitants thereof" — placed on the bell when it was first cast in 1751.

Back in Washington, I telephoned my good friend, Mary Shen, working in the USIA office in New York, in hopes she might find me a press ticket so I could come to New York on the Fourth to report to my Breakfast Show listeners on the tall ships scheduled to sail the Hudson River that day. She was unable to find me a ticket but invited me to come with her to a friend's apartment on Riverside Drive facing the Hudson. Millions of people were in New York that day to see the largest fleet every assembled of tall sailing ships. After the parade of ships, I took a bus to the airport and flew to Washington. With good luck, I arrived in time for the gigantic fireworks display on the grounds of the Washington Monument! For days after the Fourth, I was telling my listeners about watching the magnificent tall ships sailing by and my other holiday adventures walking, busing, and flying with my tape recorder over my shoulder!

A Full Mailbox

Our Breakfast Show listeners wrote often, and we answered every letter. A good part of our return letters contained scripted responses, but I always wrote with pen and ink at the bottom of each one thanking the person for listening and for writing.

Phil and I especially appreciated the letters we received from Professor Arthur Lazarus of Durban, South Africa. In one he wrote that in South Africa at that time, when a man of color woke up in the morning he never knew how his day would go. When Phil on his program or I on mine would say, "Good Morning!" Dr. Lazarus said it would change his whole day, that the program eased the burdens of living in a restricted society. When he visited me during my days at the White House, I was happy to meet him. He had earned his doctorate at Yale University and knew this country well but it was his first visit to the White House. I thought of him years later when I was in South Africa and wished he were still alive so that I might visit him.

A young girl from Tibet also visited me at the White House. She had written us at VOA from a refugee camp saying that our programs made her believe there really was an outside world worth living for. When she came to see me in her national dress she said it had been her great good fortune to come to the United States thanks to a church sponsorship, and she had called the Voice of America to learn my whereabouts.

A man in Birmingham, England, wrote frequently, and we found ourselves looking forward to his letters because he would mention specific interviews and tell us why he had enjoyed them. He would tell us all about his family and loved hearing about my Pam and Larry and being part of their lives as they grew through the years.

Dr. Gene Griffith, an American medical missionary, wrote from Vietnam, Kenya, Liberia, and other countries where he worked. He used my program as a teaching tool, he wrote, when he gathered together the Montagnards in Vietnam to tell them about America. The requested photograph on which I had written, "If you see someone without a smile, give him one of yours!" had hung on the wall of every medical ward in which he had performed operations. He visited me while in Washington to receive an award as one of the ten most outstanding young Americans of the year

More Microphone Memories

In speeches I gave to organizations in and out of Washington, I usually talked about the Voice of America and the Breakfast Show. Occasionally I tried something a little different. I would take my microphone and an engineer onto the stage and interview a guest in front of the audience, taping the interview and playing it later on my program. Thus it was that I made two close friends, both named Charlotte.

Charlotte Moton Hubbard and I had met when I first broadcast for WFAX. Like her, I became a member of American Women in Radio and Television. A tall handsome woman, Charlotte was the daughter of Dr. Robert Moton, second president of Tuskegee Institute and successor to Tuskegee's founder and first president, the renowned Dr. Booker T. Washington. After working for the Girl Scouts of America and a CBS radio station, Charlotte at the time of our interview was deputy assistant secretary of state for public affairs, the first African American woman to attain that high a rank in our government.

Many times Charlotte and I would talk about the history of her race and of her father. As president of one of the foremost black universities for fifty years, Dr. Moton was considered a leader of the Negro people. Today, of course, we say either "black" or "African American." Charlotte always preferred to be called black, saying the difference between us was that she was black and I was white. I had much to learn in those days, and Charlotte took me under her wing. Her husband, Dr. Maceo Hubbard, was an attorney in the Department of Justice. A friend had looked up Charlotte's family history at a time when everyone was looking at his or her roots, thanks to Alex Haley's best-selling book on the subject. Her friend's investigation turned up an ancestor who was an African chief and said Charlotte must therefore be of royal blood. I was not a bit surprised nor would anyone have been who knew Charlotte.

She invited me to her church in Washington to read with her some of James Weldon Johnson's poetry from his book *God's Trombones, Seven Negro Sermons in Verse*. We then did the same at my church in

Maryland. Both churches granted us the daily sermon time for the poetry reading. After our readings, Charlotte spoke of her father, reciting his stirring creed, which included the inspirational words: "I believe in the fellowship of men of good will—in their ability to live together in peace."

When I interviewed Charlotte Hubbard in front of the Army Engineer Officers' Wives Club in Washington, we talked about her responsibilities at the Department of State. She supervised publications both national and regional, worked on foreign policy conferences, and liaised with the news media, sometimes meeting with the press and acting as spokesperson for Secretary of State Dean Rusk. We kept in touch over the years, and when Charlotte died, I was asked to participate in her memorial service. Naturally, I read from James Weldon Johnson's poetry.

My other close friend Charlotte was U.S. Representative Charlotte Reid (Illinois 15th District, 1962–71), a widow with four children from Aurora, Illinois. We lived in the same apartment building. I had met her once or twice and was pleased when she agreed to my request for a VOA interview on stage in front of an audience. We talked about the scarcity of women in Congress at that time and how fortunate she felt to be one of them. I told her about my encounter with Thomas P. "Tip" O'Neill, the prominent Democratic representative from Massachusetts, later Speaker of the House, who had spoken to me about her. "She may be a Republican," he'd said, "but she is one of our most favorite persons." Representative Reid served on the House Appropriations Committee and was repeatedly reelected with bipartisan support in her Illinois district. She was the first woman to wear a pantsuit on the floor of the House of Representatives, a daring act in its day that she carried off with aplomb.

Using the stage name Annette King, Charlotte Reid, had once been the leading female singer on "The Don McNeil Breakfast Club," a highly popular radio program originating in Chicago. Even in Congress, she belonged to a singing group. We kept in close touch when she retired to Illinois, where she died in 2007.

Among my memorable interviews were several I recorded with Alex Haley, author of *Roots*, the best-selling book that stirred a widespread desire to investigate one's ancestors, whatever color or race. *Roots* tells the saga of an American family, his own family. We recorded the interviews all at once so I could air them over several weeks. He talked about the basis of his book, the oral histories passed down from generation to generation in his family. He went all the way back to his great-great-great-great-grandfather, Kunta Kinte, brought as a slave to Annapolis, Maryland, in 1767 from the Gambia in West Africa. *Roots* won the Pulitzer Prize and became a much-watched television miniseries.

Bob Hope, that great American, came to my studio for an interview I would use on the Fourth of July. What a delightful man! We think of him as a jokester, a genius at making people laugh, but on this day he was intensely serious, so the interview was unusual. He had come to Washington for "Honor America Day" ceremony, chaired by Willard Marriott. Hope explained that because of our problems in Vietnam at the time, people were ready to count their blessings. He would be the master of ceremonies for the event, to be held at the Washington Monument in the evening, which would include the Reverend Billy Graham, Jack Benny, Kate Smith, Red Skelton, and Les Brown and his "Band of Renown." The band often accompanied Bob Hope overseas to entertain our far-flung troops.

I asked Bob why his sense of humor seemed to make people so happy. He thought freedom of speech makes it possible to criticize government leaders and others without fear, and telling jokes so freely makes people laugh and relax.

Humor was his personal philosophy for living and an important quality in our lives. "It's a beautiful world," he said, "and we will lick all these problems we have. We may develop new ones but we will lick those too." When Bob Hope left my studio, I thought how natural he was, despite his fame and fortune.

In my interview with the astronaut Michael Collins, he talked about staying with the spaceship while his fellow passengers walked on the moon during that first manned moon landing on July 20, 1969. Back here on earth, he said, he often looked up at the night sky and marveled that man had made it to the moon.

The famous boxer Muhammad Ali came one day to our Voice of America studios. Previously known as Cassius Clay, he has been named the greatest heavyweight champion of all time, among his many honors. I was busy in my office on the day of his visit, but someone came to tell me I should come meet him in the director's office. I have always been glad I did. Here was a man who radiated love and goodness. He shook my hand, put an arm about me, and smiled a friendly, warm smile of the sort I spoke of in my sign-off. I have never forgotten him and can understand now why people call him "great."

In 1960, Muhammad Ali had won the Olympic gold medal in boxing. In 1996, ravaged by Parkinson's disease, he lit the Olympic torch with difficulty in Atlanta, Georgia. Watching him on television, I was saddened but full of admiration for his courage.

Interesting people were always coming to Voice of America, some for my program, others for programs going to just one area of the world. When the king of Ghana came to the African section, he was carried through the halls on a litter held high by members of his staff. I met with him at his invitation, inspired, it seemed, because many on his staff listened to the "Breakfast Show." (They intimated that the king listened, too.) He had come to America to attend a New York museum exhibition of some magnificent gold pieces from Ghana. The king himself was bedecked in gold and cut an impressive figure. Meeting him brought back memories of my own visits to Ghana.

My guests were not always kings or well-known people. Sometimes they were little-known yet important to me, such as Larkin Hart, a retired farmer from Williston, North Dakota. In our interview, we talked about how farming had changed since he first became a farmer in 1910. He had come to North Dakota from Illinois and grew hard spring wheat, which was sold all over the United States and overseas. In the beginning, he did everything by hand and used walking plows. Then, when tractors and other machines came along, many acres of wheat could be planted in a very short time. North Dakota was also cattle country, and he raised both cattle and hogs. Many farmers now live in town, he said, but continue to commute to work their farmland in the country, which would have surprised his grandfather. When I asked him why, looking back on his life, he liked being a farmer, he replied, "It's the best life yet."

Whenever possible, I would go to concerts and plays in the evenings, accompanied by Ink when he wasn't traveling. One night at the third annual All-City Choral Music Festival in Constitution Hall, we heard a group of young singers from the Washington schools. I thought right away that if Ed Sullivan could hear and see what we were seeing, he would want these young people to appear on his television program. I had interviewed Ed Sullivan back in Munich, where he told me that he was always looking for talent on his trips and if I ever had any suggestions I should let him know. He had later invited Ink and me to watch his show being televised in New York City, and we went up from Washington with our son Larry. Ed and his staff treated us royally, and that night we heard Liza Minelli, Judy Garland's daughter, on stage as a new singing talent.

The day after the concert at Constitution Hall, I telephoned Ed and asked him if he would like to have the wonderful Washington school children we had heard at Constitution Hall on his program. He arranged for buses to bring the students to New York, where the director of the D.C. Festival Chorus and her students appeared on "The Ed Sullivan Show." They were a smash hit. I told all about it on the Breakfast Show and interviewed the chorus director.

My parents always watched the Ed Sullivan Show and had been pleased when I wrote home that I had met him in Munich. They admired his program and his interest in sports (he had written a sports column long before his television days and was considered a sports authority). My mother was alone for ten years after my father died and liked to watch televised baseball games. She had just watched a World Series game before she went to bed and died. It was a blow to her family to lose her and I missed her dreadfully. It helped to recall that she always had said, "When I go, I want to go just like that," and she would snap her fingers. That's just the way it happened. I had seen her two weeks before her death and had told her what a wonderful mother she had been. How grateful I am that I told her in time.

196

Catherine Filene (Mrs. Jouett) Shouse was a frequent guest on the Breakfast Show and audiences loved her. Kay Shouse was a most unusual woman. She was the kind of "Great Lady" often referred to as a vanishing species. She had a tremendous amount of money, which her German immigrant father had earned in the clothing business in Boston, Massachusetts, founding the famous Filene's department store. She had had a fine education, attending college before most women did, and wanted to work, something women of means did not do in those days. In one of our interviews, she told of coming to Washington after college in the 1920s and getting a job with the government. Her angered father cut off her allowance, and at times she didn't have enough money for bus fare and would walk home to her little apartment.

Kay Shouse believed that women have always wanted to work not only for economic reasons but to make a contribution. Her father eventually forgave her, and she made remarkable use of her inheritance by giving the United States the Wolf Trap Farm Park for the Performing Arts, the nation's first such National Park. She not only gave the land and the buildings but also ran the place. We talked about Wolf Trap on the air, notably about the tremendous fire that destroyed almost everything just as the gigantic stage was close to completion. Standing on what remained of the stage, Mrs. Shouse had spoken to the television camera, saying we will rebuild everything and there *will* be a Wolf Trap. Now, people come from around the world to see performances on Wolf Trap's Filene Center Stage. Kay lived to be almost one hundred years old, and her indomitable spirit lives on at Wolf Trap.

On the anniversary of the birthdate in 1890 of General Dwight D. Eisenhower, his daughter-in-law Barbara Eisenhower was a guest on the Breakfast Show. I have known Barbara, a fellow army wife, for a long time. We had met when her husband John Eisenhower and Ink were stationed in Washington at the same time. I knew that Barbara and John and their four children had spent a great deal of time at the White House during the Eisenhower administration and asked her about those days. She talked about how much the president had enjoyed being with his grandchildren at the White House and at his farm, where he had horses for them to ride, and what good times they all had.

She said that the president and his wife, Mamie Eisenhower, never forgot old friends and kept up with them all through the years. His friends, she said, had made him feel it was his patriotic duty to run for the presidency. Once when Mamie was away looking after her ailing mother, Barbara accompanied President Eisenhower on an official trip, staying longest in India but visiting eleven nations in twenty-one days.

On the Breakfast Show Barbara talked about the president as the epitome of a mature person. Ike always seemed to know the right thing to do at all times, she said. The whole family was with him when he died in 1969.

One guest I asked to come to the Breakfast Show many times over the years was Esther Fannie Granton, an African American who talked about current history, the history of the Civil Rights Movement, and the history of African Americans in the United States. A dear friend of many years, Fannie Granton worked for the Johnson Publishing Company and, as mentioned earlier, had been a member of the traveling press corps on Mrs. Nixon's trips to Africa and elsewhere. On the air, we talked about civil rights and the progress or lack thereof for African Americans in this country. Once, unsure how she would answer, I asked Fannie on the air if she thought African Americans were better off today than they had been several years before.

She replied, "Yes, definitely. But there is still a long way to go."

Sitting in the studio and talking off-mike I had expressed my sympathy for her loss of a close relative. Fannie said with compassion that she'd thought of me many times and how difficult it must be without my husband of so many years. "Divorce, too, is like a death," she said, "but life has many compensations." She recommended reading Ralph Waldo Emerson's essay (not the poem) called 'Compensation,' in which Emerson explains that when you lose something in life, something else arises that provides compensation. "You have your work, Pat, which is so important for you, communicating to other people."

Fannie Granton died suddenly on June 16, 1980, and I was shaken by her death. When I later served in Africa, I took her picture with me and put it on my desk. I hoped that Fannie would approve of what I was doing.

A great happiness for me around that time occurred when my son Larry married Jamye, a young woman I could not love more if I had picked her out myself. The wedding took place in Pensacola, Florida. My niece Jeri came with me from Washington and we roomed with Pam, who came in from Colorado. It was a delightful wedding and I enjoyed sharing the details on the air with my friends all over the world! Much later, there would be two granddaughters and I would talk about them, too.

Family weddings put me in mind of my interview with the anthropologist Margaret Mead at the Smithsonian Institution's National Museum of History and Technology (as it was called then), on June 17, 1977. I had gone to hear her speak at a symposium on "kin and community," dealing with our present and looking at our future. Although the hall had been only half full during the other speeches that day, it filled to capacity when Mead walked down the aisle carrying her trademark big wooden staff. She was such a tiny woman that only her head appeared above the podium. I had my microphone with me, and we talked together after her speech.

"Some families are in isolation," she said. "We should have more older people living in our communities. Everyone should mix people, old and young." She had ideas for people with children in divorced families. "Co-parenthood is biological, but marriage is a contract and that bond can be broken. You cannot break a co-parent bond."

We spoke about generation houses and extended families, a new term at that time. "Many people will have extended families in the future," Mead said. "At times your in-laws may be of a different race or color, but even then, each of the families of the in-laws will be an extension of your own."

14

New Horizons

Dartmouth Days

President John Kemeny of Dartmouth enabled me for a brief time to attend a top-flight university, where my horizons would be permanently broadened in many directions. Not only did I learn a great deal at the Dartmouth Institute, I formed new long-lasting and valued friendships.

When I took my microphone to Dartmouth College in Hanover, New Hampshire, in the spring of 1976, I had already interviewed at Harvard University, so Dartmouth was my second stop. After I interviewed Dartmouth president Kemeny for the Breakfast Show, he invited me to return to Hanover in August to become a student at the newly created Dartmouth Institute. Based on the idea of the Aspen Institute in Colorado, it was accepting enrollment from the United States and other parts of the world, not of ordinary students but of presidents and executive vice presidents of large corporations or otherwise influential companies. The institute's objective was not about how to manage their businesses. Rather, it was how to give their minds a chance to expand in another direction. I could do interviews, he suggested, with some of these students, and he was sure it would be of benefit to them as well as to me. It was an expensive course but I would be his guest. Students had to pay double the course fee to bring their wives, and many did. At that time, few women headed large businesses, although that would happen soon.

Dartmouth provided their finest professors for the Dartmouth Institute. Professor Harry Bond was in charge of the teaching staff, and Gil Tannis, who was executive officer of the college and director of continuing education, recruited the business students. During the month-long course, we students lived in dormitories, as it was late summer and the regular college students had not yet arrived.

Harry Bond taught us English with great emphasis on the poet Robert Frost. Professor Delo E. Mook II, a physicist, taught us a great deal about the search for fusion power. Professor Vincent Starzinger talked about government, while Tom Vargish and others led us down new paths. Our class numbered about forty, and we were all wildly enthusiastic. The wives told me they had never had such a good time talking with their husbands about serious, exciting discoveries. Everyone had read the assigned books ahead of time, so we all contributed to the discussions after the lectures.

At the Dartmouth Institute I met Dan and Toby Fink. Dan was the head of the General Electric Space Center in Pennsylvania, and invited me to come and do interviews there as soon as I could. One thing led to another, and a man named Jack Elsley invited me to come to Chicago, where he said he would set up a whole group of interviews for me. Other couples stayed good friends long after that first course. Over the next several years we returned to the institute every winter for a long weekend of lectures, which meant we went on learning from the professors and from each other. Sometimes I would fly up to the winter seminars on the General Electric plane, thanks to Dan Fink, a brilliant man, who later on became a vice president of GE and then a consultant for several large corporations.

Jack Elsley was the only other single person in that first class and he would escort me to dinner and sometimes sit with me on a hill near the dormitory and watch the stars over New Hampshire. We had long discussions and became fast friends. I knew that Jack was not interested in women except as friends, but I never dreamed that someday, alas, I would be helping to make a panel for him on the AIDS quilt, which is displayed around the United States. Jack was born in Eastbourne, England, and was a graduate of Cambridge University. It was a long while before he told his family that he was gay. Thanks to Jack, I did a series of good interviews in Chicago. I met his mother, who was visiting from England. He came to

Washington several times and would telephone me a couple of times every year. He told me that a person makes few truly close friends in a lifetime, and these can be counted on one hand. He said he counted me as one of those friends.

Jack died of AIDS in the early nineties in Palm Springs, California and I was in touch with his beloved niece Judy right away. She asked me to work on the quilt panel with her. A friend, Jane Kauffman, did the actual sewing of my design, putting American and British flags on a blue panel with dates. Judy took this centerpiece and added a patchwork border from Jack's shirts, using shirt buttons to hold the top and backing together. She asked to have the panel displayed in Chicago, New York, New Jersey, and Palm Springs, as those were the places where Jack had lived. It was also displayed here in Washington on the Mall beside the Smithsonian Institution, and Judy came from Utah to join me in a visit to see the enormous quilt spread out on the Mall. I was amazed at how many people had come to see the quilt. What a sad day!

Bells Are Ringing

There was going to be a wedding, and much to my surprise it was mine. Just about the time I became used to living alone, a man named Bill Lynch came into my life and insisted we be married, the sooner the better.

Bill telephoned me one night and asked me to dinner. I had met him and his wife Jean only briefly, at two Fourth of July parties. The first time, he told me about his son Bill Jr.'s interest in radio, on which he had already found himself a job. The second time he told me that Bill Jr. was now a newsman with NBC, and the whole family was excited about it. He knew I would be interested because I was in the same business. His wife had been ill with cancer for many years, and later I heard that she had died.

When Bill called me, I was on my way to Jamaica for a short holiday with my friend Charlotte Reid. I told him I would be glad to go out with him when I returned. During our weeklong stay I remember saying to Charlotte once or twice, "I wonder what Bill Lynch is like. I hardly know him." He was a retired army officer, although I had never met him in those army years, and was now a stockbroker. He seemed like a thoughtful, kind man, rather distinguished looking, with a good sense of humor.

Larry and Jamye had left Washington and were living in Fort Collins, Colorado, where Larry was studying for his master's degree at Colorado State University and Jamye was teaching at the university. Pam was living in Denver. When it looked as though Bill and I were going to get married, we took a trip to Colorado so he could meet my children and they could get a look at him.

Meanwhile in Washington, I met Bill's daughter Katie, her husband Tony, and Bill Lynch Jr. I liked them all. Young Bill was working in Washington and had changed from NBC to CBS, where he did some television reporting from the Pentagon. Then he returned to the New York studios of CBS radio to host "The World News Roundup," the program started by Ed Murrow.

Bill and I were married in my little church in Maryland by my minister Bill Plummer. The Plummers had been especially kind to me during those years I was on my own and were delighted by this turn of events. We had a wedding reception on the lawn at Le Vesinet overlooking the Chesapeake Bay, on a glorious June day that was not too hot, not too cold, and the first without rain in well over a week. My sister Dorothy and my brother Bill were there along with all our children and many friends.

What to do about my name? I had been Pat Gates for all of my adult life and was known professionally by that name. My listeners would be confused if suddenly I turned up with another name. I finally decided that I would stay with Gates at the office, on the air, and for professional occasions, but when I was out with Bill for social events, I would add the name "Lynch," keeping the "Gates" in the middle. I have read that many professional women have a hard time with name changes. Women doctors, for example, who have established their reputation under one name can not very well discard that name when they remarry. My decision seemed to work well.

One of the guests at our wedding was Dr. Eleanor Peter, whom I interviewed soon afterward for the Breakfast Show. We talked about many of the remarkable things she had seen and heard and done in her ninety-five years of life. When I interviewed her in December 1978, around the time of the 75th anniversary of the first manned flight, we spoke about that historic flight by Orville and Wilbur Wright in Kitty Hawk, North Carolina, in a plane they had built themselves. Dr. Peter told about going with her husband to an airfield in Ohio to see the Wright Brothers, whom they knew. Her husband went up in the air on a flight with Orville Wright, but Eleanor preferred to stay on earth and watch.

She talked about seeing the horse and carriage give way to the automobile and living through many years of change to see the day when men walked on the moon. Her life was quite something to hear about. She had graduated as a doctor from the University of Chicago Rush Medical School in 1911, quite an accomplishment for a woman in those days! She then went off to China with her husband, Dr. William Peter, for fifteen years of medical missionary work. Her three children were born there. When they came back from China, they spent eight years on the Navaho Indian Reservation in Window Rock, Arizona, where her husband was medical director. Later, her husband was a professor at Yale University. When they retired, they moved to their log cabin at Scientists' Cliffs in Calvert County, Maryland, on Chesapeake Bay not far from my house.

When I met Dr. Peter after I first came to Scientist's Cliffs, she was eighty-nine years old but looked younger, and I thought she might still be working. We became fast friends and I visited her every week. One day, she told me why she must be living so long —because she was still learning something new everyday. But I think it was because she was still giving something new of herself everyday. I was fortunate to know her for six years before she died and to have her give me an interview that caused comment from people all over the world.

Pam came from Denver whenever she could, and I would go out there to see her. Emily and Sally, my granddaughters, came to visit us at Le Vesinet every summer with their mother and father, Jamye and

Larry. I would take my holiday then and the house would come alive. When Larry joined International Paper, they went on to live in Louisiana and then in Memphis, Tennessee. I was so lucky to have them assigned to an office near Annapolis for three years while the girls were teenagers. When they moved back to Memphis, we were back to occasional visits.

Bill's children and grandchildren came to visit often. Those were good years with young people around, and they went by quickly.

Presidents, Senators, and Hostages

Every now and then I returned to the White House to report on something special, like the night President and Mrs. Carter gave an official dinner for the shah of Iran and the Empress Farah. As I entered the White House gate and even from inside the walls, I heard the loud voices from Lafayette Square, across from the White House, protesting about the shah's rule and his visit here. I was reminded of my arrival in Iran in 1960, when cannons boomed to celebrate the birth of the son of the shah and his empress.

Charles Percy, chairman of the Senate Foreign Relations Committee, was a good friend and a great supporter of our Breakfast Show at the Voice of America. I had met Loraine and Chuck Percy when they had first come to Washington and we socialized together with our families. When a new nominee for director of the Voice of America would go up to the Hill for confirmation by the Foreign Relations Committee, they would usually come back to VOA and say, "Chuck Percy told us all about you when we were being confirmed! He says that you are as well known abroad as Barbara Walters is in the United States!"

Senator Percy once wrote to me from Ladakh after meeting with the commanding general of the 121st Independent Infantry Brigade Group, based at Kargil: "There are several thousand officers and men of the Indian army stationed up here along the Chinese-Tibetan Border. As we have gone along, we have asked separate groups to tell us of their favorite shortwave radio programs. Without exception, we found their favorite single show was 'The Breakfast Show.' Your name is constantly mentioned, every man seems to have established a personal identity with you, and your most frequent comment that they mentioned was, 'If you see someone without a smile, give him one of yours.' " He'd heard that the Pakistan border troops listened also.

Our nation drew firmly together when the United States Embassy in Iran was taken over in November 1979 and all the Americans inside were held as hostages. Knowing that our diplomats were in great danger on what was legally U.S. territory alarmed, angered, and deeply saddened people in this country. We worried about the hostages as though they were members of our own family in trouble, which indeed they were.

Soon the yellow ribbon became a symbol of our endangered hostages and our wish to have them home again, inspired by the song "Tie a Yellow Ribbon 'Round the Old Oak Tree." Yellow ribbons were everywhere. The tension lasted for 444 days, and the subject dominated discussion not only in the press but wherever people gathered.

The ranking hostage, L. Bruce Laingen, had been ambassador to Malta and been sent to Teheran as chargé d'affaires in early summer 1979 to run the embassy temporarily—for three or four weeks—until the president's appointee as ambassador received Senate confirmation. As events transpired, he would not return home again until January of 1981.

Bruce Laingen was just leaving a meeting in the Iranian Foreign Ministry when the news came that the United States Embassy and its personnel had been taken over by an angry crowd. He turned back to seek the Iranian revolutionary government's help and ended up being held in one room at the Foreign Ministry throughout the hostage seizure. Conditions there were little better for Laingen and the two American Foreign Service officers accompanying him than for those held in the embassy. For the last three weeks of the 444 days, Laingen and his colleagues were placed in solitary confinement.

On the Breakfast Show, Phil Irwin, Bill Reynolds, and I felt as concerned as everyone else and mentioned the situation frequently in our broadcasts. We had no idea, however, that Bruce Laingen and his two fellow captives were listening until a cable from them arrived, thanking us for the Breakfast Show. It had been relayed to us from the Department of State.

Finally, the hostages were released on January 20, 1981, the day Ronald Reagan was inaugurated as president of the United States. News of their release brought great joy from one end of the country to the other. Soon they were on their way to Washington.

I drove to work from my house in Maryland on the day the hostages were to arrive by plane at nearby Andrews Air Force Base and planned to attend the "Welcome Home" parade for them in Washington. On the way in, along Suitland Parkway, which runs past Andrews to the Capitol Street bridge near the Voice of America, I was moved to see people gathering on the hillsides in Maryland all along the parkway—old people and young people, all seriously joyful at the prospect of seeing the bus pass by carrying the hostages into Washington.

I described the parade on the Breakfast Show the next day, but I did not know then that Bruce Laingen would become a good friend. Senator and Mrs. Chuck Percy invited my husband Bill and me to dinner, and the other two guests were Bruce Laingen and his wife Penne. It was an interesting and happy evening. Sometime later, the Laingens came out to the Bay with Penne's mother to see the place I had spoken of on the air, and we sat on my little deck overlooking the Chesapeake Bay. I would see Bruce often through the years in connection with my work even after the Voice of America and I think of him and of Penne as special friends. When he retired from the Foreign Service, Bruce became president of the prestigious American Academy of Diplomacy.

I would like to share with you something Bruce wrote that means a great deal to me:

> Time can weigh heavily for a hostage; there's a lot of it to
> use up, and some days it got very heavy indeed. Sleep

helped, when we could close out the outside world and resort to whatever memories and fantasies pervaded our dreams. Even nightmares helped, and there were those too. But then mornings would come, with the prospect of a long day ahead, with hours and hours of more time to use up, with the prospect on most mornings of yet more of our hopes being dashed by the time night rolled around.

But it was not always so, thanks to something called the Breakfast Show on the Voice of America. For several months at the start of the crisis, we had access to a shortwave radio—thanks to a friendly soul in the offices of the Protocol section of the Foreign Ministry on the floor below ours. Listening to that show, we came to know someone named Pat Gates, the anchor lady of that show, and every morning it appeared, we made her a kind of hostage with us. She made our morning, she made our day.

Her voice, always sunny and bright, was a shot in the arm. We didn't know her, had never heard of her before—but while we had that radio we came to know her as a very close friend. On that show, she was talking to millions of listeners, but to the three of us, she was talking personally to us. Every morning we waited for whatever she had to say. And there was a lot—news of course, but also music and anecdotes and travelogues across the United States. As a spokesperson for the Voice, her job was to portray America, and her words and her sparkling, optimistic personality conveyed a wonderful picture. As Americans ourselves, we already knew a lot about that picture, but from where we sat as hostages, every morning she made it sound new.

We traveled with her, we laughed with her, we cried at times with her, we felt we were talking with her—especially on those mornings when she took her listeners to a historic site in the U.S., to a festival somewhere, to a sports event or to a congressional hearing. And some days she would even take us to Wall Street in New York and the workings of the stock market. There she would talk about the market, how it worked and how it was performing—the three of us lamenting we weren't there to take advantage of it. Often her commentary on the market was with someone named Bill Lynch, a thoroughly knowledgeable guy, who we assumed was up there, a trader on the floor of the market.

It was not until we returned from Iran that we learned that this person named Lynch was in fact Pat's husband and that she was Pat Gates Lynch in real life. She didn't need to travel to New York; her interlocutor was no less knowledgeable, but she could record their chat about the market right there in Washington.

Pat Gates was a Godsend to us. Hostage mornings got a lot longer when we lost that shortwave radio, which inevitably we did.

In any event, Pat, my gratitude—and I know I speak for my two colleagues too, Vic Tomseth and Mike Howland, in saying that that gratitude is as deep as ever. That Breakfast Show, and your voice in it, really did make a big difference for us, every day. Thank you.

The Road to China

It was while weeding in my father's garden in Connecticut that I first thought of the faraway land of China. My mother said that if I dug my spade all the way through the earth, I would come out in China. Realizing my spade was too small for such a task, I wondered if another way could be found to get me there. Only eleven years old, I was studying geography in a book called *Children of Other Lands*, and I wanted to visit them all! That day in the garden was a prelude to my first steps on a long road. It would be many years, after many wars had been fought in China, before that road would open up for me. The man who showed me the way would be a distinguished Chinese professor, Hubert S. Liang, whom I met via radio waves between his country and mine. So it wasn't a spade but a microphone that led me to China.

Professor Liang had taught English for close to fifty years and was renowned all over China. As a young man, he had studied journalism in the United States yet somehow had escaped any great harm during China's unsettling Cultural Revolution, when any connection with the United States was dangerous. As a loyal communist in his late seventies, he was allowed to set forth alone for America in the early 1980s, something almost unheard of then, when everyone from China had to travel in groups. His invitation to visit this country came from the University of Missouri School of Journalism in Columbia, Missouri, and other universities then invited him to talk about the new China while he gathered material for a book. When he came to Washington to talk with people in the White House and the Department of State, he was invited to visit the Voice of America.

The day I met Professor Liang, I was in the VOA cafeteria pressed for time and buying a sandwich to take back to my desk. A man from our Chinese Service approached me as I stood in line and said, "Pat, would you come over and speak with a Chinese visitor for a moment? He has asked to meet you, especially."

And so I went to meet this slight, fragile Chinese man, wearing a blue Mao shirt and trousers and a little Mao cap, with a wonderfully alert face and a twinkle in his eye. "I assign you to all my students," he said, "and we learn about the United States from you. We are eager to learn about the way you conduct business here and talk with American business leaders. Also, we learn to speak better English listening to you."

Well, I was delighted to know that VOA was getting through in far off China and being listened to, and that I was someone the professor talked about with his students. I offered to interview him about his impressions of the cities he had visited on this trip and we made a date for the next morning.

Fortunately, I had learned a great deal about the intelligence and depth of spirit of the Chinese from my dear Chinese friend, Mary Swing Shen, who had left that country many years ago. In Professor Liang, I found a new friend from China, one whose ideology was totally opposed to mine, but we shared great curiosity about and great interest in each other's country.

"You must come to China," the professor said after our interview. I told him I wanted very much to come, but it would have to be on a working status for VOA if I came. "I want to work," I told him, "for I always learn so much more about any country when I am interviewing there." Professor Liang promised he would arrange an invitation, so that his students from Nanjing University could meet me and I could see China. Somehow, when I looked at this small aging man bubbling with enthusiasm for life, I believed it might even be possible. From time to time, I received greetings from him as his stay in the United States continued, and I saw him once more when he was en route to interview former President Carter in Georgia.

Some time later a phone call came from a friend of Professor Liang's telling me that I was going to receive an invitation from the director of Radio Peking, now Radio Beijing. The invitation would be sent only after I made clear that I would accept it. I immediately said I would indeed accept and was told to contact a first secretary at the Chinese Embassy in Washington who was a former student of the professor's at Nanjing University.

The first secretary asked me what dates I would like to come—I preferred to go in the fall of that year, 1982—and what people I would like to interview. The cable from Radio Peking asked where I would like to go. I would be given an interpreter from Radio Peking and a car and driver wherever we went. It was hoped I would stay at least three weeks. Besides being allowed to do interviews, I would lecture at Nanjing University. He added that I would have to bear some of the financial burden. Fortunately for me, Voice of America was delighted by my invitation, and the deputy director agreed to use some of his end-of-year funds to send me.

My conversation at the Chinese Embassy took place in the spring and it was decided that day I would leave sometime in October. When I learned that the professor was critically ill and had been flown to Shanghai for an emergency operation, I immediately asked permission to see him when I reached Shanghai. In China at that time, you didn't decide to do something or see someone at the last minute; plans had to be made well in advance. How I looked forward to seeing the professor at the end of my trip and talking to him about

212

where I had traveled and what I was telling the rest of the world in my interviews.

It was decided by Radio Peking, the embassy, and me that I would arrive in Beijing (formerly Peking) and, after a few days there, fly to Xian and Nanjing, then go by train to Hangchow. I would also travel by train to Shanghai and take a round-trip train ride from Shanghai to Suchow. After a little over three weeks, I would depart from Shanghai for Tokyo.

Bill, my husband, was apprehensive because I would be traveling alone. "No need to worry," I told him, "I'll be well looked after and carefully watched by security people. The Chinese people are hospitable, and I know I will feel welcome."

A full moon shone on the water just outside the window of Le Vesinet, my house on a cliff at the edge of the Chesapeake Bay. It is the spot I love more than any other in the world, for to me it is as beautiful as the Indian Ocean, the Bosporous, all the beautiful places I have seen. I knew that the next time I saw a full moon, it would be over China.

Now, the road was clear. At last I was going to this ancient, mysterious land.

You Will Never Be the Same

A scholar who knew China well said to me, "Once you visit China, you will never be the same." I wondered then what he meant, but later I understood.

My interpreter, Hsiu Hua Chen, met me at the plane in Beijing, and we set off to work right away after stopping to leave my luggage at the hotel. She was a political affairs correspondent for what we now call Radio Beijing, and I was comfortable with her right away. As planned she had with her a car and a driver. In each city we visited, we would have not only a car and driver but also someone from that city to answer my questions. My plan was to do as many interviews as possible while in China, take them back to Washington on tape, and run a series on the Breakfast Show over the course of several weeks. My new friend Hsiu asked me during our journey together, "How will you use all of these interviews? You won't have time." I assured her that I would, and I did.

As another part of the plan, I made several telephone calls back to my engineer, Don Rice, in my VOA studio, which he would record and Phil Irwin would play as a direct report from China on his program that same day. It was exciting to talk to people on trains and planes who would say to me, "We heard you this morning broadcasting from China!" As the only American on these trains and planes, I was easy to find.

I had no illusions about traveling in a communist country, knowing that I would be observed at all times. At lunchtime, my interpreter would leave me, and I knew that undoubtedly she was reporting to her superiors on what we had been doing that day. My phone calls were listened to, but as I had nothing to hide, it did not worry me. In each hotel I would pass a room, always close to mine, that revealed when the door was open a uniformed security man on duty. The only time I was uncomfortable was in Shanghai, where I was being closely observed.

On one of my first stops in Beijing, at the University of Agriculture, I talked with its vice president about the newly formed Young Farmers Association for Science and Technology. Just that morning, the Chinese vice minister of agriculture had signed an agreement with the United States deputy secretary of agriculture in Washington on scientific and technical exchange projects for 1983, and we talked about that agreement in the interview.

Hsiu told me I was the first American correspondent who was not Chinese American to be invited by Radio Beijing in recent years to come and do interviews. So everywhere I went people were curious about me. Many had listened to the Voice of America for years, in English as well as in Chinese.

At the Central Conservatory of Music, I talked with a professor and afterwards asked him if I might record one of the students playing an ancient Chinese instrument. He agreed, and I taped the sound of that instrument. Each time I introduced one of my conversations in China my audience would hear that ancient Chinese music.

In Beijing I also talked with the president of the China International Trust and Investment Corporation. He told me that the corporation was then engaged in absorbing foreign investments for the domestic economy in the People's Republic of China. "A main emphasis is on the technical transformation of existing enterprises. We would like to absorb foreign investments to transform the technology of these enterprises, to meet the growing needs of the people," he said.

"Our hope is that through business exchanges, our American friends will have better understanding, more understanding about China."

We know that China has made tremendous strides in its industrial development since that 1982 interview. For me and for my listeners, it was interesting to observe the beginnings of this extraordinary development. American business firms are still searching for the best ways to do business with the Chinese. Those firms who grasp the necessity of making an effort to understand Chinese culture are those who do well in China. In Asia, our action-oriented ideas do not always go over well. It takes time and patience for American business representatives to build trust and confidence before the Chinese are ready to sign agreements with American companies.

From my firsthand experience, I came to believe the Chinese saying of "climbing a ladder to heaven" when you climb the Great Wall and walk along the narrow road at the top. When I reached the high point of the Wall, a magnificent sight lay before me. The road itself along the top of the Wall twists and turns through the craggy mountains and down into the valleys. When the astronauts were flying in earth orbit in their space capsules, they had looked down with great excitement and announced, "There below us, we can see the Great Wall of China."

The first emperor of China during the Ch'in Dynasty began the construction of the Great Wall about 221 b.c., as I learned in interviewing my guide, and each dynasty added to it. It became a strategic spot, a true fortress, with passes where battles were fought and approaching invaders were held back. The Wall contains many watchtowers and openings for weapons, and the large ones were for ancient bows and arrows. Later, the primitive weapons were replaced by cannons. During the Ming Dynasty (1368–1644), the Wall was modernized and weapons were mounted in strategic areas.

To transmit military information over the great distances between the passes, I was told, people used a signal system. Various towers and the commanding points around the Wall, as well as other towers on various hills, contained beacons used to signal when soldiers saw enemy troops coming, relying on smoke by day and fire at night.

While still in Beijing, I talked with an American student, Timothy Cheek, who had studied the Chinese language at Harvard University. Now at the University of Beijing he was collecting materials he could not find in the United States to study how the Chinese write about their own ancient history, particularly about the Ming Dynasty. Not surprisingly, he told me that the best thing about studying in China was meeting the people, particularly the scholars in his field.

Another man I interviewed in Beijing was vice president of the All China Federation of Commerce and Industry and head of the Returned Overseas Chinese. He had once headed a giant textile industry, a coal mining and shipping industry and suffered severely during the Cultural Revolution. But when I met him, China was exploiting his experience and his knowledge of the Western world. An official sat in to listen to what we were saying, and evidently everything was all right, because he did not stop us for any censorship. Several times such officials were present but only when I was interviewing someone representing the government.

The Fragrant Hills Hotel, named for a famous mountain, had just opened in Beijing. It was designed by the famous I. M. Pei, who was born in Canton, China, but left when he was eighteen to study architecture at MIT and Harvard. His many creations include the famous Ming Garden in the Metropolitan Museum in New York and the East Wing of the National Gallery of Art in Washington. The Fragrant Hills Hotel combines the Chinese national style with the modern. Pei spent a great deal of time in China choosing materials that are commonly used in that country. He kept many of the old trees, one thought to be about six hundred years old. I was fascinated by how well the hotel was situated in its natural surroundings, designed around the trees. A skylight imported from the United

States was installed in the main lobby with the assistance of American workers. The hotel has about five sections and eleven small gardens and was built in hopes of encouraging tourism.

Before leaving Beijing, I walked through the gigantic Tiananmen Square. In 1989, when I watched the upsetting television images of the deaths during the student uprising in this famous square, I was reminded of that happier day in the square when children ran by me flying their kites. It is difficult to describe the enormous size of the square, about forty hectares, or one hundred acres, in the center of the city. There I stood with my microphone in front of the monument to the People's Heroes, with the Great Hall of the People to the west, Memorial Hall on the south, and the Museum of the Chinese Revolution and Chinese History on the east. In the very north of the square is the Tiananmen Gate Tower. I think something like a half a million people can stand in the square at one time.

Beyond the square is a market place where, as in so many cities of the world, the farmers bring their products, predominantly vegetables, into the city to sell. Inside the market buildings, they sell meat and fish and other agricultural products. Many people on the outskirts of the square rode bicycles, but in the square everyone walked, with children everywhere. Cooler weather was on the way, and the wind was blowing.

When I asked to go to the zoo so I could see a panda in its native land, it caused a bit of a problem, for that was not on my prearranged schedule. The problem was soon resolved, and I did see a handsome, playful panda sitting atop his playground platform, an iron set of steps with a swing on the bottom and a great big ball for him to rotate on the top. The children were shouting, "Come down giant Panda, come down!"

Pandas usually dwell in the woods high above the sea, and they like places with enough rain and warm weather. Chinese children love watching the panda just as American children do in the National Zoo in Washington, D.C., where the pandas came from China. I did an interview about Beijing's fluffy black and white panda and hoped that my listeners would understand why I had wanted to go to the zoo!

From Beijing I flew to the ancient capital of China, Xian, to see one of the wonders of today's world, an excavated treasure of ancient sculptures discovered just outside of Xian. People come from all over the world to visit the excavation site and the Buried Sculpture Legion, a marvelous array of life-sized statues of soldiers standing in trenches in the clay where they had been unearthed. From the archaeologist I interviewed there, I learned that the Legion consisted of six hundred statues, including some horses. It was just as the emperor would have had them over two thousand years ago.

The building near these treasures looked to me somewhat like an airplane hangar, tremendous in size with skylights in the roof. By ramps built all around the excavation, we could walk over and look down into what is now the floor of the excavation site. The archeologist told me that although it is old in time, it was discovered only in 1974 when people sinking wells found three vaults, where buried sculpture legions were seen. It was a continuing excavation, which the archaeologists may have finished by now.

Some examples of this discovery traveled to the United States in a Chinese exhibit I had seen in New York. Seeing so many more of them in their original setting is an entirely different experience. The discovery at Xian is important to archaeologists, to the history of civilization, and to students of military science, who study how the guards were arranged and what weapons they used in those days. The discovery also dispelled the idea that Chinese sculpture developed only after foreign sculpture came into China, because it revealed highly skilled Chinese sculptures from before 200 B.C., long before Buddhism came into China.

Nanjing University and Beyond

One of the most satisfying times during my China sojourn was my visit to Nanjing University in old Nanking. At last, I had arrived at Professor Liang's university. He wanted me to see where he had taught for so many years, and he wanted me to lecture to the students of English. Finally, I arrived at the university, delivered my lecture, and met with some of the English professors.

In my lecture, I stopped for a moment while talking about the United States of America to describe where I lived on the East Coast. I went to the blackboard and drew a chalk outline of the United States. I am sure an American university audience would have laughed at my mediocre drawing, but here the students seemed glad to have before them an image on which to focus while I spoke of the Chesapeake Bay and everyday life there. From the questions asked when I had finished, I found the students' English pretty good. They all said they listened to the Voice of America for practice!

One English professor told me that some students at the university came from Europe, America, Japan, and other Asian countries. These students were studying Chinese history and in particular ancient Chinese history. Some students take elective classes in the evening, making a long day for the professors. Another professor had studied at Harvard and was now teaching English to science students. I asked him about some of the things that his students find especially difficult about English learned as a second language, and he said, "The grammar is so different from that of the Chinese language, the cultural background and some of the idioms can be confusing, and idiomatic usage of the English language seems extremely difficult." He described the campus as very much like a garden, with trees everywhere. There were about 5000 undergraduates, 500 graduate students, and 100 hundred foreign students, he said (probably more now).

Another professor used quite a bit of material from VOA and BBC radio broadcasts for the students to translate from English into Chinese. He liked the VOA interviews very much, hearing the voices of different people, some important or famous, in different fields.

One woman professor told me that she had to leave the teaching profession during the Cultural Revolution because it was considered wicked. Instead, she had to work in the fields planting crops. She found those years of farm labor grueling and was overjoyed that teaching was once again considered an honorable profession and she could be back at her adored University of Nanjing.

On another day in Nanjing, I visited the middle school known as the Foreign Language Institute. Here I met about 400 young students, 300 of them studying English. Both boys and girls there worked hard, with a good chance of entering the university later on. The principal of the school made me most welcome, and one of the teachers told me that students often go to libraries after class for outside reading. "They read books both in Chinese and foreign languages. They also use film projectors, slides, tape recorders in the school or in the library." A male student in the school, asked about his interest in sports, told me he liked to play volleyball, table tennis, and badminton.

My next stop was at the Nanjing Worker's Hospital to see how acupuncture was helping people. Doctors explained to me that thousands of years ago, the Chinese discovered acupuncture as a method of treating the sick and said acupuncture is widely used today in China. The rest of the world is becoming increasingly aware of results of treatment by this ancient system.

The doctors in the Nanjing Worker's Hospital took me into the clinic where patients were being treated with acupuncture needles. One patient was being treated for facial paralysis to good effect. Several doctors from different countries at the hospital were taking an international acupuncture course for foreign doctors. One doctor said to me that an American doctor had just attended the course because he had found that acupuncture is good for nervous diseases and he wanted to find out more about it.

I learned that acupuncture anesthesia is one of the methods used in this hospital for operations. The day I was there they were doing thyroidectomy operations on the neck. The doctor I interviewed said, "We are finding acupuncture is also useful for patients with cardiac palpitations, although it is not for all kinds of cardiac problems. We are now trying to combine Western medicine with Chinese medicine."

Leaving Nanjing by train, I arrived in Hangchow where the sparkling West Lake of Hangchow attracts people from all over the world. President Nixon, I was told, had visited there during his historic trip. The Chinese like to spend their holidays there. Looking out in early morning on the beautiful hills in the distance, I could see why.

I visited a silk factory in Hangchow, which is famous for its silks, and explored one of China's two foremost institutes of art. This remarkable institute has departments of national painting, oil painting, an arts and crafts department, a woodcutting department, and a department of enamel work. The school is being built up again, I was told, following the dark days of the Cultural Revolution.

Another stop on my travels was a city known all over the world for its famous gardens, the city of Suchow. The Metropolitan Museum in New York contains a replica of one of the Suchow gardens. The bell was ringing in one of China's most famous Buddhist Temples as I climbed the steps of the ancient Han Shan Temple, just outside the city of Suchow. The story goes that a monk would bang this bell 108 times on New Year's Eve, and when the 108th bell sounded, the New Year had begun. Then everyone celebrated in every village.

Suchow has very narrow streets in the old part of the city, with archways of trees, and the gardens are delightful. It is a garden city even out in the street, because weeping willows and other green trees make a sweeping pathway as you drive along. Many of the beautiful, privately owned old houses and their gardens had been confiscated by the communist government.

My last stop in China was Shanghai, one of the world's great seaport cities, which produces many of China's goods. I ventured out on a small ship on the river that flows past the city to where it meets the East China Sea. Looking towards the sea, I saw many ships lined up waiting their turn to come into the harbor. Some barges carried bricks, coal, or stones, as well as other cargo. I was pleased to see some traditional Chinese junks, the ships with the cloth sails that we in the West romanticize. Sometimes, families living on small boats, surrounded by laundry, would wave at us. The factories on the riverbanks all have polluting smoke stacks, a depressing sight to see and to breathe.

In Shanghai, I visited the enormous industrial exhibit building, with hall after hall with products made in China—furniture, textiles, toys, pianos, bicycles, television sets, and radios. Outside the building, horns honked and big trucks chugged by. It was the sound of a big city at work.

Some museums I visited in Shanghai displayed the traumatic times between the Western world and China. In this city, I was more aware than I had been elsewhere that my conversations on the phone were monitored and my actions tracked carefully.

One woman I had requested ahead of time to meet in Shanghai was Muriel Hoopes, an American woman who lived in an apartment building in rather small quarters. Her married name was Chinese, for she was the widow of a Chinese nuclear physicist, Yu Chin Tu. She was a listener of mine and had written me letters, which American visitors mailed to me when they returned to the United States. I was pleased that I could meet her.

She had suffered greatly in the Cultural Revolution, as had her husband, who died in prison, and she was now happily receiving guests such as me in her small apartment. She had lived in China for sixty-two years, longer she told me, than any other living American, though she is no longer alive. When I interviewed Muriel Hoopes then, she told me about meeting her Chinese scientist husband in New York City and coming with him to his country. She had one daughter, a cancer specialist, and a son in the United States. Here in Shanghai, she taught English in her apartment to some students. She still celebrated Christmas and kept her Christmas decorations up all year. She explained to me the meaning of a painting she had, and that was to be patient. She said we all need a great deal of patience because it is going to take a lot of time to get China up to date. She would be surprised to know how fast China is moving now.

Women in China have new roles far different from women of ancient China. When I was in Shanghai, I talked with the vice minister of international liaison of the Shanghai Women's Federation. We discussed working mothers and problems all women share no matter what their nationality. She told me how women who are busy in the office or the factory take their children to "week care." That means the children stay from Monday to Saturday afternoon, when their mothers pick them up for the weekend. She talked about the traditional custom in which three generations live together, so

222

women in some families just leave their children at home and let the grandparents take care of them.

At last, I was taken to see Professor Liang, the man who made it possible for me to come to China. He and his wife greeted me in their small apartment, and he was happy to hear all about my trip and especially about my visit to his university in Nanjing. I was distressed to see that his throat was bound in white bandages because of a major throat operation. I discovered from a painting on the wall of a tiger on velvet, that the professor, like myself, was born a tiger according to the Chinese calendar tradition, although our years were quite different. We threw our arms about each other and said good-bye for the last time. Professor Liang had touched so many lives, including mine.

Home and Family

After I had returned home to my studio and brought all my interviews to Breakfast Show listeners, I received a letter from Japan. A woman wrote, "Your China tour was the most interesting bit of reporting I've come across in a long time. I was sad when it came to a close."

People wrote from many countries thanking me for taking them to China. It was I who wanted to thank all those in China who had shared their thoughts with my listeners and me. At last, I had been able to visit this ancient land I had wanted to see since that day in my father's garden in Connecticut.

My husband, Bill, was eager to hear all about my travels in China, and I told him everything I could when my eyes weren't closing from incredible jet lag. I was so sleepy for at least two weeks that I could barely make sense on the telephone. Fortunately, I woke up at the microphone.

Now it was time to visit family members, who also wanted to hear about China. I went first to Connecticut to visit my brother Bill for one last time. I had seen him briefly before leaving for China and, after my return, would call him at his office just to say I was thinking of him. I would remind him of things he had done for me when I was still a little girl and he was much older and out in the world. Funny the things we remember, like the day he took me to see the film *Snow White*, knowing I was eager to see it but too young to go alone.

We talked about his daughter, Kay, and his regret that they were often separated after his divorce from her mother, though he had tried to see her whenever possible. Bill's late second wife had been fond of Kay, as was Evelyn, his current wife. Despite occasional upsets between him and Kay, in his last words to me he asked that I keep in touch with her. She is now a widow bringing up two fine children alone, as her husband died in a plane accident. I have always enjoyed our visits together and think of her often, just as I think of my brother, who died of cancer not long before he planned to retire and start traveling.

My older sister Dorothy lived for several years in Washington after the death of her retired navy captain husband, and we saw each other often. Luckily, my niece Jeri, so like a daughter to me, also lived in Washington. When my sister became ill, she moved in with Jeri, who decided to buy a house in New York State, not far from New York City. I was sad to see them go, and sadder still when my sister died in the fall of 2003.

We spent the Christmas holidays together with Pam, Larry, Jamye, and their girls, all eager to hear about my trip to China.

15

The Last Hurrahs

Is Anybody Listening?

When people ask me how we know about the Voice of America's impact on people around the world, I always think of Dr. Simon Rekhson. He gives me credit for changing his life, which means a great deal to me. Every VOA broadcaster hopes that he or she can "make a difference."

As Simon Rekhson told it in a General Electric Company newsletter, it all began back at the Soviet Academy of Sciences in Leningrad, when he was a senior staff member frequently working with foreign guests. "I had no trouble with French or German and I thought I was fluent in English, having studied it since the age of ten. I had read many scientific papers in English and had a good knowledge of English grammar. Then, one day an American scientist visited the academy. It was a total disaster." Dr. Rekhson discovered that he had been taught a completely incomprehensible method of pronouncing English. "I couldn't understand a word the American said nor could he understand me. Since the same style of English pronunciation is taught in all Russian schools, I had to turn elsewhere to learn it correctly. I decided to listen to the Voice of America."

Dr. Rekhson further wrote, "While VOA programs in Russian were jammed, those in English were not. The government figured it was not worth the expense to prevent 'a handful of eccentrics' from hearing them. I recorded the programs, replaying them again and again until I could separate the words. After two years, I became fluent in English. One of my favorite programs was hosted by Pat Gates. I taped many of her programs and learned a lot about America from them. She interviewed a wide variety of people—everyone from Oklahoma farmers to the president of the United States. I hoped someday I would be able to meet her."

For three years, Dr. Rekhson toyed with the idea of emigrating to America. In those Cold War days, communism still controlled the Soviet Union. "I knew communism was bad," he said, but "I didn't realize how bad. I had nothing to compare it with, for all my travels had been in communist countries. Also, as a scientist, I had one of the best positions in the Soviet Union."

When Cornelius Moynihan, a professor from Catholic University in Washington, D.C., visited the Academy of Sciences, Dr. Rekhson asked him what he should do. This conversation took place in the latter part of the 1970s. "Much to my surprise, he said that I should leave Russia as soon as possible and even offered to be my sponsor."

It was the best possible time to leave the country, as the government was permitting large numbers of its Jewish citizens to emigrate to Israel. Dr. Rekhson, his wife, and two children boarded a plane, supposedly for Israel, but when they reached Vienna, they boarded another plane bound for the United States. One of the first things Dr. Rekhson did after settling in Washington was to call me. He explained how I had helped him perfect his English and learn about America and asked if he could meet me at my office. "We had lunch together," he wrote in his GE article, "and I felt as though I had known her for years. She looked very much like I expected she would."

Dr. Rekhson taught physics as a visiting professor at Catholic University for two years. In 1979, he joined the General Electric Company in Cleveland, Ohio, as a senior scientist. After some years there, he became Chemical and Biological Research Professor at Cleveland State University. While he was still at GE, I took my microphone to Cleveland to interview Dr. Rekhson, his wife Mila, and others. Before leaving Cleveland, I gave a short speech, at which Dr. Rekhson introduced me to the people at General Electric. "If it were not for her," he said, "I would not know the meaning of real freedom."

My Solo Lecture Tour

At the Voice of America I made one last important trip. I remember the extraordinarily hard work and great pleasure of that particular journey. The United States Information Agency awarded me what is called an "Ampart Grant" and sent me off to lecture in Nepal, the Philippines, Indonesia, and Australia. Ampart means American participant and the grants are given to people who represent many different professions in the United States. Some are from universities, one was my friend, Daniel Boorstin, Librarian of Congress, another was Ambassador Max Kampelman from the Department of State. Some speakers are artists, scientists, musicians, or authors.

My lectures were to focus on the "United States Political and Social Processes" and to include: "The Future of Global Communication," "The Role of a Free Press in a Democratic Society," "The Role of Radio in Developing Societies," "International Broadcasting," "American Society in a Changing World," and "The Role of Women in America." After I was informed of this honor, I was reminded that I had to write all the speeches myself!

One thing I recall vividly was sitting at my dining room table at the Chesapeake Bay writing about the fast-moving developments in communication that would come about in the future because of the new satellites, fiber optic cables, and all kinds of electronic marvels. Just as I was writing, a large, worn-out tree fell in the ravine next to my house, crashing down with a mighty roar. Every leaf on every nearby tree was shaking, as I rushed out and made certain no one had been hurt. Unfortunately, the falling tree took our telephone line with it—our phone was no longer working, fiber optics and modern technology notwithstanding. Though our line was soon fixed, I thought the episode offered a lesson for us all. Nature continues to challenge manmade marvels! I searched a book of Robert Frost's poetry to find something appropriate to quote in the speech I was writing, and sure enough there was a poem to fit the occasion. It was called, "On a Tree Fallen Across the Road," which concludes that we will persevere and finally overcome the setbacks nature puts before us.

Nepal

My journey began in September 1983 in Kathmandu, capital of Nepal, a country I had always wanted to see. To an audience of government officials, academics, journalists, businessmen, professionals, and students I spoke about the crucial role of a free press in defending democratic principles. The question-and-answer sessions give me a chance to explain the distinction between news reporting on VOA and VOA's quite separate U.S. government editorials, and why we believe in the free flow of information across borders.

At the journalism department of the Ratna Rajya campus, I stressed to faculty members and students the unique power of radio to foster education and social change in developing countries. We examined various developments and programming aspects of radio journalism. I visited the Honorable Surya Bahadur Thapa, a Nepalese prime minister I had interviewed in Washington several months earlier during his visit to the United States. At Radio Nepal I talked about broadcasting and was interviewed on the air. Newspaper reporters also interviewed me. I tried to see as much as possible of Kathmandu in between appointments and was sorry to leave.

Although I did not meet the king when I was in Nepal, I did meet and interview him when he came to Washington on a state visit in December 1983. I apparently shocked his staff when I sat right next to him during our interview, for no one, I was later told, ever sits next to the king!

During the king's state visit in Washington, he and his queen were entertained at the White House. The next evening, December 9, Senator Charles Percy, then head of the Senate Foreign Relations Committee, hosted a small dinner party at his home for the king and queen, to which he invited Bill and me. The other guests included sixteen Americans, Nepal's ambassador to Washington Dr. Bhekh B. Thapa, and members of the king's staff. I sat at a round table with Secretary of State Henry Kissinger, the queen of Nepal, and about five other guests. It was a great evening. The Percys had some folk dancers perform for us informally in the dining room. Senator Percy explained that he wanted the king and queen to see something from rural America! Eighteen years later, I was stricken to hear the dreadful news of the fatal shooting of the king and his queen.

The Philippines

Before leaving Nepal, I was contacted by the U.S. embassy in Manila in the Philippines to see if I still planned to come there. Many official visitors were canceling because of the dangerous riots caused by anger against President Marcos. I assured the embassy people, "I will be there, danger or not!"

Certainly, I would not have missed that particular stop. It came in the midst of intense international attention on Philippine affairs because of the recent slaying of former Senator Benigno Aquino III. A fast-moving debate about what had happened faced the government and President Marcos.

In Manila, I had breakfast with members of the Professional Broadcasting Association, among whom were ten women. We had a roundtable discussion with many questions about how VOA operates and about Western media in general. We talked about international communication trends and the role of professional women in the United States. I was taken to the influential Radio Veritas, run by the Catholic Church, where most of the conversation centered on the importance of press freedom. I then met more leading women broadcasters, some of them evening news anchorwomen. Because of the current political unrest in the country, much of what we talked about centered on the difficulties confronting Philippine broadcasters forced to operate under many political restrictions.

At Maryknoll College, I talked to communication arts students and faculty. We discussed how the new technology affected communications and about broadcasting as a career. That night on the government's TV channel, I was interviewed live on a talk show for fifteen minutes. I gave another radio interview, and by the next day my voice was going fast.

My embassy escort stopped our car along the street and bought me some eucalyptus drops from a sidewalk vendor to help my throat. Remarkably, they did help, and within thirty minutes, my voice was back as strong as ever. That was a lucky turn of events because I was off that day to the Philippine city of Cebu for more speeches and discussions of free press issues. At the USIS Center in the afternoon I spoke to 130 people, including journalists and mass communication faculty and students, for about an hour and answered questions for another hour. The audience's enthusiasm made the time fly for me. Among the questions was one about my thoughts on Australia's win over America in the World Cup Sailing Race that day. I told the audience it would probably help the race in the future, as the United States had won many times consecutively, and now Australia could have the joy of victory. I was headed for Australia and looking forward to my visit there.

The question I was asked everywhere I went was: "Is President Reagan coming or not coming to visit the Philippines during this tense time when most of the country is angry with our president?" Washington had not yet made a decision, I explained, and expounded upon the long friendship of the United States and the Philippines. When I called on the American ambassador in Manila, Michael Armacost, he told me that the embassy was awaiting word from Washington.

Just before leaving the Philippines, I saw Ambassador Armacost again and told him I had what I thought could be important news for him. I had been taken to visit a capiz shell factory and during my visit the head of the factory had a telephone call from the palace of President Marcos. He told me excitedly that he was to cancel the official gift he was in the midst of making for President Marcos to present to President Reagan upon his arrival. No gift, I thought, meant no visit, and that is the way it turned out. The ambassador seemed pleased to have my clue in advance!

Indonesia

Now it was on to Jakarta, Indonesia. Never had I thought in my early years that I would visit Indonesia during my lifetime, and now here I was going there for the third time. My first visit was with President and Mrs. Nixon, my second when Phil Irwin and I made our VOA trip, and now here I was on my own.

Jakarta is a beautiful city and I worry whenever I read about trouble there. I met with the Indonesian Journalists Association and with a group of about forty women broadcast journalists from radio and television. The women asked me questions for two hours after my opening remarks. I was pleased that they made plans right then to get together again as a group. This had been the first meeting in memory of women broadcast journalists in Jakarta.

One of my talks was at the Indonesian equivalent of the National Press Club in Washington. The members of the press were especially interested in the changes electronic media and technological developments were bringing to radio, television, and satellite communication. At this press club meeting, I spoke of my personal experiences during my radio career, and the audience asked me questions for nearly three hours.

Just as we were finishing, a young reporter came in and apologized for being late. I thanked him for coming and told him I was sorry he had missed our session. "Never mind," he said, "Your smile is enough!" That is a compliment, which stayed with me for years to come because it meant that he was one of my listeners and he had heard my sign-off. I hope he is safe today, for many reporters there have been in harm's way in recent years.

On this trip, I flew to Bali, where I was in contact with a new director of TVRI, a key person in radio and television. In beautiful Bali, I had only twenty-four hours to see a sunset, a sunrise, watch volcanoes steam, and hear the waves booming in on the black sand. The flowers were blooming, the birds were singing, there was no hint of tragic times to come.

Before leaving Indonesia, I visited Surabaya for more talks, then back to Jakarta. At our embassy I enjoyed a reception given for me and met with embassy staff.

Lynn Sever, the assistant information officer at the embassy, put me on the plane. She had brought me some evaluation reports from each country I had visited so far, and I read them after the plane took off. I did not know there would be an evaluation at each stop, and when I read them, I was so happy I cried. It was a very female thing to do, as women in those days were much less sure than men about how they would be accepted.

Australia

On I flew to Australia, landing in spectacular Perth. In one direction you can look at a river and, just by turning your head, see the ocean. I visited Channel 9, one of the most modern television studios I have seen. Producer Guy Baskin had made the film series "Wonders of Western Australia" there. In my interview there, the subject of the World Cup came up right away, and someone gave me a little pin of the Australian boat that had won the race. I was able to congratulate the Australians many times.

Flying across Australia to Melbourne, I thought of my own country. We share a common language and, I think, many characteristics. Both peoples show a pioneering spirit and an outgoing attitude of friendliness towards one another and to strangers.

In Melbourne, I visited Radio Australia and was interviewed by the host of Radio Australia's popular program *Spectrum*. Between official stops, I had time to visit some of Melbourne's lovely gardens and to see some of Australia's remarkable animals, kangaroos and koalas among others. Then on to Adelaide, where I met more interesting people. One lecture I gave was to students at the South Australian College of Advanced Education, which has a good school of journalism.

In Canberra, the capital, I gave a luncheon lecture. Then on to Brisbane for a breakfast talk and a Zonta international luncheon, where I was guest of honor. My last stop was Sydney, where I enjoyed visiting the remarkable opera house. With only about eight days in Australia, I had given many more than eight lectures!

It was a great visit from start to finish. Now, I was homeward bound.

Part III

Diplomacy and Beyond

16

One Ambassador, One New Voice

Microphone to Madame Ambassador

Centuries ago, sailors aboard tall ships set sail for Madagascar from Bombay across the Arabian Sea and on into the Indian Ocean. Others rounded the Cape of Good Hope at the foot of the African continent, entered the Mozambique Channel, and headed for the port of Diego Suarez, at the northernmost point of that mysterious, exotic land of Madagascar.

Toward the end of the twentieth century, I sailed through the air on the silver wings of a Pan American Airways 747 jumbo jet from New York to Paris, then on Air France via Jeddah, Saudi Arabia, to Nairobi, Kenya. From there, Air Madagascar flew me high above where ships still set their course. My airship flew via the Comoros Islands to Antananarivo, the mile-high capital of Madagascar.

My course was charted by fate and good fortune one night in my small, windowless office at the Voice of America on Independence Avenue in Washington, after everyone in the outer office had gone home. I was often the last to leave, as I worked late preparing for the next morning's program. Just before 6:00 o'clock, as I gathered up my briefcase and snapped off the light, the phone rang. Standing in the dark, I heard the ordinary ring that would change my life.

Putting the phone to my ear I heard an operator say, "The White House is calling for Pat Gates"! Then a voice said, "This is Bob Tuttle, chief of presidential personnel. I have just left a meeting in the president's office and you have been selected as his choice to be ambassador to Madagascar."

He told me that I must say nothing yet, until after the required security clearance, financial statement, and medical exam. Next, he said that my host country would be asked for Agrément, the diplomatic term for formal acceptance of a proposed U.S. ambassador. I would have an extensive security clearance, which the White House would begin immediately, and I would be requested to fill out financial disclosure forms. When I was fully cleared and the White House was satisfied that everything was in order, I would receive a telephone call from the president asking if I would be willing to serve as his ambassador and telling me that he was sending my nomination to the Senate for its advice and consent. I would appear before the Senate Foreign Relations Committee seeking its recommendation for confirmation by the full Senate. As Bob Tuttle explained, I couldn't tell anybody except my family yet, because Congress does not like to have any news of appointments released before it has received the president's formal nomination.

At the end of our conversation Tuttle said, "Congratulations, I think you will be a fine ambassador and represent the president well."

It was an emotional moment. When I had hung up I sorted out in my mind what he had said, picked up my briefcase once again, locked the door to my office, and went downstairs, where my husband, Bill, was waiting in the car. He was delighted when I told him the news. He had known a call was on the way for the White House had tried to reach me at the apartment first. I told him how much I wished that my mother and father were still alive so they could know. They would be so happy! I have them to thank and all the people along the way. When we came back to our apartment, I telephoned Pam and Larry, but warned them that everything must be kept secret for now. They were excited!

How did it happen that a woman with no political involvement, whose principal link to the world was her international microphone, had been chosen by the president of the United States to be an ambassador? When I served in the Nixon White House I was on loan from the Voice of America, where I had faithfully served many presidents. In compliance with the Hatch Act, which proscribed political participation by civil servants, I had never campaigned for any politician nor had my husband or I ever donated money to any campaigns.

It had been a long road to this amazing appointment and a fascinating one. I thought of Ruth Bacon, a high-ranking Foreign Service officer who headed International Women's Year in the early seventies. I had worked closely with her so I might inform all of my listeners about that important year. Ruth said to me in all seriousness, "You should be an ambassador, but it won't happen because you are a woman."

It was the first time such a thought had entered my head, although on my "Goodwill Ambassador" trips, I had often been told that my experience might be effectively employed as a diplomat. I didn't see how such a thing could happen. Besides, I was sure I had the best job in the world as a host on the Breakfast Show.

It was not until after my return from China in 1982, when USIA director Charles Wick asked me to brief him on my trip that the subject came up again. He thought I would make a good ambassador and put this in a letter to the White House. Nothing came of it at the time.

The following year, during my Ampart lecture tour of Asia, the evaluations of my journey came to Wick's attention again. It was not until a year later, in December of 1984, that Arthur Burns, then our ambassador to Germany, wrote to Wick that he thought I should be an ambassador. Mr. Wick sent that letter to the White House.

At the end of January 1985, while lunching with Justice Sandra Day O'Connor in her chambers, at a little table set up beside her desk, I told her of the possibility of my becoming an ambassador. I had been approached but had never given any money to any administration and was not a political worker. The Hatch Act forbade government workers to participate in any political activities. She thought I would be a good ambassador and said, "Go for it!"

I would have to get it on merit, she said, adding that the administration needed more women. She couldn't get involved politically by writing a letter because of her status as a justice. I worried about Bill's accepting a role where his wife would be the one receiving attention. Justice O'Connor promised to call out the John O'Connor rescue squad to have lunch with Bill and explain everything.

Not long afterwards, at a small dinner party, I saw Under Secretary of State for Political Affairs Michael Armacost, who had met with me in the Philippines when he was ambassador there. That night, Sandra Day O'Connor mentioned the idea of my being an ambassador in conversation with him. He told me he thought it was a wonderful idea and State would be supportive.

Our good friends Ambassador and Mrs. Thapa of Nepal were also at this dinner. He knew I had lectured in Nepal and had met his king in Washington and had often said he wanted me to come to Nepal as ambassador. He said the king would be so pleased! Suddenly, it seemed possible though not probable.

In June 1985, after two postponements, I met at the White House with Anne Foreman, assistant chief of presidential personnel. One postponement was just before I had left my office to see her; the other was while I waited in her outer office. That time, she came out, explained to me that she was unexpectedly busy and asked me to come back a week later. I thought she must consider our appointment only a courtesy, so on the third try I was relaxed and the interview went well. She thought I had the right qualifications and something might come up later or sooner. I felt slightly optimistic when I left the Executive Office Building (EOB).

Months went by, with no word from the White House. In August, I started French lessons in my office at lunchtime with a French professor, just in case. My French needed brushing up even though I had studied it for six years in school, had lived in France, and had taken refresher lessons from time to time. After an interviewing trip to California, I heard from Pat Sieman, assistant to Director Wick, that Bob Tuttle, chief of White House personnel, would like me to come see him. By now, it was November of 1985.

I met with Mr. Tuttle in his EOB office. He started right in asking me tough, direct questions. First, what did I do at VOA? I told him about my recent California trip interviewing Bill Hewlett of Hewlett-Packard. What does VOA do? Why did I think I was qualified?

Where was my management experience? After all, an ambassador represents the president of the United States and holds a management position. Much of my management experience was in volunteer work as president of both the Washington Red Cross International Committee and American Women in Radio and Television. Women didn't often get to manage corporations then! What policies of the president did I not agree with? What did I think were my main good points? My weakest? He asked me if I had raised any funds or campaigned for the president. I explained that I was prevented by law from doing so. Would I be willing to go to Africa? Yes. We talked about thirty-five or forty minutes.

Then he said, "I think you would make an excellent ambassador, but I am not optimistic. State puts up their people for each post, and it is very difficult for us to get our people chosen."

I felt the interview had gone well and so reported as requested to Director Wick. In the waiting room outside his office, he said he was leaving the next day for Geneva and the first Reagan-Gorbachev Summit Meeting. I told him that Tuttle had said at the end of our interview that he was not optimistic, to which he replied, "Well, I'm optimistic."

At that moment, I knew there was at least a chance of success. The next day I left for Europe to see my good friends the Crookendens in England and Annabella in France. It was a wonderful time to be there watching the events of the Summit on television and hearing the pro-Reagan sentiments from everyone.

Back at work at the end of November, I knew there was a White House meeting scheduled for Friday, December 13th, at which Don Regan, the president's chief of staff, and John Whitehead, the deputy secretary of state, would go over the list of prospective ambassadors. Anne Foreman had phoned to tell me that the White House was putting me on their list for two countries: Ghana and Madagascar. I knew this was a big breakthrough.

Pat Sieman informed me that Whitehead wanted to meet with me before the December 13th meeting (he was serving as acting secretary of state as Secretary George Shultz was away that week). I was nervous. Everything seemed to be going well. In our library, I found some background material on John Whitehead and made an appointment for Thursday, December 12th, at the Department of State. I liked John Whitehead the minute I walked into his office. We chatted. He told me the important meeting had been postponed until the following week.

At the end of the interview he said, "Well, we haven't had our meeting yet but I can't imagine putting up any argument against your nomination." Nothing could be sure until the results of the meeting were announced. I went to Shreveport, Louisiana, just before Christmas for a few days with Larry, Jamye, and the children.

The meeting was canceled two more times and we were into January. Then at last I received that phone call in my office from the White House.

Late in January, I had lunch once again with Sandra Day O'Connor in her chambers, and we talked nonstop for an hour. I told her that the nomination process was under way and asked if she would do me the honor of swearing me in when the rest of the hurdles were crossed. "Of course," she said. We were both excited, and she was truly sharing my happiness. She said she and John would like to give a dinner for us after the Senate had confirmed my appointment and agreed to visit us in Madagascar.

People at my office knew only that I was going on a leave of absence to work on a special project. The security investigation was under way and Bill was working hard filling out the financial questions the White House had asked. He had requested retirement from his position as a stockbroker at Dean Witter Reynolds and was taking French lessons at the Foreign Service Institute. I was going to the Department of State every day for briefings and in between times taking private lessons at the Foreign Service Institute from an excellent French teacher.

My final Breakfast Show would be after the announcement of my appointment. Don Rice, my engineer, kept my old microphone for me until that final program. Barbara Bush, the vice president's wife, had promised to be a guest on the last day. She had broadcast with me several times in past years and did not let me down.

Days rushed by, and on March 17, Bill and I went to an all-day seminar for people going overseas. Robin Rupli, who had agreed to come to Madagascar as my assistant, also attended. The session focused on terrorism, pointing out that the ambassador is a prime target and the Embassy could be in danger. It made me acutely aware of one of my most important responsibilities and that I must check out the Embassy when I arrived to make sure it was well prepared for any trouble. Have a surprise drill with the Marines the first day on duty, I was told. Also, I must make sure the embassy drivers have had proper training. Someone would come to the Embassy to talk about disaster preparedness if I made a request, which I later did. A crisis management team came from Washington and it was most useful.

Later in March, Bill and I took the train to Philadelphia to spend the weekend with Barbara Eisenhower. Barbara has been a good friend ever since the army years. She brought out her old scrapbooks and showed us mementos from her years at our embassy in Belgium, when her husband John was ambassador there.

In April, I had an appointment to do that final program interview with Barbara Bush at the vice president's residence. We talked about her active interest in literacy and her work on programs concerned with teaching people to read. I told her my news about becoming an ambassador if all went well, warning that it was still a secret.

At last, President Reagan called. I was in my office at the Department of State late in the afternoon. The operator said, "Just a minute Ambassador Lynch for President Reagan." The president said, "I'm just calling to ask you if you will be willing to serve as United States ambassador to Madagascar and the Comoros."

Of course I said, "It would be an honor to serve you and the country, Mr. President," and I thanked him for choosing a woman.

He said, "I know something about what you have been doing these past twenty years and I think it's wonderful." Just then we were cut off! I was disappointed but sat for a moment looking out at the Lincoln Memorial thinking what a special experience I had just had. There was nothing I could do about the abrupt ending to our talk. Then, the phone rang again on a different line and I had to take it in another office. The secretary had come in and said, "This is it, this is the president."

I said, "We just talked, but we were cut off." I sat down and the operator came on the phone from the White House. "Just a moment for President Reagan."

I heard the president say, "I didn't want you to think I had hung up on you!"

"Well," I laughed, "I thought maybe that was the way it happened over there, when your time is up, someone just cuts you off!"

"No, no!" said the president.

And I replied, "I wanted to tell you about my husband. He's going with me and he's been very supportive of me. I hope there will be a chance for you to meet him before I go."

"Well, we'll have to see if something can be arranged," he said.

"My best to Mrs. Reagan. I think what she is doing on the drug problem is important."

"I'll tell her. Thank you. Please give my best to your family."

I thanked him and said, "My children can't wait to hear about this phone call. My son calls me Mamador!"

The president laughed, "Goodbye, God bless you."

I called Bill right away to tell him I had just talked to the president. Then I telephoned Justice O'Connor to tell her about the call. "Isn't it fun!" she exclaimed. She had been in her office in Arizona, she told me, when her call came from the president.

Gene Pell, director for Radio Free Europe/Radio Liberty and former VOA director, telephoned me right away because he had heard a rumor that I was going to Madagascar. He asked us to come to Munich, his headquarters, whenever possible on the way to and from Africa. We never did make it, but Gene Pell and Radio Free Europe/Radio Liberty were to be in my future.

Now my days were more filled than ever with briefings, French lessons, working at home, packing what would go to Africa with us. I spent time in my attic studio at the bay and in my closet studio at the apartment. Little by little things were getting done.

Bill and I went to a weeklong seminar at the State Department given for new ambassadors and their spouses. One of our three instructors was Shirley Temple Black. The first day, most of us were thinking to ourselves, we are actually seeing this famous child actress. But from then on, we thought of her only as Ambassador Black. She is an extremely intelligent woman and gave us excellent advice about what to do in all kinds of situations. We still keep in touch, and years later, I called her for information about Prague, one of her posts, and she was as always most helpful. She had served at the United Nations and in Ghana before we met at the Department of State. She had been one of very few women serving as ambassador, and there were still not many — only ten serving worldwide — when I went out to Africa.

What Is an Ambassador?

Many people ask me to explain exactly what an ambassador does and what the title means. I always say an American ambassador is our president's personal representative to the foreign government to which he or she is accredited. The ambassador is also the head of the American community in that country — any U.S. government employees in the embassy or attached to the embassy, Americans living in the country, and temporary American visitors.

The obligations and responsibilities of an ambassador, our chief of mission, are laid out with clarity and precision in U.S. law, 22USC3927, and explained in great detail in the American Academy of Diplomacy's excellent book, *First Line of Defense*. On the "Chief of Mission" the law states:

> A. Duties
> Under the direction of the President the Chief of Mission to a foreign country
> (1) Shall have full responsibility for the direction, coordination and supervision of all government executive branch employees in that country (except for employees under the command of a United States Military Commander); and

(2) Shall keep fully and currently informed with respect to all activities and operations of the government within that country and shall insure that all government branch employees in that country (except for employees under the command of a United States Military Commander) comply fully with all the applicable directives of the Chief of Mission.
B. Duties of Agencies with Employees in Foreign Countries

Any Executive Branch Agency having employees in a foreign country shall keep the Chief of Mission to that country fully and currently informed with respect to all activities and operations of its employees in that country, and shall insure that all of its employees in that country (except for employees under the command of the United States Military Commander) comply fully with all applicable directives of the Chief of Mission.

Many ambassadors have spent their careers in the Foreign Service of the United States. Others, about one-third of serving ambassadors, are private American citizens serving for a few years as presidential appointees. They all dedicate themselves to the United States, sometimes risking their lives, sometimes losing them. There have been many technological advances in recent years, but nothing can replace the role played by ambassadors, who provide a human channel of direct communications between governments. Relationships among nations are especially complex now with terrorism posing such a great threat.

Ambassadors rely on the men and women staffing their embassies to carry out the functions assigned to that mission. Robert R. Bowie, a former Harvard professor and State Department official, has written: "One role of ambassadors underlies all of the others and will be vitally important in the years to come. The ambassador to a given country should be the primary source of intimate, in-depth understanding of the politics, economics, and social aspects of that country and of its concepts of its national interests. An ambassador and his or her embassy staff with genuine expertise on the ground can develop the necessary understanding and feed it into the policy process in Washington so that correct decisions and policies are arrived at."

Thomas Pickering, the most senior officer in the Foreign Service when he retired in 1997, was brought back from retirement to become under secretary of state for political affairs. He raises the point that when "America's economic and political health is so closely tied to the rest of the world, it is astonishing that the relevance of diplomacy can even be raised

. . . Simply put, there are more Americans than ever whose livelihoods depend on trade and investment. There are more American tourists and students needing assistance and more American businesses that can benefit . . . The United States needs more eyes and ears out there, not fewer."

Many people ask me how many current ambassadors are career and how many non-career. The American Academy of Diplomacy has an answer.

"In 2002, there were 109 career ambassadors serving as chiefs of mission and 46 non-career ambassadors, with eleven posts unfilled. That breaks down to approximately 70 percent career and 30 percent non-career, which is about the usual proportion. The total would be 166 serving ambassadors if all posts were filled."

Non-career ambassadors bring to the diplomatic service unique knowledge and experience gained through distinguished careers in the law, education, business, the military, and public service. Many are not independently wealthy and have not contributed money to a political party. Non-career ambassadors bring fresh air to the diplomatic process. They bring their own experience to their assignment, and their expertise as administrators adds to the mission.

Two ambassadors to the United Kingdom of Great Britain and Northern Ireland in recent years came from entirely separate fields. Walter H. Annenberg was a highly innovative magazine and newspaper editor, publisher, and philanthropist before President Nixon appointed him ambassador to Britain in 1969. He used his private funds to restore the official U.S. residence in London, an area where personal funds can be a great help because the State Department budget does not always cover such renovation. A distinguished military man, Admiral William J. Crowe, Jr., was sworn in as the U.S. ambassador to Britain in 1994.

Among other non-career ambassadors was Paul Nitze, who had been special advisor to the president, director of State's Policy Planning Staff, and deputy secretary of defense, when he was appointed ambassador at large in 1986. Senator Daniel Patrick Moynihan served as U.S. ambassador to India and then U.S. Permanent Representative to the United Nations. Former senator Michael J. Mansfield served as the highly successful U. S. ambassador to Japan from 1977 to 1988. Businessman Robert D. Stuart, Jr., had been president and chairman of the board of the Quaker Oats Company for thirty-eight years and was appointed to be our U.S. ambassador to Norway in 1984.

Many of these ambassadors later join the Council of American Ambassadors, a private nonpartisan professional organization that actively supports the role of the Foreign Service in carrying out United States foreign policy.

Advice and Consent

At last, the Foreign Relations Committee set a date for the important Senate hearing. Was I nervous? You can be sure of that. I memorized all the facts and figures of our USAID program, wrote the statement I would read, and learned everything I could about Madagascar. Even then, there was no telling what questions might be asked, and I hoped I would have the right answers. As it turned out, I was not alone; there were four of us nominees, seated at a long table gazing up at our interrogators in what seemed like a high court. Large bronze torchieres with bronze wings, placed midway up the wall, illuminated the hearing room. The Great Seal of the United States hung behind the podium. It was quite a sight for a first-timer like me.

It was our good luck to have Senator Nancy Kassebaum in charge of the proceedings. She put us at ease immediately, saying she knew quite a bit about us already and would address us as ambassadors, certain we were well qualified and would encounter no big problems. Her words produced an almost audible sigh of relief, but we still faced plenty of questions.

I was to be ambassador to both Madagascar and the Comoros Islands and was prepared to answer questions on both of them. I remembered most of the figures about what my embassies would be spending and was surprised when the man next to me took out a piece of paper containing his figures. He assured me that having papers on the table was allowed, but that information came too late for me. After what seemed a long time, we were thanked and it was over! Each of us now was officially an ambassador-designate. In a few days, the entire Senate approved the committee's choices and each of us was officially an ambassador-designate. All that lay ahead was the swearing-in ceremony. First, however, there would be my last broadcast for the Voice of America.

Don Rice, my longtime studio engineer, had my microphone sitting at the table in Studio 33 when I arrived for that final program. All of us on the Breakfast Show had been blessed with wonderful engineers through the years who were very much part of the show. I was grateful to each of mine for their technical skills and genuine interest in the program. I was especially glad to have Don Rice for several years instead of different engineers for each program. We were all such good friends on the show—Bill Reynolds, Phil Irwin, Alan Silverman, Russell Woodgates, Betty Ustun, and, in the beginning, Al Johnson. Everyone helped me along the way.

At the microphone on this final day, I said my last "Good morning and welcome to the Breakfast Show. This is Pat Gates coming to you from the Voice of America in Washington." As promised, Barbara Bush was one of several guests. I talked about NASA, agriculture, sports, theater, American industry, all the subjects familiar to our audience.

It was time to say goodbye and I hoped I could get through that part without breaking. Earlier that morning, I had written some words on a yellow pad and I looked down at those words now through tears welling up. These are the words I spoke:

Now I go out to start my duties as an ambassador of the United States of America. I want to tell you how I feel about my country. I will be living in Madagascar, a country whose people, as in the U.S., come from many countries: from elsewhere in Africa, from Indonesia, from Polynesia, from China, from India, from Pakistan. They speak a common language, however, Malagasy, also called Malgache. I hope I can learn to speak it a little too. The official language is French.

Because this is my last day with you for a few years, I would like to talk for a moment about my personal feelings concerning the country I represent, the United States of America. I have traveled and taken you along all over this land. I have sat before my VOA microphone for over twenty-four years telling you about America and introducing you to its people. It is the story of our technology that spreads throughout the world. But beneath this aura of technology there beats a great heart, forged from many hearts of all nations into one nation. The people of this country, in my opinion, truly believe in the right of freedom for the individual. Sometimes we stumble, but always we go on trying to improve, striving for a better country, a better world, sharing our dreams with others in a practical and often spiritual way. I hope I've conveyed some of my belief in America as we have spent time together throughout the years. You are my family, wherever you live, whatever your nationality. My heart will always belong to you, and I thank you for the great privilege of speaking with you for a day, an hour, or for many years. I wish you good health, happiness and an inner joy to survive life's tears.

Thanks for listening and if you see someone without a smile, give him one of yours."

Goodbye Washington

At last the big day arrived! Family and friends including my grandchildren had gathered on this bright June day for my swearing-in ceremony in the Benjamin Franklin Room, one of the most magnificent rooms in all of Washington. An official reception room on the eighth floor of the Department of State, it has historic paintings on the walls, crystal chandeliers, artifacts of Colonial history, and a view of the Lincoln Memorial from the window or the balcony. It was hard to believe that Supreme Court Justice Sandra Day O'Connor would be swearing me in. Many friends had been arriving as I waited in the African bureau office downstairs for word that my time had come. I had prepared my brief acceptance speech and glanced through it one more time on the way up in the elevator. It's a good thing I did, because when I went to the podium, I had my notes in my hand but had left my reading glasses on a nearby table so I could barely see to read. I gave the speech pretty much from memory. What else could I do!

The actual swearing-in took place at the podium in the center of the room. My husband held the Bible my children had given me, as I placed my hand on it to take the oath of office. Deputy Secretary of State John Whitehead presided. Secretary Shultz was returning that day from the Philippines and had asked to see me later that afternoon in his office. After the formalities, I greeted everyone in a receiving line and we all celebrated with champagne and cookies.

Among the documents I was given proving that I was now an ambassador were two certificates of appointment, which now hang on my wall in my library. The first says:" Ronald Reagan, President of the United States of America, to Patricia Gates Lynch of the District of Columbia, Greeting: Reposing special trust and confidence in your Integrity, Prudence, and Ability, I have nominated and by and with the advice and consent of the Senate do appoint you Ambassador Extraordinary and Plenipotentiary of the United States of America to the Republic of Madagascar. " The other certificate noted, in similar words, my appointment to the Federal and Islamic Republic of the Comoros (now called the Union of Comoros).

When I called on Secretary of State George Shultz in his office, he gave me a little gold pin with the Great Seal of the United States on it. He said that this was a personal present from him and his wife and that he presented one to each new woman ambassador, of which there were few then but more now. Secretary Shultz was much loved in the Department of State because he devoted a great deal of his time and interest to running the department as well as attending to affairs of the world.

Before our fast-approaching departure for Africa, I had an important visit from a man whose life would have been snuffed out immediately if he had returned to his native Poland in 1981. General Jaruzelski's military junta, which ruled Poland, had sentenced my friend Ambassador Romuald (Romek) Spasowski to death. The ambassador had called our Department of State from his Polish Embassy Residence here in Washington just as he was about to be seized and forcefully put on a plane for Warsaw. When the FBI reached him and his wife Wanda at the Residence just ahead of the communists, he made a formal Declaration of Defection from communist Poland. He was immediately placed under FBI protection.

He and Wanda had kept in touch ever since that dramatic day. We had met when Wanda was a member of the Washington International Committee of the Red Cross. Spasowski had been a communist all his life, and his father had been a well-known communist intellectual in Poland even before the war. This was the second time Romuald had been ambassador to the United States, and we knew that he had serious doubts about the Soviet grip on his country. His wife Wanda was a Catholic and strongly anticommunist. Spasowski's fascinating book *The Liberation of One* had just been published as we were packing for Africa, and some reviewers said it was destined to be an important book on communism for years to come.

Now Ambassador Spasowski wanted to see me to talk to me about Madagascar. He explained that he was accompanied by an FBI agent at all times and would have to bring the agent with him. I suggested we meet first for lunch at Fort McNair in Washington and then go to my apartment nearby where we could talk. We had the living room to ourselves while the agent stayed in a back room. Romuald was

252

concerned about my going to Madagascar because of the strong Soviet influence there. He remembered seeing the map of Madagascar when he attended meetings concerning important Soviet goals. He emphasized that poor countries are fertile areas for Soviet subversion and that there would be many KGB agents there. The Soviets, he said, consider Madagascar a good place for training their agents because they like islands from which other countries can be reached easily. I told him how much I appreciated his counsel. I was aware of possibly difficult times ahead, but heartened that the Malagasy were not anti-American. I was looking forward to working with the president there because of signs that his government was opening up to financial restructuring with the World Bank and the IMF. We would help with development. I would heed his advice on the presence of many Soviets.

(Much later, after our return from Africa, Bill and I went to see Romuald Spasowski and Wanda in their apartment in Virginia not long before he died of cancer. I reminded him of his kindness before my departure for Madagascar and assured him that my three years there had turned out to be a remarkable experience. Madagascar had made a strong turn away from Marxism toward the West. He spoke with joy about freedom in Poland now that the Cold War was over and told us that the new ambassador from Poland had come to his bedside to visit with him.)

President Reagan had invited me to bring my family to the White House to meet with him in the Oval Office, as he did with all new ambassadors. The president let me bring a few extra family members, because he knew how much I wanted to include my little granddaughters, Emily, then seven, and Sally five. With Pam and her husband Buddy and Larry with his Jamye, Bill and I made eight. When we entered the Oval Office after gathering in the cabinet room, the president was ready with his favorite jars of jellybeans as presents for the children. The girls weren't exactly sure about the importance of a president of the United States, but they knew he must be somebody special. He was gracious as we all talked for a bit and he and I talked briefly about Madagascar. He quickly agreed to Larry's request for the White House photographer to take a picture of the president with just the two girls, in addition to a group photo. You can be sure that picture is in a place of honor in their household. I was reminded of my White House days when a White House photographer, Oliver Atkins, had asked me to sit down at the president's desk so he could take my picture, with the American flag over my right shoulder. At that time, I never dreamed I would someday have a desk of my own with the American flag over my right shoulder and the ambassadorial flag over my left.

Bill and I took off by taxi for the airport for an early morning flight for New York and Paris. Then it would be on to mainland Africa and thence to Madagascar. Reaching the airport before the airport had opened, we were deposited outside of a locked door and sat waiting on our suitcases. We laughed at how you could be in the president's office one day and sitting on a suitcase locked out of the airport the next! Then we heard the doors being unlocked and were on board in no time for the first leg of our long journey.

Ahoy Madagascar

Before we knew it, we were over the Atlantic Ocean flying halfway around the world to the Great Island of Madagascar, once called the jewel of the Indian Ocean but now, in the Soviet era, beset by poverty under a pro-Marxist government. In Paris I had some briefings at our embassy, which had always had a diplomatic interest in Madagascar. We dined with friends and, after a day or two, were off for Nairobi with a stop in Saudi Arabia.

Landing in Jeddah at 1:15 in the morning is quite an experience, one I was to repeat often. Never were we allowed off the plane. On my first landing in Jeddah, we were asked by an Air France voice on the loudspeaker to fasten our seat belts and take no pictures. The visual picture out the window, however, was something to behold, like a glittering electric factory with dancing lights neatly laid in geometric patterns. It looks like a massive city of tomorrow on another planet. As we land, there are blue lights on the runway, and as we taxi towards the airport the perimeter lights seem to move along with us, forming a long string of sparkling illuminated trains. You can see through them and know it's just a fantasy, but the giant rings do form perfect little railway cars. As the lights fade away, the luggage trucks and larger vans are waiting with flashing lights dancing on their tops like giant rotating propellers. There were no stars in the sky to compete with the manmade stars on the ground. Even the moon seemed eclipsed by the brilliance.

From our window we could see a few people disembarking, while new passengers boarded. We had been warned not to smoke at this time nor strike a match or operate a cigarette lighter. No liquor would be served. Then we ascended over the city of electric grandeur almost as a space shuttle rises up out of Florida. Even on a 747 jet it was pretty impressive, seeing lights stacked on lights, pyramids, triangles, and circles of light.

Next touchdown was Nairobi, where we spent that July 1986 night in a hotel. The next morning I had briefings at the U.S. Embassy, the same embassy that would be destroyed by terrorists several years later. The stops along the way were important, but I was eager to reach our final destination, the capital of Madagascar, Antananarivo. Bill and I arrived at the Nairobi Airport that night in plenty of time for our next flight, we thought. To my distress, I was told that the plane would not fly that night and we would have to wait until the next morning. I knew that people were planning to be at the airport to meet us and that it would not be good for us to be late. So I visited a few offices of the airline, asked more questions, and finally met a man who said, "Oh yes, your plane takes off in twenty minutes for Madagascar. I will take you to the gate!"

And so it was that we arrived on the right night, though rather late. We had stopped in the Comoros but did not disembark. I would be presenting my credentials as ambassador there but not yet. Madagascar would be my home base, and the embassy in the Comoros had a fine deputy in Chargé Ed Brynn. Now Madagascar, land of enchantment, was in sight just below us! Land ho for seamen and pirates! Captain Christian's crew knew it was on course when it sighted the Great Island from the decks of the *Bounty*. One poet called it "The land at the end of the earth."

Madagascar, approximately 10,000 miles from the United States of America, is the fourth largest island in the world, after Greenland, New Guinea, and Borneo. Lying off the southeast coast of Africa in the Indian Ocean, it is about 1,000 miles long and 360 miles across at its widest part—as large as Belgium, France, and Holland combined. Over fifteen million people live there, more than one million of them in the capital.

Madagascar is more Asian than African. It is believed that the first settlers arrived from Indonesia in around 500 A.D. It has many different ethnic groups from the coast of Africa too, but everyone speaks the same language, Malagasy, which sounds Polynesian. Madagascar had kings and queens until the late nineteenth century.

The Portuguese were the first Europeans to land, in 1504, at Fort Dauphin in the south. Later, the British came to stay for a while, then the French. On the night we flew into Antananarivo, Madagascar had been independent from France for twenty-six years. It had suffered a revolution and the disastrous effects of socialism and nationalism. There was no more rice to export, no books for schools, no homes for the poor, but there was beauty everywhere—in the houses, on the many hills of the city, in the handsome faces of the people, in the flowers, in the markets, in the sunsets, over the mountain range I could see from my window. I fell in love with Madagascar without a moment's hesitation.

Although I had sent a message from Nairobi about the flight's late arrival, I did not know whether anyone would be there to meet us. It was a great relief, therefore, to see Chargé David Rawson and his wife and the ambassador's expert and loyal driver, Albert. The long black Oldsmobile he drove for me had an American flag on its front fender. The president of the Malagasy-American Society was also there with his wife. We went to the Rawsons' house for a late supper and to stay the night. The great adventure had begun.

17

Madagascar Discovered

The staff had gathered to meet us when we drove up to the Residence, which served as both home and venue for official occasions. Here we would entertain government leaders and important visitors, and the staff made it all possible. Staff members became like family. We also met the Residence guards, who served night and day. Though I had become the embassy's ambassador, I would not be officially recognized by the president of Madagascar until I had come to the Palace to present my credentials to him.

Although I had spent many years in government, I was new to the Foreign Service. At my chancery office I met with the embassy staff, who greatly impressed me, as did the support I received from the Department of State. I also appreciated the splendid Malagasy employees working at the embassy, the Foreign Service nationals. They provide continuity as the American officers arrive and depart. After my first year there, our Malagasy economic assistant won the Department of State award as the Best Foreign Service national in all of Africa. We worked as a team, and a hard-working team at that.

The deputy chief of mission was scheduled to leave for his new assignment, and his successor would shortly arrive. The executive secretary was also leaving. Robin Rupli, who had worked with me at the Voice of America, would soon arrive to be my assistant. I had been promised a political officer, Liam Humphreys, who arrived some weeks later. I had met the administrative officer, Alex Kirkpatrick, in Washington and was glad to see him again. In Washington he had mentioned that the embassy had reported it had no tear-gas for its emergency tear-gas canisters, and at my request he managed to have procured the gas in time for my arrival.

The embassy is located on a street in the middle of the city, with the Agency for International Development (USAID) headquarters occupying half the building. I was astonished to discover that the USAID staff had no internal doorway by which to enter the main part of the embassy in case of emergency, only an exit to the sidewalk. One of my first directives during a walk-through tour was to install a passageway to our side of the embassy immediately. The marine guard posts were in our section of the building, and it was imperative that we could all be together if necessary. The United States Marines were on twenty-four hour duty to guard important papers and the Embassy itself. We were all responsible for clearing our desks and locking up our papers whenever we left the building. If the marines found an important piece of paper on our desk, we were in trouble. It happened to me just once when I left the office quickly. I made sure I didn't make that mistake again. For these young marines, U.S. embassies are special duty, for which they are handpicked. Their commander is a gunnery sergeant, who is the only one of them allowed to be married. I cannot give enough praise to the marines. They are absolutely superb, and I was sorry each time one left at the end of his one-year tour of duty.

Every day, I was up at 5:30 a.m., reached the office by 7:30 a.m., and went home for the two-hour lunch break from 12:30 p.m. to 2:30 p.m. One reason I went into the office before most of the staff had arrived was to see the cable traffic coming in from Washington. I had been told at the State Department that it was important for me to read every cable from Washington for a while to learn about everything going on in the Embassy, however minor. It takes about six months, the African Bureau chief had told me, for a new ambassador to feel at home with his or her responsibilities. That's about the same length of time, I thought, for a business executive entering a new position of responsibility.

An ambassador is responsible and accountable for everything going on at the Embassy, even in our small commissary. I had learned that sometimes when the commissary would run out of money, it was necessary although not obligatory to provide a loan, which I consistently did. Once when the paychecks for the Foreign Service nationals did not arrive from Paris on time, my husband Bill and I covered for the paychecks and were reimbursed later. These may not seem like earth-shaking events, but they can be pretty important when people have to eat. Speaking of eating, at first, the American staff said they would like to have a shorter lunch break and go home earlier (I did not require that someone stay late just because I did). So we took a vote on it and, much to everyone's surprise, hardly anyone voted in favor of shortening the lunch hour.

My experience as a communicator proved tremendously valuable. A television camera was always present whenever I gave a speech, visited one of our projects, or attended anything important. So the U.S.A. was up there on the nightly news, sometimes several times a week. With only one TV station, I had a captive audience. Communicating in French made media interviews more difficult there than in the States, but all the basics of my profession served me well regardless of the language. An interview I did in English with a reporter from the *Economist* led to the only time I have ever been quoted in that magazine. I told the reporter that in Madagascar "politics is rice."

Politically, Madagascar was a perfect example of a failed economy under strict socialist practices. As the fourth largest island on earth, with an area larger than that of France, Madagascar has good harbors, ample natural resources, and a long history of exposure to the West. Once one of the most prosperous countries of the Indian Ocean, now times were hard.

The socialist revolution had begun after a violent uprising in 1972 overthrew the government that had ruled Madagascar since its independence in 1960. Didier Ratsiraka consolidated that revolution when he became president in 1975. He took out high-cost foreign loans to pay for nonproductive capital projects, just when world trade was turning against Malagasy exports. The socialist bloc saw an opportunity and moved in. By 1980, Madagascar was broke, and President Ratsiraka had to change policies abruptly and come to terms with the IMF and the World Bank.

If his government meant what it said about economic reform, the United States would move quickly to implement a sound long-term development program. Washington was alarmed by the Ratsiraka government's anti-Western stance, particularly because of Madagascar's strategic location on the major shipping lane through the Mozambique Channel. When Ratsiraka indicated his willingness to resume dealing with the West and commit to economic reform, we decided to focus our help on supporting the IMF–World Bank policy package, with emphasis on rice.

Rice is the staple of the Malagasy people's diet, the basis of most Malagasy families' breakfast, lunch, and dinner. Surprisingly, the Malagasy per capita consumption of rice surpasses even that of the Chinese. Before the revolution, Madagascar had exported a very high quality of rice, but by the end of the 1970s the country found it necessary to import rice. Unfortunately, its agricultural sector was severely affected by policies adopted by the socialist-oriented governments of the 1970s and 1980s. These policies consciously depressed the price of rice received by the rural farmers in order to maintain an unsustainably low price for the large urban population. Over the years, the government acquired a dominant control in the marketing of the crop. The distortions brought about by the government's intervention effectively subsidized prices to urban consumers at the expense of the rural rice growers.

Poor agricultural seasons in the mid-1980s ultimately led to the depletion of the country's rice reserves. By the time of my appointment to Madagascar in 1986, the country, once confidently self-reliant in rice production, faced the need to rely on substantial imports. Unfortunately, it lacked the foreign currency resources to pay for such imports.

In response to the country's rice shortage, the United States, shortly prior to my appointment as ambassador, agreed to provide a significant shipment of rice under the 1985 Food for Progress program. On my first visit to the east coast port of Tamatave soon after my arrival, I witnessed the off-loading of the first such shipment of rice. While donors such as the United States and the United Nations' World Food Programme could provide limited rice supplies as a stopgap measure to avert immediate catastrophe, the essential need for fundamental reform of the country's agricultural marketing policies was evident.

Under World Bank leadership, a number of Madagascar's principal foreign partners worked closely with the government's agricultural, economic, and planning agencies to develop a comprehensive program of reform, to be implemented over many years. The program's principal goal was to liberalize agricultural marketing and restore a free, competitive, and open market. In the long term, this would raise the price of rice paid to growers and encourage them to sustain or even increase production. Over time, it would also prompt investors to develop a more effective production and marketing infrastructure.

The international community recognized that the cost of a desperately needed reform program would lead, in the short term, to reduced government revenue, the dismantling of government-operated marketing structures (with a consequent loss of employment for their cadres), and a gradual increase in the price of rice to consumers. To offset the shock of these anticipated hardships and provide hard currency to fund the country's essential imports, donors agreed to provide significant cash incentives to the Malagasy government upon the adoption of the stipulated reform measures.

Our own foreign assistance program, the U.S. Agency for International Development, reached a pioneering agreement with the Malagasy government for the implementation of significant elements of the agricultural marketing reform program. Under the terms of the agreement, the government committed itself to adopt and implement specific reform measures on an agreed schedule. In return, the United States agreed to make substantial foreign currency disbursements for the Malagasy government to make available to importers, to enable the country to obtain such essentials as transportation and agricultural equipment, agricultural supplies, and fuel.

In contrast to USAID's more narrowly defined projects in Africa, this was one of the agency's earliest examples of policy-based assistance programs. As such, it was viewed at the time as USAID's highest priority initiative in Africa. It was followed by a range of policy-based initiatives in such fields as environmental preservation and health. Altogether, the funds we supplied from 1981 to 1988 totaled over $65 million.

Trooping the Line at the Palace

A week or two went by with no word from the president concerning my credentials. The British ambassador, Malcolm McBain, called me early on and said he and his wife Audrey would like to give a dinner party for us, even though it was rushing protocol a bit. His post before Madagascar had been in Houston, Texas, as consul general. We became friends, and Malcolm and Bill often played golf together at the only golf course in the country!

Finally, the call came to present my credentials on Wednesday, August 6, 1986, at the palace, the home of President Didier Ratsiraka. Located in the very center of the city the palace had once been the French Embassy. The Malagasy protocol people arrived about 10:00 a.m. to pick me up in a big Mercedes sedan, with U.S. and Madagascar flags flying from the front fenders and a motorcycle escort. Four of my staff accompanied me. At the palace, a military honor guard stood at attention, and I was invited to "troop the line" by inspecting the waiting troops while a band played appropriate military airs. Then, the band played both national anthems as we all stood at attention. Standing in the courtyard listening to my national anthem being played so far from home was an emotional moment. Then it was into the palace for the presentation ceremony. No one knew that I had been practicing in my kitchen at the Residence what my first words would be when I spoke with the President in front of the television cameras.

I wanted to say, "I am happy to be in Madagascar" so I worked with Jean Clair, the cook, as my coach, to say that phrase in Malagasy. Over and over, trying to remember each word, I said, "Faly aho tonga eto Madagascar." I had my formal speech in French on cards in my hand to glance down at it as I presented my credentials, but my Malagasy was in my head and the words were the first I spoke to the president.

Of all the speeches I gave during the next three years, I think those few words proved to be the most important. For years, people would say to me, "We remember when you first spoke with our president on television, you spoke in Malagasy and we were most touched."

After the official ceremonies I had an hour-long private chat with the president, who told me he didn't much like the United States, or words to that effect. I resolved to change his mind as time went by. Leaving the palace, I passed by the honor guard as the band played. Bill had not been invited to the ceremony, but we watched it together on the local TV news, which carried the entire thing as the lead item that night in both French and Malagasy.

Cigars and Brandy

We had maintained a rather low profile until I presented my credentials to President Ratsiraka, but now that would change. As the first woman American ambassador, I was the subject of much curiosity. When people would address me as Madame Ambassadress, I would correct them politely, "It is Madame Ambassadeur. We use ambassador for a woman just as for a man."

At our first official dinner, I know I must have been a concern to the dean of the diplomatic corps, the Japanese ambassador, who always invited the ambassadors for conversation after dinner in a separate room, where cigars and brandy were passed around. Bill, as my spouse, had been asked by the ambassador to join the wives in the sitting room, and he ventured forth with aplomb. He had a good time, and it turned out to be quite an adventure for me too. The other ambassadors on this night sat very quietly at first while we waited for our host to join us. There was a rather uncomfortable silence while they all wondered what to say.

Finally, one of them spoke up and said, "I'm having a good bit of trouble with my leg. At night, the cramps are almost unbearable."

"Oh," said I. "Do you know about using wine corks to relieve the pain?" Every one looked at me rather startled.

I went on to say, "We have just been in England, and our British hostess told my husband, who also has leg cramps, that the British solution is to put wine corks in your bed. She told us to put two corks between the sheets and a blanket at our feet. For some amazing reason, it works. My husband, of course, did not believe what she was saying. But, armed with two wine corks he gave it a try, and believe it or not, his leg cramps have disappeared. We brought the corks with us to Madagascar and are still using them. They are still working, so you might give it a try."

To say that my listeners were flabbergasted is putting it mildly, but they all agreed that there are many things we can accept without understanding. The Japanese ambassador had arrived to join us, and we went directly from corks to politics. At the end of a good discussion, very helpful to me because the Japanese ambassador had a fine sense of what was going on in the country and shared his knowledge with the rest of us, we joined the spouses. All the ambassadors rushed up to their wives to tell them about the corks. Bill looked absolutely delighted. Our first formal diplomatic dinner had been a success!

The Residence

The Residence had a life of its own. It was a beautiful house built before the country's independence in 1960 by a wealthy French family. When the French were no longer thriving there, they sold it to the American embassy.

The house sat on top of a hill in an area called Cité Planton. I discovered on a walk one day that the entire hillside had been owned by the Planton family, who lived in a huge stone house on the way up the narrow, winding road toward the top. Over time they sold parcels of land until gradually the hills were packed with houses. The only real expanse of land was around the Residence. The old Planton house of red stone is now a nursery school, and every day on my way up or down the hill in my official car I would pass cars driven by parents bringing their children to and from the school.

Returning home after dark was always a pleasure. Rakoto or Martin would meet me at the car carrying in my briefcase and other packages. Willy, our Malagasy shepherd dog, would run down the long steps to meet me and then to take his brief ride in the car as Albert backed into the carport. I would walk up the stairs under the blue canvas canopy where my husband might be waiting or still be inside reading in the library. I would hurry to the kitchen to say good evening to Jean Clair, the cook, who always had a big smile, a warm heart and a good dinner waiting.

Jean Clair, a small man, even shorter than I, was very special to me. I have never met anyone quite like him before or since. One night the smile was gone, and we were all heartbroken because word had come that Jean Clair's oldest son had been killed in a truck accident while out in the countryside with the army, inspecting roads. He was about to graduate from the university as an engineer, quite an achievement coming from a family of nine children with very little income. We suffered with Jean Clair, for he and the others really were family there. We paid for a car to take Jean Clair some four hours to the southwest to pick up the body. We visited the family, we mourned — all we could do. It was a hard time.

We liked everyone on our household staff. Martin was the head houseman. Rakoto, another houseman, took especially good care of our houseguests, in his quiet way, as well as helping with everything else. Though not young, he worked hard. Noeline, one of two maids, did the laundry, and Marie-Angele cleaned the rather large house with the help of Noeline. Two gardeners, Pierre and Gabrielle, tended the fairly large grounds, which were not elaborate but were quite lovely. We had white ducks in a little pond and two large tortoises. We fed the tortoises meat and rice, and they grew even larger during our three years there.

In our last year, the pretty collie that lived with a Malagasy family outside our back gate had puppies. One of the puppies looked like a combination shepherd and collie, what some would call a border collie. We started to feed him breakfast when he was six weeks old when he slipped through the back gate. Our dog Willie enjoyed playing with him, and our attachment to this puppy grew even as he grew. After several months, he was the only puppy out of the litter that had not been given away, and we asked if we might keep him. We called him Tolliver or Tollie, because he was so tolerant when our big dog pushed him around a bit. We brought both dogs home to America with us, and although Willie did not live long, Tollie lived beyond the turn of the century and was an important, much loved family member.

Many nights I would come home with just enough time to change clothes to host dinner guests or a reception or attend an official affair. Other nights, we would watch the news on the only television station. The first newscast was in Malagasy, so that was difficult to understand, but the news was repeated in French, which we could understand. We lived in every room in the house, even enjoying our formal living room, with its handsome Venetian chandeliers, which also hung in the dining room. Some excellent paintings hung on the wall, on loan from our friend Olga Hirshhorn and other collectors, some from what is called "The Arts in Embassies Program." One small treasure was a painting of Camp David by Dwight David Eisenhower, painted when he was president. His son John, grandson David, and the Abilene, Kansas, Museum enabled us to borrow that one. It was everyone's favorite and was admired by visiting Malagasy school children.

In the cold winter months, June through September, we would always light a fire in the living room fireplace. Fortunately, at the last minute we had decided to bring our winter clothes and would have frozen that first Malagasy winter if we hadn't. Eventually, the embassy ordered some electric radiators for the house, which helped tremendously. I remember the Indian ambassador told me that he usually wore two pairs of socks when he went for dinner at an ambassador's residence. The houses had no heat of their own, and the temperature dropped to only a few degrees above freezing. It never snowed, yet on some days I needed a heavy coat. At the end of September, it would start warming up.

We enjoyed our music on CDs we played in our library, and there was a piano in the drawing room. It was a happy place and never more so than when we had family and friends from home to share this remarkable country with us, or when we would entertain the Malagasy, the diplomatic corps, and members of the embassy staff. A week seldom went by without dinners or receptions. We would stand in our center hall receiving guests and never grow tired, for people seemed so delighted to be in the Residence, some for the first time. That center hall had marble floors, and we were glad we had brought with us a Persian rug from Teheran to stand on while greeting our guests. When the weather was fine, the guests would often go onto the large stone terrace overlooking the gardens, where we would sometimes have dinner served.

We received government representatives from the prime minister on down. President Ratsiraka never went to embassy affairs, even though I saw him often in the Palace. He told me he would like to come, but if he went to one he would have to go to all.

Our guests at the Residence came from all over Madagascar, sometimes from the University in Antananarivo, sometimes they were business people or American missionaries resident in Madagascar. Two visitors from Washington who stayed with us at the Residence were Dr. Dillon Ripley, then director of the Smithsonian Institution, and his wife Mary. When a yellow fly flew into Mary's iced tea at lunch, she asked Jean Clair to preserve it in some Vodka because it was rare and she wanted to take it home!

Some of our visitors were Americans on World Wildlife tours, professors, industry consultants, and Malagasy scientists. Once, American navy pilots and crew on a worldwide oceanographic research project stopped off. Another time we had American Seabees working with the Malagasy military.

Another visitor, Henry Mitchell, gardening expert for the *Washington Post,* wrote stunning articles on Madagascar when he returned to the U.S.A., articles that helped us communicate the need for focus on this country's environmental problems as well as its great economic needs. I recall that one or two of those articles appeared on the front page of the *Post.*

One who stayed with us, Allison Jolly, wrote informative and exciting *National Geographic* stories on Madagascar, especially about that remarkable, lovable little primate, the lemur. Perhaps, say some scientists, the lemur is the oldest relative of man. Today the continuing existence of the lemur is threatened, as the forests are burned for planting crops and the lemurs' tree homes and food sources disappear. As Loren Eiseley often wrote, man is the only animal that lays waste to his own environment.

We bought shoes and warm jackets for the Residence guards, so they would not have to wear blankets around their shoulders at night to keep warm. Bill arranged for some lockers in the garage so they could leave the jackets there, but the shoes they kept so they could walk home in comfort. Some of them were studying English and Bill enjoyed talking with them. When I kept the household staff late because of official entertaining, I always had them taken home by car because they had miles to walk and the roads were not entirely safe.

Through a tall, narrow window in our bedroom, I had a fairy-tale view of the city of Antananarivo, with the Andringitra Mountain range in the distance. I could see houses nestled together on descending levels and church steeples. Off to the left, if I got very close to the glass, I could glimpse the queen's palace perched on the highest point in the city. It was the ever-changing sky that made the view through that window my favorite. In the early morning, I would open the draperies to see if the mountains were visible. When they were hidden by fog, I knew we would have sun later in the day. But if it was stormy in that direction, we were in for a dark day. On a Sunday, Tuesday, or Thursday when the rising sun was brightly reflected across the valley, I knew the early morning flights from Paris and Nairobi could land. There was no instrument flying here; it was all by sight. In the evening, if I were home before the "coucher du soleil" (literally, the going to bed of the sun), I would go to my window and stay for a moment or two to watch the glorious glow hovering over the hills with the darkening blue of the African sky weaving the city into a magnificent tapestry. I thought of it as an enchanted city, here on the Great Red Island that has intrigued navigators and explorers for centuries.

Exploring the Country

My very first day at the Embassy, I found a friendly letter on my desk from a Doctor Jacobson, welcoming me to the Great Island and inviting me to come to the city of Antsirabe for the opening of a new school by some Lutheran missionaries in a few weeks' time. I accepted. When the time came, Bill and I headed south in a four-wheel-drive vehicle rather than my usual car, with Albert at the wheel. It was good to have a four-wheel drive because the road was decent for only half the way, the other half resembling a washed-out riverbed. In addition to the school, we planned to visit a couple of USAID projects near the city.

Antsirabe had been a favorite summer resort area of the French, when they had occupied Madagascar, and there were many old villas that had once been quite lovely. After many years of neglect due to limited resources, the city had fallen on bad times. We stayed in what was once a French resort hotel, with roughly one hundred rooms, few of them occupied. Although we did have a bath, there was no seat on the toilet, only a lid. It turned out that only four rooms in the establishment had one. Apparently seats were a favorite target for people passing through, as they are unattainable in the country. We found a toilet seat in the basement of the Residence when we returned and thenceforth took it along whenever we visited a new city.

The important thing missing from our Antsirabe hotel was heat of any kind, and it was one of the coldest days of the year. We wore all of our clothes to bed, survived what really were insignificant inconveniences, and had a good time.

The visit to the school was a great pleasure. I gave a speech in which I noted, among other things, that "a new school means a place where we can satisfy the curiosity of our minds. It means a place to explore the many wonders of our world, a place where teachers lead us by the hand for awhile and give us tools for learning our whole life long." Certainly, I was still learning.

In Antsirabe we took a tour in a couple of "pous-pous," which translates into "push-push," which look like rickshaws. Unlike

Antananarivo, the city is quite level and this is the primary source of transport for everyone. We had a grand trip home from Antsirabe on a train that looked exactly like a bus on rails, hood, fender, and all. It carried nineteen passengers in comfortable wicker chairs, the same as seen on countless verandas. We had bought some French bread, cheese, and fresh fruit for our evening meal, as it was a four-hour journey. The train moved slowly on single, narrow-gauge track, and we cranked down the windows and waved to everyone we passed on the way home. Surely, the passing of that train is the biggest event of the day in many of their villages.

I was already planning another trip, this time to Tulear, down on the southwest coast, to visit some USAID projects with two men from USAID. Because it was quite a distance away, two and a half days by car, we would fly by commercial air and a four-wheel-drive vehicle would be driven down from the embassy in advance to meet us when the plane landed.

Safari into Lemur Territory

Madagascar is sometimes referred to as the original Garden of Eden. It has rain forests, a desert, long coastlines, extraordinary plants and trees — and lemurs. Lemurs are prosimians, lower primates. As Allison Jolly had noted, these are amazing little mammals, and it is sad that the lemur population is rapidly declining as the human population on the Great Island continues to increase. Their habitat in recent years has been destroyed as population pressures and agricultural needs translate to burning forests and making food hard to find for the lemurs.

Madagascar contains many wonders, such as chameleons with long tails seemingly hand-painted by God in beautiful designs and colors, and radiated tortoises like the ones in my garden. Best of all, I love the lemurs, with their big, round, sensitive eyes. These animals adapt to their surroundings. In the Spiny Desert, with its wonderland of plants, the lemurs find flowers for food even when surrounded by thorns. Lemurs come in various shapes and sizes, and I would be hard pressed to say which species of lemur I find most enchanting.

Some scientists say that Madagascar broke away from mainland Africa, probably as many as 165 million years ago, and that long afterwards the lemurs probably came to Madagascar by "rafting" across the Mozambique Channel from Africa on tangles of vegetation. Ian Tattersall, a paleontologist and primatologist, says "By the time human beings arrived less than 2,000 years ago, the island was home to at least 45 lemur species ranging in body size from the two-ounce mouse lemur to a 400-pound Archaeo-Indris, as big as a large gorilla. Those huge ones are gone now, but there are over twenty species still in existence."

My first sighting of a lemur was in Beza Mahfaly at the Ala Tahry Reserve, on the trip to Tulear on the southwest coast with Dick Macken and Tony Pryor of USAID. Our Land Rover automobile was waiting for us at the airport with our sleeping bags and supplies, the driver having left Antananarivo three days before. We left the airport around 3:30 p.m. and drove inland, stopping for a few minutes at the city market for bread, oranges, and a little tin charcoal stove. We drove for five hours and what an adventure!

Most of our driving was in the dark and the mostly dirt road was unbelievable. It would disappear completely, or it would be so eroded that we would have to descend very carefully to avoid upsetting. Occasionally we would pass through a little village of huts with people standing in doorways. Only once did we go through a village that had electricity. We saw men carrying spears along the road but realized with some relief that the spears were only for hunting or gathering fruit. And so we traveled on, hour after hour, under a star-filled sky that seemed even more glorious than the view we have in our own hemisphere. We doubted that the road could continue but were reassured by our guide, Professor Rakotomanga Pothin of the University of Madagascar. Suddenly, we doubted even his word when we rounded a bend and saw the road abruptly end at a river. We were certain we would have to go back.

"Ah," said the professor. "We can proceed, the river is not profound." So we drove through the river and proceeded on our journey. We arrived at the Ala Tahry Reserve, which is a clearing in the forest at 8:15 p.m, and the villagers greeted us, about thirteen of them, mostly children. They knew we were coming but had expected we would have tents, so immediately; they took shovels and brooms and cleared out one of their mud huts with a thatched roof. This became our home and was actually quite comfortable. The two zebus, Madagascar cattle, standing in front of the hut were moved around to the back, Looking out of my glassless window next morning, I saw them munching on straw beside an old wooden cart reminiscent of a Van Gogh painting. The zebu is a huge animal with horns and a big hump on its back. I am fond of these zebus and have seen hundreds of them in Tulear province, the heart of zebu country.

Next evening, I sat under a thatched roof in a forest clearing, with six children beside me, one a little girl about six years old carrying a baby about one year old. They were curious about my pen and notebook as I wrote by the light of the fire. These were the villagers' children, and we had watched them at play and at work that afternoon. They had two toys made of wood, roughly hewn; one a little bus, one perhaps a wagon with a string to pull it.

The villagers shared their food with us, giving us fresh pineapple for breakfast and rice to go with our dinner. We ate the rice with bread, cheese, crackers, and wine that we had brought with us in a big basket. We also had baked beans, tuna fish, cookies, and oranges. What more could one want?

Although we had no tents, we did have sleeping bags with us and I had a large mosquito net with a ring at the top tied to a stick that went across a corner of the hut under the roof. It looked almost like the royal hangings on the bed of Henry VIII in this tiny hut hung over my sleeping bag. It is quite practical, although fortunately there didn't seem to be many mosquitoes. We were always on the alert for the malaria-bearing mosquito when away from Antananarivo. My two USAID companions had no mosquito nets and put their sleeping bags in a corner of our one-room hut.

On our first morning walk in Beza Mahfaly, we saw one sifaka lemur, with a baby on its stomach. When it leaps through the trees, it jumps with its hind feet, looking like a kangaroo with its pouch out in front. Its hands and toes look human, with apposite thumbs like ours. The sifaka is mostly white with what looks like a black mask on its face, little black ears, a black tail, and other black markings on its body. Soon we saw the ring-tailed Maki lemurs, with grey fur and long bushy tails with black and white stripes. It too is handsome and seems to have quite a sense of humor. When we first saw some Makis, they were walking along a path with their tails swaying, pointed straight up in the air. As the lemurs were not frightened of us, we were able to get quite close, although we mostly watched at a distance with our field glasses.

In the afternoon, we drove to the Spiny Desert not far from our camp, where we saw the most amazing variety of desert plants and trees, many in bloom. It was springtime and although the land was arid, in the springtime desert one or two rains in recent weeks had been enough to produce beautiful flowers. Even in the prickly trees we saw some lemurs.

The forests have been disappearing from burning or cutting, making the danger of extinction for the lemur real. The World Wildlife Fund financed this vital reserve area project. The fund was looking into improving the road for the transportation of rice from the countryside into the city of Tulear and studying the effects of charcoal-making. In many villages along the road getting wood to make charcoal rapidly destroys the forests. USAID was trying to improve the charcoal burners' efficiency to reduce the amount of charcoal needed. That is why Dick and Tony had bought a sample tin charcoal burner in the market place.

On the second night in our camp, I spent some time with villagers, who are the guardians of the reserve. I watched two little girls, four or five years old, using long poles to pound rice in a cutout log. The pounding separates the rice from its shell and takes about half an hour. The girls had carefully placed baskets on four sides of the log and spilt very little on the ground. The open fires seemed to be going constantly under kettles of rice or meat. A large rooster paraded around at all times, impressing two chickens. There were only three huts other than mine, but three more were being built on twig frames for expected research students.

At one point, three men arrived from the neighboring village carrying their spears and sitting down some distance away, I walked over to shake hands with each of them. The chief, or leader, of the region carried a royal spear and wore a handsome red and white shawl over his clothes. He said he had come to pay his respects to me, and I told him I wished to pay my respects to him.

Late in the evening of the second day we went on a night walk. Although we heard the lemurs, we could see only sets of eyes peering at us from the trees. The lemurs have large, bright round eyes. These remarkable creatures, whose cries sound almost human, have friendly inquisitive natures. I am sure they were intrigued by the beams from our flashlights.

Saturday morning it was time to pack up and head back to Tulear. We were sorry to leave the reserve, in spite of its remoteness. Although it was primitive, very cold at night, and as hot as 105 degrees Fahrenheit during the day, we had survived quite well. Our return trip took about six hours, as we stopped frequently to take pictures and to enjoy a picnic lunch under a tree, spreading our blankets over the thorny ground.

When we reached our hotel in Tulear, a shower became the high point of the day. Soon we were back in the Land Rover, headed for a 5:00 p.m. courtesy visit with the vice president of the province, standing in for the president, who was out in another part of his province. We were warmly greeted and spoke for about ten minutes with the vice president and three members of the cabinet in the town hall. Then we drove through the market to the beach, where we watched the sun disappear magnificently over the Indian Ocean. It is sad to see the poverty and deterioration of a city where there is so much natural beauty. With the proper infrastructure, it could be a tourist paradise.

The dinner at our hotel of local wine and shrimp with rice and bananas flambé for dessert seemed a feast after the plain food in the field. After an early night, I was up with the sun next morning to finish my report before flying home. What an unforgettable journey!

Visiting My Comoros Embassy

On my first visit to my other ambassadorial responsibility, the Comoros Islands, I was flown in a small plane and spent three days. The Union of Comoros is located between Mozambique and Madagascar on a strategic sea route. A former French colony long known for political intrigue, the Comoros Islands would become even better known shortly after my three- year tour because of a coup attempt with an unhappy outcome for President Abdallah. The country is predominately Muslim, with a culture that combines Islam and East Africa and retains a strong French influence. The three islands — Anjouan, Moheli, and Grande Comore, site of the nation's capital Moroni — gained independence from the French in 1975. A fourth island, Mayotte, elected to remain under French administration. President Abdallah had been elected the first president in 1975, been overthrown once, and was then restored to office. It was rumored that a French mercenary, a soldier of fortune, I was told, was resolved to do him in one day.

The chief of protocol met me at Hahaya Airport on this first visit and took me immediately to the Residence, which was occupied by the deputy chief of mission (DCM), Edward Brynn, a remarkably capable Foreign Service officer. Whenever I visited Moroni, it became my Residence, but Ed Brynn was in charge when I was in Madagascar, where I spent most of my time. He kept in touch with me by cable and telephone. After his assignment in the Comoros Islands, it wasn't long before he was appointed an ambassador.

We drove in the president's car to meet with President Abdallah and present my credentials. During our brief visit, the president showed me a glass case displaying a rare "living fossil" called the Coelacanth (Greek for "hollow spine"), a fish whose body plan has not changed in hundreds of millions of years. Since its discovery over fifty years ago, scientists have been excited about it. Rarely sighted east of Madagascar, Coelacanth are not pretty (quite ugly as a matter of fact), but I certainly was interested in seeing a fish that went back three hundred million years. Imagine it being discovered alive today!

After meeting the president, I was taken on a short tour of Moroni and paid a courtesy call on the French ambassador.

The staff at the American Embassy in Moroni was small, and I was delighted to meet everyone, including Elka Hortoland and her husband. Elka was secretary to DCM Brynn and became my secretary for my last year in Antananarivo. We rushed around a good bit after luncheon, going to a "CARE" Garage Project and paying courtesy calls on the minister of the interior and the deputy chief of mission of the People's Republic of China, Zhao Jian. Fortunately, I was still full of energy for the reception held that evening for me with about seventy-five Comorian officials and diplomats and the dinner that followed, given by President Abdallah.

We were on the go all the next day, with courtesy calls and a flight to the island of Anjouan, where we met the village elders and a wise man known as the Sage of Mbeni. Returning to the Grande Comore, we drove to a major export operation, a Ylang Ylang plantation, where they grow aromatic flowering trees used in making perfume. We ended our busy day by returning to the Embassy in Moroni via the coastal route, with quick stops at more projects. Finally, we had a private dinner at the Residence served on an outdoor balcony, where large upside-down-hanging bats looked at us with great black eyes from the trees above. It was the first time I realized that bats could have sweet faces!

From the Comoros I traveled on to Mauritius, joined by Bill for this part of the trip. Mauritius is part of the Commonwealth and reveals its British influence by the cars driving on the left side of the road. With a population predominately of Indian extraction, the island is quite prosperous. I made several semiofficial calls on local officials, as well as on my counterparts in the diplomatic community. We enjoyed it so much that we later returned to Mauritius for a short holiday.

It was always good to get back to Madagascar, our home now, with the staff there to greet us and Willie barking enthusiastically. We were soon entertaining visitors from the States, members of the World Wildlife Fund interested in the preservation of the lemur and its habitat. Several of the group stayed with us, though they were in and out on trips to the field. To our delight, one of these was Olga

Hirshhorn. Now she could see the paintings she had loaned us as they hung on our walls.

18

On the Diplomatic Front Line

A Woman in the Lion's Den

At the Department of State when I was preparing for my assignment, someone who had been stationed in Madagascar said, "You'll find it very difficult being a woman in Madagascar. The president is a macho man and will be condescending to you." It was not so at all. President Ratsiraka never made me feel he was talking down to me; rather, he expected me to measure up as well as any man. He was always courteous to me, and we had many lively and substantive discussions. Actually, I think being a woman was an asset, for he made an effort not to condescend to me.

Margaret Thatcher, the former prime minister of Great Britain, when asked what it felt like to be a woman prime minister said, "I don't know what it feels like, I've never experienced the alternative!" I believe that would go for a woman ambassador, too.

When the time came for me to enter the lion's den, the office of the president of Madagascar, it did not take me long to realize that President Didier Ratsiraka was an extremely complex man. He was definite in his opinions and did allow me to work on changing them, or at least he gave that impression. At our first one-on-one conversation in his office (I never took an interpreter with me), I made it clear that I differed with him politically and that I would like to convince him that Marxism was not good for any country.

The president, I recognized, was a brilliant man. A graduate of the French Naval War College, l'Ecole Navalle de Brest, he had always gone to good schools, had been a captain in the Malagasy navy, and had served on a French navy frigate, the *Jeanne d'Arc.* He was a remarkable linguist, speaking Russian, Italian, Spanish, French, and

English, and was studying Hebrew, he told me. Although his English was good, he wanted us to speak together only in French. We agreed that when I missed the subtlety of something he might say, he would explain it to me in English. He would correct my French when necessary. He asked me to correct his English, and we kept our agreement without any apologies or hesitations.

President Ratsiraka was known to have a highly mystical side. He spoke to me once about studying spiritual development to improve his own "power." He was a skilled politician, often bringing his enemies into the fold. Born in the tiny village of Vatomandry, he was an ethnic Betsimisaraka and lived in the city of Tomatove in the east coast region of the country. His moods were ever-changing, sometimes charming, sometimes depressed, sometimes short-tempered, although not with me. He always seemed especially depressed when the weather was bad. I was not there to analyze the president, however, but to do business with him.

President Didier Ratsiraka had headed the Malagasy government since 1975 as chief of state, head of government, and president of the Supreme Revolutionary Council. After the assassination of Lieutenant Colonel Ratsimandrava, a provisional government was put in place with Major General Andriamahazo in charge. Then, Didier Ratsiraka, who had been foreign minister, formed an interim government, instituted major reforms through the charter of the Malagasy socialist revolution, and became the leader of what he called the Democratic Republic of Madagascar.

Ratsiraka's hero was the head of North Korea, Kim Il Sung. Four North Korean MIG-17 jets were on loan to Madagascar, complete with North Korean crews, and the Soviets gave him twelve MIGs and some transports with their crews. The North Koreans helped President Ratsiraka build a new presidential palace and trained his palace guards.

During my time in Madagascar, I managed to engage our military in arrangements with the Malagasy military. Thanks to help from our military command in Hawaii, Malagasy forces were soon involved in training exercises with U.S. forces. In addition, at my request, the

American Seabees came to Madagascar for some construction projects that proved highly satisfactory.

By the time I arrived in Madagascar, President Ratsiraka had recognized the failures of his socialist policies and decided to pursue reforms and a policy of nonalignment, becoming more moderate and accepting Western aid to improve conditions in his country. We discussed continuing the policy of not allowing either Soviet or U.S. ships to be stationed in his big northern Diego Suarez port.

When we met in his office, he sat at his wide desk with me seated at the other side of the desk. During our talks he would smoke large Cuban cigars, gifts, he said, from the Cuban ambassador. Now, I am sensitive to both cigarettes and cigar smoke, and one day when we were interrupted by a telephone call, he put his cigar in an ashtray. The heavy smoke blew more strongly than usual right at me, and I started to cough and sneeze. A week or two later, when I returned to his office, he asked about my cold, remembering that I had coughed during our last visit. I never told him the cause. I only thought, each time I sat there enveloped by cigar smoke, what I will do for my country!

We talked about his cooperation with the IMF and the World Bank and possible plans for reforming the industrial sector. I urged him to consider more free trade and to make his textile industry more profitable, as nearby Mauritius had done. He never wanted to relax his strict export rules much and would always say that he didn't want too much commerce with other countries because he wanted to keep drugs out. He was worried about AIDS, especially if too many tourists came. We discussed world affairs, and he was well informed on international events. Once he told me he was going to Libya for its national day because he wanted to keep the door open with its leader, Muammar Qadhafi. I had a theory, as did some others in Washington, that Ratsiraka perceived the military might of the United States as going downhill, especially after Vietnam, and that of the Soviet Union as going up. Therefore, he was sticking more closely to the Soviets than to us. His opinions began to change, I thought, as we became stronger militarily, and I think he was influenced by our bombing of Libya a few months before I arrived. Always around the anniversary of that bombing, our Embassy would receive threats, to which the marines were especially alert.

The president and I discussed the feasibility studies underway with U.S. private enterprise concerning ferrachrome deposits. Madagascar is rich in minerals, such as graphite and mica, iron ore, bauxite, and others. The Canadians began some titanium development during my time, and AMOCO and others had been exploring for suspected heavy oil deposits. President Ratsiraka hoped that the discovery of oil would solve all his problems, but it didn't turn out that way.

For development, Madagascar needs infrastructure, roads, and docks. Western countries like France, Germany, Japan, and the United States are all trading partners of Madagascar, with vanilla a big export. I urged the president to allow the Peace Corps to come to Madagascar, as had ambassadors before me, but he refused. He later changed his mind, and the Peace Corps finally came to the country after I had left.

We spoke about the importation of American rice to Madagascar, and always I would bring up the subject of the environment. We wanted to know how the government was going to pull all of the environmental elements together and persuade people not to burn off agricultural land. I asked if the president would take an active personal interest, and he agreed to follow the situation closely.

We sometimes discussed philosophy and world exploration. I presented the president with the French edition of Daniel Boorstin's book *The Discoverers,* and he said he enjoyed reading it. After my return to the United States, I met the Pulitzer Prize–winning author for the first time and he was pleased to learn that I had given his book to the Madagascar president. The Boorstins became good friends, and we spent many happy times together at our house on the bay and theirs on the Potomac. I visited Dan Boorstin at the hospital a few hours before he died in February 2004. He was a great man, Librarian of Congress Emeritus and author of many books translated into thirty languages. I remember him best as the devoted husband of Ruth, a loving father and grandfather, and a dear friend.

President Ratsiraka liked to talk about the navy, and I told him I planned to visit his port city of Diego Suarez, the largest natural deep-water harbor in the world. How the Soviet Union wanted that harbor! I remembered my Polish ambassador friend telling me the Soviets were hungry for the island.

Some years later, then deputy secretary of state Strobe Talbott said he was considering sending another woman ambassador to Madagascar and asked me if I thought another woman would be well received. I assured him that the answer was yes and that the Malagasy accepted women in many walks of life. I added that there had been a nineteenth-century queen, Ranavalona, who had despised Christians and had them thrown off a high cliff. I had stood at the top of that rugged cliff and looked down. It was a long way to fall, and I could see that there was no climbing back up.

President Ratsiraka did not push people over a cliff, but in many ways he was feared. The end of his reign of power was not a happy one. In 2002 it was determined that he had lost an election, but he caused great problems for the country before the new president, Ravalomanana, managed to take over. It brought to my mind a day when I sat with President Ratsiraka in his palace shortly after there had been riots in the country. I asked him, "Do you ever wish that you could retire and give up having to face so many problems? You could go to France and have a comfortable life."

President Ratsiraka looked at me, held up his hands and said, "But what would I do?" Even with its burdens, it was no different now than through centuries past. "Power" is not given up easily.

Diplomatic Diversity

I have already mentioned that some scientists believe that Madagascar was once attached to the African continent and separated from it some 165 million years ago. Other scientists disagree as to when it broke off from the mainland and drifted out into the Indian Ocean. Some say that the widening Mozambique Channel caused the split more than 150 million years ago, others that the landmass broke away about 65 or 70 million years ago. Most historians believe that in the year 1500, the Portuguese were exploring Madagascar and tried to establish trading posts. French and British ships also explored Madagascar. In the sixteenth and seventeenth centuries under the Malagasy kings and queens, it was known as the Merina kingdom.

Pirates operated in Madagascar in the seventeenth and eighteenth centuries, headquartered on the Malagasy island of Saint Marie. Some history books called it the greatest pirate stronghold of all time. The British government had been influential in Madagascar but changed its attitude to the area when the Suez Canal opened in 1869. It no longer considered Madagascar as a strategic location. Then Great Britain and France made a deal: Britain was given control of Zanzibar, freeing the French to deliver an ultimatum in 1894 to the Malagasy government, demanding unconditional capitulation to France. After various revolts, in 1896 Madagascar became a French colony. The French abolished the merina monarchy in 1897 and sent the queen into exile, first to Réunion and then to Algiers.

During World War II, the British captured Madagascar's port city of Diego Suarez from the control of Vichy France. The British feared that the Japanese might take Madagascar to use as a base in the Indian Ocean. British warships sailed into the harbor and took control of the occupied naval base after two days of fighting. Soon the government of the island was turned over to the Free French. After the war, the French violently suppressed the revolts that erupted and stayed in control until Madagascar regained its independence. In 1960, the popular Malagasy, Philibert Tsiranana, became its first president. After several ups and downs in 1975, the revolutionary naval officer, Didier Ratsiraka, became president.

Anyone coming to visit the Embassy of the United States of America in Madagascar flies into its capital, Antananarivo. From the airplane window, one's first view is of the mountains and the red soil that gives Madagascar its name, the Great Red Island. This city of one million people is built on many hills. Its streets run up and down the valleys, with buildings of red clay or concrete. The U.S. Embassy, located right downtown, was guarded in my day by a six-man detachment of United States Marines, who greeted me each morning at 7:00 a.m. My office was on the second floor, and everything above the first floor was called the secure area, where only American staff had access without an escort. It was a cheerful place.

From my office, I had a good view of the city. During my first few weeks, I was startled to find hundreds of bats swooping by my window at twilight. They had been nesting in the top of the building. One night when the bats were out flying about, we boarded up their nesting place. They had to look for another home where they would be safe, and we were free of the dark cloud of bats passing overhead.

"Country team" meetings, cables, travel, decisions, receptions — every day was different. The country team, which consisted of the leaders of the various sections of the embassy, met in a safeguarded, secure room to exchange news of what each person was doing and plan the immediate future. We discussed the importance of maintaining and building good trade relations between Madagascar and the United States. Country team members included, among others, the head of USAID, the director of USIS (the United States Information Service), the navy attaché, the embassy's deputy chief of mission, and its political, economic, and administrative officers. It was a strong, articulate team, and I always looked forward to the meetings.

Staff at our meetings would often hear me discuss the vital subject of security, stressing that such a thing as a "low-risk" post no longer existed. Our regional security officer, stationed in Nairobi, visited us, and State's Bureau of African Affairs, at my request, eventually assigned us our own security person. Unlike at some other posts, I had the marines report directly to me, which worked for us. The marine colonel in charge of all marines in Africa said he thought our way worked best. The cable traffic was never-ending, both incoming and outgoing.

The deputy chief of mission is an extremely important person in every embassy. He or she takes charge of the post when the ambassador is out of the country, greatly helps the ambassador keep well informed at all times about everything going on in the embassy, and works closely with the staff. If you think of it in business terms, I would say that the ambassador is president and CEO and the DCM is the executive vice president. I was fortunate to have the highly capable Marilyn Hulbert as my DCM. I had started off with someone else but he and I did not agree on our respective roles, and the State Department assured me it was better to make a change. I didn't have to go back to Washington to find the right person as she was already on the embassy staff as head of USIS, and I asked to have her assigned to the embassy as DCM. Marilyn Hulbert and I were the first two-woman team to head an embassy, and the first where one was white and one was African American. We had both been pioneers before we arrived and were delighted, always, to be pioneers in embassy folklore!

Our first big reception at the Residence was held in late July to mark the official beginning of my duties as ambassador, a tradition with all incoming U.S. ambassadors. About five hundred people attended, and as the newspaper said, all of Antananarivo was there— members of the supreme council of the revolution, friends of the United States, ministers, diplomats, and business men and women. We needed ten additional waiters, and Jean Clair had worked a week ahead of time preparing the food. The weather was fine, and the guests filled the terrace and main salon. Receptions are not just for fun. They are good opportunities for all members of the embassy staff to meet and talk with the persons with whom they do business.

This might be a good time to say that I had been preceded by some excellent ambassadors, who had laid the groundwork for several projects I would be working on over the next three years. An ambassador never finishes all projects before leaving, and sometimes the new ambassador gets credit for a predecessor's hard work. In the end, it all works out as the credit just keeps passing along.

Our first houseguests were from the United States, my cousin Betty Brickley who had been one of the first women U.S. Marines of World War II, and her friend Maria Allen who spent a week with us. Betty was particularly impressed with our marine detachment, as were they with her. Betty and Maria accompanied me on one short official field trip. We drove west about 120 kilometers to the village of Ampefy, where I formally pushed the button to start the operation of a mini-hydroelectric plant funded by USAID, the World Bank, and the International Monetary Fund. It was the first time this village of 500 persons and 100 houses had had electricity. The villagers had put in about two thousand hours of labor to help construct a pipe funneling water to a turbine to make electricity for the village and for a millstone to grind rice. This time, my speech was in French, English, and a bit of Malagasy.

Our guests all wanted to go to the big outdoor market known as the *zoma*, which offered unusual fruits and vegetables and gorgeous flowers for sale, along with Malagasy games and little handmade wooden figures. My Malagasy teacher, Aurelie, accompanied the visitors and translated when necessary. Aurelie was a first-grade teacher at the American School and enjoyed taking our guests to the *zoma* when she could and watching out for pickpockets there. Aurelie also took many of our guests to the old summer palace out in the countryside and to the palace on top of the highest hill in the city. I loved that city palace, which displayed in one of the glass cases a letter from Queen Victoria to the queen of Madagascar. I would read it every time I went there, as it was written in Queen Victoria's own hand. To my great regret and to the sorrow of everyone in the city, the palace burned down after I had left. Recently, I asked the Malagasy ambassador in Washington about that letter and he told me it vanished forever in the flames.

Almost every month I would invite all of the embassy staff and their spouses to the Residence for lunch, where a Malagasy speaker would share something about the culture of the country. One such speaker was a daughter of the first Malagasy president, Tsiranana. Another was Yvette Ranjevo, a professor at the University of Madagascar and the wife of its president, Raymond Ranjevo. The Ranjevos were our next-door neighbors and good friends. Today, Raymond Ranjevo is a judge on the International Court at The Hague.

My automobile was always parked by the Embassy's front door with Albert nearby, ready at any time to take me to an appointment. It was thanks to that car and driver that I was able to accomplish so much each day, both inside and away from the Embassy. When Robin, my assistant, would come into my office and say, "Time to go," I would hurry down the stairs, jump into the backseat of my waiting automobile, briefcase in hand, and take off over the winding city roads. My schedule was heavy, and I enjoyed its diversity.

It is customary for American ambassadors to call on the government ministers of the host country. This is something I did soon after my arrival. One of my calls was on the minister of revolutionary art and culture, Madame Gisele Rabesahala, a communist who had not previously been involved with our embassy. I wanted to call on her not only because she was a minister but because she was a woman. She seemed surprised when I arrived in her office and told me I was the first American ambassador ever to call on her. I said that although we differed completely in our political views, I was delighted to see that Madagascar had chosen a woman as a minister. I found her to be an outgoing person and our cordial relations seemed to help in various ways.

After my meeting with Minister Rabesahala, embassy officers and I were invited to several official art and cultural events at which we had not previously been included. In the spring of 1989, the Museum of Natural History in New York sponsored a magnificent exhibit called "Madagascar—Island of the Ancestors." I wanted very much for Minister Rabesahala to come to the opening in New York City, and she did. Another visitor who came from Madagascar to that exhibit was the University of Madagascar's director of art and archeology. I made a special trip home for the event, remaining briefly in Washington for some additional meetings.

Chester Crocker, assistant secretary of state for African affairs, called the exhibit a rare opportunity for Americans to be exposed to the culture of a distant country, part of Africa but an island with its own special quality. He and I discussed moves toward economic liberalization in Madagascar and the winds of change occurring at that time in China and the Soviet Union.

The exhibit later traveled to London when I happened to be in England, so I went to see it again with my old friend Malcolm McBain, Great Britain's ambassador to Madagascar during my tenure. When the time came for Ambassador McBain to leave Madagascar, we hosted a dinner for him at the Residence, inviting many ambassadors from other countries. I wanted to do something different and remembered having seen a silent film of a western melodrama, something original to the United States, some years before.

One evening, I sat down and wrote, "The Saga of Little Nell on the Lone Prairie." In the traditional melodrama, Little Nell works hard but cannot pay her rent. As always, a villain lusts after her and threatens to carry her away with him, and a hero rescues her just in time. The story takes place out on the prairie in the western territory in North America. Here in a little log cabin owned by the rich and mean Simon Legree lived Little Nell with her young baby.

I had the script written out in both English and French so that our guests would understand it. In this melodrama the actors never speak; it is all in exaggerated mime. I was the narrator and the players members of the embassy staff, with my assistant as Little Nell. The rehearsal at the Residence generated great excitement. How would we show that it was wintertime and that Little Nell might die struggling through the snow? We came up with the idea of using, of all things, the tiny bits of white paper from our shredding machine, as it could be tossed in the air over the characters. No one would be hurt or cold and no one would recognize from whence these minute snowflakes had come!

The night of our party, our after-dinner entertainment was ready with the players waiting to emerge from the Residence library. I introduced the event, announcing, "The Last Chance Saloon presents a romantic melodrama: 'THE SAGA OF LITTLE NELL ON THE LONE PRAIRIE,' starring the Red Rose of Texas, Robin Rupli, as our heroine the widow, Little Nell; Sir Stephen Holgate as Simon Legree, our villain; and special guest star John Wayne McBain, as our hero, Ranger John. Our stage manager is Faithful Felicia Holgate, and our special effects man is my husband Wild Bill Lynch."

At the very end of our production, the narrator says, "Little Nell takes the hand of her Hero, Ranger John, and together they go off into the sunset to live happily ever after. The End." After thunderous applause by our dinner guests, I asked French ambassador Alain Bry why he seemed to be laughing so often as I was narrating. "Was my French not good enough?"

"No," he replied, "your French was fine. I was laughing because it was so incongruous to hear an American melodrama narrated in French."

Another day, at lunchtime, I hurried over to the marine house where I had called to ask if one of the off-duty marines would be available to play a few games of ping-pong with me. I explained that we were going to have dinner with the Chinese ambassador, Yang Guirong, and his wife at the Chinese embassy that evening and I had heard that the ambassador always invited his guests to a game of ping-pong before dinner. It was time for a little ping-pong diplomacy. It just so happened that when I was growing up in Connecticut, my father and I had played a good bit of ping-pong together on the table in our sunroom. I was out of practice but knew if I could spend a little time at a ping-pong table with a marine, I would not fall on my face representing my country! When I finally played a game with the Chinese ambassador, he led me on for quite a while with long volleys before decisively scoring the winning points. The Chinese are famously masters of ping-pong, and pretty good at diplomacy too!

The United States Marines are also good at diplomacy, and were strutting their stuff at embassies around the world and in Madagascar on November 10, 1986, their 211th anniversary. The Continental Congress in Philadelphia, Pennsylvania, had resolved at Tun Tavern in 1775 that two battalions of Marines be "raised for service," and John Adams signed the resolution. In Madagascar, our marine security detachment put on a magnificent ball, having spent the entire year raising funds (holding movies, Sunday pancake breakfasts, barbecues, and tennis matches) to help defray expenses for this one annual gala event.

The ball was held in the main Ballroom of the Hilton Hotel—yes, there was a Hilton Hotel in Antananarivo—and included an impressive "Presentation of Colors" ceremony, a sit-down dinner, a band, and dancing. Over two hundred people attended, including members of the diplomatic community and many Malagasy guests. Many of the men wore dinner jackets, the women long gowns, and the marines full dress uniform. I was called upon to give a speech and did so in both French and English. Then the marine gunnery sergeant, the noncommissioned officer in charge, asked me to dance, and we circled the floor to open the dancing. Some guests asked if it would be possible for the marines to have two birthdays a year! During my time there, I was able to participate in two more such birthday balls. Though I had greatly enjoyed my first marine ball many years before in Paris, this ball in far off Africa I enjoyed even more.

The Exorcism

One of my most challenging experiences at the Embassy involved plunging into the unknown. I was prepared to grapple with emergencies but lacked training in dealing with the devil's use of evil spirits.

A well-educated local employee of the embassy had for some time not been getting on well with her Malagasy colleagues or the American staff. I knew I would have to let her go, so we worked out an arrangement. She would immediately take early retirement but continue to draw her pay for a year, when she would become legally eligible to retire. She left, and everyone was relieved. There was more to come.

For several weeks we had been renovating the first floor offices, where our Malagasy employees worked. These Foreign Service nationals are invaluable, with their long-term knowledge of past years, their considerable skills, and their loyalty. They deserve nice surroundings and were delighted by our efforts to redesign and paint their work areas. From my office on the second floor I would walk downstairs from time to time to see how the renovation was going. On one of my trips downstairs I passed the office of our departed employee and noticed her overturned desk and general disarray. Nothing had been painted or fixed. When I inquired why no work had been done on this office, I was told that before the employee had been "shown the door," she had invoked evil spirits to move into her office. Consequently no workman would enter it. I knew I must take action and that it would not be ordinary!

Alone in my office, I telephoned my friend the Episcopal bishop and asked him to come to see me, that I had a problem I needed to discuss with him. He arrived within the hour. I asked him if he would perform an exorcism to expel the evil spirits in one of my offices. I explained that in America we sometimes would ask a minister, a priest, or a rabbi to come to a newly built house and bless it, and I would like him to bless the new offices and work space for the Malagasy employees. At the same time, would he perform the exorcism? I had never dealt with a situation like this one before, I explained, but was pretty sure it was the right thing to do.

Bishop Remi agreed but asked, "Aren't you afraid that people will think you a strange American to believe in evil spirits and exorcism?"

"No," I told him, "I do not have to believe it myself to respect the fact that other people believe."

"Good," he said, "I would like to bring two of my priests with me and we will have a full ceremony." He asked who would escort them to all the offices, and I assured him I would do it myself. Not one soul did I tell ahead of time. I hoped that the Malagasy would approve what I was going to do with the help of the Malagasy bishop.

The next day I asked everyone in the embassy, Americans and Malagasy, to come to our main foyer where the marines' desk was located. When everyone had assembled, I introduced the bishop and explained that he would be blessing their new working quarters.

Bishop Remi led the ceremony. When he started singing a well-known hymn and everyone joined in, I knew all would go well. He invited all of the Malagasy employees to follow us as we visited the new office space. He carried a bowl of water and flowers with him. When we passed the office with the overturned desk, he entered and recited special prayers, as did his priests. Everyone in the procession watched as we then proceeded with all the blessings. The highest-ranking of the employees asked if he would please bless her office.

When the ceremony was over, I asked Bishop Remi to come up and bless my office too. An extra prayer, I believe, is always helpful. He did.

The next day, workmen were painting and hammering in the office that had been burdened by evil spirits. The bishop had accomplished his mission. The exorcism was complete!

A Star for Christmas

As our first Christmas in Madagascar approached, so did our own Christmas star, Annabella. In France, Annabella was truly revered as a great film star throughout her lifetime and especially in the days of the famous director, Rene Clair. Just a few years earlier, a retrospective celebration of Rene Clair's work at the Museum of Modern Art in New York featured Annabella's films, and Annabella had been there. I was there too. Now, because she was such a dear friend of so many years, she was to visit us at the Residence for about ten days over Christmas.

Annabella was especially proud of being an American citizen as well as being French, and during World War II, she had starred in Broadway plays while her husband, Tyrone Power, served as a pilot in the United States Marine Corps. She even went to Italy with the military's USO program to appear in Noel Coward's *Blithe Spirit*. On that assignment to Italy, she proudly wore an army captain's uniform. French ambassador Alain Bry expressed delight when I told him that Annabella would be coming for Christmas, as she had always been his favorite film star. Because the French had spent many years in Madagascar, many Malagasy officials were also familiar with her. We hosted several parties in her honor and were in turn feted at the residences of the French, British, Chinese, and Egyptian ambassadors.

Prior to her leaving Paris, we had asked Annabella to send us videotapes of some of her films. These became the theme of our dinner parties, with the showing of a different film each evening after dinner. We entertained all of the embassy staff one night with the feature film *Suez*, costarring Annabella and Tyrone Power. The following night, along with the prime minister and forty other top government officials and their spouses we invited ambassadors of many countries. The film was *Wings of the Morning (La Baie du Destin* in French), in which Annabella starred with Henry Fonda. On another night we showed the French film *Paris — Mediterranée* costarring Jean Murat. We had had programs printed with photos of Annabella and the title of the film for the evening. Before and after each screening, Annabella talked about the making of the film and about meeting Tyrone Power on the set of *Suez* and later marrying him.

We decorated the artificial tree we had brought from Washington with all the lights and trimmings to recreate as much as possible a traditional Christmas at home. We did not need to buy poinsettias, the national flower of Madagascar, which bloomed wild everywhere, even on our terrace. We gave a Christmas party for our household staff and their families, including Albert, my driver, and his family. Almost everyone had many children so although the household staff consisted of only six people, with their families we had thirty-eight people for the celebration. My husband Bill played the role of Santa Claus in a Santa costume mailed to us by my niece Jeri. Reluctant at first to be Santa Claus, once he'd done it, he loved it and repeated the performance each Christmas we were there. He was, of course, that day called "Père Noël." We had candy gifts for all the children, gifts for the adults, and gifts of food for our two gardeners and twelve resident guards. Although we missed having our own children there, we loved this household staff. It was great fun for us all, including Annabella.

Throughout the holidays, we entertained everyone at the embassy, and Bill appeared several times as Santa Claus. Another year we invited the ambassadors of other embassies and asked them, if they were used to singing carols at home, to sing a Christmas carol of their country for us all to enjoy. It was touching to hear the East German and West German ambassadors, separated politically, sing together some of their similar Christmas carols. The West German ambassador was saddened that while he was fortunate indeed to be on the western side of the Berlin Wall, his colleague had had the bad luck to be on the eastern side.

Annabella left before New Year's so the two of us had a quiet New Year's Eve. I was continuing to work about ten hours a day in the office during the week and going in for just a couple of hours on the weekends. I didn't mind the hard work, that's what I was there for, and that's what most of the other ambassadors in Antananarivo did. We kept in good touch with each other to learn from one another what was really going on inside Marxist Madagascar.

As we entered a New Year, I had been there long enough now to have a pretty good idea of the Foreign Service. At times, I felt I must have been serving at embassies all of my life!

Lemurs and Riots

When it is winter in Washington, it is summer in Madagascar. I never minded the rains that came late in the afternoon because that heavy monsoon rain was good for the earth. It could be hot if you were on the coast, however, rather than in our mile-high city, and it was Malagasy-summer hot when Bill flew with me down to Fort Dauphin on the southeastern tip of the island. We were going to one of the earliest European settlements, dating well back into the sailing ship era. Many of the early inhabitants were shipwrecked sailors who stayed on.

Fort Dauphin has for many years been a base of operations for U.S. Lutheran missionaries, and the primary reason for our trip was for me to participate in the thirtieth anniversary celebration of a hospital the Lutherans maintained there. The town is small, with beautiful coves and beaches, unfortunately polluted, and breathtaking ocean views. There is little oceanfront building because of the devastating Indian Ocean cyclones.

While at Fort Dauphin we went out to Berenty, a privately owned and financed lemur preserve, armed with bananas to lure the lemurs out of hiding. We hadn't gone fifty yards into the forests when we were covered by ring-tailed lemurs, on our heads and shoulders and climbing up our legs, trying to get to the bananas. In just a few hours we saw several types of lemur, but the ring-tailed were the most friendly. Berenty is an oasis of green in the middle of a desert, with plantations of sisal. It is a paradise of nature kept alive for many years by Dr. and Mrs. Jean De Heaulme and family. Several months later, I went back for a visit to Berenty, staying in the old plantation house and waking to the sounds of lemurs calling to each other from tree to tree.

Our next important visitors were our British friends, Pat and Napier Crookenden, known more formally as Lt. General Sir Napier Crookenden and Lady Crookenden. They helped us greatly in our relations with the Malagasy military, who were impressed by this distinguished couple, both of whom had a keen sense of humor and genuine interest in the country. When I spoke of our friend, the Bishop of the Episcopal Church, Pat recalled that an uncle of hers in earlier times had been the Anglican bishop in Madagascar and was pleased when she met his Malagasy successor. The Crookendens spent about two weeks with us and traveled with us whenever possible.

On one such trip, we were accompanied by my USAID director Sam Rea and his wife Julie. I felt so blessed to have him working there with me that I despaired when he had to leave. Never, I thought, would I have another director as capable as he but I was wrong. Another splendid man arrived, Baudouin de Marcken, who was just as capable and just as good a friend. Their wives, Julie Rea (who worked for USAID) and Gail de Marcken (a painter and author), were also great additions to embassy life. I had long heard of great rivalry at embassies between the USAID directors and the ambassador, because USAID had its own power base in Washington. I never found such rivalry at my embassy. The USAID funds for the many projects we undertook jointly were of tremendous help to the accomplishment of my mission. How else could I be making a speech in which I might be giving away millions of dollars provided by USAID for a good cause in Madagascar?

While the Crookendens were with us, we had a series of dinner parties, one of which was for the top generals and colonels of the Madagascar military. Many of these men, eager for more contact with Western military leaders, wanted their country to become more democratic. Napier was in rare form and had the entire group roaring with laughter during a short speech, replete with some of his favorite jokes, all in French. One of the Malagasy generals played the piano, and it turned out to be a great evening.

We planned a brief holiday trip to Mauritius with the Crookendens. The U.S. embassy in Mauritius had helped us rent a car and an attractive house right on the beach. After a day or two, however, the nonfunctioning plumbing became a problem, and the porous roof leaked rainwater on us even as we slept. The house had a brightly painted metal roof, over which hung a large tree branch. The tree bore hard fruit about the size of a lemon, which throughout the night would drop onto the roof with a loud crash and noisily cascade down to the gutter. We decided it was time to move out. As we had warnings of a pending cyclone, we transferred to a hotel up the beach. The feared cyclone veered just before hitting the island, but the winds rose to 75 miles per hour, accompanied by large waves and horizontal rain. We could not get to the airport because no cars were allowed on the road and the storm lasted three days.

I was impatient to get back to Madagascar, as I had received word from Washington that some trouble was brewing in the countryside there. We felt lucky we had not been washed away and left for Antananarivo as soon as the first plane flew. Before the storm, we had been entertained by the Australian high commissioner to Mauritius and the U.S. ambassador, Ronald Palmer. We were well looked after but felt it was rather unreasonable to be involved with a cyclone while paying holiday hotel rates.

Back in Madagascar, signs of unrest and reports of burning and looting in Antsirabe, Tulear, and other cities came in. I was glad to get back before the situation became ugly. The Indian merchants, and there are many, were the targets of these attacks, and many Indians fled the country temporarily. Refugees poured into the capital. Fortunately, we were spared any attacks on the embassy, although troops were out in the streets for several weeks. We quickly checked on the situation of the Americans living in the troubled areas, but all remained well with them, I was happy to be able to assure them they would receive help from us if needed. The crisis management team had just visited our embassy, so we had had a good practice session of what to do in an emergency. The Madagascar desk officer at State, Eunice Reddick, had come for an official visit at the time of the unrest and watched it all with us firsthand. Shortly after her visit, David Fischer, head of the department's East Africa Bureau, spent a few days with us. He had been U.S. ambassador to the Seychelles, but this was his first visit to Madagascar. I was to take him for an official visit to President Ratsiraka. It enabled me to bring firsthand news of Washington to the president and show him our interest in the progress of his sometimes questionable financial restructuring.

We combined a Chiefs of Mission meeting coming up in Washington with some home leave. Coming back to Madagascar, we stopped in Paris, where I had appointments at the American embassy and Bill went to the Paris Air Show. After a reception at the Embassy, we decided that although it was certainly grander and more spacious than ours, we wouldn't want to trade. When we reached our own Residence in Madagascar, it was time to prepare for our National Day reception.

Celebrating the Fourth of July, the United States Constitution, and More Visitors

The Fourth of July is a big event at U.S. embassies around the world. For a week ahead of ours, the weather was overcast and quite cold, but turned cloudless on the Fourth. At midday all five hundred invited guests filled our house, the terrace, and the gardens. We had bought a compact disc of John Phillips Sousa marches and placed loudspeakers on the terrace so that music would blare forth for all to hear. Everyone tapped toes to this red, white, and blue music. The Marine Security Detachment outdid itself in a spectacular Presentation of the Colors ceremony. They marched through the garden, up the terrace steps, skillfully maneuvering into position on the terrace for the playing of our national anthem and the Malagasy anthem, all on cassettes. At the end of the anthems, wanting to be different, I had arranged for a hundred red, white, and blue helium balloons we had bought in Washington to be released from beneath a net on the lawn to soar forth into the sky. I did not give a speech because I felt the day belonged to the Declaration of Independence and the United States Marines.

The next day, we had a family picnic for all in-country Americans at the marine house. The Americans came in from all over the island, played tennis and volleyball and swam and, for the hardy, there was a one-mile marathon. A puppet show in French was put on for the children by Malagasy professionals. We served hamburgers, baked beans, and potato salad. That might sound ordinary at home, but far from home it was special.

Our old friends Lord Kindersley of Great Britain, chairman of the Commonwealth Development Corporation, and his wife paid us a visit while looking into a possible economic fit between his organization (something like USAID) and the local government. On one weekend we looked for and found the large lemurs, the spectacular black and white indri, at Perinet, a reserve about 130 kilometers east of Antananarivo. The largest of the lemurs, indris are accomplished jumpers, making consecutive leaps of as far as sixteen feet. When they call to each other, they make a loud, eerie, haunting sound to signal territorial ownership. To me, they sounded like whales. We all stood transfixed at the sight and sound of these rare and endangered creatures.

Another World Wildlife Fund group visited, and we made sure that they met with the Malagasy government people most involved with the environment. Many of our guests from the United States had never been in an Embassy Residence, and it was great fun to have them for supper with the Malagasy.

My niece Jeri, who is like one of my own children, came to visit us, and it was a great treat to have her there. She speaks good French from her days living with us in France and used her language skills often during her visit. She fell in love with Madagascar and joined the World Wildlife Group for the last three days of its tour, which was spent in Nosy Be, a unique island off the north coast.

Lt. General Charles Bagnal, the commanding general of the Military Western Command out of Hawaii, visited us for five days. It was his first visit to the Indian Ocean sector of his command, and I was eager to take him to talk to President Ratsiraka. I hoped to convince the general to provide some funds for certain university buildings, which the president badly wanted. The army had told me it would pay only for roads, but I wanted to convince the general that the buildings would be better for us to give, and for the president to receive, than roads. Lt. General Bagnal and his wife Pat were delightful people, and he assured me he would talk to the president and me with an open mind.

We had a successful visit with Ratsiraka, who explained that the University of Madagascar was in dire need of new buildings for incoming students, because he couldn't get some of the old graduates out of the present residential quarters without fomenting an all-out crisis. The general understood the problem and agreed to have the buildings built. It was a great victory for our country, the students were aware that the United States was helping them. When I spoke at the dedication ceremonies for the buildings and on the opening day of the university, there were loud cheers from the students for the USA.

The visit of the Bagnals coincided with the two hundredth anniversary of the signing of the U.S. Constitution on September 17, 1787. For a celebration on September 17, 1987, we invited a hundred people to the Residence for the evening. As the guests mounted the stairs to the main entrance, they were flanked by two rows of Malagasy violinists playing appropriate airs. After all the guests had arrived the musicians moved indoors and played "America, the Beautiful." I must admit that I borrowed the idea for violinists from my friend, Bhekh Thapa, who had been the ambassador of Nepal to the United States when the king and queen of Nepal visited Washington. At the reception for the royal couple, Ambassador Thapa had had violinists on the steps as the guests arrived.

For our bicentennial celebration of the Constitution, we showed the film, *1776*. Though it is in English, I introduced it in French, and the music made it easy to understand. The film is really a musical about the Declaration of Independence, but in my introductory remarks, I wove the story of the Declaration into the signing of the Constitution eleven years later. The Malagasy ministers and other guests seemed to enjoy the film hugely and even the British ambassador, whose country had lost its colony through all these signings, had nice things to say about it!

The Seabees Land in Madagascar

Gen. Charles Bagnal's official visit to Madagascar brought us many dividends. First, he sent a U.S. Navy Seabee (Construction Battalion) training team from the U.S. Northwest to work for several weeks with a Malagasy engineers' unit for operation and maintenance of large construction equipment. It was vital that they keep in practice to help in any wartime emergency, as they had in Vietnam. The navy agreed that this posting would be good for both the Seabees and the Malagasy military. The project site was about fifty kilometers east of Antananarivo at a local military base, and the Malagasy were delighted to have them in their country. When the Seabees came into Antananarivo in uniform to shop or to sightsee, they were greeted with many smiles and words of welcome.

As the Seabees' program neared completion, they planned a ceremony to turn over to the Malagasy military some large new construction equipment that had just arrived by ship. This road-construction equipment included front-end loaders, Caterpillar tractors, and an immense 40–50 foot-long, 16-foot-high Caterpillar motor grader, with a huge blade beneath and a large operator's cab on top. I was asked to host this ceremony, to which all top Madagascar military people were invited. In the best U.S. navy tradition, the Seabees brought me a size small navy fatigue uniform with my name on it, complete with Seabee patches and a cap. The Seabees decided to put four stars on the cap, knowing that an ambassador has the equivalent rank of four military stars. I was quite pleased by their thoughtfulness and wore the shirt, trousers, boots, and cap (without the stars) for the ceremony.

The Malagasy newspaper and television people covered the event and hoped I would go up into the high cab of the large Caterpillar

Motor Grader. After all the speeches, I was indeed hoisted up to the cab, along with the Malagasy deputy secretary of defense and army chief. As the engine started, I told my two guests that they were putting their lives in my hands, but that a qualified operator would sit behind me. I actually managed to handle the machine by myself, despite being half-terrified, half-exhilarated as I started off and drove for a short distance. The Seabees and the press were delighted, and most of that evening's news was devoted to the ceremony and to the American ambassador building a road. As I passed the press, I had waved, and that's how the program ended. Thousands of people in Madagascar saw that television program. All seemed pleased except perhaps some of the East Bloc ambassadors, who had probably dreamed of driving such a vehicle all their lives!

19

Real Life Continues

Children, Grandchildren, Elephants, and Giraffes

When you are far, far from home and children and telephone calls are difficult, nothing is more exciting than a family visit. First my daughter Pam and her husband Buddy came to Madagascar, then my son Larry, his wife Jamye, and my granddaughters Emily and Sally came for our second Christmas. Our niece Jeri's visit was a great event, too.

Pam and Buddy arrived during a time of unrest on the university campus and in the city, but I had decided it was safe enough for them to come. While they were visiting us, Pam met the Soviet ambassador one evening at a reception. He told her, "Because of the recent riots, we weren't too sure what was going to happen here in the capital. But when I heard that you were still coming to visit your mother, I cabled Moscow that things must not be too bad, the American ambassador is having her daughter come visit!"

Pam came for three weeks, Buddy for only the last two weeks. I had registered her at the Alliance Française for French lessons every morning, knowing that she was eager to practice her French. She had started a refresher course before leaving Denver. I had to spend every day at the office but during the afternoons, my Malagasy teacher, Aurelie, showed Pam around, sometimes with Bill along. She loved going to the outdoor market, the zoma, which means "Friday" in Malagasy. The market was open every day, but more things were for sale on Friday than any other day. Pam was impressed by the intricate and delicate work on the linens, the baskets, the games, and just about everything else and bought little presents for all her friends. When Buddy came, he bought things for his geologist colleagues in Denver. An excellent golfer, Buddy went off to the golf course with Bill as often as possible.

They were both afflicted with the familiar Madagascar stomach problems but continued with most activities, like the guitar concert at the Hilton Hotel. Sid Spears, the headman of the AMOCO oil operation, which he was closing up, invited us to his office. He was disappointedly heading home to Texas as their fifth well again proved dry. We took Pam along to a dinner at the home of the prime minister. He was delighted that she carried on a good conversation with him in French, something many visitors cannot do. She loved the evening and bravely tried smoked eels for the first time.

Threats of disturbances persisted in the city. Much of the unrest was caused by the anger of university students over government threats to move them out of their dormitories, to which they clung even though they had graduated sometimes years before. I couldn't make it home for lunch one day because marching students blocked the roads.

The Indian chargé entertained us at his home, as did our USAID director. Pam and Buddy saw their first lemurs while on a special tour of the zoo. They saw more lemurs when the four of us flew up to Nosy Be for the weekend. Pam found the beaches at Nosy Be some of the most beautiful she had ever seen. I have always considered it an untouched Hawaii, a paradise, a separate world. Back in the capital, we entertained all the marines for dinner at the Residence.

The Egyptian ambassador, Ibrahim Youssri, an especially good friend and extremely knowledgeable, had us over with Pam. I once took a high-ranking Department of State visitor to his house for breakfast, explaining that the ambassador would be the right person to answer his questions. Ibrahim's opinions and evaluations of the situation in Madagascar were enormously useful to me and would be, I knew, to my visitor.

Pam and Buddy met almost all of my colleagues during their visit. One, Jose Bronfman, the World Bank representative, was always helpful to me. He has remained in Madagascar, where his wife Monique exports first-rate Malagasy-made hats and bags to France and the United States.

We sent Pam and Buddy to the village of Perinet with Bill's car and driver to see the rainforest, the large indri lemurs there, and the village itself. The hotel at Perinet is also the railroad station, so you hear trains coming and going just under your window during the night. They watched farmers harvesting rice, cutting it by hand, and carrying it on their heads to big flat rocks, where they would beat the rice on the rock to thrash it. At the only graphite mine in Madagascar, the French manager took them to the open pit, an initial crushing operation, and then to the redefining operation, where the graphite ore is further crushed, washed, strained, dried, and sacked. Inside the building there were beams of tiny sunlit flakes of graphite suspended in the air that looked like sparkle dust, almost magical. Perhaps the pencils we use are filled with graphite from Madagascar!

Most thrilling were the wonders of nature, exotic trees, and bushes they encountered in the dense, dark forest. They found the indri in the trees above, heard their earsplitting screams, and agreed with us that the indri are spectacular!

One night as we dined out quite far from the Residence, a riot broke out in the city, apparently starting at a soccer game at the stadium. Bottles and rocks were thrown, several shops were burned, and we heard some shooting. The four of us spent that night at the home of the hospitable British ambassador, as it was too risky to drive home.

After three weeks that passed too quickly, Pam and Buddy flew to Kenya for a safari before returning to Denver. The large house always seemed empty after our family and friends had left.

Almost everyone stationed in Africa goes on safari. Though we could not go to Kenya with Pam and Buddy, Bill and I determined to go with Larry and his family, whom we met on their arrival in Nairobi, Kenya. From there we left immediately for Little Governor's Camp, an hour's flight from Nairobi. In the wilderness we lived under the stars in tents, using flashlights and candles for light. Each family had two tents, with all the equipment for a full bath in the smaller tent. We drove for two days through the bush with our driver-guide, seeing many of Kenya's best-known animals, including giraffes, lions with cubs, elephants, zebras, rhinos, hippos, jackals, cheetahs, warthogs, baboons, antelopes, impalas, and hyenas, all in their natural habitat and all almost within touching distance.

We were warned not to leave our tents at night because of the dangerous cape buffalo or to leave our Land Rover to take pictures of lions, which could move a lot faster than we could. Every now and then, a foolish tourist would lose the race! Crossing a river in a boat, one of the guides told us not to put our hands in the water as they might be bitten off by a crocodile. We carefully respected all advice. Our four-wheel-drive vehicle had a top that opened so it was a perfect way to view the country and its wildlife. Our grandchildren, only eight and six years old, were intrigued by the animals, the African sky, the entire adventure. They still enjoy the movies we took on the safari. Suddenly, their world had new horizons! The time went by all too quickly for we had only three days before heading home to Madagascar.

We had decorated the house for Christmas before going to meet the children and were all ready for the festivities. Once again, Bill donned his Santa Claus suit. The grandchildren were surprised that Santa had found them in such a faraway place, even without snow for his sled. On one-day trips to see the countryside and the lemurs, Jamye, a professional watercolor artist, busily photographed everything for her brush and palette once she returned home.

I joined Larry and his family on the Antananarivo-Paris flight because I had business at our Paris embassy. We had a day in Paris together before they flew back to the States. It had been a glorious time.

We had a bad scare in the spring of 1988 when Pam called from Denver to say that her doctors informed her that she had a brain tumor. An alert ear specialist had discovered it, and the surgery was scheduled for mid-March. It took me six separate flights to get to Denver, because I was traveling on my own as inexpensively as possible. I arrived in Denver the day before Pam's operation, although my suitcase did not.

Pam had two excellent Denver doctors and an outstanding hospital, St. Joseph's. Happily, the operation, a difficult one, went well. What a relief! She did lose the hearing in one ear, but the nonmalignant tumor had been caught just in time before doing extensive, possibly fatal damage. We parents never stop worrying about our children, no matter how old they are! Pam was home before I left, and Buddy took good care of her. Her positive attitude throughout the ordeal was a big help, and she was eager to get back to work.

I had to wear Pam's clothes, rather a snug fit, at the hospital and in her house. Lo, my suitcase, mislaid in Nairobi, finally arrived in Denver just in time for me to take it back home with me! Soon I was back at my desk, after flying a total of twelve airplanes to go from Madagascar to Colorado and back.

Glasnost in Madagascar

Working at the Embassy provided real life experiences with the KGB and some historic moments too. When the summit meetings between Presidents Reagan and Gorbachev were held in Washington at the end of 1987, I invited the Soviet ambassador, Pavel Petrik, to my office for champagne. It was a small meeting with just my deputy chief of mission, Marilyn Hulbert, a political officer who came with the Soviet ambassador, my husband, Bill, the champagne, and the cake. We toasted the summit in Washington and its hope for peace between the Soviet Union and the United States. We talked about our families and what peace would mean to them, and I shared pictures of my children I had brought to the office that morning.

It was an interesting moment in my relationship with the Soviet ambassador and opened up considerable contact between his embassy personnel and mine. In a very short time, he invited the same small group back for a private celebration in his Residence, which was usually closed to the West. We had more champagne, a delicious cake his wife had baked herself, and more pictures, this time of Ambassador Petrik's family. Some time later, I invited all the people from behind those high Soviet compound walls for a picnic at the Residence. We had many games set up outdoors—croquet, badminton, horseshoes. Ambassador Petrik really enjoyed his first game of horseshoes! We had all kinds of food and a merry time, even when it started to rain. I invited everyone inside out of the rain, and those whom I knew to be KGB people were stunned.

One of them said, "You are really inviting us to come inside your Residence?" I assured him I was doing just that and he was free to look around and make himself at home.

There was much more Soviet-American contact in Madagascar, thanks to Mr. Gorbachev's initiatives, but it was mostly on the cultural side. We still stepped cautiously and circled each other. They still pursued their old ways and we needed to protect our flanks even as we hoped for a better future. The world moves on and changes occur slowly, but they do occur.

Our next joint venture was a day of games in the Soviet compound, which boasted a tennis court and a swimming pool. Later on, when we had a fine American pianist, Michael Caldwell, coming to perform in Madagascar on his African tour, I approached my friend the minister of cultural affairs. Would she support a joint event at the Soviet-Malgache Friendship House at Antananarivo, which had a splendid piano, with our pianist entertaining both Soviets and Americans, along with invited guests of the Malagasy government? The answer was a resounding yes, and what a grand evening it was!

About this time, our old friend, Richard Dinning arrived from Washington to spend a couple of weeks with us. He had recently retired as a vice president of U.S. Airways and had been a bomber pilot in the U.S. Army Air Force during World War II. His plane had been one of those cheered by our soldiers on the ground as they broke through the clouds over the Battle of the Bulge. Richard arrived just in time to accompany us to the big evening of music at the Soviet Friendship House. He was politely questioned by a Soviet sitting next to him, who seemed to know all about him. Richard guessed the Soviets assumed he must be a spy from Washington. Once they were satisfied he was not, they relaxed, and so did he.

More Travels, and Champagne for a New Bridge

While Richard was visiting, we returned to Nosy Be and continued on to Diego Suarez. This was our first visit to that magnificent natural harbor on the northeast tip of the island. It is truly one of the finest natural harbors in the world, bigger than Pearl Harbor in Hawaii. During the period of French control, it served as a major naval base and repair facility, but today it is a ghost harbor.

We flew on a Sunday afternoon, with Richard at the controls for a time, to the famous Island of Saint Marie, off Madagascar's east coast, the home of many pirates in past years. Even the famous Captain Kidd spent a great deal of time here once he decided to become a real pirate.

Shortly after Richard returned to the United States, we flew off to the Seychelles, an independent island nation several hundred miles northeast of Madagascar. Though beaches were everywhere, I was, alas, too busy to enjoy any of them. The new Sheraton Hotel we stayed in reminded us of Hawaii. The island remains unspoiled, and tourism is their main source of foreign exchange. While there, we visited a U.S. Air Force satellite-tracking station manned by a small contingent of U.S. military and many civilian technicians. All of them hoped they would be stationed in this island paradise forever!

After the Seychelles, we flew down to Mauritius for our third visit. I was on official business again so Bill had to enjoy the beach without me. We were fortunate to have a small U.S. Air Force plane this time for our travels, and the entire trip took less than a week.

No sooner had I returned to Madagascar than it was time to pack up for another trip to the Comoros. The embassy there had a new deputy, Karl Danga, who kept everything in good order for me. Though we kept in touch by cable and telephone, I was both eager and obligated to check in personally from time to time. The former DCM there, Edward Brynn, was later ambassador to Burkina Faso and Ghana and a deputy assistant secretary of state. I had pushed hard for him to get his own mission.

Back in Madagascar, I was saddened that many of my staff were now rotating to other posts. Their normal time at a post is two years, whereas I was there for three. The marines changed every year and deserved many thanks for their service. I well remember Gunnery Sergeant Timothy Bedwell, because he was one of the best marines I have known. His wife also worked hard for the post, as did many of the Foreign Service officers' spouses. One of those moving on was economics officer Bill Kuhn, who had lived in Le Vesinet, France, as a young boy when his father was assigned to the Embassy in Paris. Amazingly, it turned out that the house the Kuhns had rented in Le Vesinet was the very one we had lived in when Ink was stationed at SHAPE headquarters. (Sadly, Bill Kuhn died of hypothermia while hiking in the mountains of Kazakhstan not too many years after leaving Madagascar.)

The embassy's new economics officer, Don Koran, was excellent. My administrative officer, Alex Kirkpatrick, was granted an extension and continued his duties. There were so many changes that I can't name them all, but I can say that I was fortunate to have a good staff from start to finish. Robin Rupli, my assistant, returned to Washington after two years and she was a great loss but happily, I was able to convince Elka Hortoland to replace her when her tour of duty was up in the Comoros. She had been commended officially as one of the best secretarial assistants in the Foreign Service.

While in Mauritius, I invited the U.S. ambassador there, Ronald Palmer, to visit us in Madagascar, which he and his wife Intan had never seen. She is a Malaysian princess Ron met when he had been assigned to Kuala Lumpur. While they were visiting us, he came to our Embassy for briefings. Mauritius was Ron's third ambassadorial post, so he was an old hand and was helpful to me as a neighboring ambassador.

At the dedication of the Namakia Bridge in the Mahajanga region, President Ratsiraka used the occasion to launch his campaign for reelection. I was pleased that he had decided to come to Namakia, as this bridge was paid for by the United States and we wanted people to know about it. It is the second longest bridge in Madagascar; 300 meters long, the length of three football fields. It is a Bailey Bridge, a type of temporary bridge of prefabricated, interchangeable steel truss panels bolted together. It was named after a British engineer and used with great success by engineers of the Allied forces during World War II.

I had brought along a bottle of champagne wrapped in a plastic bag so the glass would not fly through the air. The president, as a former navy man, smashed it expertly on the side of the bridge after we had walked part way across. It splattered a little, but missed us both. It was a memorable day; with big press coverage of the event. During his speech, President Ratsiraka thanked the United States for the bridge and, turning to me said, "Give Mr. Reagan and Nancy my thanks for their message of sympathy on the death of my father."

Later in his campaign, we opened a low-cost housing unit in Antananarivo together, where we had to walk down a steep, rather muddy slope. He gave me his hand to help me down. People were pleased watching him on television and thought it was a true gesture of amity between our two countries. On camera, we discussed plans for distribution of the low-cost housing, and the president said there was quite a rush on for the space. In my best ad lib French, I suggested holding a lottery. I later returned to see the houses we were sponsoring and saw that they had been well built by the Malagasy military. Gifts such as those houses make a bigger impression on the population than do military buildings.

The president's campaign continued for quite awhile. He knew that the Socialist route had plunged his country into economic disaster, but he wanted to stay in power. Hardly anyone in power, it seems, ever wants to leave; it is addictive. The president feared for his life, knowing that many factions were against him. He said many times that he wanted to bring his country back economically to show that he could change with the times. In the next few years, he would take many downslides, then bounce up again. The bad ending came in 2002, when he at first refused to step aside after an election declared Ravalomanana president. Finally, Ratsiraka's power was gone. The United States was the first country to recognize the new government.

Sandra Day O'Connor Visits Madagascar

When Justice Sandra Day O'Connor says she'll come to visit you, she means it, and come to Madagascar she did. She wowed the Malagasy from President Ratsiraka on down, and she worked hard. She was the highest-ranking woman in the United States government, and I was honored that she visited us. More than just an important person, she is a close friend.

As almost everyone knows, Sandra Day O'Connor is the first woman to serve as an Associate Justice of the Supreme Court of the United States. When I gave a reception for her at the Residence, inviting a hundred outstanding women of Madagascar, they could hardly believe that when she graduated magna cum laude from Stanford University and third in her law school class, California law firms refused to employ her as a lawyer, offering her only a secretarial job. In her talk to these guests she told how she kept on trying. Returning to her home state of Arizona, she was elected to the Arizona State Senate and eventually became majority leader, the first woman in that role anywhere in the country. Born in El Paso, Texas, the daughter and granddaughter of pioneers and cattle ranchers, she was raised on her parents' cattle ranch, the Lazy B, on the Arizona-New Mexico border. Like other homes of the time and place, their house had no indoor plumbing, running water, or electricity. At age six she went to live with her mother's parents in El Paso, where she attended school, but spent a great deal of time with her parents on the ranch. After high school in Texas, she had studied at Stanford University in California, where she had met her lawyer husband, John O'Connor.

I had mapped out a heavy work schedule for the justice, beginning on the day she arrived with a visit to President Ratsiraka in his palace office. The president had insisted that she be escorted at all times when traveling around the city by about eight motorcycles driven by a group of friendly young officers.

Another day, we met with Honoré Rakotomanana, president of the High Constitutional Court, which ranks above the Supreme Court of Madagascar. Justice O'Connor had agreed to address the members of his court on "The Organization and Structure of the U.S. Judicial System." At the same meeting, the High Counselor, Mrs. Berthe Rabemahefa, spoke on the Malagasy High Constitutional Court. In Madagascar women hold important positions at all levels of government.

The next day Justice O'Connor spoke on "Judicial Review: Freedom's Shield" at a colloquium of the Malagasy High Constitutional Court attended by the University of Madagascar law faculty, the Malagasy Academy, jurists, government officials, and students. All seemed pleased to hear the views of one of America's most distinguished jurists. She noted that although our Constitution was designed for us, some of its points could be useful for Madagascar as they planned their new Constitution.

DCM Marilyn Hulbert gave an enjoyable reception at her home to introduce Justice O'Connor to the Embassy staff, who were excited about meeting her. I had earlier shown the staff a video of an interview I had done with her several years before to give them an idea of what she was like. In addition to the reception at the Residence for the prominent Malagasy women, we hosted another reception and a dinner, so there was hardly a moment for rest. However, at her advance request, we made time for Bill and the justice to play a round of golf. They had played golf together in the United States, but playing in Madagascar was a whole new experience. The motorcycle escort insisted on going the whole way to the golf course and then waiting there, giving the other golfers a most unusual day.

One day we went to the zoma, departing at the crack of dawn. There was no way we could go there with the motorcycle escort and not be noticed, so we put bandanas on our heads (to disguise ourselves!) and had Bill's driver meet us with the Peugeot at the back gate, where a road led down to the main hill. Off the two of us went to the market. The escort arrived at the Residence shortly after we had left, not knowing we were not at breakfast, and waited patiently. We felt a little guilty but had a great time and Sandra picked up several gifts to take home. Once we arrived back at the Residence, we took off our bandanas, donned our workday clothes, and went down to my car, to Albert, and the waiting motorcycles.

We took the weekend off to enjoy ourselves at Nosy Be, our own special Tahiti. With bungalows on the beach, we could swim without fear of sharks, which were known to stay beyond the reefs. We visited the Center of Oceanographic Research, not far from our bungalows, to see how the government studied its fishing resources. The Malagasy want to know whether they are exploiting their shrimp-rich sea too fast, or if an abundance of crevettes enables them to export ever-growing quantities. Japanese fishing boats are hauling away great quantities of fish and crevettes in Mahajanga on the West Coast, but under a business agreement with Madagascar this territory up north is being preserved for the Malagasy themselves. When the big fish come to eat the little fish, as they do in great numbers, the fisherman has no trouble making a good catch.

We went by boat to two small islands. One boasted plentiful lemurs, which rested on our shoulders to eat the bananas we offered. Some were black, some red. Sandra fell for these lovable creatures, which have been known to make nice pets, although that is now forbidden. When a human to whom a lemur has become attached leaves for good or even for a long vacation, the lemur dies of sorrow. It is thus far kinder to make friends in the forest and say goodbye before the attachment grows too strong.

On the second island our little group disembarked for snorkeling and a sumptuous picnic on the beach. Some men on the beach were busy cutting fresh coconuts when we arrived and we were able to drink right from the husks. Our picnic feast included a rice and vegetable dish with meat cooked on skewers and plates full of fresh pineapple and mangoes for dessert. On the voyage back we viewed an ever-changing sky and many new little islands. Sandra was reminded of a boat trip she had taken off the coast of California, when she had seen many porpoises. I had never seen a porpoise in the waters around Madagascar, but no sooner had she spoken than a porpoise sailed high into the air beside the boat and gracefully disappeared into the sea. We were speechless. Why that porpoise had appeared at that particular moment remains a mystery. I never saw another.

Back at Nosy Be, we sat for awhile in little beach chairs waiting for the sun to set. The palm leaves snapped as the wind rose. The sunset created a reflecting "coucher du soleil" over the distant outline of Madagascar proper, its glow stretching across the horizon. Then the moon lit up the Southern Cross and all its stars. Standing at the water's edge, we watched with wonder the beauty of the sunset and the stars. That moment remains in my mind's eye.

Back to Antananarivo on Sunday, the end of the weekend vacation also spelled the end of the visit of Justice O'Connor. Before her departure, we had tea at the next-door home of University President and Mrs. Ranjevo, the one who became vice president of the International Court in the Hague. His wife Yvette is now Madagascar's ambassador to UNESCO in Paris. Their hospitality provided a warm ending to a remarkable visit.

20

Out of Africa

Home Leave and Pearl Harbor

Africa is far from home, and I always urged everyone on my embassy staff to take advantage of their home leave time. So it seemed like a good idea to take a trip ourselves. Bill and I spent the first two weeks of our annual leave in Europe. We flew to Zurich for two days on the lake in Locarno with our old friends, Felix Schnyder, the much-admired former Swiss ambassador to the United States, and his wife Sigi. I am so glad we stopped in Switzerland, because not long afterward Felix died. We saw Sigi several more times, in Washington and Switzerland, before she drowned, in 2002, in a dreadful accident in a car that plunged into Lake Locarno.

When we stopped in Munich, I noticed changes from my last visit several years earlier. Despite the many new shops, much of the charm of the old city remained. I visited with Anni, my former housekeeper, and saw Dr. Peter Maurer, who had lived next door in Munich when he was a boy. We visited U.S. Consul General David Fischer, who had come to Madagascar while he was chief of the African Bureau at the State Department. On we flew to Paris and to St. Jean de Luz, on the Bay of Biscay in southwestern France, where we relaxed with Annabella and her daughter, Anne, before returning to Paris for appointments at the American embassy.

In England, we visited our close friends, Pat and Napier Crookenden, who had visited us in Madagascar. We saw the dreadful destruction of trees caused by one of Britain's worst hurricanes ever. Over five million trees were uprooted or shattered throughout southeastern England, especially in Kent where we were. On one of my many visits several years later, I was surprised to find no sign of the trees having been destroyed. Nature had taken care of the situation with new trees. If I hadn't seen the original destruction, I would not have believed it had ever happened.

One of the vistas I like best in all the world is from an upstairs window overlooking a meadow where sheep sometimes grazed at "Twin Firs," the Crookendens' house in Four Oaks, Kent. Though not large, the house is cozy and delightfully situated. In days gone by, the meadow was called the Park, at the far edge of which stands an old manor house. In World War II the Canadian army kept tanks in the park and billeted troops on the very spot where my friends lived. One night during the war, a German warplane heading home via the Channel rid itself of a leftover bomb that landed on the farmhouse below, totally destroying it. It was the new farmhouse that was built that the Crookendens bought and fixed up as their retirement home, and where I found my favorite English window.

Flying into Washington, Bill and I were met by my niece Jeri at Dulles Airport and then spent several days with Loraine and Chuck Percy in their guest cottage. I had business at the Department of State, and we attended to medical and dental appointments, as diplomats do while on leave. We saw old friends, visited our families, and before we knew it, it was time to head for home in Madagascar. We stopped in Denver to see Pam, who had made a great recovery from her surgery but still suffered from violent headaches.

Homeward bound, we flew to Hawaii for two days, the distance to Madagascar being about the same via the Pacific as via the Atlantic. The U.S. Navy had been urging me to stop in Honolulu for a briefing, as Madagascar is in their area of responsibility. I enjoyed my series of conferences and briefings immensely. Admiral Ronald J. Hays, then Commander-in-Chief, Pacific, and his staff briefed me themselves in a large, impressive conference center at Pearl Harbor, and entertained us at a dinner party of naval officers and key civilians. I had other briefings at the senior army headquarters.

When we arrived in Hong Kong for a one-day stay, we were exhausted. From there we flew to Singapore for a plane change to Mauritius, spending a couple of hours in the middle of the night in

Singapore's handsome new airport. I was reminded of my stop in Singapore some years before, when I visited the Kidney Center at the hospital. In Mauritius we again arrived in the middle of the night, then flew to Réunion, a small French island, for a brief rest near St. Denis, the capital, and an appointment with the French governor of the island. A volcanic island with magnificent mountains, Réunion gives France a position in the Indian Ocean and is a good trading partner.

Along the street near our hotel, I could see the palm trees bordering the ocean and watch the waves rolling in. I have often mused, when standing on the point where my house looks out over the Chesapeake Bay, that it looks as beautiful as the Indian Ocean. Now, gazing at the Indian Ocean, I thought, it looks as beautiful as the Chesapeake Bay. Though they are quite different, on each of them I can imagine the ships of the explorers and sense the great wheels of commerce turning.

Finally back in Antananarivo, we were glad to touch down and return to our own residence. We had been on and off eighteen airplanes of different carriers, which, remarkably, in every case, left and arrived on time with all of our baggage intact. Though returning via the Pacific rather than the Atlantic was a bit more difficult, I was happy that we had made the effort and appreciated the navy's briefings in Hawaii, which were enlightening and helpful to me at my post.

The French Warship

We were on our way to Mahajanga on a turbo prop plane with Alain Bry, the French ambassador, and his wife, together with my embassy naval attaché and political officer. It was raining in Antananarivo, but flying above the clouds on this hourlong trip we could look down and see the green terraces and villages below. The land looked most beautiful in this rainy season, as the roads wound crookedly through the valleys, between rolling hills sometimes scarred by erosion. Rocks formed a crazy pattern on top of some hills, probably some of Madagascar's many valuable minerals.

Soon we were heading into unpopulated territory. Every now and then, we saw a village, almost always with churches, usually one Protestant and one Catholic. I thought of the many missionaries who spend most of their lives in Madagascar, one of whom, Dr. Quanback, had been at the airport with his wife, heading for Nairobi to attend a course in continuing medicine. The Quanbacks had been in Madagascar for many years, and his father for many years before him. They loved this country and the people who lived there. Dr. McKenzie, another Lutheran we saw at the airport, was a dentist in the city of Antsirabe who treated Malagasy patients in the hospital there.

I was making my first visit to the Northwest port city of Mahajanga, once one of the finest ports in the country. Since the revolution in 1975, it had gradually filled up with silt from lack of maintenance. Ships had to anchor outside and use small boats to get to and from the land, as we would be doing later this day to board the French frigate, *Doudart De Lagrée*.

I was glad to see Ambassador Bry, seated just across the aisle from me, taking a catnap. He worked long hours, and we had all been up at 5:00 a.m. He is a remarkable, intelligent, caring man, a great and helpful friend. He had invited Bill and me to share in this special day on which a French warship had been allowed to come into port. My joining him aboard would show a unity between our two countries, and that would send a strong signal to the Malagasy of friendship between us and with them.

I was holding in my lap a six-day-old *International Herald Tribune* from Paris, the latest to reach us. We had the VOA, BBC, and Radio France, but there had been no time that morning to tune in.

As we descended for a landing, the wide river below looked bigger every moment. The ocean, I knew, was ahead on the other side of the hills, but I could not see it. The earth became a delta, with water everywhere, and occasionally I could see a little wooden boat. Suddenly, there it was, the city and the ocean beyond, spread out

320

before us, and soon we were on the airfield taxiing in past clumps of grass.

Numerous representatives of the city met us, and then we all loaded up in our car. We drove to the Zaha Motel, which received us, royally, and checked into our bungalow on the beach. The heat was intense, but the Indian Ocean was in sight. We left in convoy, Ambassador Bry, his wife, and his military attaché in their cars leading the way, with Bill and me following.

Just ahead looking beautiful in the harbor lay the *Doudart De Lagree*, the first French warship in fifteen years to be allowed to go into a west coast port in Madagascar. From Mahajanga it would travel around to the east coast of Africa before returning a few weeks later to its normal duty in the Persian Gulf.

We took the ship's gig from the dock out to the ship for luncheon on board at noon. When the gig reached the frigate, Ambassador Bry explained the boarding procedure and I waited while he was piped on board. I watched as the bosun stood at the top of the steps blowing on a tiny pipe. VIPs such as admirals, generals, and ambassadors receive this special piped salute while boarding. Once Ambassador Bry had greeted the captain and reviewed the officers he came back to the top of the ladder to greet me. I too was piped on board, a first for me. The world had turned into France. Later, the ambassador said with a smile that he had thought of Lafayette as I came up the ladder!

The hospitality was superb, the ship shining for the occasion. At luncheon in the captain's quarters, the French conversation was good practice for me. (I was improving each year, fortunately.) The *capitaine* spoke excellent English but on this occasion spoke French. He talked to me about the frigate's upcoming trip to the Persian Gulf, where he would be watching carefully for treacherous mines. His ship, with two large guns and smaller ones for antiaircraft, had experienced other journeys into danger. The *capitaine* told me of the camaraderie between French and American crews in the Gulf. They even wave to the Soviets as they pass, for they all have the same mission, to keep the Gulf open for international shipping.

After a leisurely luncheon, we headed for shore, and dropped everyone off. My driver took me to the home of the governor, a

Muslim leader of the province. At the time Muslims were only about 7 percent of Madagascar's population. The governor and I discussed the economic situation in his area (not good but showing some signs of life), the region's crops— vanilla, coffee, cloves—the fertile land, the outstanding variety of rice they would like to export as in years gone by, and those valuable minerals just waiting to be brought out of the earth.

Then, back to the hotel to change for a reception on the deck of the *Doudart De Lagree*. There we saw many French citizens and Malagasy representatives. A canvas cover turned the deck into a tent, with flags draped along the sides. After the reception we stayed for supper back in the capitain's quarters, the doors open to the room where music played for dancing. As we departed and looked back from our small boat, the *Doudart De Lagree* was a magnificent sight, lights blazing, the moon shining hazily above, the star-filled sky outlining the shore. I stood the whole way back to shore to take my last view of the ship through the open roof of our small boat.

I asked Alain if the ship goes lighted or in darkness when in the Gulf. He said, "At first lighted, but now no lights burn. The target opportunity is too great." Silently, I wished her well, along with our own allied ships, risking all to keep the oceans free.

From the Ngong Hills to the Andringitra Mountains

When I found it necessary to travel to Kenya to talk with people at the American embassy there, I would always try to save a short time to go a few miles from the embassy to visit the Karen Blixen Museum. There I would sit in the garden, a perfect place to relax and to think. I'm not sure why it had such a pull for me, perhaps because I could sit in the garden undisturbed by anyone at all and look off into the Ngong Hills. I had traveled much closer to those hills by car and from a great height had looked down into the valley, home of the Masai, a proud tribe now threatened by civilization's push for more land; but it was from Karen Blixen's garden that I could see the blue haze of the hills and watch the clouds settling just beyond them. Above the clouds, that endless expanse of blue African sky has always mesmerized people in love with Africa. A legend about the Ngong Hills tells of a great giant who terrorized the Masai people. Finally, the Masai went to the termites and asked them to rid them of their enemy. One night while he was sleeping, the termites buried the ferocious giant but his hand and arm were left exposed. It is this hand that is said to have formed the Ngong Hills.

The garden is simple and beautiful, and I liked to sit on the stone terrace. A stretch of grass preceded a rock garden with flowering bushes backed by candelabra-like trees. Then beyond laid a natural forest, perhaps leading to a valley I could not see, and finally, in the distance, the hills I love.

Karen Blixen (who wrote under the pen name Isak Dinesen) came to Africa from Denmark in about 1917, living there until 1931. The house I saw is a replica of the original and was built for the filming of *Out of Africa,* starring Meryl Streep and Robert Redford, which made the house famous. The original house was built when Karen Blixen started a coffee plantation there on six hundred acres of land. She worked hard along with the workers and opened a school for little children, but her hopes of making a fortune were never realized. Sometimes drought brought famine to the area, and the coffee trees would not grow.

Inside the house, her riding boots stood in a corner. There were lace curtains at the windows, a leopard skin on the floor, and an old metal bathtub. Old photographs were everywhere. The cedar floors sported a Persian carpet. A desk had her typewriter on it and added to the strange feeling of her presence. I can see why it is now one of the national museums of Kenya.

The guide in the house told me that Karen Blixen adored her Karen Coffee Company, co-owned by the Swedish African Coffee Company, and the view from the verandah, where she could gaze at the Ngong Hills. The story goes that just outside her front door she would hang a lantern to signal to her lover, Denys Finch Hatton, that she was at home. He was killed in a plane crash and buried in those hills. Karen Blixen sold the farm and returned to Denmark, where she wrote her book *Out of Africa.* She became a respected writer and died in 1962 at the age of seventy-seven. What a fascinating person she must have been!

I learned that the Gabra people of the north were similar to the Masai and wanted to learn about these people because I have a painting titled "The Gabra Man" by an artist friend, Lunda Hoyle Gill, who painted people from vanishing tribes. She is highly regarded by the Smithsonian Institution, where some of her paintings used to hang. When Lunda gave me that painting, she said she had listened to me on "The Breakfast Show" while painting in faraway countries. "The Gabra Man" hung in my office in Madagascar and hangs in my living room today in the United States.

Back in Antananarivo, I had my own special view of the Andringitra Mountain Range. At the office, there were problems to tackle, as always. I say very little here of the difficult decisions I had to make and the occasional crises that arose. I held many discussions with President Ratsiraka and with my colleagues about the progress of the World Bank structural reforms. The main goals of the reforms included initiating and effecting economic viability and debt relief and improving the country's infrastructure, agricultural production, and the people's quality of life.

Sometimes, I would hear Westerners say they thought colonization was the answer for the world's poor countries, that only under the control of a more educated regime could they thrive. I do not think that colonization is the answer for poor countries, even though I cannot come up with an alternative formula for what would work. In Madagascar, I could see that the Malagasy people had absorbed and admired much of the French culture. Musicians would play French music, the schoolchildren wear a French styled blue *tablier*, the same smocks my own children had worn at school in France. Now, the Malagasy breathed the air of freedom, the breath of life, without French control. Years before in France, a French general, a friend, in commenting on the war then raging between the French and the Algerians, told me the Algerians would fight until they were free. This same General Allard would lose a son in that war and would himself be temporarily in trouble with General DeGaulle during a threatened uprising by French paratroopers in France.

When not long ago, I read Albert Camus' last book, *The First Man,* about his childhood in Algeria, I understood better the ever-growing tension between Algeria, the occupied, and France, the occupiers. And I understood why a revolution had come to this country and the Malagasy had to be free. The tragedy lay in the revolutionary President Ratsiraka's embrace of Marxist ideology.

The Malagasy people I worked with were intelligent, industrious, and eager to learn but lacked management skills. The prime minister had discussed this point with me and how their problems might be solved — certainly not by rioting against Indian merchants. There are those who think it will take generations for people freed of domination to manage themselves effectively. We worked hard on our USAID programs and were already bringing in some management experts, hoping that self-development and freedom would work hand in hand.

What do you do to let your hair down when you are the ambassador and people expect you to be decorous at all times? One source of relaxing moments came when we were invited to a party at the Bardays. It was a step into another land. The Bardays are third generation Indians in Madagascar, highly successful import-export entrepreneurs. Their house on a hill is not large, yet it is beautifully and imaginatively designed. Askar Barday explained that his father built the house in 1940. On one particular September night, the dinner party was about eighteen people, a bit larger than usual. We climbed many stone steps, each with a ceramic-encased candle, and emerged in a small garden, where we were warmly greeted by Serene Barday, a gracious woman. It was cold this night on the last foray of winter in the Southern Hemisphere, so dinner was planned indoors. When I stepped inside, there was candlelight everywhere and a fire burning in the stone corner fireplace. From the window, I could see a tiny secret garden with more candles, an oriental carpet covering the concrete floor, orchid plants and greenery everywhere. When the host took me out through the French doors, I was delighted to see that this intimate city garden seemed as beautiful as that of an enormous estate.

At dinner in the library, I was seated at a round table with the host and Jose Bronfman, the charismatic head of the World Bank headquarters in Madagascar, and Monique Bry, wife of French ambassador Alain Bry. We discussed many subjects: Madagascar's problems, the malaria, the liberalization, the World Bank's structural reforms, opera in Argentina, the American election. The conversation was part serious, part light, in French and English. Dessert was served in the entrance hall, buffet style, with at least seven desserts and a large gourd in the center of the table filled with intriguing sparklers. After dessert, music filled the house. The dessert table had disappeared and the front hall became a tiny, perfect dance floor. The conversation, one on one, was good. It was all so relaxing, so much fun, and over so soon, a rare occasion for us, and we felt suspended in time.

That night was one of the magic moments of Madagascar, a country that should have everything, with its talented people, its resources, its beauty, and yet was plunged into poverty. We who dined together had spoken of trying to bring the country out of its Socialist disaster into a world where each man and woman would have enough to eat and live better. It is good to be reminded of how there can be relaxing moments after work, with friends who are aware of the difficult situation we face and with a common goal for Madagascar.

U.S. Election

Not many tourists came to Madagascar while we were there, and visitors to the Residence were always welcomed, not only by us but also by everyone we knew. We took them around with us while they were our guests so they would begin to understand this amazing country of Madagascar.

Good friends who lived near us in Scientists' Cliffs, Maryland, came to visit, as did my old radio partner, Rosanne McQuarrie Broughton of Washington. Some visitors arrived just in time for the 1988 U.S. presidential election night celebration at the Hilton Hotel.

We took them along so they could see how our embassy gave people an idea about our election process.

The embassy staff, especially Phil Breeden, new director of our USIS post, had worked hard to prepare little voting booths with curtains across the opening to the booths and to create as festive an atmosphere as possible, as in an election campaign. We invited many people in Antananarivo to come see what an American election is like. Though we were many hours ahead of what the time at home would be, this evening was as close as we could make it to the actual election going on in the United States. George H. W. Bush was the Republican party candidate and Michael Dukakis, governor of Massachusetts, the Democratic candidate. While I was in the United States on leave, I had bought balloons, small flags, and little straw hats with red-white-and-blue bands on them, typical of some of the hats worn at our political conventions, and the hats became prime souvenirs for our guests. We wanted to show something of the American political system and have fun doing it. We had posters, videotapes playing on television sets, and pictures of the two candidates all around the room.

We asked all the guests to participate in the voting and invited some of the foreign ambassadors to supervise the counting of the votes afterward. The Soviet ambassador took great care to see that everything was done honestly and well. I showed him one of our voting booths and explained how he should step inside and I would draw the curtain so that his voting would be completely private and no one would ever know how he voted. Pencil and paper were provided inside the voting booths, and everyone seemed eager to participate in the voting. Remarkably, the election at the Hilton Hotel that night came out percentage-wise about the same as the real election, whose results were announced on the Voice of America, with Bush, the winner, becoming president of the United States. That year, the Americans had chosen a Republican president and a Democratic Congress. The election party we gave was part convention, part election day, and exciting for us all!

Welcome Peace Corps in the Comoros

One of my best visits to the Comoros occurred when I joined Peace Corps director Loret Ruppe on her visit to the corps' newest outpost. To welcome Loret and me and Peace Corps chief of staff David Scotton, my deputy at our embassy in Moroni held a big reception. Comorian officials and the Peace Corps volunteers, who had been there for about four months and were feeling very much at home, attended the reception. Having the Peace Corps director come out all the way from Washington for a formal inauguration of the latest Peace Corps presence abroad was a big event warranting the presence of the American ambassador, me.

The volunteers were an unusually fine group of young people, enthusiastic about the pupils in their English classes and about their life on the islands. They knew that the name "Comoros" comes from the Arab word *kamar,* or *kumr,* meaning "moon," and they were learning about Islamic culture. Most of them were on Grande Comore, the largest island, in houses provided by the Comorian government. The houses had the basic essentials, down to mini-refrigerators in the kitchens. Other volunteers lived on the nearby islands of Maheli and Anjouan and also seemed pleased with their welcome and their lives. I had come over to greet them when they had first arrived for their initial training, after which they had gone right into the school year.

Loret and I visited some of the schools where the Peace Corps members were teaching. She was eloquent in a classroom situation, making an informal speech to the English students and encouraging the teachers. She spent the rest of the day with her group while I went to the island's main hospital to dedicate a new, badly needed room for which the United States had paid.

Sometime later, Loret Ruppe left the Peace Corps to become the United States ambassador to Norway. I saw her there briefly when I was in Oslo for a meeting, and we became friends, sharing our memories when we would see each other at meetings of the Council of American Ambassadors. I was one of many who grieved when she died much too young, while celebrating the great deal she had accomplished.

Back in Antananarivo it was time for the annual bazaar in which almost all ambassadors and embassy staffs participate. The Wednesday Morning Group, a charity-oriented international women's group, sponsors the bazaar and raises considerable money for the poor from the profits. Bill and I had loaned $1,700 of our own money (hoping to get it all back which we did) to help buy what our embassy would sell at the bazaar. Our committee had ordered T-shirts, hats, tennis balls, French-English dictionaries, and other popular items. Every year, our booth made a good profit. All the embassies sold items made in their own countries, and all did well. Every such fund-raising effort helps and we all admired the work of the international women's group. When the bazaar opened, even the new Soviet political officer was there taking it all in with his penetrating eyes and strictly business manner.

As the year-end holiday time rolled round again, our Episcopal Christ Church in Port Republic, Maryland, which sent us money every month, helped sponsor holiday activities in our little village outside Antananarivo. One year, people at the church had sent clothes for the fifty children between five and ten years old. My Malagasy teacher and I had spent several lunch hours in our cellar sorting the clothes and putting them in festive bags. This year, Aurelie, my teacher, suggested we buy yards of material at the market and have the dressmaker make fifty or sixty outfits for the children in the village. She would do sizes according to the children's ages. The church sent the extra money, and we bought the material at amazingly small prices. We put each present in a panier basket with a toy, marked with the child's name. Bill and I went together to present the gifts.

It was really Bill's project, for he took an immense bag of rice and dry vegetables to the village every week to enable the minister's wife to cook one meal a day, seven days a week for the children. We also helped with supplies, notebooks, and blackboards for the school attached to the church, which had no books. Bill would arrive with his own bags of hard candy and the children would follow his car up the winding hills to the village, knowing he would have candy for them all. Sometimes, the people in the village would ask him to take a basket of fresh eggs home for me. To this day, Christ Church takes up a collection once a year, and I send the money to the bishop in Madagascar for some village projects.

The Pope Comes to Madagascar

Several weeks after our U.S. election, Madagascar experienced an explosive presidential election as President Ratsiraka sought another term. Not everyone was pleased when Ratsiraka won, and riots broke out in the streets, with rock-throwing crowds of thousands around the embassy and throughout the city. The constant danger was hard on the Malagasy people. Fortunately, none of the anger was directed at us. The president's opposition charged vote fraud. Deputy Assistant Secretary of State Irvin Hicks had come from Washington to represent the Department of State at President Ratsiraka's inauguration. While I was showing him a gathering crowd at the top of a nearby hill, the crowd suddenly turned and started toward our Embassy. We raced to get back inside, where the marines on duty were getting ready to rescue us. As the mob rushed by the Embassy, rocks in hand, someone looking up at the American flag shouted, "Look, Americans!" and everyone cheered. Those cheers were welcome to our ears!

In the midst of the rioting, an important visitor came to Madagascar, Pope John Paul II, and a great effort was made to fill in the many potholes in the roads that would be used by the Pope during his visit. We were concerned about his coming during so much unrest, but the Papal Nuncio, the Vatican's ambassador to Madagascar, told us the Pope never stayed away just because of trouble. It was remarkable to see what a soothing effect he had on the rioters, with no more outbreaks while he was there. In Madagascar, approximately 50 percent of the Malagasy are Christian, half Protestant and half Catholic. About 45 percent practice traditional ancestor worship, and a small percentage are Muslims.

At an intimate reception for diplomats at the home of the Papal Nuncio, the Pope greeted each ambassador and spouse. I was impressed that he spoke a few words to each of us in our own language, whether English, German, Chinese, Arabic, or other. He also delivered a short speech in the drawing room, explaining that when he spoke to a group such as ours, he was reaching people in many countries, not only the country in which he stood.

In 2002, I was in Toronto, Canada, when the same Pope came to speak with 22,000 young people gathered for a meeting of the World Youth Council. Many of these friendly and well-mannered young people told me how much it had meant to them to be close to the Pope in this tremendous crowd. I remembered how fortunate I had been to be in a small room meeting this pope, whose presence was magnetic indeed.

Quite unexpectedly, I had to go to Pretoria, South Africa, for some dental work, as required by the medical policy of the embassy. That's how I happened to have my education considerably broadened. As I would have to be there for two weeks, with my weekends free while the dentist's office was closed, I was able to spend one weekend in Swaziland with the American ambassador there, Mary Ryan, and then in Capetown with U.S. ambassador Edward Perkins and his wife. I met with many people so that I might learn about the South African government and Capetown. Ambassador Perkins lent me his car and driver for an entire day to visit a township, which was depressing, and see the city. At that time, South Africa had 3 million whites, 26 million blacks, 2.5 million so-called coloreds, and 5 million Asians. I was happy when apartheid ended in South Africa some years later.

Ed Perkins, a distinguished ambassador, was the first African American sent as ambassador to South Africa. I believe he deserves great credit for bringing about a new outlook in South Africa. He was greatly respected by the white government, which reportedly had always doubted it could do high-level business with anyone not white. Perkins had been there for six months before people of color came to trust him, he said, and to bring their problems to him. He was able to take their grievances to the political table and make some diplomatic progress between the white government and the black leadership. I am oversimplifying a complex problem, but I could see that Ambassador Perkins made a tremendous impact while he was there. Later, when Ambassador Perkins was director general of the Foreign Service, he held a retirement ceremony for me in his office. Referring to my broadcasts on the Voice of America (he said he had always listened), he called me "a legend in my own time." I didn't know whether to feel a bit aged or extremely pleased so I chose the latter!

Time Grows Short

Only a few months remained until we would be leaving Madagascar to return to Washington. I didn't know how we could possibly get everything done in time, but we would give it a good try.

As the days rushed by, I was surprised to awaken one morning at 4:30 a.m. to the sound of what seemed like the roar of a train engine forging through our bedroom. The dogs barked, and we jumped out of bed wondering what was happening. Was it an earthquake? Had someone blown up the palace? I sleepily rushed to the window, looked for any sign of fire in the sky, and listened for sounds of excitement, but all was dark and silent. Only the floodlights on the grounds of the Residence were lighting up the distant hills separating us from a view of the city. The train sound was gone, and we went back to a state between sleep and semi wakefulness. The next morning I learned that there had indeed been an earthquake one hundred miles away. Damage was slight, but the impact was widely felt. Many people in Antananarivo had heard the ear-shattering noise.

Each day when our alarm went off at 6:00 a.m., we listened with pleasure to the usual early morning sounds. The guards in the carport beneath our bedroom window would turn on their radio, and the languid Malagasy music would float upwards on the wind. An embassy vehicle would drop off Albert at the gate. To be there in time to drive me to work, he had to get up around 4 a.m., like most Malagasy. Ever so faintly, I would hear Martin in the kitchen. Our bedroom wing was in what was called a "safe haven," at the end of a hallway secured by a steel door that we would lock at night, in case of an unlikely attack from outside. The Malagasy are fond of Americans and posed little danger. But an unfriendly foreign group might be more of a possibility.

I would hear Jean Clair the cook and Rakoto the house man coming in at the gate after a long bus journey The kitchen and the house would wake up to their busy, loving hands, and breakfast would be ready at an early hour. Working at the Residence was a job to be valued, and this staff had been there for years. I loved each one and knew about their families and their many children. In a poverty-stricken country, even the small salary we paid made the difference between a miserable life and a decent one.

Later, back home on the Chesapeake Bay, I would recall these sounds and the sights I saw en route to the office: little shops at the foot of my hill and watercress paddies where women washed clothes. We would wind up the hill past once-grand houses to the city's tunnel entrance. Just before the tunnel was a somewhat optimistic sign proclaiming "Le Supermarket." Downtown was an old French monument just beyond the park. The Jacaranda trees in bloom, loaded with purple flowers that seemed to bloom for months, always lifted my spirits.

Cars abounded in the town, many of them small and needing repair along with some large Mercedes Benzes in good condition. We passed the Roxy Movie House, the jewelry shops, the Bata shoe store not far from the railroad station. Turning left, then up the cobblestone street, up, up, in a circular pattern brought us to the church on the hill, from where we looked down into the zoma, the market place, with its tall parasols. Every morning I found new sights to see and old sights to treasure. The many rice fields on the way to the airport contained small wooden rice-storage sheds, set on stilts to keep the rats from getting at the rice. The little kiosks in front of crumbling houses were illuminated at nightfall by candlelight and were an enchanting sight.

Bill accompanied me on a last-minute journey to a part of Madagascar we had not seen and where there were several USAID education and food projects. We flew to Manakara, a pleasant small city on the southeast coast and the terminus of a railroad that winds its way to the high plateau city of Fianarantsoa, our destination. After arriving by air in Manakara, we took this four-and-a-half-hour scenic rail trip on what was actually a diesel yard engine, with a driver and room for four to six passengers. And was it scenic! The train climbs the steep escarpment through a rain forest with many tunnels, waterfalls, and steep drops. So sparse was the traffic on this line that at noon we were able to stop the train beside a waterfall and eat our picnic lunch. As beautiful as we had been told the ride would be, it was also bumpy and rough, so our arrival in Fianarantsoa was not unwelcome.

The next morning we drove up to Ranomafana, deep in a heavily forested area, where the Duke University Primate Center has a field research station. They were conducting lemur research, their primary focus, in the lemurs' natural habitat. We spent the night there and met Professor Ken Glander, visiting from Duke, and many other devoted American students and faculty members. We learned a great deal and were sorry to leave. When I met Ken Glander back in the United States, he invited me onto the visitor's board of the Primate Center at Duke, which has several hundred lemurs. The valuable research done there is helping solve the environmental problems of keeping lemurs alive in Madagascar. Thanks to Duke University, the area around Ranomafana that we had visited was to become a Madagascar national park.

On our last, unforgettable Independence Day celebration in Madagascar I was able to give the Malagasy a truly BIG present. One of the long-lead-time projects initiated on my watch was the presentation to the Malagasy Air Force of a World War II vintage DC-3 cargo plane, completely rebuilt from nose to tail and looking like new. A DC-3, still flown in the United States, is a perfect aircraft for the Malagasy environment, easy to maintain, virtually indestructible, and fast enough for local purposes. Included in this gift from the United States were spare parts for several long-deadlined DC-3s owned by the local air force but not operational. The gift plane had been completely rebuilt in Michigan under private contract and flown to Madagascar for the presentation. Two civilian contract pilots took sixty-six hours of flying time to make the trip via a circuitous route from the United States.

The ceremony late in the afternoon of the Fourth of July included honored senior guests, an honor guard, a band, and of course speeches. The USA really dominated the local television and print media that day with the aircraft ceremony, our Independence Day celebration at the Residence in the morning, and a lengthy film about America on the night of the Fourth.

Just before our departure we were fortunate to be invited to a family ceremony called the Famadihana, "The Turning of the Dead." The ceremony is a Merina custom, in which the shroud-wrapped bodies of dead family members are removed from the family tomb at intervals of years and displayed at a big family celebration before being wrapped in a new shroud and put back into the tomb. I had read about the Famadihana before going to Madagascar and thought it sounded like an unhappy occasion. I was wrong. The custom probably comes from Indonesia, reflecting the Indonesian roots of many Malagasy people. The slash-and-burn rice cultivation is also said to come from Indonesia.

The burial ceremony we attended was given by a wealthy Malagasy family, who seated us on top of a big hill overlooking the family's stone burial tomb. With us was a visitor from Great Britain, Mervyn Brown, who had been his country's ambassador to Madagascar in 1967 and who wrote one of the best books ever written about that country, *Madagascar Rediscovered*. It was in reading his book that I first learned about the burial ceremony we would witness together. Although he had researched and written about the Famadihana, he confided that he had never seen an actual ceremony until that day!

Sitting atop the hill, we watched a parade of musicians and people as they wound their way up the long path from the village. When the family had gathered at the tomb, the bodies were removed one by one but never completely uncovered. Their descendants held them in their arms and deftly wrapped them in new silk shrouds called *Lamba mena*. Mervyn Brown said the families sang stories about their ancestors so the children present would know more about them. I thought that a good idea, for I often wished that my parents had lived long enough to know my grandchildren, and here in another way were people making such a connection. It was not at all an unhappy or dismal ceremony. There was even dancing after the bodies were returned to the tomb.

Funeral rites concern power and prestige. Families are distinguished by how far back they can trace their ancestors, a custom not unknown in the West. Burial ceremonies absorb enormous amounts of time and money and are difficult for people with little money who have to save for years for the Famadihana. In Madagascar's society, where funeral rites vary considerably, Famadihana ceremonies are unique to the plateau area.

Another day, I visited a large herbal plantation where the Malagasy were exploring the capabilities of plants as healing drugs. As we know, plants and animals are constantly acquiring new applications in medicine, science, agriculture, and industry. The rosy periwinkle of Madagascar, a great triumph in plant medicine when its marvelous properties were discovered, is the source of a drug called Vincristine. Before the discovery of Vincristine, leukemia was almost always fatal in children but thanks to the rosy periwinkle, children with leukemia now have a 95 percent chance of remission. The Malagasy had been using it in their folk medicine for thousands of years. I wondered as I looked around the plantation if I might be looking at a plant that would some day cure some other life-threatening disease. The Malagasy have proven that modern scientists are sometimes wrong to think that something like a periwinkle is only another example of witchcraft. Botanist Larry Morse has written that some Nature Conservancy botanists are intrigued by the rosy periwinkle story.

It was time for me to pay an official farewell visit to the Comoros Islands' President Ahmed Abdallah, who had ruled the Comoros for all but three years since 1972. Little did I know as I said good-bye that in approximately three months' time he would be assassinated in the presidential palace in Moroni, the capital. It was never clear just who shot the president, but some time later in France, a French mercenary was arrested and imprisoned on a charge related to that 1989 assassination. Some reports claimed that Abdallah was slain by an army soldier who had had a dispute with him.

Back in Madagascar, I had a call from the Papal Nuncio, His Excellency Monseigneur Marchetto, inviting Bill and me to come to his house for a small farewell dinner. At the dinner I was pleased when our host called attention to the dedicated work Bill had done with the church in Madagascar. He spoke of Bill's interest in the soup kitchen run by the Catholic Sisters and of his work with the children of Saint Peter's Anglican Church in the village of Anjazafohy, which was sponsored by our Episcopal church in Maryland. Although he included me in his remarks, the dinner was really a much-deserved tribute to Bill. We spoke of the day we had met with the Pope in this same house. We were sorry to say goodbye to Monseigneur Marchetto, who went on to serve in the Vatican.

Another invitation meant a great deal to us, this one from His Excellency Bishop Remi Rabenirina asking if he might give a special evening service for us at the Episcopal Cathedral of Saint Laurent the week of our departure. The service was a memorable event. Although I had visited many churches of all denominations in Madagascar, it was with this cathedral and the bishop and his wife Elizabeth that we had become involved in the village where Bill would take rice every week to feed the children.

Many people came to the cathedral that evening, and the bishop gave a touching speech to us as his sermon. He presented me with a beautifully embroidered blue satin banner with the outline of the cathedral on it, a gift, he told me, for Christ Church in Port Republic, Maryland, where it now hangs on a brass stand. The women of the cathedral had stayed up two nights embroidering it.

When a U.S. ambassador leaves his or her post, it is the custom to submit a report to the State Department explaining the embassy's achievements during one's time there. Together with my splendid team, we prepared a long list about what our embassy had accomplished. It is to the Foreign Service officers, to many of their spouses who worked for us, and to the remarkable Malagasy people who worked in the embassy that I owe my thanks, and to the United

States Marines, the members of USAID and USIS, and everyone who helped me. Everyone came to the farewell party for us at the embassy, and I was sorry to be leaving.

The Malagasy newspaper was extravagant in its coverage of our embassy's accomplishments, mentioning once again the road-grading equipment the U.S. had given the Malagasy military and my driving the army chief of staff aboard the highest truck!

Au Revoir, Veloma, Farewell

The time had come for the farewell reception given me by the minister of foreign affairs. He bade me farewell in a most generous speech and placed around my neck the National Order of the Democratic Republic of Madagascar at the rank of commander.

I had prepared my remarks with care, for there was much I wanted to say from a personal as well as an official point of view. I began by expressing our respect for Madagascar, with whom U.S. relations went back more than a hundred years. I spoke of my traveling throughout the country as much as possible during my three years there; touched on the many places and people I had met and admired, and expressed my high regard for diplomatic colleagues. Then I said to my Malagasy friends:

> Now, it is time for us to say goodbye, to go back to Washington and turn my world globe so Madagascar can be seen at all times.
> Madagascar, land I will carry in my heart forever, *Au Revoir, Veloma,* Farewell.

The day arrived when for the last time the car flying the flag of the United States awaited me at the foot of the Residence steps. Another car would bring members of the household staff to the airport to wave goodbye. The dogs were already at the airport in their new pet carriers. Bill and I took one long last look at the house we had lived in for three unforgettable years and were on our way. My driver said to be sure to watch alongside the road, for his family planned to be there. Sure enough, Albert's wife and children stood there waving as we passed. At the airport, the embassy staff had all gathered to wait with us. When our plane arrived, we had last-minute goodbyes and tears when I left the household staff, especially when I hugged Jean Clair, who had wanted to come to America to work for us. Later, when his family wrote to me that he had died, there was a hole in my heart. He was one of the sweetest men I have ever known.

We boarded the Air Madagascar plane and the great adventure was over.

Had being an ambassador gone to my head? No, because I am well aware that some day in the future, I will be just a picture in a frame in my son's and daughter's houses. But I will admit that, before going into that frame, I have had a great love affair with life, and the chapter marked "Madagascar" was one of the best.

Veloma, to you, Enchanted Island.

Part IV

The Radios

21

Once Again a New Career

Into the Corporate World: RFE/RL

Almost as soon as I left Africa in late summer 1989, along came a new career that combined everything that had gone before. I had been home only five days when Gene Pell, president of Radio Free Europe/Radio Liberty, called from Munich to ask me to work for him in Washington. We would communicate by phone and e-mail from his office at RFE/RL headquarters in Munich to my office in Washington. I would represent RFE/RL in the United States, have management responsibilities in Washington, supervise the language services in the Washington Bureau, and work with the Washington and worldwide press corps. No broadcasting for me now that I was on the management side of the microphone. As director of corporate affairs, I was to be responsible for all public relations and communications for RFE/RL. I would sit in on board meetings and attend all European advisory council meetings. Because I knew something about the vital work of RFE/RL, I did not hesitate to say "yes" when asked to join the Radios.

Before becoming president of RFE/RL, Gene Pell had directed the Voice of America, where I first knew him. At lunch several days after that phone call, he spoke of exciting times for the Radios, with Poland having confirmed Lech Walesa, Solidarity's noncommunist head, as its new leader and signs of change in Hungary even as we spoke. Little did we know how fast things would happen in Europe once communism collapsed.

RFE/RL constitutes the home stations for the states of the former Soviet Union and Eastern Europe, now more often referred to as Central Europe. RFE/RL programs, broadcast in the languages of the receiving countries, provide world news and an objective perspective on their own domestic affairs. They also give practical information and useful ideas to people eager to learn how to restructure their governments into democracies.

I began work for the Radios in October 1989, when I traveled to Norway for a meeting with Gene Pell and our Western European Advisory Committee. From then on, I attended all the committee's meetings, held in different parts of Europe and hosted by the local board members.

From Norway I went to Munich for briefings at the Radios' headquarters, where I heard about the big events then unfolding. The Iron Curtain was beginning to crack. The Hungarians agreed to create a multiparty system. Then the Berlin Wall came tumbling down. The Bulgarian government, although still run by communists, agreed to hold multiparty elections in June. The tyrant Ceausescu was executed in Romania. And in Czechoslovakia, playwright Vaclav Havel became the first noncommunist leader in more than four decades. The Baltic States pressed for their freedom, and other winds of change were blowing in the Soviet Union. During this upheaval, RFE/RL broadcasters, researchers, writers, and engineers worked long hours, awestruck and enthusiastic, in our offices in Munich, Washington, and New York. The Romanian Service was broadcasting twenty-four hours a day.

With all the pressures of the moment, we were reporting accurately what was happening as the communist world unraveled. Only at the time of the Azerbaijan and Armenian problems in Baku in Central Asia did we run into problems, as the Armenians claimed our Azerbaijan service was biased in its reporting. Some mistakes had been made but steps were taken immediately to correct them.

The cessation of jamming meant we could get through to our audiences more clearly and quickly. Phones rang continuously in all the Munich language services, with listeners calling in to report news of what was happening in their countries. Both governments and opposition leaders asked us to air their views, and we did. We acted as megaphones for people who could not get their words heard across their own countries.

More than a decade later, listeners still ask our advice on how to form new governments, how to "do democracy." They want to know how to organize an election, how to set up free-market systems, how to learn about constitutional law. All those systems we take for granted had for them been swept away. It appears that the Radios will continue to be needed for as many years as democracy is still consolidating.

Estonian foreign minister Lennart Meri said at the time his country became free that "Radio Free Europe has been shining like a lonely star in a very dark night for years."

Pope John Paul II, upon learning of the August 1991 coup in Moscow, was quoted as saying, "Thank God there is a Radio Free Europe and Radio Liberty."

Boris Yeltsin said, "I would dare say that Russians learned more correct information about the work of the Russian Supreme Soviet, about its leadership, and about the Russian government from Radio Liberty than from our own media."

Much of the credit for Radio Free Europe/Radio Liberty's help in bringing down communism belongs to its superb leader and president, Gene Pell. I watched him lead his staff of many nationalities and personalities with a brilliance equal to that of the best chief executive officer of any large American industry. Instead, he chose to serve his country in a time and at a place where his skills were most needed.

Gene is a dynamic, complex, and completely honest man, whom I greatly admire. His magnificent deep voice instantly commands attention, but underneath his forceful exterior is an extremely sensitive man. He was proud of his talented, capable, loyal, and effective workers and was sad when it came time for him to move on. By then, he had received Germany's highest civilian award for his leadership, which, though exercised in their country, inspired all the world. Though I wished that the United States would give this extraordinary man an award, he really didn't need one, because the leaders of the countries of Eastern Europe and the former Soviet Union had been exceedingly vocal in their thanks and praise, as was each member of the Radios' European Advisory Committee, which included highly influential European leaders.

Another remarkable man with whom I worked was the chairman of the bipartisan Board for International Broadcasting (BIB), Malcolm S. Forbes, Jr., known as Steve Forbes. The board oversaw RFE/RL and channeled the congressionally appropriated funds for the Radios as grants to RFE/RL. Receiving a grant instead of direct support from the government made the Radios more independent.

Steve Forbes, best known as the president and chief executive officer of Forbes Incorporated and editor in chief of *Forbes* magazine, also ran for the presidency of the United States. Many people were unaware of his extensive knowledge of foreign affairs. As the active chairman of BIB, he visited with many of the Western countries' leaders and later with leaders of Eastern Europe. I believe that Steve wanted to be president because he wanted to serve.

I accompanied Chairman Forbes to the White House one day to see President George H. W. Bush's chief of staff, John H. Sununu. I had set up the appointment and knew that its main purpose was to ask to have Lane Kirkland's term of office on the Board for International Broadcasting extended. Kirkland was then president of the AFL-CIO and a tremendous asset to the board. He and his member unions had worked hard to aid the Solidarity movement in Poland and had been effective in helping Poland break away from the Soviet Union. We had heard from the White House that he would no longer be on our board, and Steve was hoping to change the president's mind. I said nothing during the meeting until the moment we were told that President Bush had something important in mind for Lane Kirkland.

At that point I said, "I am sure there is nothing the president could offer Lane Kirkland in the way of another board that would mean as much to him as serving on the board of RFE/RL," and the chairman backed up my statement. We knew we had been heard when shortly after our meeting, Steve received word from the White House that Lane Kirkland would be kept on the Board for International Broadcasting!

Steve Forbes gave a small dinner, which I attended, at the *Forbes* magazine headquarters in New York to thank former President Reagan for his strong support of the Radios. In his after-dinner speech, President Reagan told some of the jokes the people in the Soviet Union had told each other during the years of oppression. They were funny, politically loaded stories, and the president told them well. He was still in good health and scarcely needed his notes. Tragically, it was not too long afterward that he announced to the world that he was becoming a victim of the dreaded Alzheimer's disease.

I thoroughly enjoyed working for RFE/RL. It was exciting to be a part of it when the Berlin Wall fell and when the hammer-and-sickle flag came down from the Kremlin. After he had become president of Poland, Lech Walesa came to Washington and gave a great speech to a joint session of Congress. I invited Steve Forbes to come with me. Walesa opened the speech with the words "We the People," and the House and Senate erupted with applause and a standing ovation. Afterwards. President Walesa came to visit our RFE/RL headquarters on Connecticut Avenue, and we were all delighted to have this Nobel Prize winner there.

Looking back on those days in my Connecticut Avenue office, I remember my initial shock at seeing a computer and knowing I had to learn how to use it. Thanks to the help of my two splendid assistants during my five years with RFE/RL, I did learn. The first, Elizabeth Davidson, was a gem. A Foreign Service wife, she was well versed in international relations and helped me find a firm footing in the corporate world. Then I was most fortunate to have Dr. Natalie Doyle-Hennin work for me. She helped me with the computer, set up conferences, and gave me the time to think rather than spending all of my hours over a machine. She enjoyed working with the press as much as I did and had a great sense of humor.

RFE/RL's vice president of financial affairs, Michael Marchetti, whose office was at the other end of the corridor from mine, was a joy. During the lunch hour he would reminisce about how his family came to the United States from Italy and how hard his father worked to get his family launched. Now here was Michael, a vice president of a big corporation and always appreciative of what had been possible for him to achieve in this country.

Larisa Silnicky, the chief of the Russian Service in Washington, whose office was next to mine, taught me a great deal about Russia. When Dr. Roald Sagdeev, who had married Susan Eisenhower, would come in to be interviewed by Larisa, we had good talks. Among other visitors Larisa would bring to my office were new ambassadors from the Soviet Union to the United States, the wife of Soviet dissident Andrei Sakharov, and Galina Starovojtova, a member of the Russian Parliament who was assassinated in Moscow several years later.

After I retired from RFE/RL, I was invited to its new headquarters in Prague, capital of the Czech Republic. In a twist of history, this important international Radio Center was located in the Communist-built Parliament building on Prague's famous Wenceslas Square. Prague had been the capital city of Czechoslovakia before the Czechs and the Slovaks split into two countries.

Although I have traveled a great deal, beautiful Prague was unlike any place I had ever visited. This proud city has suffered so many occupations that it was a pleasure to see the people of the country and its president embrace Radio Free Europe/Radio Liberty and welcome its presence.

Why the move to Prague when the Munich headquarters I knew so well seemed a good place to stay? The answer: lack of money! Munich was expensive, and the German unions are so strong it was almost impossible to save money by firing anyone.

Congress had cut the budget drastically for all international radio and voted to join RFE/RL to the Voice of America. Then to the rescue came Czech president Vaclav Havel, who invited the Radios to move to Prague. He would give them the old Parliament building for a very reasonable rent (which turned out to be $12 a year!).

President Havel said, "These Radio stations are significant even after the end of the Cold War, not only because human rights are not fully respected and democracy has not fully matured, but also because they set a goal for the new independent media by creating a healthy and competitive environment."

On March 10, 1995, RFE/RL made its first broadcast from Prague. Sadly, the management had been cut 77 percent, the support staff 66 percent; and the budget itself had been slashed from $218 million to $75 million, which was all that Congress would grant.

When I arrived in Prague to see with my own eyes this remarkable feat of saving costs while maintaining high broadcast quality, I brought my pen and notebook and talked with many of the language chiefs and broadcasters. I had the run of the building and was impressed by its facilities and its new digital broadcast technology. The enormous satellite uplink sat high in the courtyard in the center of the building. The communists would have been surprised to see the wonders in their former Parliament building. In one room I saw, journalists from all areas of the former Soviet Union were meeting for a training session. An American foundation, the Fund for America Studies, pays for this course, which was in such demand that five hundred people had applied for the one hundred places. The curriculum was designed by George Mason University in Virginia and Georgetown University in Washington.

Each morning for the five days I was there, I attended the regular morning meetings at which all the service chiefs discuss the important local news to broadcast to their countries and to hear what worldwide news reports the Radios will be emphasizing that day. The variety of facial types of the many ethnic groups gathered about the long oval table was striking.

Looking back on that trip, I am encouraged that Radio Free Europe and Radio Liberty are alive and well in Prague. I hope that our Congress will continue to understand how important it is that our international Radios keep sending out that vital signal.

Death Takes No Holiday

Bill had a severe stroke in October of 1997, which left him brain-damaged and blind. He was in George Washington University Hospital in Washington for four weeks, followed by six weeks at Potomac Center Nursing Home in Arlington, Virginia. During this traumatic time, I was there every day. He seldom said anything, but I think he heard my daily patter:

> Bill, it's October 20th and it's raining outside. . . .
> It's the 1st of November and the wind is blowing
> the leaves from the trees. . . .
> It's Thanksgiving Day and the children are coming
> from Annapolis. . . .
> It's the 3rd of December and it's snowing. . . .
> It's the 6th of December and your children, Katie
> and Bill, and your brother, Joe, are here along with
> the rest of your family . . .
> It's the 15th of December and Christmas is coming.
> I've put a card up on the wall and it's Santa Claus in
> a sled . . .

It's the 16th of December and it's Ruth Boorstin's birthday. Dan is giving a luncheon for her at the Library of Congress and I'm invited, but I'll be back. Jeri is coming to see you, she comes almost every day.

I'm here beside you again, but I'm leaving now because it's almost dark and I want to cross the bridge in daylight.

It's 10:30 p.m. and I'm here again, but you've gone. You're waiting for the horses and the caisson. . . .

It's the 6th of January and the horses are here. The black riderless horse with the one boot turned around in his stirrup, is for you. The band is here before the Old Fort Myer Chapel and the troops are standing at attention. Inside, every row is full. There's Supreme Court Justice Sandra Day O'Connor and John. There's an admiral, Ed Waller and his wife, Marty. The six of us had good times together at our house on the Bay.

There are many old army friends, other friends and family from all over. There's Gene Tucker singing "On Eagle's Wings" for you, and Father Daniel Morrissey in his Dominican Friar's habit speaking directly to you in an Ecumenical Service.

There's a long line of cars driving through Arlington Cemetery to the place where your stone stands. It has your name on it and that of your other wife, Jean—you're back with her now. I am alone and know not what lies ahead. I know it was a beautiful ceremony—I hope you liked it. The soldiers' rifle volley echoes through the rows of gravestones. I hold the American flag you have earned. It is like the flag you always put up at the Community House at the Bay.

It is over.

Life Goes On

Retirement, I think, is often a myth. I have kept busy since retiring and have enjoyed having more time to spend with my family and friends. It had been good luck for Bill and me when Larry and Jamye and my two granddaughters, Emily and Sally, then still in high school, had come to live in Severna Park, Maryland, just outside of Annapolis, only a little over an hour away from my house on the Chesapeake Bay. About this time, a new member of the family came to live with us. We were adopted by a tiny black kitten, which we called Samantha. She didn't mind our dog as long as we appreciated *her* as someone very special, and we did! Several years later, it was a blow to Samantha, the cat, as well as to me when our Malagasy dog, Tollie, departed this world. A few months later Samantha died. Happily, I now have an entrancing Welsh corgi which helps fill the void.

Because Larry worked for International Paper, I knew that his time living so close to us would not last long. But I relished those three years we had before the company called him back to Memphis, Tennessee.

Soon my granddaughters were ready for college. Sally headed off to Franklin and Marshall College in Lancaster, Pennsylvania, while Emily went south to Auburn University in Alabama. After two years at Franklin and Marshall, Sally transferred to Auburn to pursue some courses. And Auburn is not far from their mother and father in Memphis, so it was easy for both girls to go home for holidays. They had summer jobs in Memphis to help with their expenses, and now they have graduated and are out in the world. Daughter Pam still lives in Denver, Colorado, but comes to visit me twice a year. Whenever I can, I visit Denver and Memphis.

Weekends are spent at Le Vesinet, my house on the Chesapeake Bay. I sold my apartment in Washington and bought another in nearby Virginia. My Virginia neighbors have lived all over the world, so I find it a stimulating atmosphere. The apartment is not far from Mount Vernon, the home of George Washington.

From 1998 to 2005 I was chairman of the board of the Association for Diplomatic Studies and Training (ADST) at the Foreign Service Institute. ADST is a non-governmental organization helping the

Institute as it seeks to educate diplomats of today and tomorrow. I also serve on other boards concerned with foreign affairs, and I have come to know one of the great diplomats of our age, former Secretary of State, Colin Powell, who has been a strong supporter of education for the Foreign Service. Seldom have I seen a man so honored by everyone around him or as giving of himself in this country and around the world. His successor, Condoleezza Rice, is another Secretary of State much admired and respected.

Suddenly, all Americans became brutally conscious of foreign affairs when on the morning of September 11, 2001, terrorists crashed two passenger-filled airplanes into the World Trade Center's twin towers in New York City and a third into the Pentagon near Washington. A fourth plane was believed headed toward the White House or the Capitol building in Washington when it was brought down in a field in Pennsylvania, intentionally, it is believed, by courageous passengers. I had been planning to drive in to Washington that afternoon and go to New York two days later. Needless to say, all my plans were canceled. All across the United States, American flags appeared on front porches, out in the yards, on buildings and bridges, and President George W. Bush rallied the country.

Several months later, while in New York, I visited the platform overlooking the remains of the World Trade Center. I well remembered the day I had done an interview for "The Breakfast Show" in the "Windows on the World" restaurant at the top of one of the towers. I also recalled having taken my granddaughter, Sally, in 1998 to the top of the World Trade Center for her first view of New York. There was nothing quite like it for its panoramic view of the rivers, the Statue of Liberty, and all of the city. Now I was back, in the year 2002, but the only view was of broken buildings and construction crew equipment.

Along the fence of St. Paul's church, which stands near Fulton Street just off lower Broadway beside the wooden ramp leading up to the platform overlooking the remains of the Center, people had posted messages, hand-made flags by school children, and photographs of fathers and mothers who would no longer be coming home to their families. Coming down the ramp, I heard a volunteer

New York City policeman, there to help with the crowd of visitors, say to one of us, "This is sacred ground."

I wanted to say something to him but found I was unable to speak.

Why this attack, I ask myself as everyone else asks. How can there be such hatred for this country when we struggle to do what is right, sometimes failing but always trying, when we welcome people from all over the world, when we have freedom of religion? All those years I was broadcasting and receiving thousands of letters from every part of the world, from people of every religion, I would read these messages from listeners telling me of their admiration for this country and how much they liked meeting Americans of every kind on my program.

When our space ship *Columbia* exploded with seven remarkable human beings on board on February 1, 2003, I recalled the January day in 1986 when our space expert, John Hammersmith, came to my VOA studio for an interview. Afterwards, he hurried back to his office at NASA to watch the *Challenger* lift off. When he had gone, I hurried out to Independence Avenue to catch a taxi to an appointment. On the taxi radio the announcer said, "Something is wrong, the *Challenger* has exploded!"

I still remember the sorrow I felt that day and again when the *Columbia* exploded seventeen years later. On "The Breakfast Show," we had always talked about the American space program's benefits to mankind, the scientific discoveries for medicine; osteoporosis, cancer. Astronaut John Glenn, the first American to orbit the earth, had been a Breakfast Show guest. I thought of all the pictures of astronauts walking on the moon I had been shown by school children in India, Pakistan, and other countries.

The War on Terrorism and the War in Iraq have made it more important than ever for all citizens to keep up on world affairs. I am pleased that I can be a part of spreading the word in this country on why our Department of State matters to us all.

This little girl from Connecticut has sailed from one century into the next, and the voyage continues to amaze me.

Coda

In the second half of the twentieth century, my hours were spent capturing the voices of people crossing a remarkable stage setting, the stage of life itself. I found something special in each person. Sometimes it was a dream, a talent, a challenge met, a sorrow, or a joy. These voices have been broadcast outward into space for others to hear, from one end of our world to the other. I hope that the scientists are correct who believe these voices do not vanish but continue to drift through the spheres, waiting to be discovered by other worlds, other forms of life.

Now in the first years of the twenty-first century, I am still involved with what is going on around me. Staying engaged with what is happening in my own country and around the globe makes life so worthwhile that I wonder why the days are not longer.

How fortunate I am to be a woman living in a time and place where so much is possible! In this splendid nation, I have discovered that doing the best you can with what you have, wherever you are, will give you, woman or man, the notes with which to write your own song.

The music of my song now comes to me here at Le Vesinet, at the edge of the cliffs of Calvert where my garden overlooks the Chesapeake Bay. The waves come into shore, driven by a northern breeze. They are waves of velvet this morning as I write, celebrating a day without the recent oppressive heat. The sun is shining where I stand, but the clouds further out have turned the deep Chesapeake channel into a black hollow, awaiting the ocean-bound ships that will soon come into view.

My hand rests atop my hat, to hold it fast, and for a moment, I think I am the Monet "Lady with a Parasol" looking out to sea. In reality I am wearing a floppy canvas hat with a cord under my chin, a rough white cotton shirt, and old blue cotton pants, with the newspaper carrier bag over my shoulder. I have just come back from the top of the lane where I have fetched the *Washington Post* for my neighbor and myself, from the newspaper-warrens clustered along the road. Fun, to pretend you are in a painting, however absurd! It's like thinking you can dance just like that when you watch Fred Astaire, the best of them all, in an old film. Well, at least I have known what it was like to run (float, I thought) with my hand in Fred Astaire's, as we hurried to the elevator after my interview with him.

Whenever I look out at the Bay, odd thoughts cross my mind, as the water lapping on the shore below brings with it bits and pieces of days gone by. Older friends tell me that it is very hard to lose good friends as the years pass. Now, as I grow older, I am seeing this happen. I have always thought life was like the game of musical chairs we played as children. Empty chairs are placed in a circle, and the children circle the chairs as music is played. When the music stops, another chair is pulled away, and each time fewer chairs are left for the children to sit on. At the end, only one chair is left. Life is like that, I think, as your friends go one by one, with only one or two people left at the end of the game.

How well I remember the people who sat in those chairs, people I have talked to you about. What remains are the memories, taking the place of the people for whom the music has stopped. But I have been lucky, for there are new circles of chairs bringing new faces, new friends, and this new century.

In the beginning, Connecticut was my whole world. Looking back over the years of my life, I realize that after I left Connecticut the whole world was my home. My love for people has never diminished, and they have cast a warming glow for me over the shadow of mortality.

Listen with me to the music of the Bay.

Thank you for listening.

Bibliography

Astaire, Fred. *Steps in Time.* New York: Harper & Brothers, 1959.

Berg, A. Scott. *Max Perkins.* New York: Thomas Congdon Books, E.P. Dutton, 1978

Boorstin, Daniel J. *The Seekers.* New York: Random House, 1998

Brown, Mervyn. *Madagascar Rediscovered.* London: Damien Tunnacliffe, 1978.

Bunge, Frederica M., ed. *Indian Ocean — Five Island Countries.* 2nd ed. Foreign Area Studies/The American University. Washington, D.C.: The Series, United States Government Printing Office, 1983.

Chevalier, Maurice. *I Remember It Well.* New York: Macmillan, 1970.

Century in the Post Series. *Washington Post*, August 7, 1999.

Compton, Arthur Holly. *Atomic Quest.* New York: Oxford University Press, 1956.

Davis, Nuel Pharr. *Lawrence & Oppenheimer.* New York: Simon and Schuster, 1968.

Eisenhower, Julie Nixon. *Pat Nixon: The Untold Story.* New York: Simon and Schuster, 1986.

Garment, Leonard. *Crazy Rhythm.* New York: Random House, Times Books, 1997.

GE News. Nela Park, East Cleveland, Ohio. Volume 10, Number 11, July 6, 1984.

A Glance at Madagascar. Tananarive: Edition Librairie "Tout pour l'Ecole," 1973.

Griffith, Aline, Countess of Quintanilla. *The Earth Rests Lightly.* New York: Holt Rinehart and Winston, 1963.

Henry, Neil. "Comoro Islands Leader Shot to Death" *Washington Post*, November 28, 1989.

Johnson, James Weldon. *God's Trombones.* New York: Viking Press, 1927.

Keeley, Robert V., ed. *First Line of Defense: Ambassadors, Embassies and American Interests Abroad.* Washington, D.C.: American Academy of Diplomacy, 2000.

Kerensky, Alexander. *Russia and History's Turning Point.* New York: Duell, Sloan and Pearce, 1965.

Laingen, L. Bruce. Personal letter to author, February 16, 2000.

Lynch, William D. Personal Letters from Madagascar to the United States, 1986–1989.

Mandelstam, Nadezhda. *Hope Against Hope: A Memoir*. New York: Atheneum, 1970.

Nichols, K. D. *The Road to Trinity, A Personal Account of How America's Nuclear Policies Were Made*. New York: William Morrow, 1987.

Polmar, Norman, and Thomas B. Allen. *Rickover*. New York: Simon and Schuster, 1982.

Shklovskii, I. S., and Carl Sagan. *Intelligent Life in the Universe*. San Francisco: Holden-Day, 1966.

Shirer, William L. *The Nightmare Years 1930–1940*. Boston: Little, Brown, 1984.

Spasowski, Romuald. *The Liberation of One*. New York: Harcourt Brace Jovanovich, 1986.

Tattersall, Ian. "Madagascar's Lemurs," *Scientific American*, January 1993.

The World Book Year Book. Chicago: Field Enterprises Educational Corp., 1967.

Index

A

Abilene, KS	266
Abdallah, Pres., Comoros	275, 276, 336, 337
Abrams, Creighton, Gen.	154
Abidjan, Ivory Coast	173
Aburi, Ghana	173
Accra, Ghana	173, 176, 177
Adams, John, Pres.	290
Adelaide, Australia	232
ADST (see also Association for Diplomatic Studies and Training	351
Advise and Consent, film	75
AFL-CIO	346
AFN	77, 89, 96, 104, 115, 116
Africa	50, 168, 170, 171, 191, 237, 241, 244, 245, 250, 252, 254, 256, 261, 271, 283, 285, 305, 317, 321, 323, 343
Agency for InterNational Development (see also USAID)	258, 261
Aida	101
AIDS	202, 203
AIDS Quilt	202
Aim for the Stars	82
Air Force	59, 89
Air Force Band	
Air France	237, 254
Air Madagascar	237
Ajabshar, Iran	83, 84, 85
Akufo Addo, Mrs.	173
Akufo Addo, President	173

Alabama	134, 351
Alamogordo, NM	24
Ala Tahry Reserve, Madagascar	271, 272
Albert, U. S. Embassy driver, Madagascar	256, 265, 269, 287, 294, 314, 338, 339
Albertazzie, Ralph, Colonel, Pilot, Air Force One	153, 154
Aldrin, Edwin E., "Buzz"	164
Algeria	284, 324, 325
Algiers	284, 324
Ali, Muhammad (Cassius Clay)	195
Allard, General	324
Allen, Maria	286
All India Radio	181
Alps	49, 79, 81, 90, 92
"(I'll Be Loving You) Always"	187
A Man for All Seasons	73
America	106, 127, 187, 191, 211, 219, 225, 226, 230, 250
"America, the Beautiful"	300
American Academy of Diplomacy	208
American Red Cross, International Committee, Washington, DC	174, 175, 240, 252
American University, DC	68
American Women in Radio and Television	131, 241
AMOCO	282, 304
Ampefy, Madagascar	286
Anderson, Elaine	6

Andrews Air Force Base, Maryland — 161, 170, 171, 174, 188, 208

Andriamahazo, Maj. Gen. — 280

Andringitra Mountains, Madagascar — 268, 322, 324

Anjazafohy, Madagascar — 337

Anjouan, Comoros Islands — 275, 276, 328

Annenberg, Walter H., Amb. — 247

Andrea Doria — 65

Ankara, Turkey — 89

Annabella — 5, 6, 7, 20, 21, 60, 61, 114, 241, 293, 294, 295, 317

Annapolis, MD — 194, 206, 349, 351

Antananarivo, Madagascar — 237, 255, 256, 267, 268, 270, 271, 272, 276, 284, 286, 290, 295, 297, 299, 301, 306, 308, 311, 315, 319, 324, 327, 329, 332

Antananarivo, University, Madagascar — 267

Antarctica — 158

Antsirabe, Madagascar — 269, 270, 297, 320

AP — 158

Apollo II — 164

Aquino, Benigno, III, Sen. — 229

Arabian Sea — 237

Arizona — 205, 244, 312

Arizona State Senate — 312

U.S.S. Arizona — 175

Arctic, the — 99

Arctic Circle — 116

Argentina — 326

Arlington Forest, VA — 67

Arlington National Cemetery, VA — 350

Arlington, VA — 40, 41, 67, 133, 349

Armacost, Michael, Amb. — 230, 240

ARMCO Steel Corp. — 128, 129

Armed Forces Network (see also AFN) — 115

Armed Forces Special Weapons Project (AFSWP) — 40

Army — 75

Army Air Force Strolling Strings — 164

Army Chorus — 164

Army War College — 118, 119, 126

Army Engineer School — 52

Armstrong, Mr. & Mrs. M. O. — 15, 22

Armstrong, Neil A. — 164

Arnold, Bob — 136

Asheville, NC — 22

Ashoka Hotel, New Delhi — 157

Asia — 151, 215

Asse-djan, Nana, Chief — 173

Association for Diplomatic Studies and Training (see also ADST) — 351

Aspen Institute, CO — 201

Astaire, Adele — 75

Astaire, Fred — 74, 75, 356

Astronauts — 164

Atlanta, GA — 195

Atkins, Oliver — 254

Atlantic Coast — 168

Atlantic Ocean — 10, 254, 318, 319

Auburn University,

AL 351
Aurelie, Malagasy
  language instructor 287, 303,
  320, 329
Aurora, IL 193
Australia 227, 230,
  232, 233
Austria 77, 79, 91,
  110, 226
Azerbaijan 344
Azerbaijan Service 344

B

Bacon, Ruth 239
Bad Tolz, Germany 49
Bagnal, Charles,
  Lt. Gen. 299, 300, 301
Bagnal, Pat 300
Bailey Bridge 310
Baku 344
Baldwin, Faith 19
Bali, Indonesia 231
Balmain, Paris 113, 114
Baltic States 344
Balzac, Honoré de 58
Bangkok, Thailand 153, 156
Bangladesh 182
Barday, Askar 325
Barday, Serene 325
Bardays, the 325
Basie, Count 150
Baskin, Guy 232
Bavarian Alps 81
Bay of Biscay 317
BBC 104, 219, 320
Bednowicz, Eleonore,
  Cmndr. 32
Bedwell, Mrs.
  Timothy 310
Bedwell, Timothy,
  Gunnery Sgt. 310
Beebe, William, Dr. 52
Begum Liaquat Ali
  Khan 178
Beijing, China (see
Peking) 172, 212,
  213, 214,
  215, 216,

Beijing, University
  of 216
Belgium 56, 87, 243,
  256
Bellson, Louis 150
Benny, Jack 194
Berenty, Madagascar 295, 296
Bergen, Norway 116
Berlin, Germany 93, 94, 95,
  113
Berlin, Irving 20, 186, 187
Berlin Wall, Germany 93, 94, 95,
  294, 344, 347
Bermuda 10, 12, 21,
  52
Beza Mahfaly,
  Madagascar 271, 272
Bethesda Naval
  Hospital 31
BIB (see also,
  Bipartisan Board
  for International
  Broadcasting) 345, 346
Biltmore Hotel, NYC 13
Bipartisan Board
  for International
  Broadcasting (BIB) 345, 346
Birmingham,
  England 191
Black, Shirley
  Temple, Amb. 245
Blanchard, Kate 41
Blithe Spirit 293
Blixen, Karen (Isak
  Dinesen) 322, 323
Blum, Leon 110
Bodo, Norway 116
Bohan, Marc 113, 114, 115
Bolshoi Ballet 100
Bolshoi Theatre 101
Bolt, Robert 73
Bombay, India 179, 180,
  181, 237
Bond, Harry, Prof. 201, 202
Bonn, Germany 63
Boorstin, Daniel, Dr.,
  Librarian of
  Congress, Emeritus 227, 282, 350
Boorstin, Dr. and

Mrs. Daniel J.   282
Boorstin, Ruth   282, 350
Borneo   256
Boston, MA   197
Bosporus   213
Bounty, The   255
Bowie, Robert R.,
   Prof.   246
Boyd, Forrest   169
"Breakfast Show,
   The"   126, 127,
    135, 136,
    137, 157,
    167, 174,
    175, 176,
    177, 178,
    179, 180,
    181, 182,
    189, 190,
    195, 197,
    198, 201,
    205, 206,
    207, 208,
    209, 210,
    213, 222,
    239, 242,
    249, 324,
    352, 353
Breeden, Phil, USIS
  Director,
   Madagascar   327
Brezhnev, Leonid   101
Bremerhaven   118
Briarcliff College   130, 133
Brickley, Betty   286
Brisbane, Australia   233
Britain (see also
  Great Britain)   248
British
  Commonwealth   276
Brodin, Theodore,
  Maj.   52
Brodin, Yvonne   52
Bronfman, Jose   304, 326
Bronfman, Monique   305
Brown, Fannie   30
Brown, Les   194
Brown, Mervyn,
  Amb.   335
Brown, Staunton,

Bry, Alain, Amb.   289, 293,
    319, 320,
   321, 322, 326
Bry, Alain, Mrs.
  (Monique)   319, 321, 326
Brynn, Ed., Chargé
  Amb.   255, 275,
    276, 309
Bucharest, Romania   136, 160
Buchwald, Art   114
Buchwald, Art, Mrs.   114
Budapest Airport   104, 107
Budapest, Hungary   77, 96, 97,
    104, 105,
    106, 107
Buddy (Sprague,
  husband of Pam
  Gates)   303, 304,
    305, 307
Buffalo, NY   27
Bunker, Carol Laise,
  Ambassador   154, 155
Bunker, Ellsworth   57, 154
Burkina Faso   309
Burma   17, 20, 21,
    22, 23
Burns, Arthur, Amb.   239
Bush, Barbara   242, 243, 249
Bush, George H. W.,
  President   120, 327, 346
Bush, George W.,
  President   120, 352
Bush, William, H. T.
"Bucky"   120

C

Cagney, James   108, 109
Caldwell, Michael   308
California   16, 17, 66,
    148, 162,
    188, 203,
    312, 314
Calvert County, MD   205, 355
Campbell, Carroll   183
Campbell, Ivan   183
Cambridge
  University, England   202
Camp David, MD   266

<table>
<tr><td colspan="2">

Lynch

</td></tr>
<tr><td>Camp McCoy, WI</td><td>12, 14, 16, 66</td></tr>
<tr><td>Cam Rahn Bay, Vietnam</td><td>132</td></tr>
<tr><td>Camus, Albert</td><td>325</td></tr>
<tr><td>Canacho, Governor</td><td>151</td></tr>
<tr><td>Canacho, Mrs.</td><td>151</td></tr>
<tr><td>Canada</td><td>56, 331</td></tr>
<tr><td>Canberra, Australia</td><td>233</td></tr>
<tr><td>Canton, China</td><td>216</td></tr>
<tr><td>Cape of Good Hope</td><td>237</td></tr>
<tr><td>Capetown, South Africa</td><td>331</td></tr>
<tr><td>Capitol Building, DC</td><td>40, 41, 133, 189</td></tr>
<tr><td>Carlisle, PA</td><td>118, 125, 126</td></tr>
<tr><td>Caron, Leslie</td><td>72</td></tr>
<tr><td>*Carousel*</td><td>5</td></tr>
<tr><td>Carpenter, Les</td><td>74</td></tr>
<tr><td>Carpenter, Liz</td><td>74, 140, 141, 158</td></tr>
<tr><td>Carter, Jimmy, Pres.</td><td>206, 212</td></tr>
<tr><td>Carter, Mrs. Jimmy</td><td>206</td></tr>
<tr><td>Catherine the Great</td><td>99, 100</td></tr>
<tr><td>Caterpillar (tractors)</td><td>301</td></tr>
<tr><td>Catholic Church (Philippines)</td><td>229</td></tr>
<tr><td>Catholic University of America</td><td>226, 230</td></tr>
<tr><td>Cavin, Patty</td><td>75</td></tr>
<tr><td>CBS</td><td>8, 100, 159, 192, 204</td></tr>
<tr><td>Ceausescu, Nicolae, President</td><td>160, 344</td></tr>
<tr><td>Cebu, Philippines</td><td>230</td></tr>
<tr><td>Center of Oceanographic research, Madagascar</td><td>314</td></tr>
<tr><td>Central Asia</td><td>344</td></tr>
<tr><td>Central Europe</td><td>344</td></tr>
<tr><td>Ceylon (see Sri Lanka)</td><td>182</td></tr>
<tr><td>Century Plaza Hotel, Los Angeles</td><td>164</td></tr>
<tr><td>Chaffee, Roger B., Astronaut</td><td>164</td></tr>
<tr><td>*Challenger,* NASA vehicle</td><td>353</td></tr>
<tr><td>Champaign-Urbana, IL</td><td>35, 37, 39,</td></tr>
</table>

<table>
<tr><td colspan="2">

Thanks for Listening

</td></tr>
<tr><td></td><td>40</td></tr>
<tr><td>Chancellor, John</td><td>100</td></tr>
<tr><td>Channel 9, Perth, Australia</td><td>232</td></tr>
<tr><td>Chang, Y. C. (Eugene)</td><td>39</td></tr>
<tr><td>Checkpoint Charlie, Berlin</td><td>94</td></tr>
<tr><td>Charles, Jeri</td><td>53, 54, 58, 60, 63, 119, 126, 199, 224, 294, 299, 303, 318</td></tr>
<tr><td>Chattanooga, TN</td><td>15</td></tr>
<tr><td>Cheek, Timothy</td><td>216</td></tr>
<tr><td>Chesapeake Bay</td><td>55, 178, 181, 204, 205, 208, 213, 219, 227, 319, 333, 350, 351, 355, 356</td></tr>
<tr><td>Chevalier, Maurice</td><td>59, 71, 72, 73</td></tr>
<tr><td>Chicago, IL</td><td>14, 30, 136, 202, 203, 205</td></tr>
<tr><td>Chicago, University of</td><td>205</td></tr>
<tr><td>*Children of Other Lands*</td><td>210</td></tr>
<tr><td>China</td><td>39, 136, 171, 173, 174, 188, 193, 205, 210, 211, 212, 213, 214, 215, 217, 218, 221, 222, 223, 224, 239, 250, 276, 288</td></tr>
<tr><td>China-Burma-India Theatre</td><td>17</td></tr>
<tr><td>Chicago, IL</td><td>17, 34</td></tr>
<tr><td>Chopin</td><td>103</td></tr>
<tr><td>Christ</td><td>91</td></tr>
<tr><td>Christ Church, Port Republic, MD</td><td>329, 330, 337</td></tr>
<tr><td>Christian, Spencer, Captain</td><td>255</td></tr>
</table>

Churchill, Winston 27
Citizen Kane 28
Clair, Rene 293
Clay, Cassius
 (Muhammad Ali) 195
Cleveland, OH 226
Cliburn, Van 98
Cold War 81, 98, 348
Colette 72
Collins, Michael 164, 194
Colombo, Sri Lanka
 (Ceylon) 182
Colorado 199, 201,
  204, 307
Colorado State
 University 204
Columbia, MO 211
Columbia, NASA
 vehicle 353
Commonwealth
 Development
 Corporation 299
Comoros, The (see
 also The Comoros 237, 243,
 Islands) 249, 251,
  255, 275,
  309, 310,
  328, 336

Comoros Islands
 (see also The 237, 243, 249
 Comoros) 251, 255, 275
"Compensation"
 (essay) 198
Compton, Arthur
 Holly, Dr. 25, 26, 34
Compton, Betty 25, 30
Compton, Karl, Dr. 26, 30
Conger, Clem 146, 147
Congress 193
Connecticut 3, 5, 9, 13,
  24, 37, 40,
  42, 63, 65,
  79, 87, 120,
  130, 133,
  145, 210,
  223, 289,
  290, 353, 356

Connecticut Avenue,
 DC 347
Conover, Willis 150

Constitution Hall,
 DC 196
Contremundo,
 France 60
Copeland, Verne 155
Copen, Bruce, Prof. 138
Copenhagen,
 Denmark 117
Corps of Engineers 21, 33
Cotton, Hamilton 149
Council of American
 Ambassadors 248
Count de Quintan-
 illa 61
Countess de
 Quintanilla (see
 Also Aline Griffith) 61
Covington, Ann 97
Coward, Noel 293
Cox, Edward Finch 169, 170
Coxes, the 170
Cox, Patricia Nixon 148, 169, 170
Cushing Bookshop 18, 19, 75
Crocker, Chester,
 Asst. Sec'y of State 288
Crookenden, James 58
Crookenden, Jane 58, 62
Crookenden, Lt. Gen. 58, 59, 60,
 Sir Napier, 241, 296,
  297, 317, 318
Crookenden,
Patricia, Lady 58, 59, 60,
  62, 241, 296,
  297, 317, 318
Crookendens 59, 296, 297,
  318
Crowe, William J.,
 Jr., Amb. 248
Crown Prince Cyrus
 Reza, Iran 85
Cushing, Edward 18
Cushing, Mary
 Watkins 19
Cyrus Reza, Crown
 Prince of Iran 85
Czechoslovakia 245, 344, 348
Czech Republic 348

D

Dacca, Bangladesh	182
Dachau	48, 108, 109, 110, 111
Dallas, TX	74
Danga, Karl, DCM	309
Danube River	81, 107
Dartmouth College	33, 34, 38, 201
Dartmouth Institute	33, 38, 201
Davidson, Elizabeth	347
Davies, Marion	28, 38
Davis, Sammy, Jr.	186
D-Day	62, 63
Deane, John Russell, Jr,, Gen.	93, 94, 95
Dean Witter Reynolds	242
Dear Ruth	20
Death of a Salesman	20
DeGaulle, Charles, Pres.	116, 324
De Marcken, Baudouin	296
De Marcken, Gail	296
Democratic Republic of Madagascar (see Also Madagascar)	280
Denmark	56, 117, 323
Denver, CO	204, 205, 303, 304, 305, 306, 307, 318, 325, 351
Department of State (See also, State Department)	193, 211, 227, 242, 243, 244, 245, 251, 252, 279, 298, 304, 318, 353
"Desiderata"	177, 179
Diego Suarez, Madagascar	237, 281, 282, 284, 309
Dietrich, Marlene	18

Dinesen, Isak (see Karen Blixen)	323
Dinning, Richard	308, 309
Dior, Christian	113, 114
Dior, House of	111, 113, 114, 115
"Discoverers, The"	282
District of Columbia	251
"Don McNeil Breakfast Club, The"	193
Donnelly, Harold C. Lt. Gen.	53, 59, 63
Don Quixote	100
Doudart de Lagrée	320, 321, 322
Dover, England	62
Doyle-Hennin, Natalie	347
Drake, Frank D.	135
Duchess of Windsor	59, 114
Dukakis, Michael, Gov.	327
Duke Universiy	148, 334
Duke University Law School	148
Duke University Primate Center	334
Duke of Windsor (see also Edward VIII)	59
Dulles Airport, VA	131, 132, 318
Dulles, Eleanor	81
Dulles, John Foster, Sec'y of State	81
Dunkirk, France	49
Durban, South Africa	191

E

East Africa	275, 298
East Berlin	93, 94
Eastbourne, England	202
East China Sea	221
East Coast (U.S.)	219
Eastern Europe	343, 345
Ebony	173
Economist, The	259
Edward VIII, former Monarch, England	59
Eddy, Nelson	72, 73

"Ed Sullivan Show,
  The" 196
Eisenhower, Barbara
  (Barbara
  Eisenhower Foltz) 42, 118, 197,
  198, 243
Eisenhower, David 147, 266
Eisenhower, Dwight
  D., President 42
  57, 72, 109,
  118, 197,
  198, 266
Eisenhower, John,
  Amb. 118, 119,
  197, 243, 266
Eisenhower, Julie
  Nixon 147, 148, 163
Eisenhower, Mamie
  (Mrs. Dwight D.) 198
Eisenhower, Susan 347
Eiseley, Loren 268
Eleventh Armored
  Cavalry 82
Ellington, Duke 130, 149, 150
Ellington, James
  Edward 149
Ellington, Miss Ruth 150
El Paso, TX 312
Elsley, Jack 202, 203
Elsley, Judy, niece of
  Jack Elsley 203
Ely, Nevada 148
Elysées Palace, Paris 59
Emerson, Ralph
  Waldo 198
Empress Farah, Iran 85, 206
236th Engineer
  Combat Battalion 14
England 5, 45, 59, 60,
  62, 66, 73,
  89, 138, 156,
  161, 191,
  202, 264, 317
English Channel 45
Esme, Keith 15
Estremadura, Spain 61
Europe 7, 17, 43, 45,
  52, 53, 56,
  65, 76, 105,
  151, 219, 317

European Theatre 41

F

Fallon, Joe 21
Falls Church, VA 67, 72, 130,
  131
Fermi, Enrico 34, 35
Fianarantsoa,
  Madagascar 334
Filene's, Boston, MA 197
Fink, Dan 202
Fink, Toby 202
First Line of Defense 245
First Man, The 325
Fischer, David, U.S.
  Consul General,
  Ambassador 298, 317
Fitzgerald, F. Scott 18
Florence, Italy 51
Florida 119, 120,
  199, 255
*Flowering Cherry,
  The* 73
Fonda, Henry 294
Forbes Magazine 346
Forbes, Malcolm S.
  "Steve" Jr. 345, 346, 347
Foreign Service 208, 246,
  247, 248,
  257, 258,
  295, 310,
  332, 337, 351
Foreign Service
  Institute 242, 351
Foreman, Anne 240, 241
Fort Belvoir, VA 12, 41, 42,
  43, 52
Fort Benning, GA 113, 119, 120
  121, 125, 131
Fort Collins, CO 204
Fort Dauphin,
  Madagascar 256, 295
Fort Leavenworth,
  KS 64
Fort McNair, DC 252
Fort Myer, VA 349
Fouchet, Paris 114
Fountain City, TN 25, 27

Four Oaks, Kent,
  England   318
Fourth Armored
  Division   80, 81
Fourth of July   298
Fragrant Hills Hotel,
  Beijing, China   216, 218
Frankfurt, Germany   115, 148
France   56, 59, 65,
                         66, 76, 77,
                         93, 110, 256,
                         259, 282,
                         283, 284,
                         293, 299,
                         305, 317,
                         319, 324, 325
Frankfurt, Germany   115, 148
Franklin & Marshall
  College   351
Fraser, Harvey, Brig.
  Gen.   29
Fraser, Jean   29
Free French (WW II)   284
From Here to Eternity   18
Fremstad, Olive   19
Frost, Robert   202, 227
Furtseva, Katherina,
Mme.   101

G

"The Gabra Man"   324
Gabra people   324
Gabrielle,
  Madagascar
  Embassy employee   265
Gailey, C. K., Gen.   70
Gare St. Lazare,   113
  Paris
Gagarin, Astronaut   99, 164
Gajaneh   93
Gandhi, Indira,
  Prime Minister,
  India   157
Gargarin, Yuri   99
Garment, Leonard   150
Garmisch, Germany   49, 50
Gates, Bernard   22, 53
Gates, Emily   205, 253,

                         303, 306, 351
Gates, Fran   24
Gates, Clayton   22
Gates, Jamye   199, 204,
                         205, 224,
                         242, 253,
                         303, 306, 351
Gates, Lawrence
  Alan   41, 42, 45,
                         46, 47, 48,
                         51, 53, 58,
                         63, 65, 66,
                         76, 77, 78,
                         91, 92, 93,
                         108, 109,
                         115, 118,
                         120, 127,
                         130, 133,
                         137, 174,
                         175, 188,
                         191, 199,
                         204, 206,
                         224, 238,
                         242, 244,
                         253, 303,
                         305, 306,
                         351
Gates Lynch,   58, 107, 127,
  Patricia, Amb.   137, 174,
                         176, 181,198,
                         204, 208,
                         209, 210,
                         225, 228,
                         237, 243,
                         249, 251,
                         321, 329
Gates, Mahlon "Ink"   7, 9, 10, 11,
                         12, 13, 14,
                         17, 21, 22,
                         23, 26, 29,
                         30, 32, 36,
                         37, 38, 39,
                         40, 41, 42,
                         43, 46, 47,
                         49, 51, 53,
                         54, 59, 60,
                         61, 62, 63,
                         64, 65, 66,
                         67, 75, 76,
                         78, 79, 83,

	84, 85, 118, 119, 120, 126, 130, 131, 132, 133, 134, 141, 171, 174, 197
Gates, Marge	119
Gates, Mrs. Elsie, (Sr.)	13, 53, 119, 129
Gates, Mr. Sam, (Sr.)	13, 53
Gates, Pamela Townley (Sprague)	29, 38, 42, 45, 46, 47, 48, 51, 54, 63, 65, 66, 75, 76, 77, 78, 92, 93, 109, 115, 116, 118, 120, 127, 130, 133, 137, 174, 175, 191, 199, 204, 205, 224, 238, 253, 303, 304, 305, 306, 307, 318, 351
Gates, Sally	205, 253, 303, 306, 351, 352
Gateses, Mr. & Mrs. Sam	11
Gatlinburg, TN	27
Gayler, Kay	175
Gayler, Noel, Adm., CINCPAC	175
Gatlinburg, TN	27
General Electric	4, 225, 226
General Electric Space Center, PA	202
Geneva, Switzerland	34, 24
Genevieve, nurse to Dr. Tkach	188
George Mason University, VA	349
Georgetown Univer-	

George Washington University Hospital, DC	359
Georgia (U.S.)	125, 195
Germaine	56, 57
German-Czech border	80
Germany	33, 43, 49, 50, 53, 54, 62, 76, 78, 79, 89, 104, 115, 239, 282
Gettysburg, PA	118
Ghana	171, 173, 176, 195, 241, 245, 309
Gibraltar	60, 61
Gielgud, John, Sir	73
Gigi	71, 72
Gill, Lunda Hoyle	324
Giuliani, Rudolf, Mayor	109
Glander, Ken, Prof.	334
Glenn, John, Astronaut, Senator	118, 353
"God Bless America"	187
God's Trombones, Seven Negro Sermons in Verse	192
Goldberg, Max, M.D.	15
Goldberg, Sid	15
Golestan Palace, Iran	84
Gorbachev, Premier	241, 307, 308
Gorme, Eydie	75
Graham, Billy	171, 172, 194
Grambling College Band, LA	172
Grande Comore, Comoros Islands	275, 276, 328
Granton, Esther Fannie	173, 197, 198, 199
Great Britain	27, 60, 70, 82, 247, 248
Great Smoky Mountains	27
Great Wall of China	215, 216
Green, Don, DDS	15
Greenland	256

Green, Marshall,
Asst. Sec'y State 154
Grenada, Spain 61
Griffith, Aline (see 61
also Countess de
Quintanilla)
Griffith, Eugene, Dr. 191
Griffiths, Charles,
Vice Admiral 32
Grissom, Astronaut 164
Groce, Cliff 126, 127
Groves, Leslie, Gen. 24, 35
Grozier, David 80
Gruenther, Alfred,
Gen. 53, 57, 58
Gruenther, Grace 57
Guam 151
Guderian, Heinz 119
Guirong, Yang, Amb. 290
Guirong, Yang, Mrs. 290
Gulf of Finland 98
Gulf War, First 133
GUM Department
Store, Moscow 101
Gunther-Hasse,
Hans, Amb. 95

H

Hadsel, Fred,
Ambassador 173
Hague, The 287
Hahaya Airport,
Comoros Islands 275
Haindel, Anni 47, 48, 51,
53, 54, 57,
58, 63, 83,
89, 91, 115,
317
Haldeman, Robert 147
Hale, Nathan 5
Haley, Alex 192, 193
Hammersmith, John,
NASA VOA space
expert 353
Hamid, Abdul,
Director 183
Hanford Reservation 24, 29
Hangchow, China 213, 220, 221

Hanoi, North
Vietnam 188
Hanover, NH 201
Harding, Warren G.,
President 149
Harlem, NYC 150
Harriet 20
Harris, Julie 69
Hart, Larkin 195
Harvard University 180, 201,
216, 219
Hasanlu, Iran 87
Hatch Act 238, 239
Hatton, Dennis Fitch 323
Havel, Václav 344, 346
Hawaii 131, 132,
133, 151,
175, 280,
299, 304,
309, 318, 319
Hawaii 132
Hayes, Helen 20
Hays, Ronald J.
Adm., CINCPAC,
USN 318
De Heaulme, Jean 296
De Heaulme, Mrs. 296
Hearst, William
Randolph 28
Hedy, hotel maid,
Munich 47
Heidelberg, Germany 53, 95, 115
Heidi 79
Hemingway, Ernest 18
Henry VIII 162, 272
Herbert, Victor 72
Hermitage, the 99
Hess, Rudolph 95
Hewlett-Packard 240
Hewlett, Bill 240
Hicks, Irvin, Dep.
Asst. Sec'y State 330
Hidayatulla, M.,
Acting President,
India 157
Hilton Hotel,
Antananarivo, 290, 304,
Madagascar 308, 326, 327
290, 319,
326, 327

Himmler 110
Hines, Earl "Fatha" 150
Hiroshima, Japan 24, 28, 33
Hirshhorn, Olga 266, 276-7
Hitchcock, Alfred 148
Hitler, Adolf 3, 7, 8, 48, 50, 51, 104, 110
Hoboken, NJ 43
Holgate, Felicia 289
Holgate, Stephen 289
Holland (see also, the Netherlands) 45, 52, 62, 256
Holland, Mike 210
Hollywood 60
Holocaust 108, 112
Hong Kong 318
Honolulu, HI 318
Hoopes, Muriel (Mrs. Yu Chin Tu) 222
Hope Against Hope 4
Hope, Bob 186, 194
U.S.S. Hornet 151
Hortoland, Elka 276, 310
Hotchkiss School 130
Hotel George V, Paris 113, 114
Hotel Ivoire, Abidjan 173
Hotel Tilden-Hall 37
Hotel Ukrainian 99
Hotel Von Steuben 50
Horne, Mary 26
House of Representatives 193
Houphoet-Boigny, Felix, Mrs. 173
Houphoet-Boigny, Felix, President 173
Houston, TX 132, 262
"How Is the Weather in Paris?" 72
Howland, Mike 210
Hsiu Hua Chen 213, 214
Hubbard, Charlotte Moton 192, 193
Hubbard, Maceo, Dr. 192
Hudson River, NY 7, 190
Hudson Valley, NY 24
Hughes, Don, Gen. 154

Hulbert, Marilyn, DCM 286, 307, 313, 285, 286, 307, 313
Humphrey, Hubert, Vice President 130, 140
Humphrey, Muriel 130
Humphreys, Liam 257
Hungary 77, 96, 104, 105, 107, 343
Hunter, Alice 14, 66
Huntsville, AL 82, 134

I

Iceland 56
"(I'll Be Loving You) Always" 187
Illinois 36, 65, 97, 193, 195
Illinois, University of 36
IMF (see also International Monetary Fund) 259, 260, 281, 286
"I'm Glad I'm Not Young Anymore" 72
India 17, 27, 136, 156, 157, 178, 180, 181, 182, 197, 198, 248, 250, 353
Indian Ocean 213, 237, 254, 256, 259, 274, 283, 284, 295, 299, 300, 319, 321
Indian Red Cross 179
Independence Hall, Philadelphia 190
Indonesia 156, 183, 227, 231, 232, 250, 335
International Herald Tribune 320
International Monetary Fund (see also IMF) 259, 281, 286

International Paper 351
International
Women's Year, 1975 139
Iran 75, 76, 77,
78, 83, 85,
87, 88, 89,
118, 206, 207
Iraq 353
Ireland 45
Irwin, Phil 126, 135,
168, 176,
177, 178,
179, 181,
183, 182,
189, 190,
191, 208,
214, 231, 249
Israel 226
Italy 51, 56, 77,
118, 293, 347
It Isn't All Mink 114
Ivan the terrible 100
Ivory Coast 171, 173

J

*Jacobowski and the
Colonel* 21
Jacobson, Dr. 269
Jakarta, Indonesia 136, 152,
183, 231, 232
Jamaica 203
Janus 66
Japan 28, 33, 139,
219, 223, 282
Jaruzelski, General 252
Jean Clair,
Madagascar
Embassy employee 262, 265,
267, 286,
333, 339
Jeanne d'Arc 279
Jeddah, Saudi
Arabia 37, 254
Johnson, Al 126, 127,
135, 162,
167, 249
Johnson, Dorothy,
(Mrs. Harold K.) 41, 189

Johnson, Harold
K., Gen. 41, 42, 189
Johnson, James
Weldon 192, 193
Johnson, Jeff 87
Johnson, "Lady Bird" 75, 129, 139,
158
Johnson, Luci
Baines 141
Johnson, Lynda Bird 140, 141, 170
Johnson, Lyndon B.,
Pres., 74, 129, 140
Sen. 74
Johnson, Mr.,
American
construction chief,
Marand, Iran 84, 87
Johnson Publishing
Company 198
Jolly, Alison 267, 270
Jones, James 18
Johnson, Jeff 87
Johnson, Mr., Iran 84, 87
Joint Chiefs of Staff 130
Jourdan, Louis 72

K

Kaduna, Nigeria 177
Kalb, Marvin 100
Kampelman, Max,
Ambassador 227
Kampung Mindah,
Malaysia 182
Kampung Sungai,
Malaysia 182
Kansas 64, 65, 66,
266
Kansas City 66
Karachi, Pakistan 177
Karen Blixen
Museum 322
Karen Coffee
Company 323
Kargil, India 206
Kassebaum, Nancy,
Sen. 248
Kathmandu, Nepal 228
Kauffman, Jane 203

Kaye, Danny	139
Kazakhstan	310
Kelly, Grace (Princess Grace of Monaco)	78
Kemeny, John, Pres. Dartmouth	201
Kemp, Clark	85
Kennedy Center	100
Kennedy, Jackie	146
Kennedy, John F., President	28, 74, 84, 120
Kent, England	317, 318
Kenya	177, 191, 237, 305, 306, 322, 323
Kerensky, Alexander	19
KGB	253, 307, 308
Khan, Yahya, Pres., Gen.	158
Khachaturian, Aramilich	93
Khrushchev	97
Kidd, Captain	309
Kiel, Germany	116
Kiev, U.S.S.R.	77, 97, 98
Kiev, University of	97
Kim Il Sung	280
Kindersley, Lord Hugh	62, 299
Kindersley, Nan	62, 299
King, Annette (Rep. Charlotte Reid)	193, 203
Kirkland, Lane	346
Kirkpatrick, Alex	257, 310
Kissinger, Henry, National Security Advisor, Sec'y of State	154, 185, 188, 228
Kitty Hawk, NC	205
Kleimans, Paul	85
Knill, Eddie	6
Knoxville, TN	23, 25
Kohmeini Airport, Iran	89
Kolhapur, India	181

Komorov, Astronaut	164
Koran, Don	310
Korea	43
Kovanov, Vladimir, Dr.	102
Kremlin, the	100, 347
Kremlin Museum, the	100
H. M. S. Kron Prins Harald	116
Kuala Lumpur, Malaysia	182, 310
Kuhn, Bill	310
Kulkanthorn, Chalit, Lord Mayor	153
Kunta Kinte	194

L

La Baie du Destin	294
La Bohéme	116
La Crosse, WI	14
Ladakh, India	206
Lady in the Dark	5
"Lady with a Parasol"	355
Lafayette, Marquis de	321
Lafayette Square, DC	206
Lagos, Nigeria	177
Lahore, Pakistan	158
Laingen, L. Bruce, Ambassador	207, 208
Laingen, Penne (Mrs. L. Bruce)	208
Lakeville, CT	79, 130
Lane, Rex	85
La Louque	72
Langner, Armina Marshall	5, 60
Langner, Lawrence	5, 60, 61
Laughton, Charles	75
"La Vie En Rose"	74
Lawrence, Bill	5, 17, 18, 204, 224
Lawrence, Charles	3, 42, 51, 52, 63, 86, 196
Lawrence, Dorothy	5, 204, 224
Lawrence, Ernest O., Dr.	26, 27, 35

Lawrence, Evelyn — 224
Lawrence, Gertrude — 5
Lawrence, Kay — 18, 224
Lawrence, Molly
  (Mrs. Charles) — 3, 27, 42, 51, 52, 63, 119, 174, 196
Lawrence, Molly
  (Mrs. Ernest) — 27
Lawrence, Steve — 75
Lazarus, Arthur, Prof. — 191
Leavenworth, KS — 65, 66
Lebanon, TN — 16
Lech, Austria — 90, 91, 92
l'Ecole Navalle de Brest — 279
Le Havre, France — 65
Lehrer, Jim — 70
Leigh, England — 62
Lenin — 98, 100
Leningrad, U.S.S.R., (St. Petersburg) — 77, 97, 98, 99, 100, 225
Lerner, Alan J. — 72
LeSueur, Larry — 8
Le Vesinet, France — 54, 55, 59, 62, 63, 71, 114, 310
Le Vesinet, Maryland — 204, 205, 213, 329, 351, 353, 355
Lewine, Fran — 158
Liang, Hubert, Prof. — 210, 211, 212, 218, 223
Liberation of One, The — 252
Liberia — 129, 171, 172, 191
Liberian Suite — 130
Liberty Bell, Philadelphia — 190
Library of Congress — 350
Libya — 281
Liliom — 5, 6, 7
Life with Father — 20
Lijorndet, Norway — 116
Lincoln, Abraham, President — 105, 189
Lincoln Memorial, DC — 42, 189, 243

Lincoln, Nebraska — 43
Little, Frank — 42, 43, 45, 46, 62, 63
Little Governor's Camp, Kenya — 305
Little, Kay — 42, 43, 45, 46, 62, 63
Little, Stephen — 62, 63
Locarno, Switzerland — 317
Lodge, Henry Cabot, Ambassador — 130
Loire Valley, France — 60
Lom, Norway — 117
London, England — 9, 81, 172, 247, 288
Long Binh, Vietnam — 155, 156
Long Island Sound — 9
Longworth, Alice Roosevelt — 170
Los Alamos, NM — 24, 27
Los Angeles — 163
Los Angeles Times — 182
Louisiana — 206, 241
Louvre, the, Paris — 99
Love Me Tonight — 72
Lowe, Frederick — 72
Luce, Clare Boothe, Amb. — 175
Luxembourg — 56
Lynch, Jean — 203, 350
Lynch, Katie — 204
Lynch, Patricia Gates — 198
  (see also Gates Lynch, Patricia
Lynch, William — 203, 204, 206, 208, 210, 213, 223, 228, 238, 240, 242, 243, 244, 251, 253, 254, 255, 259, 262, 263, 264, 268, 269, 276, 289, 294, 295, 298, 303, 304, 305, 306,

	307, 309,
	313, 317,
	318, 320,
	321, 329,
	333, 337,
	338, 349,
	350, 351
Lynch, William, Jr.	203, 204
M	
MacDonald, Jeanette	72, 73
Mackay, Ellin	187
Macken, Dick	271, 273
Madagascar (see also Democratic Republic of Madagascar)	52, 237, 241,
	242, 243,
	244, 248,
	249, 250,
	251, 252,
	253, 254,
	255, 256,
	257, 259,
	260, 261,
	262, 264,
	267, 269,
	270, 271,
	275, 276,
	279, 280,
	281, 282,
	283, 284,
	285, 287,
	288, 289,
	290, 293,
	294, 295,
	296, 297,
	298, 299,
	301, 302,
	304, 305,
	306, 307,
	308, 309,
	310, 313, 314
	315, 317,
	318, 320,
	321, 324,
	326, 329,
	330, 332,
	333, 334,

Madagascar Rediscovered	335
Madison, Dolley	144
Madrid, Spain	61
Madras, India	181
Mahajanga, Madagascar	314, 319, 320, 321
Mahajanga Region, Madagascar	310, 314, 319
Maheli, Comoros	328
Malagache, language, (see also Malagasy)	250, 256, 262, 263, 265, 266
Malagasy Academy	313
Malagasy, language, (see also Malagache)	250, 256, 262, 263, 265, 266
Malagasy, the	267, 330, 332, 334, 336
Malagasy High Constitutional Court	313
Malaysia	182
Malta	207
Manakara, Madagascar	334
Manchester (U. K.)	48
Mandarin Hotel, Bangkok	156
Mandelstam, Osip	4
Mandelstam, Nadezhda	4
Manhattan Project	23, 27, 28, 30, 33, 34
Manila, the Philippines	229
Mansfield, Michael J., Amb.	248
Marand, Iran	87
Marchetti, Michael	347
Marchetto, Msgr.	337
Marcos, Ferdinand, Pres.	152, 229, 230
Marcos, Imelda	151-2
Maregeh, Iran	88

Marie-Angele,
  Madagascar
  Embassy employee   265
Marine Band   164
Marine Drum and
Bugle Corps   164
Marine Orchestra   186
Marriott, Willard   194
Marnes la Coquette   72
Marshall, Armina
  (see Langner)   5
Marshall, George C.,
  Gen.   11
Marshall Space
  Flight Center   82

Martin, Madagascar
Embassy employee   265, 332
Maryknoll College,
  Manila   229
Maryland   40, 55, 193,
    204, 205,
    206, 208,
    326, 329,
    337, 351
Maryland, University
  Of   89
Masai   322, 323
Massachusetts   197, 327
Massachusetts
  Institute of
  also MIT)   216
Mauldin, Patti   74, 75
Maurer, Erika   48, 49, 77,
    78, 89, 91,
    92, 118
Maurer, Eva   48, 78, 92
Maurer, Georgi,,   48, 49, 77,
Professor Dr.   78, 92, 102,
    118
Maurer, Peter, Dr.   49, 317
Maurers, the   47, 48, 92,
    118
Mauritius   276, 281,
    297, 309,
310, 318, 319
Mayotte, Island in
  Comoros Chain
  (Fr. Admin.)   275
McBain, Audrey   262

McBain, Malcolm,
  Amb.   262, 288, 289
McCain, John S., III,
  Sen.   186
McChesney, John   79, 80
McChesney, Molly   79, 80
McKenzie, Dr.   320
McQuarrie, Jock   67, 93
McQuarrie
  Broughton,
Rosanne   66, 67, 68,
    69, 70, 71,
    76, 93, 326
Mead, Margaret   199
Mehrabad Airport,
  Iran   89
Melbourne,
  Australia   232
Memphis, TN   206, 351
Meri, Lennart,
  Foreign Minister   345
Mesnil, Colette   59, 115
Mesnil, Marie Rose   59
Mesnil, Maurice,
  Monsieur   59
Mesnils   59
Metropolitan
  Museum, NY   216, 221
Metropolitan Opera
  House, NY   130
Metz, France   53
Mexico   66, 169
Michener, James   132
Michigan   334
Middletown, Ohio   128
Midwest (U. S.)   39
Mildenhall Air Force
Base, England   161
Miller, Arthur   11, 20
Milwaukee, WI   141
Minelli, Liza   196
Minor, Fran   61
Minor, Tony   61
Missouri   211
Missouri, University
  of   211
MIT (see also
  Massachusetts Ins-
  titute of
  Technology)   216

Mitchell, Cameron 19
Mitchell, Henry 267
Mittenwald, Germany 49, 50
Mo i Rana, Norway 117
Molnar, Ferenc 19
Monaco 79
Monet, Claude 355
Monte Carlo 114
Monteiro, Ernest, His
Excellency, Amb. 183
Montgomery,
Bernard, General 57
Monrovia, Liberia 172
Mook, Delo, II, Prof. 202
Moore, Beech 129
More, Sir Thomas 73
Moroni, Comoros
Islands 275, 276,
328, 336
Morrissey, Daniel,
Rev. 350
Morse, Larry 336
Moscow, Soviet 48, 77, 98,
Union 99, 100, 101,
102, 103,
136, 172,
281, 303,
345, 346,
347, 348
Mother Teresa of 139
India
Moton, Robert, Dr. 192
Mount Vernon, VA 351
Mozart, Wolfgang
Amadeus 101
Mulligan, Jerry 150
Mount Eagle-in-the-
Mountains, TN 7, 8
Moynihan, Daniel
Patrick, Amb. 248
Moynihan, Cornelius,
Prof. 226
Mozambique 275
Mozambique
Channel 237, 260,
271, 283
Munich, Germany 43, 46, 47,
48, 49, 51,
53, 76, 77,
78, 79, 80,

81, 82, 82,
83, 85, 87,
89, 90, 91,
92, 93, 96,
98, 100, 107,
108, 111,
115, 117,
118, 125,
126, 196,
244, 317,
343, 344, 348
Munich, University of 79
Murat, Jean 294
Murrow, Edward R. 8, 9
15, 16
204
Museum of Modern
Art, NY 293
Museum of Natural
History, NY 288
Mutual Network 169

N

Nagasaki, Japan 24, 28
Nairobi, Kenya 177, 237,
254, 255,
256, 268,
285, 305,
307, 320
Namakia Bridge,
Madagascar 310
Nanjing University,
China 212, 218,
219, 220,
222, 223
Nanking, (Nanjing) 212, 213,
China 218, 220
NASA 82, 127, 164,
249
Nashville, TN 15
National Aeronautics
and Space
Administration 82
National Gallery
of Art, DC 216
National Geographic 267
National Museum of
History and

Technology, DC   199
National Press Club   231
National Theater   67, 69, 126,
National Zoo, DC   217
NATO   56, 57
Nautilus   32
Naughty Marietta   72
Navaho Indian
   Reservation   205
Navy Band   186
Nazis   82, 109
NBC   76, 77, 79,
   82, 84, 86,
   87, 88, 89,
   90, 100, 115,
   126, 153,
   155, 165, 203
Nebraska   42, 43, 63
Nepal   154, 227,
   228, 240
Nepal, King of   228, 229, 240
Nepal, Queen of   228, 229
Netherlands, the (see
   also Holland)   43, 45, 46,
   56, 92
Nevada   148
Neva River, Russia   98
New Canaan, CT   3, 6, 12,
   18, 21, 66
Newcomb, Genevieve   67, 68
Newcomb, Lamar   67, 70, 71
New Delhi, India   156, 157,
   158, 178, 179
New England   18, 19
New Guinea   256
New Hampshire   202
New Jersey   42, 203
New Mexico   24, 312
*News Hour with Jim
Lehrer, The*   70
Newsweek   172
New York City, NY   12, 13, 21,
   24, 30, 65,
   73, 76, 90,
   118, 148,
   190, 195,
   203, 209,
   216, 217,
   218, 221,
   222, 224,

*New York Herald
Tribune*   7, 12
New York State   224
Ngong Hills, Kenya   322, 323
Nichols, Kenneth D.,
   Maj. Gen.   24, 26, 27,
   28, 34, 35,
   40, 42
Nicholses, the   28, 42
Nigeria   177
Nitze, Paul, Amb.   248
Nixons, President
and Mrs. Richard   130, 141,
   143, 149,
   150, 152,
   153, 154,
   157, 164,
   168, 170,
   185, 188, 231
Nixon, Patricia
(ne Thelma
Catherine Patricia
Ryan)   143, 144,
   145, 146,
   147, 149,
   150, 151,
   152, 153,
   154, 155,
   156, 157,
   158, 159,
   160, 161,
   162, 163,
   167, 168,
   169, 170,
   171, 172,
   173, 174,
   185, 188, 198
Nixon, Richard,
President   143, 148,
   149, 150,
   151, 153,
   154, 155,
   156, 157,
   158, 160,
   161, 164,
   168, 169-
   170, 171,

172, 174,
185, 186,
187, 188,
189, 221,
238, 247

Noeline, Madagascar
  Embassy employee 265
Normandy, France 63
North America 289
North Carolina 205
North Dakota 195
North Korea
Norway 56, 77, 97,
115, 116,
117, 248,
328, 344
Nosy Be, Madagascar 299, 304,
309, 312,
314, 315
Northern Ireland 247
Nuremberg 109, 110, 111

O

Oklahoma! 6
Oak Ridge Journal 24, 30, 33
Oak Ridge, TN 23, 25, 26,
27, 28, 29,
30, 31, 32,
33, 34, 36,
37, 128, 134
Oberammergau, 90, 91
  Germany
O'Brien, Pat 75
O'Connor, John 240, 242,
312, 350
O'Connor, Sandra
  Day, Justice 239, 240,
242, 244,
250, 251,
312, 313,
314, 315, 350
O'Connor, William
  "Bucky", Dr. 29
O'Flaherty, Liam 19
O'Neill, Thomas P.
  "Tip," Speaker of
  House 193
Ohio 226

Oklahoma 225
Oklahoma, musical 6
"On a Tree Fallen
  Across the Road" 227
"On Eagle's Wings" 350
Opera, Paris 59
Oppenheimer, J.
  Robert, Dr. 27, 35
Oregon 163
Osborne, Ralph, 93
  Gen.
Oslo, Norway 116, 117, 328
O.S.S. 18, 35, 61
Otopeni Airport,
  Romania 160
Out of Africa 323

P

Pacific Ocean 149, 151,
168, 318, 319
Pakistan 138, 156,
157, 159,
160, 178,
182, 207,
250, 353
Palmer House Hotel,
  Chicago 14
Palmer, Intan, former
  wife of Amb. Ronald
  Palmer 310
Palmer, Ronald,
  Amb. 297, 310
Palm Springs, CA 203
Pan Am (see also Pan
  American Airways) 157, 176
Pan American
  Airways (see also
  Pan Am) 157, 176,
237
Papal Nuncio 330, 331, 337
Paris 51, 52, 53,
54, 56, 58,
59, 60, 63,
64, 65, 72,
74, 78, 99,
109, 113,
115, 116,
121, 237,

254, 259,
268, 291,
293, 298,
306, 310,
315, 317
Paris-Mediterranée　294
Pascualete, Spain　61
Patterson, Marvin
　Breckenridge　8
Patton, George, Gen.　81
Peace Corps　328
Peacock Throne, Iran　84
Pearl Harbor, HI　9, 175, 309,
317
Pearl River, NY　61
Pei, I. M.　216
Peking, China (see
Beijing)　172, 213
Pell, Gene　244, 343,
344, 345
Pennsylvania　87, 118, 126,
202, 352
Pennsylvania Ave.,
　DC　41
Pennsylvania Hotel,　14
　NYC
Pennsylvania, State
　of　24, 126, 190,
352
Pennsylvania, Uni-
　versity of　87
Pensacola, FL　199
Pentagon, The　40, 42, 53,
67, 95, 126,
130, 132, 352
Percy, Charles, Sen.　206, 208, 228
Percys, Sen. Charles
　and Mrs.　228, 318
Percy, Loraine (Mrs.
　Charles　206, 208
Perinet, Madagascar　299, 305
Perkins, Edward,
　Amb.　331, 332
Perkins, Edward,
　Mrs.　331
Perkins, Maxwell　18
Perkins, Louise　18
Perlman, Kahl　18, 21, 22
Persia　85, 86
Persian Gulf　321

Perth, Australia　232
Peter, Eleanor, Dr.　205
Peter the Great　98, 100
Peter, William, Dr.　205
Peterson, A. V. "Pete"　29
Peterson, Esther,
　Asst. Sec'y of Labor　107
Peterson, Marie
　Louise　29
Petrik, Mrs. Pavel　307
Petrik, Pavel, Amb.　307, 308
Petrov, Boris A., Prof.　102
Pettersen, Luli　116
Pettersen, Thor,
　Adm.　116
Philadelphia, PA　190, 243, 289
Philippines, the　41, 151, 227,
229, 230,
240, 251
Phillips, Nancy　97
Piaf, Edith　74
Pickering, Thomas　247
Pierre, Madagascar
　Embassy employee　265
Plummer, Bill　204
Plummers, Mr. &
　Mrs. William　204
Poland　3, 30, 31, 77,
96, 103, 104,
252, 253,
343, 346
Polynesia　250
Ponnamperuma,
Cyril　136
John Paul II, Pope　330, 331, 345
Pius XII, Pope　52
Port Republic, MD　329, 337
Portugal　56, 61
Pothin,
　Rakotomanga,
　Prof.,　271
Potomac River　71, 282
Powell, Colin, Sec'y
　of State　352
Power, Tyrone　5, 6, 21, 59,
60, 75, 293,
294
Prague,
　Czechoslovakia
　(now Czech

Republic) 245, 348, 349
Presley, Elvis 72
Pretoria, South
  Africa 331
Prince, Buck 76
Princess Beatrix 92
Princess Caroline of
  Monaco 79
Princess Grace of
  Monaco (Grace
  Kelly) 78
Project Head Start 139, 140
Pryor, Tony 271, 273

Q

Qadhafi, Muammar 281
Quaker Oats Co. 248
Quanback, Dr. 320
Quanback, Mrs. 320
Queen Elizabeth II 49
  as Princess, 70
Queen Victoria 287
Quintanilla, Count 61
  de
Quintanilla, Count
  and Countess of 61

R

Rabemahefa, Ms.
  Berthe, High
  Counselor 313
Rabesahala, Gisele,
  Minister 288
Radio Australia 232
Radio Beijing (Radio
Peking) 212, 213, 214
Radio France 320
Radio Free Europe 80, 81, 82,
  95, 96, 104,
  244, 343,
  344, 345,
  346, 347,
  348, 349
Radio Liberty 80, 95, 244,
  343, 344,
  354, 349

Radio Nepal 228
Radio Pakistan 178
Radio Peking (Radio
Beijing) 212, 213
Radio Republik
  Indonesia (RRI) 183
Radio Times of India 182
Radio-TV Singapore 183
Radio Veritas 229
Rakoto, Madagascar
  Embassy employee 265, 333
Rakotomanana,
  Honoré, Pres. High
  Constitutional Ct. 312
Randall, Ann Hagen 125
Ranomafana,
  Madagascar 334
Rapid City, SD 29
The Rainbow Bridge 19
Ramhurst Manor 62
Ranavalona, Queen 283
Ranjevo, Raymond,
  Pres., U. of Mada-
  gascar; and Justice 287, 315
Ranjevo, Yvette, Prof. 287, 315
Ratna Rajya, Nepal 228
Ratsimandrava, Lt.
  Col. 280
Ratsiraka, Didier,
  Pres. 259, 260,
    262, 263,
    267, 279,
    280, 281,
    282, 283,
    284, 298,
    300, 310,
    311, 312,
  324, 325, 330
Ravalomanana, Pres. 283, 311
Rawlings, Marjorie
  Kinnon 18
Rawson, David,
  Chargé, Amb. 256
Rawson, David, Mrs. 256
Raymond, Daniel,
  Maj. Gen. 110, 111
Rea, Julie 296
Rea, Sam 296
Reagan, Nancy (Mrs.
  Ronald) 244, 311

Reagan, Ronald,
President   164, 165,
                          208, 230,
                          237, 238,
                          241, 243,
                          244, 251,
                          253, 254,
                          307, 311, 346
Rechts Am Isar
  Hospital, Munich   48, 49
Red Cross (American)   17, 18, 33
                          57, 174, 175,
                          179
Red Cross (Tokyo)   33
Reddick, Eunice   298
Redford, Robert   323
Reid, Charlotte, U. S.
  Representative   167, 193, 203
Regan, Don   241
Rekhson, Mila (Mrs.)
  Simon   226
Rekhson, Simon, Dr.   225, 226
"Remember the Night
  That We Met"   187
Remi Rebenirina,
Bishop   292, 337
Remi Rebinirinia,
  Elizabeth   337
Reston, LA   172
Réunion   284, 319
Reynolds, Bill   167, 176,
                          208, 249
Reynoldses, of
  Champaign-
  Urbana, IL   37, 38
Rezaiyeh, (Urmia)
  Iran   85, 86, 87
RFE/RL (see also
  Radio Free Europe
  and Radio Liberty)   80, 96, 104,
                          105, 106,
                          343, 344,
                          345, 346,
                          347, 348
Rice, Condoleezza,
  Sec'y of State   352
Rice, Don   214, 242, 249
Richland, WA   24
Rickover, Hyman
  "Rick," Admiral   30, 31, 32,

                                         33
Ripley, S. Dillon, Dr.   267
Ripley, Mary   267
Rise and Fall of the   108
Third Reich, The
Rissersee Hotel   50
Riverside, CA   17
Robb, Charles, Sen.
  and Gov.   141, 170
Robin, Bernard   79
Rocquencourt,
  France   55
Roddis, Louis,
  Cmndr.   30
Rogers, Adele
  (Mrs. William)   151, 170
Rogers, Ginger   75
Rogers, William,
  Sec'y of State   170
Romania   156, 180
Romanovs, the   100
Romberg, Sigmund   72
Rome, Italy   51, 52, 99,
                                         118
Rondel, Mme.   54
Rose Marie   73
Rotterdam, the
  Netherlands   43, 45, 46
Roosevelt, Eleanor   156
Roosevelt, Franklin
  D., President   7, 9, 25, 27,
                                         149
Roots   193, 194
Rupli, Robin   243, 257,
                                         287, 289, 310
Ruppe, Loret, Dir.,
  Peace Corps., Amb.   328
Rush Medical School,
  Univ. of Chicago   205
Rusk, Dean, Sec'y of
  State   130, 193
Russia   31, 347

Rusk, Mrs. Dean   130
Ryan, Kate
  Halberstadt Bender,   148
Ryan, Mary, Amb.   331
Ryan, Kate Halber-
  Stadt Bender   148
Ryan, Thelma (Mrs.

Richard Nixon) 148
Ryan, Will 148
Ryndam, S.S. 43, 45

S

"Saga of Little Nell on
  The Lone Prairie" 289
Sage of Mbeni 276
Sagdeev, Roald, Dr. 347
Saigon, Viet Nam 154, 155
St. Basil's Cathedral,
  Moscow 100
St. Cloud, France 60
St. Denis, Réunion 319
St. Jean de Luz 317
St. Joseph's
  Hospital, Denver 307
Saint Marie, Mada-
  gascar 284, 309
St. Moritz,
  Switzerland 79, 80
St. Paul's Church,
  NYC 352
St. Petersburg,
  U.S.S.R., 97, 98, 99,
  (Leningrad) 100
Sakharov, Andrei 347
San Clemente, CA 149, 169
Sandburg, Carl 53
San Francisco, CA 66
Saroya 85
Saudi Arabia 237, 254
Schnyder, Felix,
  Amb. 317
Schnyder, Sigi 317
Scientists' Cliffs, MD 205, 326
Scotton, David, Chief
  of Staff, Peace
  Corps 328
Scouten, Rex 146, 188
Scribner's 18
The Seeker
  (magazine) 138
Seine River 55, 114
Semaramis Hotel,
  Teheran 83, 84, 88,
  89
Senate, U. S. 238, 248

SETI 135
Seven Corners, VA 70, 71
1776, film 300
Sever, Lynn 232
Severna Park, MD 351
Seychelles, the 298, 309
Shah of Iran 75, 76, 83,
  84, 88, 206
Shakespeare, Frank 143, 144
Shanghai, China 4, 212, 213,
  214, 221, 222
SHAPE (Strategic
  Headquarters, Allied
  Powers Europe) 53, 56, 57,
  59, 72, 94,
  95 116, 310
Shen, Mary Swing 128, 129,
  190, 211
Sheraton Hotel,
  Seychelles 309
Shirer, William L. 7, 8, 108
Shoemaker, Ray Lt.
  Gen 109, 110, 111
Shoreham Hotel, DC 73, 74, 75
Shouse, Catherine
  Filene (Mrs. Jouett) 197
Shreveport, LA 242
Shubert Theater, DC 71, 72
Shultz, George, Sec'y
  Of State 241, 251, 252
Sieman, Pat 240, 241
Silverman, Alan 249
Silnicki, Larisa 347
Simon Legree 289
Sind 178
Singapore 183, 318, 319
Sirikit, Queen 153
Skelton, Red 194
Smith, C. Rodney,
  Maj. Gen. 80
Smith, Helen McCain 161, 162, 167
Smith, Kate 194
Smithsonian
  Institution, DC 199, 203,
  267, 324
Smyser, Dee Prather 132
Snow White 224
Sogndal, Norway 117
Solidarity Movement,
  Poland 346

Sorrell, Maurice 173
Sorrento, Italy 51
Sousa, John Phillips 298
Southern California,
    University of 148
Southern Cross 315
South Africa 191, 331
Southhampton, U.K. 45
Soviet Union 25, 57, 58,
    77, 93, 95,
    96, 97, 98,
    105, 113,
    226, 281,
    283, 288,
    307, 343,
    344, 345,
    346, 347, 348
South Asia 178
South Australian
    College of Advanced
    Education 232
South Dakota,
University of, School
of Mines 29
Southern
    Hemisphere 325
Spain 60, 61
Spandau Prison,
    Berlin 95
Spanier, Ginette,
    Mme. 114
Sparta, WI 66
Sparta Hotel, La
    Crosse, WI 14
Spasowski, Romuald
    (Romek), Amb. 252, 253
Spasowski, Wanda 252, 253
Spears, Sid 304
Spectrum 232
Spiny Desert,
    Madagascar 270, 273
Sprague, Buddy,
husband of Pam
Gates 303, 304,
    305, 307
Sputnik 99
Sri Lanka (see
    Ceylon) 182
Stalin, Joseph 98, 100, 105
Stamford, CT 9, 12, 13, 14,

15, 19, 20,
67
Stanford University 312
Starzinger, Vincent,
    Prof. 202
Starovojtova, Galina 347
State Department
(see also,
    Department of
    State) 160, 227,
    244, 247, 257
298, 317,
318, 330,
337, 353
Statue of Liberty 65, 352
Steinbeck, John 6
Stella Maris College,
    India 181
Steps in Time 74
Stewart, Jimmy 186
Strasberg, Lee 6
Streep, Meryl 323
Stuart, Gilbert 186
Stuart, Robert D.,
    Jr., Amb. 248
Studio One 61
Stuttgart, Germany 43, 62, 63
Straubing, Germany 82
Suchow, China 221
Suez 293
Suez Canal 284
Suharto, Mrs. 152
Suharto, President 152
Sullivan, Ed 196
Sunday Breakfast
Show 135, 137
Sununu, John H.,
    White House Chief
    of Staff 346
Supreme Court,
    Madagascar 312
Supreme Court, U.S. 164, 312
Surabaya, Indonesia 232
Surrey, England 73
Sussex, England 138
Suvretta House, St.
    Moritz 79
Swaziland 331
Swedish-American
    Coffee Company 323

Swing, Raymond
Graham 128
Switzerland 8, 49, 77, 79,
80, 317
Sydney, Australia 233

T

Tabriz, Iran 85
Tahiti 314
Taj Mahal, India 179
Talbott, Strobe, Dep.
Sec'y of State 283
Tamatave,
Madagascar 260, 280
Tannis, Gil, Dir. 202
Tan Son Nhut
Airport, Vietnam 154, 156
Tata, J.R.D., Mr. 181
Tata, J.R.D., Mrs. 181
Tattersall, Ian 271
Taylor, Billy 150
Taylor, Maxwell D.,
Gen., Ambassador 130
Teheran, Iran 78, 83, 85,
207, 267
Teheran, University
of 84
Terracina, Italy 118
Tennessee 22, 23, 36,
37, 206
Texas 132, 262,
304, 312
"Thank Heaven for
Little Girls" 72
Thapa, Bhekh B.,
Dr., Ambassador 228, 240, 300
Thapa, Mrs. Bhekh
B. 240
Thapa, Surya
Badahur, Hon. 228
Thatcher, Margaret,
Prime Minister 279
Thayer Hotel, West
Point, NY 13
*The Stork Didn't
Bring You* 41
This is the Army 24, 36
20

Thomas, Helen 158, 163
Tiananmen Square,
Beijing 217
"Tie a Yellow Ribbon
Round the Old Oak
Tree" 207
Tilley, Miss 38

Tibet 191
Tkach, Walter, Dr. 158, 187, 188
Today Show, The 70
Tokyo, Japan 33, 213
Tolbert, Mrs. Wm. R.,
Jr. 172
Tolbert, William R.,
Jr., President 171, 172
Tomah, WI 16
Tomseth, Vic 210
Tonbridge, England 62
Tony, husband of
Katie Lynch 204
Torbrau Am
Isartorplatz,
Munich 47
Toronto, Canada 331
Torremolinos, Spain 60, 61
Trondheim, Norway 116, 117
Truman, Harry S.,
President 23, 27, 28,
33, 42, 188
Tsiranana, Philibert,
President 284, 287
Tubman, President,
Liberia 129
Tubman, William 130
Tucker, Gene 350
Tucson, AZ 66
Tufty, Esther Van
Wagoner 81
Tulear, Madagascar 270, 271,
273, 274, 297
Turkey 89
"The Turning of the
Dead" 335
Tuskegee Institute 191
Tuttle, Bob 237, 238,
240, 241
TVRI Radio and
Television,
Indonesia 231

TWA   157
Tyrone, PA   13, 22,42,
                                 131

U

UCLA Medical School   28
Ukraine   97
UNESCO   315
Union Station, DC   40
United Kingdom of
  Great Britain and
  Northern Ireland   56, 247, 288,
                                 299, 335
United Nations   245
United Nations
  Atomic Energy
  Commission   34
United Nations
Children's Fund   139-140, 248
United States (see
also U.S.A.)   5, 14, 21,
                                 24, 25, 27,
                                 28, 30, 31,
                                 33, 35, 39,
                                 51, 56, 57,
                                 65, 70, 74,
                                 75, 76, 78,
                                 81, 84, 85,
                                 86, 89, 93,
                                 95, 96, 99,
                                 104, 105,
                                 107, 125,
                                 127, 137,
                                 152, 153,
                                 161, 168,
                                 170, 177,
                                 181, 183,
                                 184, 185,
                                 191, 201,
                                 202, 208,
                                 209, 211,
                                 212, 214,
                                 216-17, 217,
                                 218, 219,
                                 222, 225,
                                 227, 228,
                                 229, 230,
                                 238, 245,
                                 246, 248,
                                 250, 251,
                                 253, 259,
                                 260, 262,
                                 263, 280,
                                 281, 282,
                                 284, 286,
                                 299, 300,
                                 305, 306,
                                 307, 309,
                                 310, 311,
                                 312, 313,
                                 324, 327,
                                 328, 334,
                                 335, 343,
                                 345, 346,
                                 347, 352
USAID   248, 258,
                                 261, 269,
                                 270, 271,
                                 272, 273,
                                 285, 286,
                                 296, 299,
                                 304, 325,
                                 333, 338, 345
United States
  Information Agency
  (see also USIA)   125, 143,
                                 176, 190,
                                 227, 239
United States
  Information Service   177, 178, 183
  (see also USIS)   230, 285
United States
  Military Academy   7
S.S. United States   65
Universal Studios   148
University of
  Agriculture, Beijing   214
University
  of Madagascar   287, 288,
                                 300, 313
University of
  Southern California   148
University of Teheran   84
UPI   158, 271
Urmia, (Rezaieh) Iran   85, 86, 87
U.S.A. (see also
  United States)   259, 267, 326
U. S. Agency for

International   258, 261,
Development)   269, 270
US AID (See also
  Agency for
  International
  Development)   258, 261,
                            269, 270
U. S. Air Force   309
U. S. Airways   308
U. S. Army   34
U. S. Army Corps of
  Engineers   75
U. S. Army Air Force   308
United States Atomic
  Energy Commission   34
USIA (see also   125, 143,
  United States   176, 190,
  Information Agency   227, 239
USIS (see also
  United States
  Information
  Service)   178, 230,
                            285, 286
U. S. Lady Magazine   68
U. S. Lady on the Air   68, 70, 76
USO   17, 73, 293
U. S. Navy   318, 319
U. S. Navy Seabees   301, 302
U. S. Northwest   301
U. S. Signal Corps   144
Ustun, Betty   249
Utrecht, NL   46

V

Vals, Monsieur   71
Van der Heuvel,
Gerry   143, 153
Van Gogh, Vincent   272
Van Thieu, Nguyen,
Mrs.   155
Van Thieu, Nguyen,
President   155
Vargish, Tom, Prof.   34, 202
Variety   74, 140
Vatican, The   52, 330
Vatican Museum, the   99
Vatomandry,
  Madagascar   280

Venezuela   147
Verdi, Giuseppe   101
Verdun   58
Verity, Wm., Sec'y of
Commerce   129
Versailles   58
Vichy France   284
Vienna, Austria   106, 226
Vietnam   130, 131,
                            132, 133,
                            134, 140,
                            141, 153,
                            154, 155,
                            156, 185,
                            186, 191,
                       194, 281, 301
Vietnam, South   133
Vincent, Francine   78, 79
Vienna, Austria   107
Vincents, the   78
Virginia   12, 67, 127,
                            131, 141,
                            189, 349,
                       351, 343, 353
Virginia, University
of   174
VOA (see also Voice
of America)   90, 104, 107,
                            125, 126,
                            127, 128,
                            132, 135,
                            136, 137,
                            138, 139,
                            144, 167,
                            168, 169,
                            176, 177,
                            180, 181,
                            183, 188,
                            191, 193,
                            195, 206,
                            208, 209,
                            211, 212,
                            214, 219,
                            225, 227,
                            228, 229,
                            231, 237,
                            238, 240,
                            241, 244,
                            250, 257,
                       320, 343, 353

Vogel, Hans Johann,
  Hon.   90
Vogue Magazine   4
Voice of America
(see also VOA)   31, 86, 87,
                                   90, 107,
                                  125, 126,
                                  128, 130,
                                  135, 137,
                                  138, 141,
                                  150, 157,
                                  161, 169,
                                  171, 176,
                                  180, 183,
                                  191, 195,
                                  206, 209,
                                  211, 212,
                             214, 219, 225
                                  226, 238,
                                  249, 327,
                                  332, 344
Von Braun, Werner,
  Dr.   82, 83
Von Hase, Karl-
  Gunther,
  Ambassador   95
Von Plato, Gen.   56
Von Schuschnigg,
  Kurt, Chancellor   110
Voss, Norway   117

W

Walesa, Lech   343, 347
Waller, Edward,
  Adm.   350
Waller, Marty, (Mrs.
  Edward)   350
Walter Reed Hospital   41
Walters, Barbara   162, 206
Walthour, Chaplain   13
Warren, Jerry   153
Warren, Stafford, Dr.   28
Warren, Vi   28
Warsaw, Poland   77, 97, 103,
                              104, 105, 252
Warsaw Ghetto   104
Washington, Booker
  T., Dr.   192

Washington National
  Cathedral, DC   189
Washington,   12, 28, 31,
DC   37, 40, 41,
                                48, 56, 67,
                               68, 73, 100,
                                  118, 119,
                                  121, 125,
                                  126, 131,
                                  133, 134,
                                  139, 140,
                                  141, 158,
                                  161, 174,
                                  180, 183,
                                  188, 189,
                                  190, 191,
                                  192, 193,
                                   194, 197
                                  199, 202,
                                  203, 208,
                                  212, 213,
                                  216, 217,
                                  226, 228,
                                  230, 237,
                                  243, 246,
                                  249, 251,
                                  257, 258,
                                  260, 281,
                                  287, 288,
                                  294, 295,
                                  297, 298,
                                  299, 307,
                                  308, 310,
                                  317, 326,
                             328, 332,338,
                                  343, 344,
                                  347, 348,
                                  351, 352
Washington
  Monument, DC   189, 190
Washington, George,
  President   186, 189, 351
Washington Post, The   267, 356
Washington Red
  Cross International
  Committee (see
  American Red
  Cross International
  Committee)   241
Washington Univ.,

St. Louis, MO	26
Watergate	185
Waters, John K., Gen.	82
Wayne, John	186
Welles, Henry	4
Wenceslas Square, Prague	348
West Berlin	93, 94
Westinghouse International Atomic Power Company, Ltd.	34
West Point, NY	7, 10, 11, 12, 13, 21, 22, 23, 25, 60-61
Westport, CT	5, 7
Westport Country Playhouse	6, 8, 60
WETA	126
WFAX	67, 68, 69, 70, 71, 75, 76, 77, 89, 125, 130, 135, 192
Whitehead, John, Dep. Sec'y of State	241, 242, 251
White House, The	25, 42, 68, 70, 95, 129, 130, 139, 140, 141, 143, 144, 145, 146, 148, 149, 150, 155, 156, 158, 161, 162, 163, 164, 167, 168, 169, 170, 173, 185, 186, 187, 188, 189, 191, 197, 206, 211, 228, 237, 238, 239, 240, 241, 242, 244, 253, 254, 346
Whittier, CA	148
Whittier, CA High School	148
Whittington, Robert, Sir	73
Wick, Charles, Director, USIA	239, 240, 241
Widmer, Mlle.	114
Williams, Donald, Col.	70
Williams, Joe	150
Williams, Madge	29
"Willis Conover Jazz Program"	127, 150
Williston, ND	195
Wilson, Harold, Prime Minister	161
Wilson, Woodrow, President	26
Winchester, Lucy	162, 164
"Windows on the World"	352
Windsor, Duchess of	59, 114
Windsor, Duke of	59
Window Rock, AZ	205
Wings of the Morning	294
"Wonders of Western Australia"	232
Woodgates, Russell	249
"World News Roundup, The," CBS	204
World Bank	253, 259, 260, 261, 281, 285, 304, 324, 326
World Trade Center	109, 352
World War I	3, 7, 59
World War II	6, 24, 56, 59, 81, 82, 97, 103, 109, 130, 131, 284, 293, 308, 311, 318
World Wildlife Fund	273, 276, 299
Wolfe, Thomas	18
Wolf Trap Farm Park	197
WPA	126
Wright, Orville	205
Wright, Wilbur	205

Wyeth, Andrew   146

X

Xian, China   213, 218

Y

Yale University   191, 205
Ylang Ylang   276
Youssri, Ibrahim,
  Amb.   304
Yu Chin Tu   222
Yugoslavia   87

Z

Zaha Motel,
  Mahajanga,
  Madagascar   321
Zanzibar   284
Zhao Jian, Dep.
  Chief of Mission   276
Zarathustra   86
Zoroaster   86
Zurich, Switzerland   317